The Audit Committee Handbook

THE AUDIT COMMITTEE HANDBOOK

Third Edition

LOUIS BRAIOTTA, JR., C.P.A.
School of Management
State University of New York at Binghamton

JOHN WILEY & SONS, INC.

New York • Chichester • Weinheim • Brisbane • Toronto • Singapore

Copyright © 1999 by John Wiley & Sons, Inc.

Library of Congress Cataloging-in-Publication Data

Braiotta, Louis, 1943–
    The audit committee handbook / Louis Braiotta, Jr. — 3rd ed.
        p.   cm.
    Includes index.
    ISBN 0-471-34576-8 (pbk. : alk. paper)
    1. Audit committees.   I. Title.
    HF5667.15.B7 1999
    658.15—dc21   99-22088
                                      CIP

Printed in the United States of America

10 9 8 7 6 5 4 3 2

*To the Adopters of the second edition
and dedicated to the memory
of my father, Louis Braiotta, Sr.*

From the Forewords of the Previous Two Editions . . .

Excerpt from the foreword to the second edition:

"Members of audit committees will find this second edition an invaluable resource in meeting their oversight responsibilities and give them an increasing awareness of their current duties as well as an insight into future developments."

> Richard S. Hickok, CPA
> Chairman, Hickok Associates, Inc.,
> and Chairman Emeritus of KMG/Main Hurdman
> (now KPMG Peat Marwick)

Excerpt from the foreword of the first edition:

"Audit committee members will find this book a useful reference in performing their oversight responsibilities. It should also help them develop a constructive relationship between their function and the activities of the full corporate board, management, and internal and external auditors."

> John C. Biegler, CPA
> Chairman Emeritus, Price Waterhouse International
> (now PricewaterhouseCoopers)

Preface

Since the publication of the second edition of *The Audit Committee Handbook* in 1994, audit committees in a global securities marketplace continue to respond to the investing public's demand for oversight protection. (See Appendix B.) Such committees not only help engender a high degree of integrity in both the internal and external audit processes and financial reporting process, but they also help provide for an efficient and transparent securities market. For example, many countries with developed equity markets or emerging markets have adopted audit committees through public and/or private sector initiatives to ensure price protection of their securities to investors. Moreover, the recent initiatives to develop and adopt harmonized international accounting and auditing standards accentuate the need to achieve uniformity in oversight protection to investors. It should be noted that companies will use the endorsement of these standards by the International Organization of Securities Commissions in their stock offering documents to raise capital in a global securities marketplace.

Although many countries have recognized that the establishment and benefits of audit committees help to ensure integrity in the corporate accountability process, it is imperative that such committees conduct their activities in an efficient and effective manner to help their boards of directors discharge their financial and fiduciary responsibilities to stockholders. As noted in the text, the important recommendations of the Blue Ribbon Committee on Improving the Effectiveness of Corporate Audit Committees will influence significantly how boards of directors through their audit committees can meet their oversight responsibilities in both the auditing and financial reporting areas. This third edition provides comprehensive guidance to all functions, duties, and responsibilities of audit committees as well as their direction in the corporate governance context. It retains the thrust of the second edition, focusing on current trends and developments that maximize the effectiveness of audit committees. Numerous references are made to the pronouncements of leading organizations in both the public and private sectors to bring an element of authority to the handbook.

Recognizing that audit committees interact with the internal auditor, independent auditor, chief financial officer, internal legal counsel, and independent legal counsel, the third edition continues to offer practical guidance in developing a constructive relationship between the committees' jurisdictional responsibilities and the activities of these executives. This revised professional reference work enables the aforementioned parties to help audit committees plan their agendas and achieve their mission in corporate governance. It provides a perspective that will help the members of the audit committee develop the appropriate requisite knowledge with respect to such matters as:

1. Understanding the role and responsibilities of the audit committee with a general update and reality check on auditing cycle activities.
2. Identifying the developments that impact audit committee practices and the latest techniques and strategies for committee meetings.
3. Understanding the latest authoritative sources that enable audit committee members to develop a repertoire of effective strategies to help the board of directors discharge its fiduciary responsibility to the stockholders.
4. Developing a comprehensive professional development program that enables committee members to prepare a periodic assessment of their activities and an informed review of both audit processes and financial reporting process.
5. Understanding the legal aspects of the audit committee and role of legal counsel as well as fraudulent financial reporting.

The book is divided into four parts. Part 1 is devoted to the audit director's basic responsibilities and includes a discussion on corporate accountability, the external users of accounting information, and the legal position of the audit committee. In addition, the broad framework of generally accepted auditing standards and their integration with generally accepted accounting principles are dealt with in one chapter to show their interrelationship.

Part 2 covers the planning function of the audit committee. An initial overview of the concept of audit planning is presented and followed with a discussion of the audit director's role in planning the audit. This part includes a discussion of the selection or reappointment of the public accounting firm.

Part 3 describes the monitoring and reviewing functions of the audit committee. Here the book focuses on the system of internal control, the internal audit function, accounting policy disclosures, management fraud, and sensitive business practices.

Part 4 covers the reporting function of the audit committee. Special attention is initially given to an overview of the independent auditor's opinions and reports. The final chapter explains the purpose of the audit director's report and discusses the guidelines for preparing it.

This book seeks to provide useful information and guidance for the audit committee and to point out opportunities for auditors and management to better serve the audit committee.

LOUIS BRAIOTTA, JR., C.P.A.

Binghamton, New York

Acknowledgments

I want to express my appreciation to Dr. Glenn A. Pitman, Dean of the School of Management of Binghamton University (State University of New York), for his encouragement in the preparation of the manuscript. Also, I want to thank my faculty colleagues, accounting practitioners, and students for their encouragement and support.

I am grateful to the American Institute of Certified Public Accountants, the Institute of Internal Auditors, the American Bar Association, and the Association of Certified Fraud Examiners for their permission to use certain materials subject to their copyrights.

My sincere thanks to Mrs. Betty Regan for her fine typing work and to Colleen Hailey, senior assistant librarian. My thanks to the people at John Wiley & Sons for their production and editorial assistance.

Contents

Part One

Getting Acquainted with Your Responsibilities

Chapter 1

Your Role in the Auditing Process

The major purpose of this chapter is not only to examine the organizational and functional characteristics of the audit committee but also to introduce the nature and importance of the external and internal auditing processes. Conceptually, one should understand the following:

1. The basic considerations in forming the audit committee
2. The basic audit committee functions
3. The role of the audit directors with respect to the external and internal auditing processes[1]

ORGANIZATION OF THE AUDIT COMMITTEE

Nature of the Audit Committee

In view of the complexity of the modern corporation and the increased demands for corporate accountability, the audit director's role has become an increasingly important consideration in the conduct of corporate affairs.[2] As defined by the American Institute of Certified Public Accounts, "An audit committee should be

---

[1] The terms *audit director* and *audit committee member* are used synonymously throughout this book.
[2] With respect to critical issues, Korn/Ferry International found in its annual survey of 327 CEOs that:

> According to our respondents, chief executive officers believe their attention should focus on financial results, followed by maximizing shareholder value and executive leadership. Eighty-five percent ranked financial results as most deserving of their time and 83 percent ranked maximizing shareholder value as most important. Executive leadership was seen as the most important issue by 81 percent of responding CEOs. (p. 12)

In a more recent survey of 1,020 directors, Korn/Ferry International found that among the greatest challenges facing boards of directors are "board independence, shareholder value and effective strategic planning" along with two dominant challenges, namely, "management succession and recruiting good directors" (p. 5). As Richard M. Ferry, chairman of Korn/Ferry International points out:

organized as a standing committee of the board composed mainly of nonofficer directors."[3] In contrast to the other standing committees of the board, such as the executive or finance committees, the audit committee is unique since it consists of outside or independent directors. Independent directors are individuals who are not directly involved in managing the corporation. For example, the chief executive officer and chief financial officer are considered management directors because not only are they immediately involved in managing corporate affairs, they are also employees of the corporation. Thus the independent audit committee is composed of individuals who are nonmanagement directors.

The Corporate Organization Policy Committee of The Business Roundtable concluded that the board of directors should be served by an audit committee because it would allow committee members to focus their attention on corporate matters in greater depth than would be practical for the full board. Moreover, a Conference Board study on audit committees found that "93 percent of the surveyed companies have such a committee. The recent action of the New York Stock Exchange requiring the 1,200 or so listed companies to establish by mid-1978 such a committee made up solely of directors independent of management reinforces this development."[4] See also Appendix B.

In a subsequent survey of 692 companies (628 companies compared with 1978), the Conference Board found a significant increase in the audit committee's involvement in such activities as reviewing the internal audit function and the independent status of the outside auditors, approving both audit and nonaudit services and related fees, and preparing a written agenda in advance of the meetings. They concluded that:

> Audit committees are larger: median sizes are now 4 members for manufacturing and nonfinancial services companies—up from 3 in 1978—and 4.5 for financial firms, up from 4.

Two overwhelming trends are cited as the most important developments during the past 25 years in board policy and structure—the emerging independence of the audit, compensation and nominating committees and the presence of fewer inside directors. Other major changes are the rise in formal evaluations of CEO [chief executive officer] performance, the increased strictness regarding directors with conflicting interests, the increasing popularity of corporate governance committees, the increasing diversity of board composition and, somewhat surprisingly, the trend toward paying directors in stock. (p. 9)

See Korn/Ferry International, *Twentieth Annual Board of Directors Study,* and *Twenty-fifth Annual Board of Directors Study,* New York: Korn/Ferry International, 1993 and 1998.

[3] American Institute of Certified Public Accountants, *Audit Committees, Answers to Typical Questions About Their Organization and Operations* (New York: American Institute of Certified Public Accountants, 1978), p. 11.

[4] The Business Roundtable, *The Role and Composition of the Board of Directors of the Large Publicly Owned Corporation* (New York: The Business Roundtable, 1978), pp. 21–22.

Their members include fewer directors with relationships that might interfere with the exercise of independent judgment, especially former executives of the company and directors affiliated with banks serving the company. Ninety percent of the committees have *no* members with such a potential conflict of interest.[5]

Notwithstanding the Conference Board survey results, the National Commission on Fraudulent Financial Reporting (NCFFR) endorsed the principle that "the board of directors of all public companies should be required by SEC rule to establish audit committees composed solely of independent directors."[6] The Commission recommended that senior management set the tone for the corporation's control environment, which includes an effective audit committee of the board of directors. The Commission asserted that "Audit Committees should be informed, vigilant, and effective overseers of the financial reporting process and the company's internal controls."[7]

Ray Bromark and Ralph Hoffman note that the role of the audit committee is expanding because of its value to the board of directors and to management and because of the need to meet the challenges of constantly changing business conditions. They point out that the audit committee has the following primary responsibilities:

Assisting the board to fulfill its oversight responsibilities as they relate to the financial reporting process and the internal structure

Maintaining, by way of regularly scheduled meetings, direct lines of communication between the board, financial management, the independent accountant, and internal audit

Additional responsibilities include the following:

Reviewing corporate policies relating to compliance with laws and regulations, ethics, conflict of interests, and the investigation of misconduct and fraud

---

[5] Jeremy Bacon, *The Audit Committee: A Broader Mandate,* Report No. 914 (New York: The Conference Board, 1988), p. vii.

[6] National Commission on Fraudulent Financial Reporting, *Report of the National Commission on Fraudulent Financial Reporting* (Washington, D.C.: National Commission on Fraudulent Financial Reporting, 1987), p. 40.

Moreover, a recent American Society of Corporate Secretaries study on current board practices found in a survey of 804 companies that most respondents (85.6 percent) have no management director on the audit committee (p. 12). In a subsequent survey of 648 companies, they found that such a board practice continued to rank high among the most commonly adopted practices (p. 14). See American Society of Corporate Secretaries, *Current Board Practices* (New York: American Society of Corporate Secretaries, 1996), and *Current Board Practices, Second Study* (New York: American Society of Corporate Secretaries, 1998).

[7] Ibid., p. 41.

Conducting periodic reviews of current pending litigation of regulatory proceedings bearing on corporate governance in which the corporation is a party

Coordinating annual reviews of compliance with corporate governance policies through internal audit or the company's independent accountants

Performing or supervising special investigations

Reviewing executive expenses

Reviewing policies on sensitive payments

Reviewing past or proposed transactions between the corporation and members of management

Reviewing the corporation's benefits programs

Assessing the performance of financial management[8]

Making the Audit Committee Effective

To organize an effective and efficient audit committee, consideration should be given to the proper delegation of responsibility and authority as well as to its membership and size.

Delegation of Responsibility and Authority   As a prerequisite to the effective performance of the committee, the board of directors should formulate a clear definition of the committee's responsibilities and authority. Moreover, the board should either pass a formal resolution or amend the bylaws of the corporation in order to document the establishment of the committee. Wayne Zetzman reports that an audit committee can best serve a corporation when "it is a viable, independent group with a definite mission and it has full access to the company's financial information."[9] A recent study noted that 51 companies with financial reporting problems, namely Securities and Exchange Commission (SEC) enforcement actions and/or material misstatements of quarterly earnings, were much less likely to have audit committees consisting solely of outside directors. Additionally, the researchers found that accounting and finance knowledge as well as frequent meetings are minimum steps needed to improve the quality in financial

[8]Ray Bromark and Ralph Hoffman, "An Audit Committee for Dynamic Times," *Directors and Boards* 16, No. 3 (Spring 1992), pp. 52, 53, 60.
[9]Wayne Zetzman, "How to Organize and Use the Audit Committee," *Financial Executive* 5, No. 4 (July/August 1989), p. 54.

reporting.[10] In addition to both the internal and external auditors' guidance and assistance, Zetzman notes that the chief financial officer must educate and guide the audit committee to enable it to serve the company effectively.[11]

An example of the board's delegation of responsibility and authority to the audit committee is that of the Bristol-Myers Squibb Company:

> The duties of the Audit Committee are (a) to recommend to the Board of Directors a firm of independent accountants to perform the examination of the annual financial statements of the Company; (b) to review with the independent accountants and with the Controller the proposed scope of the annual audit, past audit experience, the Company's internal audit program, recently completed internal audits and other matters bearing upon the scope of the audit; (c) to review with the independent accountants and with the Controller significant matters revealed in the course of the audit of the annual financial statements of the Company; (d) to review on a regular basis whether the Company's Standards of Business Conduct and Corporate Policies relating thereto has been communicated by the Company to all key employees of the Company and its subsidiaries throughout the world with a direction that all such key employees certify that they have read, understand and are not aware of any violation of the Standards of Business Conduct; (e) to review with the Controller any suggestions and recommendations of the independent accountants concerning the internal control standards and accounting procedures of the Company; (f) to meet on a regular basis with a representative or representatives of the Internal Audit Department of the Company and to review the Internal Audit Department's Reports of Operations; and (g) to report its activities and actions to the Board at least once each fiscal year.[12]

In addition, the activities of the audit committee are further disclosed in the annual stockholders' report, which states in part:

> The Audit Committee of the Board of Directors is comprised solely of non-employee directors and is responsible for overseeing and monitoring the quality of the company's accounting and auditing practices. The Audit Committee meets several times during the year with management, the internal auditors and the independent

---

[10] See Dorothy A. McMullen and K. Raghunandan, "Enhancing Audit Committee Effectiveness," *Journal of Accountancy* 182, No. 2 (August 1996), pp. 79–81. Also see Eugene M. Katz, "Keys to an Effective Audit Committee," *Credit World* 86, No. 4 (March/April 1998), pp. 21–23; Krishnagopal Menon and Joanne D. Williams, "The Use of Audit Committees for Monitoring," *Journal of Accounting & Public Policy* 13, No. 2 (Summer 1994), pp. 121–139; F. Todd De Zoort, "An Investigation of Audit Committees' Oversight Responsibilities," *Abacus* 33, No. 2 (September 1997), pp. 208–227; Robert Lear, "The Decline of the Audit Committee," *Chief Executive,* No. 111 (March 1996), p. 10; William W. Warrick and Duncan J. Galloway, "The Governance Audit: How Can We Make Sure We Don't Get Surprised?" *Directorship* 22, No. 5 (May 1996), pp. 1–4.

[11] Zetzman, "How to Organize and Use the Audit Committee," p. 57.

[12] Bristol-Myers Squibb Company, *Notice of 1998 Annual Meeting and Proxy Statement,* pp. 5–6.

accountants to discuss audit activities, internal controls and financial reporting matters. The internal auditors and the independent accountants have full and free access to the Audit Committee.

The appointment of Price Waterhouse LLP as the company's independent accountants by the Board of Directors was ratified by the stockholders. Price Waterhouse LLP's Report to the Board of Directors and Stockholders of Bristol-Myers Squibb Company appears on this page.

Charles A. Heimbold, Jr.   Michael F. Mee
Chairman of the Board and   Senior Vice President and
Chief Executive Officer   Chief Financial Officer[13]

Membership and Size of the Audit Committee   The effectiveness of the audit committee depends on the backgrounds of the members and of the chairman.

As defined by the New York Stock Exchange, the membership qualifications are as follows:

> Each domestic company with common stock listed on the Exchange, as a condition of listing and continued listing of its securities on the Exchange, shall establish no later than June 30, 1978 and maintain thereafter an Audit Committee comprised solely of directors independent of management and free from any relationship that, in the opinion of its Board of Directors, would interfere with the exercise of independent judgment as a committee member. Directors who are affiliates of the company or officers or employees of the company or its subsidiaries would not be qualified for Audit Committee membership.

> A director who was formerly an officer of the company or any of its subsidiaries may qualify for membership even though he may be receiving pension or deferred compensation payments from the company if, in the opinion of the Board of Directors, such person will exercise independent judgment and will materially assist the function of the committee. However, a majority of the Audit Committee shall be directors who were not formerly officers of the company or any of its subsidiaries.

Supplementary Material

In order to deal with the complex relationships that arise, the following guidelines are provided to assist Boards of Directors to observe the spirit of the policy in selecting members of the Audit Committee.

A director who has been or is a partner, officer or director of an organization that has customary commercial, industrial, banking or underwriting relationships with the company which are carried on in the ordinary course of business on an arms-length basis may qualify for membership unless, in the opinion of the Board of Directors, such director is not independent of management or the relationship would interfere with the exercise of independent judgment as a committee member.

[13] Bristol-Myers Squibb Company, *1997 Annual Report,* p. 45.

A director who, in addition to fulfilling the customary director's role, also provides additional services directly for the Board of Directors and is separately compensated therefore, would nonetheless qualify for membership on the Audit Committee. However, a director who, in addition to his director's role, also acts on a regular basis as an individual or representative of an organization serving as a professional advisor, legal counsel or consultant to management, would not qualify if, in the opinion of the Board of Directors, such relationship is material to the company, the organization represented or the director.

A director who represents or is a close relative of a person who would not qualify as a member of the Audit Committee in the light of the policy would likewise not qualify for the committee. However, if the director is a close relative of an employee who is not an executive officer or if there are valid countervailing reasons, the Board of Directors' decision as to eligibility shall govern.

While Rule 405 under the Securities Act of 1933 may be helpful to the Board of Directors in determining whether a particular director is an affiliate or a close relative for purposes of this policy, it is not intended to be so technically applied as to go beyond the spirit of this policy.[14]

Furthermore, the National Association of Securities Dealers has adopted a requirement for issuers of securities listed on the NASDAQ National Market System, which states that "each NASDAQ/NMS issuer shall establish and maintain an audit committee, a majority of the members of which shall be independent directors."[15] It should be noted the American Stock Exchange has adopted a similar requirement. The standard of independence is also disclosed in other legislative acts (Federal Deposit Insurance Corporation Improvement Act [FDICIA] and the Ontario Business Corporation Act and reports, as noted in the historical perspective. See Appendixes B, C, and E.

Recognizing the importance of the standard of independence rules, David Vicknair, Kent Hickman, and Kay C. Carnes investigated proxy statement data from the period 1980 to 1987 of 100 New York Stock Exchange companies to determine "grey" area director representation on audit committees. Proxy statements report such grey areas as interlocking directorships, related-party transactions, affiliations with the firm's bank, lawyers receiving fee income, service by retirees of corporation, consulting fees, and kinship relationships. They found that "approximately one-third of the 418 audit committee members could be classified

---

[14]New York Stock Exchange, Corporate Responsibility: Audit Committee, Section 303.00 of *New York Stock Exchange Listed Company Manual* (New York: New York Stock Exchange, 1983). For further discussion on the independence, membership, and size of the audit committee, see the recommendations of the Blue Ribbon Committee on Improving the Effectiveness of Corporate Audit Committees as indicated in Chapter 14, Exhibit 14.3.

[15]National Association of Securities Dealers, *NASD Manual* (Chicago: Commerce Clearing House, 1987), Part III, section 5(d) of Schedule D of the NASD bylaws.

as 'grey' area directors. Interlocking directorships (12 percent) and other related-party transactions (11.5 percent) individually account for more than ten percent of the directors." The remaining categories individually account for approximately 3 percent or less. They concluded that such directors may be a potential source of violations of audit committee independence.[16]

In addition to those outlined in the New York Stock Exchange's statement, other basic qualifications of the audit director are as follows:

1. A general understanding of the company's industry and the social, political, economic, and legal forces that affect the industry
2. A knowledge of the company with respect to its history, organization, and operational policies
3. An understanding of the fundamental problems of planning and control, as well as the fundamentals of the functional aspects of the company.

In short, the membership of the committee should consist of both financial and nonfinancial people so that the board can draw upon members from various professions such as accounting, economics, education, psychology, and sociology. As Richard T. Baker, retired managing partner of E&W (now E&Y) and now a member of several audit committees, points out:

> Having one or two nonfinancial people can make a committee more effective. They bring a different and useful perspective. Over the years I have come to greatly respect these people. . . . They add balance to a committee.[17]

Thus, a committee that has members with diverse backgrounds is advantageous since it provides the audit directors with the kind of perspective and experience desirable in assessing both the internal and external audit functions.

Equally important, the chairman has a critical role in coordinating the committee's task. The success or failure of the operation could depend on the chairman, and therefore such an individual should be chosen with great care. Specifically, the chairman should possess the same basic qualifications listed earlier as well as the following:

1. The ability to stimulate the audit directors' thinking without dominating the meeting
2. The ability to retain not only each member's personal interest in the work of the committee but also the willingness to contribute to its objectives

---

[16] David Vicknair, Kent Hickman, and Kay C. Carnes, "A Note on Audit Committee Independence: Evidence from the NYSE on 'Grey' Area Directors," *Accounting Horizons* 7, No. 1 (March 1993), pp. 55–56.
[17] Ernst & Whinney, *E&W People* (1980), p. 7.

3. A general understanding of the objectives and jurisdictional aspects
4. The ability to plan the agenda and to coordinate and disseminate information to the committee and the board members

In a study of 42 publicly held companies dealing with leadership styles of audit committee effectiveness, William D. Spangler and Louis Braiotta, Jr. report that transformational leadership and active management by exception have a substantial impact on the performance of audit committees. They found that "correlations of transformational leadership (charisma, intellectual stimulation, and individualized considerations), contingent rewards, and active management by exception with effectiveness were significant in the predicted positive direction and passive management by exception was nonstatistically related to audit committee effectiveness as predicted."[18] Their findings and conclusions were based on Bernard M. Bass's theoretical leadership perspective, which states: "Transformational leadership is somewhat independent of organizational structure and relies on the personality, beliefs, and behavior of leaders and subordinates. Indeed, transformational leaders are likely to emerge in times of crises when traditional organizational and social structures and values are weak."[19]

With respect to the size of the audit committee, the American Institute of Certified Public Accountants indicates that:

> A survey of corporations with audit committees revealed that nearly 90 percent had audit committees of three to five members. In general, the audit committee should be large enough to have members with a good mix of business judgment and experience, but not so large as to be unwieldy.[20]

This survey is further supported by the Conference Board survey, which reports that the median sizes are now 4 members for manufacturing and nonfinancial service companies and 4.5 for financial firms.[21]

Although there is general consensus regarding the size, obviously, the number of members will vary from corporation to corporation. The number of members depends not only on the committee's responsibility and authority but also on the size of both the board of directors and the corporation. For example, Bristol-Myers Squibb Company has 11 members on the board of directors. Five are non-

---

[18]William D. Spangler and Louis Braiotta, Jr., "Leadership and Audit Committee Effectiveness," *Group and Organization Studies* 15, No. 2 (June 1990), p. 134. See also Lawrence Kalbers and Timothy J. Fogarty, "Organizational and Economic Explanations of Audit Committee Oversight," *Journal of Managerial Issues* 10, No. 2 (Summer 1998), pp. 129–150.

[19]Bernard M. Bass, *Leadership and Performance Beyond Expectations* (New York: Free Press, 1985), p. 37.

[20]American Institute of Certified Public Accountants, *Audit Committees,* p. 12.

[21]Bacon, *The Audit Committee: A Broader Mandate,* p. 5.

employee directors who are also members of the audit committee. Furthermore, Bristol-Myers Squibb's audit directors are individuals from the fields of investing, education, and industry.[22]

THE AUDIT COMMITTEE FUNCTIONS

Audit Committee Functions as Defined by the American Bar Association

The Committee on Corporate Laws of the American Bar Association has defined the functions of the audit committee as follows:

> In its capacity as the communication link between the board of directors as representative of stockholders, on the one hand, and the independent auditors, on the other hand, the audit committee should have prime responsibility for the discharge of at least the following four functions:
>
> 1. To recommend the particular persons or firm to be employed by the corporation as its independent auditors;
>
> 2. To consult with the persons so chosen to be the independent auditors with regard to the plan of audit;
>
> 3. To review, in consultation with the independent auditors, their report of audit, or proposed report of audit, and the accompanying management letter, if any; and
>
> 4. To consult with the independent auditors (periodically, as appropriate, out of the presence of management) with regard to the adequacy of internal controls, and if need be, to consult also with the internal auditors (since their product has a strong influence on the quality and integrity of the resulting independent audit).[23]

More recently, the Committee on Corporate Laws expanded its definitions to include in substantial part the American Law Institute's Principles of Corporate Governances:

1. Recommend which firm to engage as the corporation's external auditor and whether to terminate that relationship.

2. Review the external auditor's compensation, the proposed terms of its engagement, and its independence.

3. Review the appointment and replacement of the senior internal auditing executive, if any.

[22] Bristol-Myers Squibb Company, *1997 Annual Report,* p. 49.
[23] American Bar Association, *Corporate Director's Guidebook* (Chicago: American Bar Association, 1978), pp. 32–33.

4. Serve as a channel of communication between the external auditor and the board and between the senior internal auditing executive, if any, and the board.

5. Review the results of each external audit, including any qualifications in the external auditor's opinion, any related management letter, management's responses to recommendations made by the external auditor in connection with the audit, reports submitted to the Audit Committee by the internal auditing department that are material to the corporation as a whole, and management's responses to those reports.

6. Review the corporation's annual financial statements and any significant disputes between management and the external auditor that arose in connection with the preparation of those financial statements.

7. Consider, in consultation with the external auditor and the senior internal auditing executive, if any, the adequacy of the corporation's internal financial controls. Among other things, these controls must be designed to provide reasonable assurance that the corporation's publicly reported financial statements are presented fairly in conformity with generally accepted accounting principles.

8. Consider major changes and other major questions of choice regarding the appropriate auditing and accounting principles and practices to be followed when preparing the corporation's financial statements.

9. Review the procedures employed by the corporation in preparing published financial statements and related management commentaries.

10. Meet periodically with management to review the corporation's major financial risk exposures.[24]

In addition to the American Bar Association's definition on the function of the audit committee, the National Commission on Fraudulent Financial Reporting recommends the following functions:

As part of its ongoing oversight of the effectiveness of internal controls, a company's audit committee should review annually the program management establishes to monitor compliance with the code of conduct. (p. 35)

All public companies should develop a written charter setting forth the duties and responsibilities of the audit committee. The board of directors should approve the charter, review it periodically, and modify it as necessary. (p. 42)

Audit committees should have adequate resources and authority to discharge their responsibilities. (p. 43)

Audit committees should oversee the quarterly reporting process. (p. 47)

Management and the audit committee should ensure that the internal auditors' involvement in the audit of the financial reporting process is appropriate and properly coordinated with the independent public accountant. (p. 39)

[24]American Bar Association, *Corporate Director's Guidebook* (Chicago: American Bar Association, 1994), pp. 28–29.

The audit committee should review management's evaluation of factors related to the independence of the company's public accountant. Both the audit committee and management should assist the public accountant in preserving his independence. (p. 43)

Before the beginning of each year, the audit committee should review management's plans for engaging the company's independent public accountant to perform management advisory services during the coming year, considering both the types of services that may be rendered and the projected fees. (p. 43)

All public companies should be required by SEC rule to include in their annual report to stockholders a letter signed by the chairman of the audit committee describing the committee's responsibilities and activities during the year. (p. 46)

Management should advise the audit committee when it seeks a second opinion on a significant accounting issue. (p. 47)[25]

Basic Audit Committee Functions

In addition to the preceding conclusions on the functions of the audit committee, the basic functions should include:

1. The planning function
2. The monitoring function
3. The reporting function

The Planning Function   Since the primary objective of the committee is to oversee and monitor the financial accounting and auditing processes, it should adopt its own coordinated plan of administration that is consistent with this objective. Such a plan should be designed to provide assurance to the full board of directors that both the internal and external resources allocated to the audit function are adequate and used effectively. The Committee on Corporate Organization Policy of The Business Roundtable agreed on two core functions of the board that are directly related to the committee's planning function:

> 1. Although the board cannot effectively conduct day-to-day operations, the board does have a major role in, and a major accountability for, the financial performance of the enterprise. This clearly requires a continuing check on corporate financial results and prospects.

---

[25]National Commission on Fraudulent Financial Reporting, *Report of the National Commission on Fraudulent Financial Reporting,* 1987. For further discussion, see the Committee of Sponsoring Organizations of the Treadway Commission (COSO), *International Control-Integrated Framework,* 4, Committee of Sponsoring Organizations of the Treadway Commission (1992), pp. 8–10.

2. Directors and top management cannot be the guarantors of the lawful conduct of every employee or manager in a large organization. . . . Policies and procedures should be designed to promote corporate law compliance.[26]

Thus, in view of the committee's oversight and advisory capacity, its plan should include[27]:

1. A review and appraisal of the overall purpose, objectives, and resources available for the entity's overall audit plan in accordance with the committee's charter as well as the committee's recommendation of the audit goals and objectives to the board for its approval
2. A review and consolidation of the audit plans of the internal and external auditing groups
3. An appraisal of the corporate audit plan annually

Furthermore, the committee should consider an integrated approach whereby its plan is oriented toward the segments of the auditing cycle, which are: (1) initial planning segment, (2) preaudit segment, and (3) postaudit segment. For example, during the initial planning segment, it should develop a basic understanding of the entity's business and its industry. Such an understanding of the qualitative characteristics of the entity and its position in the industry will enhance the committee's ability to discharge its responsibilities more effectively. In addition, during the preaudit and postaudit segments, it should develop an understanding of management's business risk assessment process and the audit risk assessment process related to financial reporting risk as well as the analytical review process with respect to the financial statements.

The Monitoring Function Obviously, the audit committee cannot participate in the accounting and auditing functions on a day-to-day basis, because such a task is contrary to its overall purpose. However, since the board of directors has the ultimate responsibility for these functions, the audit directors should monitor the corporation's activities based on their jurisdiction. The monitoring function should be administered so that the planning function is accomplished. Consequently, the committee can assist the board by obtaining information from the

---

[26] The Business Roundtable, *The Role and Composition of the Board of Directors of the Large Publicly Owned Corporations,* pp. 10–13.

[27] See Chapters 6 and 7 for more information on the committee's role in the planning function. It should be noted that the chairman of the audit committee usually will ask the audit engagement partner, the director of internal audit, and the chief financial officer to suggest agenda items for the committee meetings. These individuals are a major source of guidance and information to the committee. In addition, it is essential that agenda and supporting documents are prepared and distributed in advance for each meeting.

accounting and auditing executives in order to discharge the board's responsibility. The consensus seems to be that the audit directors should monitor the following:

1. The internal auditing function
2. The internal control system and related business risks
3. The financial reporting disclosures
4. Conflicts of interest, ethics audit, and fraud audit activities
5. Corporate perquisites
6. Corporate contributions[28]
7. Information technology systems
8. Other tasks as requested by the board

In administering the monitoring function, it may be advisable for the committee to retain the necessary professional expertise, such as the corporation's outside legal counsel or outside data processing experts.

The Reporting Function[29]   The audit committee should report directly to the board of directors and not to the chief executive officer. Since the members are independent or nonmanagement directors, they provide an objective appraisal of management's accounting and auditing performance. Furthermore, the reporting function is directly related to both the planning and monitoring functions. The general content of the audit directors' report should be based on the review programs regarding the planning function. Although the minutes of the committee meetings are a record of the proceedings, the nature of its function warrants a formal report. The report should contain a summary of its findings and recommendations with the appropriate figures and narrative remarks. In developing the reports for the board, the committee should focus its attention on the board's interests in such matters as:

1. The financial accounting policies and the related industry accounting practices (e.g., depreciation methods, inventory pricing, basis for consolidation)
2. The reports of the independent auditors and the internal auditors (e.g., the auditors' opinion on the system of internal control)
3. The reports of legal counsel with respect to significant commitments, contingencies, and governmental compliance
4. The reports of a special investigation concerning the review of the corporation's financial affairs, such as political contributions

---

[28] The board of directors may request that the audit committee review corporate contributions to ensure compliance with the corporate giving policy.
[29] For further discussion, see Chapter 14.

In short, the report of the audit committee may vary in form; however, the committee should render a concise report that fulfills the needs and interests of the board.

THE EXTERNAL AND INTERNAL AUDITING PROCESS

The Nature of External Auditing

External auditing is the process not only of examining the financial statements but also of testing the underlying accounting records of the company. The examination is conducted by the independent auditors, who express an objective opinion regarding the fairness of presentation of the financial statements. The audit examination is conducted within a predetermined set of generally accepted auditing standards that are promulgated by the Auditing Standards Board, formerly named the Auditing Standards Executive Committee of the American Institute of Certified Public Accountants (AICPA).[30] Since the audit examination is performed by certified public accountants who are independent of the company's management, the objective opinion of the independent auditing firm strengthens the reliability and credibility of the company's financial reporting practices.

More specifically, corporate management has full responsibility for the financial statements because such statements represent a report on management's stewardship accountability to its outside constituencies. The Auditing Standards Board of the AICPA asserts:

> The financial statements are management's responsibility. The auditor's responsibility is to express an opinion on the financial statements. Management is responsible for adopting sound accounting policies and for establishing and maintaining internal control that will, among other things, record, process, summarize, and report transactions (as well as events and conditions) consistent with management's assertions embodied in the financial statements. The entity's transactions and the related assets, liabilities, and equity are within the direct knowledge and control of management. The auditor's knowledge of these matters and internal control is limited to that acquired through the audit. Thus, the fair presentation of financial statements in conformity with generally accepted accounting principles is an implicit and integral part of management's responsibility. The independent auditor may make suggestions about the form or content of the financial statements or draft them, in whole or in part, based on information from management during the performance of the audit. However, the auditor's responsibility for the financial statements he or she has audited is confined to the expression of his or her opinion on them.[31]

[30]As noted in Chapter 13, the name of this committee has been changed to the Auditing Standards Board. However, the former name of this group will be used in connection with the appropriate Statements on Auditing Standards as discussed in the text.

[31]AICPA, *Professional Standards, U.S. Auditing Standards/Attestation Standards,* vol. 1 (New York: American Institute of Certified Public Accountants, 1998), AU Sec. 110.03.

Increasingly, management's responsibilities for financial statements are typically acknowledged in a Report of Management in the annual stockholders' report, which states in part:

> Management is responsible for the accompanying consolidated financial statements, which are prepared in accordance with generally accepted accounting principles. In management's opinion, the consolidated financial statements present fairly the company's financial position, results of operations and cash flows. In addition, information and representations included in the company's Annual Report are consistent with the financial statements.
>
> The company maintains a system of internal accounting policies, procedures and controls intended to provide reasonable assurance, given the inherent limitations of all internal control systems, at appropriate costs, that transactions are executed in accordance with company authorization, are properly recorded and reported in the financial statements, and that assets are adequately safeguarded. The company's internal auditors continually evaluate the adequacy and effectiveness of this system of internal accounting policies, procedures and controls, and actions are taken to correct deficiencies as they are identified.[32]

The audit opinion is presented in the independent auditors' or accountants' report. Such a report may be addressed to the board of directors, to the stockholders, or to both the board and the stockholders. For example, if the independent auditors were employed by the stockholders, then the report would be addressed to them. It should be noted that the report is included in the corporate annual report.

The report consists of three paragraphs. The first is the introductory paragraph, which sets forth the responsibilities of management and the auditors. The second is the scope paragraph, which describes the nature of the audit, and the third paragraph states the opinion. The standard form of an unqualified audit report is as follows:

(Introductory paragraph)

We have audited the accompanying balance sheets of X Company as of December 31, 19X2 and 19X1, and the related statements of income, retained earnings, and cash flows for the years then ended. These financial statements are the responsibility of the Company's management. Our responsibility is to express an opinion on these financial statements based on our audits.

(Scope paragraph)

We conducted our audits in accordance with generally accepted auditing standards. Those standards require that we plan and perform the audit to obtain reasonable assurance about whether the financial statements are free of material misstatement. An

---

[32]Bristol-Myers Squibb Company, *1997 Annual Report,* p. 45.

audit includes examining, on a test basis, evidence supporting the amounts and disclosures in the financial statements. An audit also includes assessing the accounting principles used and significant estimates made by management, as well as evaluating the overall financial statement presentation. We believe that our audits provide a reasonable basis for our opinion.

(Opinion paragraph)

In our opinion, the financial statements referred to above present fairly, in all material respects, the financial position of X Company as of [at] December 31, 19X2 and 19X1, and the results of its operations and its cash flows for the years then ended in conformity with generally accepted accounting principles.[33]

In the introductory paragraph, the auditors indicate that they are responsible for their audit report and that management has primary responsibility for the financial statements. In regard to the scope of the examination, the auditors state that they have performed not only certain auditing procedures based on their professional judgment but have also conducted their examination within the general guidelines or standards set forth by the AICPA. This scope paragraph communicates to the reader of the financial statements that the auditors' compliance with auditing standards provides reasonable assurance that such statements are free of material misstatements and/or omitted material facts. Furthermore, in the opinion paragraph, the auditors state that the financial statements have been prepared in accordance with accounting principles that are widely accepted in the practice of accounting and, therefore, that such statements are fairly presented. An illustration of the auditors' report follows.

To the Board of Directors
and Stockholders of
Bristol-Myers Squibb Company

In our opinion, the accompanying consolidated balance sheet and the related consolidated statements of earnings, comprehensive income and retained earnings and of cash flows present fairly, in all material respects, the financial position of Bristol-Myers Squibb Company and its subsidiaries at December 31, 1997, 1996 and 1995, and the results of their operations and their cash flows for the years then ended in conformity with generally accepted accounting principles. These financial statements are the responsibility of the company's management; our responsibility is to express an opinion on these financial statements based on our audits. We conducted our audits of these statements in accordance with generally accepted auditing standards which require that we plan and perform the audit to obtain reasonable assurance about whether the financial statements are free of material misstatement. An

---

[33] "Reports on Audited Financial Statements," *Statement on Auditing Standards, No. 58* (New York: American Institute of Certified Public Accountants, 1988), par. 8.

audit includes examining, on a test basis, evidence supporting the amounts and disclosures in the financial statements, assessing the accounting principles used and significant estimates made by management, and evaluating the overall financial statement presentation. We believe that our audits provide a reasonable basis for the opinion expressed above.[34]

Price Waterhouse LLP

1177 Avenue of the Americas
New York, New York 10036
January 22, 1998

Role of the Audit Directors   The work of the audit directors and the independent auditors is very closely related because both groups have common objectives regarding the financial affairs. The audit directors are responsible for overseeing the independent audit examination as well as the recommendations of the independent auditors. The audit directors must assure themselves that the financial statements and the system of internal accounting controls are based on acceptable accounting principles and procedures. Moreover, the audit directors need assurance that the executives and their staff are reasonably competent and trustworthy.

Although the extent of the audit committee's activities has led to some controversy, it is clearly evident that its effectiveness has been increased by the U.S. Securities and Exchange Commission (SEC), the U.S. Congress (FDICIA), and other private-sector initiatives (National Commission on Fraudulent Financial Reporting, the MacDonald Commission (Canada), and the Cadbury Committee, Hampel Committee, and Committee on Corporate Governance (UK). The reality of the situation is that the Foreign Corrupt Practices Act, the Private Securities Litigation Reform Act, and the aforementioned initiatives place greater responsibilities on the audit committee. Thus, it is critically important that the committee keep a perspective and focus on its oversight role for the system of internal control and financial reporting areas of the company. If the audit committee becomes too deeply involved in management's operational activities, its effectiveness will be diluted. As Ray Groves, E&Y former managing partner, has indicated:

> This does not mean a committee cannot rely on management and the internal and external auditors to see that controls are in good order. The committee's responsibility is to satisfy itself that these groups are performing and the necessary documentation exists.[35]

The audit directors are in an excellent position to contribute to the external auditing process. For example, the independence of the auditing firm is enhanced

---

[34] Bristol-Myers Squibb Company, *1997 Annual Report,* p. 45.
[35] Ernst & Whinney, *E&W People,* p. 7.

because the independent auditors establish a line of communication to the board of directors through the audit committee. In addition, since the audit directors nominate and select the auditing firm, they are in a position to examine the qualifications of this firm as well as to assess the results of the audit examination.[36]

In a survey of 34 publicly held companies dealing with the effectiveness of audit committees as perceived by both external auditors and audit committee members of those companies, Lawrence P. Kalbers found that practicing audit committees are not uniformly effective and that the auditors rate committee members significantly lower than do members on responsibilities, attributes, and effectiveness. He concludes that the audit committee, management, and auditors need to work toward the right balance of the committee's involvement with audit fees, audit scope, audit results, and internal controls. He believes that training and educating the committee members can help them meet their responsibilities.[37]

The Nature of Internal Auditing

As defined by the Institute of Internal Auditors,

> Internal auditing is an independent appraisal function established within an organization to examine and evaluate its activities as a service to the organization. The objective of internal auditing is to assist members of the organization in the effective discharge of their responsibilities. To this end, internal auditing furnishes them with analyses, appraisals, recommendations, counsel, and information concerning the activities reviewed. The audit objective includes promoting effective control at reasonable cost. The members of the organization assisted by internal auditing include those in management and the board of directors.[38]

For example, internal auditors may evaluate the internal control of a company as well as review management's adherence to the company's policies. They can also help the audit committee with special investigations and compliance audits.

However, it is important to recognize that the internal auditing group is not completely independent from corporate management, because the members of the group are employees of the company. To enhance their independence and objectivity, the Institute of Internal Auditors recommends that the director of

---

[36] For further discussion on communication with audit committees, see Chapter 5.

[37] Lawrence P. Kalbers, "An Examination of the Relationship Between Audit Committees and External Auditors," *The Ohio CPA Journal* 51, No. 6 (December 1992), p. 27. Similarly, Price Waterhouse noted that: "The single most important findings, and the key to audit committee effectiveness, is: background information and training." See Price Waterhouse, *Improving Audit Committee Performance: What Works Best* (Altamonte Springs, FL: Institute of Internal Auditors, 1993), p. 2. For further discussion on training and educating audit committee members, see Chapter 7.

[38] The Institute of Internal Auditors, Inc., *Standards for the Professional Practice of Internal Auditing* (Altamonte Springs, Fla.: Institute of Internal Auditors, 1998), p. 105.

internal auditing should be responsible to an individual whose authority is sufficient to promote independence and provide the necessary internal auditing coverage.[39] Thus, the director of internal auditing should report not only to a senior executive, such as the chief financial officer with access to the chief executive officer, but also to the independent audit committee. To ensure the independence of the internal auditing group, the director must have free access to meeting regularly with the committee. The internal audit function is discussed more extensively in Chapter 9.

Role of the Audit Directors[40]   The interface between the audit directors and the internal auditing group provides a logical relationship because these groups have common goals. It is important that both groups establish a working relationship which is not counterproductive. More specifically, to maximize the productivity of the internal auditing group, the audit directors should do the following:

1. Assist in the overall internal auditing policy determination and approve such policies to ensure that the internal auditing group has authority that is commensurate with its responsibilities
2. Review the coordination of the work and schedules of the internal and external auditing groups
3. Review not only the qualifications of the director of internal auditing and his or her support staff but also the professional development activities of the group
4. Review the copies of the internal auditing reports and critically evaluate findings, recommendations, and management's response

In this overview of the audit director's role in the auditing process, it is interesting to note some general observations:

1. The audit committee has become an integral part of the corporate framework to help fulfill the board of directors' stewardship accountability to its outside constituencies.
2. The work of the audit committee is dynamic since the accounting and auditing processes are subject to change.

[39] Ibid., p. 11.

[40] For further discussion of the audit committee's role, see *Internal Auditing and the Audit Committee: Working Together Toward Common Goals* (Altamonte Springs, FL: Institute of Internal Auditors, 1987); and Barbara A. Apostolou and Raymond Jeffords, *Working with the Audit Committee* (Altamonte Springs, FL: Institute of Internal Auditors, 1990). Also see the video, *Audit Committees and Internal Auditing: An Essential Alliance for Effective Governance* (Altamonte Springs, Fla.: Institute of Internal Auditors, 1994).

3. Authoritative bodies at home and abroad, such as the U.S. Congress, the national stock exchanges, the Cadbury Committee, the Hampel Committee, and the Committee on Corporate Governance (UK), have established standards for both the board of directors and the auditors to improve the financial reporting process. (See Appendix B.)

4. The audit committee is fundamental to the concept of corporate accountability.

SOURCES AND SUGGESTED READINGS

American Bar Association, *Corporate Director's Guidebook* (Chicago, IL, 1978).

American Bar Association, *Corporate Director's Guidebook* (Chicago: American Bar Association, 1994).

American Institute of Certified Public Accountants, *Audit Committees, Answers to Typical Questions about Their Organization and Operations* (New York: American Institute of Certified Public Accountants, 1978).

American Institute of Certified Public Accountants, Professional Standards, U.S. Auditing Standards/Attestation Standards, Volume 1. New York, 1998.

American Society of Secretaries, *Current Board Practices* (New York: American Society of Corporate Directors, 1996).

American Society of Corporate Secretaries, *Current Board Practices,* 2nd Study (New York: American Society of Corporate Directors, 1998).

Bacon, Jeremy, *The Audit Committee: A Broader Mandate,* Report No. 914 (New York: The Conference Board, Inc., 1988).

Bass, Bernard M., *Leadership and Performance Beyond Expectations* (New York: Free Press, 1985).

Bristol-Myers Squibb Company, *1997 Annual Report.*

Bristol-Myers Squibb Company, *Notice of 1998 Annual Meeting and Proxy Statement.*

The Business Roundtable, *The Role and Composition of the Board of Directors of the Large Publicly Owned Corporation* (New York: The Business Roundtable, January 1978).

Committee of Sponsoring Organizations of the Treadway Commission, *Internal Control-Integrated Framework* (New York: American Institute of Certified Public Accountants, 1992).

Ernst & Whinney, *E&W People,* Booklet No. 46302.

Hoffman, Ralph and Ray Bromark, "An Audit Committee for Dynamic Times." *Directors & Boards,* **16,** No. 3 (Spring 1992), pp. 51–53, 60.

The Institute of Internal Auditors, Inc. *Standards for the Professional Practice of Internal Auditing* (Altamonte Springs, Fla., 1998).

Kalbers, Wayne P., "An Examination of the Relationship Between Audit Committees and External Auditors." *The Ohio CPA Journal,* **51,** No. 6 (December 1992), pp. 19–27.

Korn/Ferry International, *Twentieth Annual Board of Directors Study* (New York: Korn/Ferry International, 1993).

Korn/Ferry International, *25th Annual Board of Directors Study* (New York: Korn/Ferry International, 1998).

National Association of Securities Dealers, *NASD Manual* (Chicago: Commerce Clearing House, 1987).

National Commission on Fraudulent Financial Reporting, *Report of the National Commission on Fraudulent Financial Reporting* (Washington, D.C.: National Commission on Fraudulent Financial Reporting, 1987).

New York Stock Exchange, Corporate Responsibility: Audit Committee, Section 303.00 of the *New York Stock Exchange Listed Company Manual* (New York: New York Stock Exchange, 1983).

Price Waterhouse, *Improving Audit Committee Performance: What Works Best* (Altamonte Springs, Fla.: Institute of Internal Auditors, 1993).

Spangler, William D. and Louis Braiotta, Jr., "Leadership and Audit Committee Effectiveness." *Group and Organization Studies* **15,** No. 2 (June 1990), pp. 134–157.

Statement on Auditing Standards No. 58, "Reports on Audited Financial Statements" (New York: American Institute of Certified Public Accountants, 1988).

Vicknair, David, Kent Hickman, and Kay C. Carnes, "A Note on Audit Committee Independence: Evidence from the NYSE on 'Grey' Area Directors." *Accounting Horizons* **7,** No. 1 (March 1993), pp. 53–57.

Zetzman, Wayne, "How to Organize and Use the Audit Committee." *Financial Executive,* 15, No. 4 (July/August 1989), pp. 54–57.

Chapter 2

Corporate Accountability: How to Keep It in Perspective

To properly understand the importance of the corporate director's position on the audit committee, one must understand the nature and importance of the concept of corporate accountability. Therefore, the major objectives of this chapter are as follows: first, to explain the meaning and significance of corporate accountability; second, to examine the historical developments in corporate accountability; third, to show the impact of corporate accountability on the audit committee and its corporate relationships; and fourth, to review the recent developments in corporate governance.

THE NATURE AND IMPORTANCE OF CORPORATE ACCOUNTABILITY

The Meaning of Corporate Accountability

Strictly speaking, the concept of corporate accountability may be stated as follows:

> The board of directors is charged with safeguarding and advancing the interest of the stockholders, acting as their representatives in establishing corporate policies, and reviewing management's execution of those policies. Accordingly, the directors have a fiduciary responsibility to the stockholders. They have an obligation to inform themselves about the company's affairs and to act diligently and capably in fulfilling their responsibilities.[1]

---

[1] American Institute of Certified Public Accountants, *Audit Committees, Answers to Typical Questions About Their Organization and Operations* (New York: American Institute of Certified Public Accountants, 1978), p. 7.

The board of directors is charged with protecting the interests of the stockholders because the position of the board is determined by the state laws. The powers and responsibilities of the board are defined in the corporate charter and the corporate bylaws. Therefore, from a legal point of view, the basic purpose of corporate accountability is to provide a legal framework within which the directors must discharge their stewardship accountability to the stockholders. Furthermore, the board is directly answerable to the stockholders because the stockholders, as the owners of the enterprise, have entrusted their capital resources to the management of the corporation. (See Appendix G.)

The Business Roundtable described corporate accountability as follows:

> The board of directors is ultimately accountable to the shareholders for the long-term successful economic performance of the corporation consistent with its underlying public purpose. Directors are held accountable for their performance in a variety of ways.

> First, there is the powerful accountability imposed by markets. The impact of consumer dissatisfaction with products and services is quick and visible. Financial markets also quickly reflect their evaluation of the quality of accountability through the price of equity and debt.

> Accountability is also imposed through the numerous statutes and regulations enacted by governmental bodies to limit and control corporate action. Directors are held accountable to regulatory mechanisms.

> There is also a body of law—part statutory, part court-made—which defines the duties of directors and the principles and boundaries within which they must keep their decisions. If they overstep, their decisions are subject to reversal by the courts. Directors can also be held personally liable, without limitation, to the extent of their personal assets if they violate their duty of loyalty to the corporation.

> A final form of board accountability comes through the election of directors by the shareholders at the corporation's annual meeting. Annual meetings may also include shareholder resolutions which are a form of governance by referendum.

> Each of these forms of accountability is dynamic, not static. The developing specifics of each form of accountability must be judged as to its overall potential to contribute to the successful long-term performance of the corporation. Each specific new item of accountability carries with it the potential for harm as well as good.[2]

With respect to establishing and maintaining corporate policies, the board of directors is responsible to the stockholders for assuring that management fulfills its responsibilities in the execution of the corporate policies. For example, the board can authorize the establishment of an audit committee in order to assist the

---

[2] The Business Roundtable, *Corporate Governance and American Competitiveness* (New York: The Business Roundtable, 1990), pp. 15–16.

board with the development of the financial accounting policies. In addition, the audit committee can be authorized to review the preparation of the financial statements as well as to select the independent auditors. Although the board has the power to delegate authority to the various standing committees, such as the audit committee or the executive committee, the board must render an accountability to the stockholders. In short, the board has a fiduciary relationship with the stockholders and, as a result, must periodically report on the status of the corporation's economic resources.

As John Shandor points out:

> Audit committees have become crucial to the audit process. Also, the audit committee has been considered essential in an organizational approach to making boards of directors more effective in their interaction with financial management and chief executive officers as well as with internal audit staff and independent auditors.[3]

In addition to the directors' fiduciary responsibility, they are expected to attend board meetings and their appropriate standing committee meetings. A director must keep informed on the affairs of the corporation and use reasonable care and diligence in the performance of his or her duties. It is imperative that the director keep abreast of the corporate developments since he or she is directly responsible for participating in the decisions that affect the management of the corporation. Thus the director may be held liable for losses sustained by the corporation as a result of his or her neglect.

Practically speaking, the concept of corporate accountability extends not only to the stockholders but also to the other constituencies of the board of directors, such as credit grantors and governmental agencies. The extension of corporate accountability to the other constituencies is evidenced by a meeting of the American Assembly. The discussion leaders focused their attention on questions central to running the corporation vis-à-vis its many constituencies. With respect to a framework for corporate accountability, the participants generally agreed on the following:

> Boards of directors have a primary role in interpreting society's expectations and standards for management.
>
> The five key board functions are:
>
> (a) Appraisal of management performance and provision for management and board succession;
> (b) Determination of significant policies and actions with respect to present and future profitability and strategic direction of the enterprise;

[3] John Shandor, "Audit Committees Take a Broader Role in Corporate Policy," *Corporate Controller* 2 (November/December 1989), pp. 46–48.

(c) Determination of policies and actions with a potential for significant financial, economic, and social impact;

(d) Establishment of policies and procedures designed to obtain compliance with the law; and

(e) Responsibility for monitoring the totality of corporate performance.

Boards should continue to be the central focus in improving the way corporations are governed.[4]

In addition to the American Assembly's recommendations, to establish and maintain a successful program of corporate accountability, the following prerequisites are necessary:

1. The board of directors and the officers must assume prime responsibility for corporate accountability as well as define and clarify the objectives and responsibilities concerning the different levels of the organization. Therefore, the individuals who are assigned responsibility at the middle and lower management levels should be held accountable for their activities.

2. The organization chart of the corporation is central to establishing corporate accountability since the jurisdiction for each area within the corporation must be defined. Also, the extent of authority should not only be clearly outlined but also commensurate with the individual's responsibilities.

3. Executive management should create a management environment whereby the middle and lower management levels understand the nature of corporate accountability. Thus management should maintain an effective communications network within the organizational structure.

As a case in point, Bruce W. McCuaig and Paul G. Makosz report that Gulf Canada Resources, Ltd., has developed a new approach to corporate governance through the use of an internal control assessment strategy. Such a strategy was developed based on a clear definition of internal control as a combination of (1) organization controls, (2) systems development and change controls, (3) authorization and reporting controls, (4) accounting systems controls, (5) safeguarding controls, (6) management supervisory controls, and (7) documentation controls. With the implementation of a management-by-objectives framework and related control mechanisms, the authors observed that the board of directors and senior management are far better informed.[5]

---

[4]The American Assembly, *Corporate Governance in America,* Pamphlet 54 (New York: Columbia University, April 1978), p. 6.

[5]Bruce W. McCuaig and Paul G. Makosz, "Is Everything Under Control? A New Approach to Corporate Governance," *Financial Executive* 6, No. 1 (January/February 1990), p. 25.

The subject of corporate accountability is a dynamic concept in the governance of the corporation. It is dynamic because the directors must not only assess the changing needs of their constituencies but also render a stewardship accountability based on legal pressures from their constituencies.

The Need for Corporate Accountability

In view of the size and scope of modern corporations as well as the increasing demands in the legal and regulatory environment, the need for corporate accountability has become very important in the evaluation of the performance of the board of directors. For example, the sales figures of these corporations amount to billions of dollars, which far exceed the gross national product of several countries. In addition, large corporations have control over the major economic resources of society. Furthermore, the board of directors is subject to numerous public laws, such as the Environmental Protection Act, the Occupational Safety and Health Act, federal securities laws, and antitrust laws. Thus many of these corporate enterprises play a significant role in the future of our society, since the decisions of corporate management have a direct impact on the economy.

Unfortunately, corporations are confronted with the problem of a lack of credibility because they often have been subject to corporate self-interest as opposed to the public interest. As one former executive partner of Price Waterhouse International asserts:

> We have all been stunned by the shocking disclosures of alleged improper payments and similar activities, not by funny fly-by-night firms nobody ever heard of, but by some of the finest names on the roster of American enterprise. . . . As one inevitable result, reinforced by uneasy business conditions, public confidence in American business has plunged to its lowest level since the great depression. It is as if these events simply confirmed a gathering suspicion that such transgressions are not exceptional—a suspicion that American business is built on bribery and deceit.[6]

To compound the problem of the credibility gap, the standards of corporate accountability have not been defined or codified into basic precepts by a recognized professional body. For example, the performance of a professional person, such as a medical doctor, can be measured against the standards established by the American Medical Association. Therefore, directors of publicly held corporations are more vulnerable to lawsuits as well as to the increased risk of liability, since they are unable to find shelter in a formal set of standards of corporate accountability. (See Appendix I.) As a result, many qualified persons are reluctant to accept a position on the board.

[6]John C. Biegler, "Rebuilding Public Trust in Business," *Financial Executive* 45 (June 1977), p. 28.

The need to resolve the credibility gap is evident. Corporate management must adopt standards of corporate accountability. As one proponent points out:

> Every corporation's business is conducted by some standard. If it is not formulated systematically at the top, it will be formulated haphazardly and impulsively in the field. And top management will be called on to defend practices that were unnecessary and unintended.[7]

Consequently, the need for corporate accountability is not only apparent but essential in shaping and projecting a corporate image to the public.

Shaun F. O'Malley, former co-chairman of Price Waterhouse World Firm (now PricewaterhouseCoopers), points out that dramatic changes have occurred in the roles of boards of directors, auditors, and management and in the relationships between these groups. Corporate accountability is a question of balance among the three groups as well as between government and the private sector. Shareholders and other constituencies of the company will continue their demands for protecting the company from fraud along with communicating warning signals of possible business failures.[8]

Daniel J. McCauley and John C. Burton comment on the changing expectations of director responsibility and audit committees as follows:

> The limited responsibility of the directors for financial matters, as it formerly existed, has been significantly changed in recent years. The public's loss of confidence in the business community has been accompanied by a correlative demand for greater director vigilance over company financial integrity. This oversight function of the board has been promoted as one of the means for restoring business's image.[9]

IMPORTANT DEVELOPMENTS IN CORPORATE ACCOUNTABILITY[10]

It is important to review the historical developments in corporate accountability and their relationship to corporate financial reporting. Such a review is in order since financial reporting is fundamental to the concept of corporate accountability. In short, the corporation must report its accomplishments not only to its principal constituency, the stockholders, but also to other outside constituencies.

---

[7] Ibid., p. 29.
[8] Shaun F. O'Malley, "Auditing, Directors, and Management: Promoting Accountability," *Internal Auditing* 5, No. 3 (Winter 1990), p. 3.
[9] Daniel J. McCauley and John C. Burton, *Audit Committees,* C.P.S. No. 49 (BNA, 1986), p. A-3.
[10] For further discussion, see Appendix B, "Historical Perspective on Audit Committees."

Public Sector Initiatives

The United States Congress and the Securities and Exchange Commission have imposed several financial reporting requirements and have proposed several requirements to emphasize the fair presentation of financial information and corporate disclosure. The developments of particular importance are summarized in the following paragraphs.

Foreign Corrupt Practices Act of 1977 In regard to the Foreign Corrupt Practices Act of 1977, Estey and Marston point out:

> One of the more ambitious ventures in the post-Watergate morality, the bill sailed through Congress after more than 300 major U.S. corporations had made gingerly disclosures of millions in "questionable" or "dubious" foreign payments—and after revelation of the payoffs by Lockheed had rocked governments in the Netherlands, Italy, and Japan. In passing the legislation unanimously, Congress labeled corporate bribery "bad business" and "unnecessary." President Carter pronounced it "ethically repugnant" as he signed the bill into law.[11]

On December 9, 1977, the United States Congress enacted the Foreign Corrupt Practices Act.[12] The purpose of this legislation is to prohibit U.S. companies, including directors, officers, stockholders, employees, and agents, from bribing foreign governmental officials. In addition, the law provided for the establishment and maintenance of a system of internal accounting control and record-keeping requirements with respect to all publicly held corporations. Accordingly, the law amended the Securities and Exchange Act of 1934.

Specifically, the law states that with the exception of facilitating (grease) payments, which are small payments for custom documents or minor permits, a direct or indirect payment or offer that is intended to promote business interests constitutes foreign bribery. Moreover, the corporation can be fined not more than $1,000,000, and individuals, such as directors, officers, or stockholders, can be fined up to $10,000, or imprisoned for up to five years, or both. Furthermore, publicly held companies must do the following: (1) devise and maintain a system of internal control sufficient to provide reasonable assurance that transactions are appropriately authorized and recorded and (2) maintain accounting records that in reasonable detail accurately and fairly reflect the financial activities.[13]

---

[11] John S. Estey and David W. Marston, "Pitfalls (and Loopholes) in the Foreign Bribery Law," *Fortune* 98, No. 7 (October 1978), p. 182.

[12] The act is contained in Title I of Public Law No. 95-213, December 19, 1977. See Appendix D.

[13] See Chapter 8 concerning the role of the audit committee and the internal accounting control aspect of the act.

As a case in point, on March 11, 1978, *The New York Times* observed the enforcement provisions of the Foreign Corrupt Practices Act.

> Mr. Matusow, Mr. Hyman, and several companies controlled by them have misappropriated and diverted at least $1.24 million of corporate assets. Aminex filed false and misleading annual and quarterly reports with the SEC. Finally, the defendants were charged with disguising the misappropriated funds "by means of false and improper accounting in the books and records of Aminex."[14]

Although the court granted a temporary restraining order and appointed a receiver to protect the company's assets, the SEC's actions indicate that it has the authority to regulate the internal affairs of the company.[15]

Furthermore, in February 1979, the SEC issued release no. 34-15570, which prohibits not only the falsification of corporate records but also false statements by the directors and officers to the corporate accountants, internal auditors, and external auditors. With respect to maintaining records, the SEC stated:

> The concern expressed with respect to inadvertent and inconsequential errors is unwarranted. The statute does not require perfection but only that books, records and accounts "in reasonable detail, accurately and fairly reflect the transactions and dispositions of the assets of the issuer." In addition, the legislative history reflects that "standards of reasonableness" are to be used in applying this provision.

As a result of the Foreign Corrupt Practices Act, an increasing number of companies are including a management report in the corporate annual report. As D. R. Carmichael, former vice president of auditing, American Institute of Certified Public Accountants (AICPA), reports:

> The management report is a development in corporate financial reporting that can be implemented now with relative ease. It offers management an opportunity to simultaneously improve corporate communication and demonstrate accountability. Widespread adoption of management reports would also demonstrate the ability of voluntary disclosure to be innovative and responsive to the needs of users of financial information.[16]

Thus, through the management report, management acknowledges its responsibility for the content of the corporate annual report.

---

[14] Judith Miller, "SEC Sues Aminex and 2 Ex-Officers Under the New Law," *The New York Times,* (March 11, 1978), p. 29, Column 3.

[15] See Chapters 8 and 12 for some possible implications of this law.

[16] D. R. Carmichael, "The Management Report," *Financial Executive* 46 (November 1978), p. 50. *Illustrations of Management Reports on Financial Statements* may be obtained from the AICPA.

In August 1988, the act was amended as part of an omnibus trade bill. Basically, individuals who knowingly fail to comply with the internal control standard can face criminal penalties on a limited basis. In addition, the amendments to the act clarify the definition of bribery and increase the penalty for bribery. For example, the amendments define what constitutes routine government actions, such as obtaining permits to do business in a foreign country. However, if a foreign official encourages or influences a decision to award or continue new or old business, then such action is not considered routine. Moreover, the corporation can now be fined a maximum of $2,000,000, and individuals up to $100,000.[17]

Federal Deposit Insurance Corporation Improvement Act of 1991[18]

On December 19, 1991, the United States Congress enacted the Federal Deposit Insurance Corporation Improvement Act. The major objective of this banking reform legislation is to strengthen the internal control environment of financial institutions and improve compliance with laws and regulations. The law provided for the establishment of independent audit committees and internal control reporting by management and the outside auditors. The law is applicable to insured depository institutions that have total assets of $150,000,000 or more. (See Appendix E for further details.)

In response to the banking law, the AICPA issued two Standards for Attestation Engagements that deal with reporting on the internal control structure and compliance attestation. (See Chapter 5 for further discussion.)

As Joseph F. Moraglio and James F. Green conclude:

A quick reading of the new law's audit and accounting provisions demonstrates it isn't purely about depository institutions. Congressional faith in the value of the audit function has driven, among other things, a mandate for annual audits and an increase in management reporting, with accompanying attestation about management's assertions by CPAs.

This trend toward increasing CPAs' role to attest to management's representations—in addition to financial statement audits—is likely to continue. The nature and form of the services specified in the new banking law may prove to be the model for future legislation.[19]

In addition to the aforementioned legislation related to corporate accountability, the audit committee should be aware of other congressional legislation, such

---

[17]The amendments are contained in Title V of Public Law No. 100-418, August 23, 1988. See Appendix D.

[18]The act is contained in Title 1 of Public Law 102-242, December 19, 1991.

[19]Joseph F. Moraglio and James F. Green, "The FDIC Improvement Act: A Precedent for Expanded CPA Reporting," *Journal of Accountancy* 173, No. 4 (April 1992), p. 71.

as the Racketeer Influenced and Corrupt Organizations Act (RICO), the Federal Sentencing Guidelines for Organizations, the Insider Trading Sanctions Act, the Insider Trading and Securities Fraud Enforcement Act, and the Private Securities Litigation Reform Act. Such legislation is applicable to officers, directors, and outside auditors because of their legal liability and allegations by plaintiff's bar that they knew or failed to know what they should have known of material misstatements of financial statements.

Securities and Exchange Commission Corporate Governance Rules

The SEC has been deeply concerned about corporate accountability. The rapid increase in the numerous disclosures of questionable and illegal payments has raised many questions concerning corporate governance. As a result, the SEC embarked on a review and study of the rules regarding corporate governance.

In July 1978, the SEC released a proposal (Number 34-14970) on the corporate conduct of the board of directors. Essentially, the proposal centered on ways to strengthen the independence of the board. For example, the SEC proposed that corporations disclose the identity of each director and nominee in terms of his or her nonmanagement or independent capacity. Accordingly, the SEC is attempting to define the director's affiliation in order to determine the director's dealings with the corporation. Thus, a banker who is affiliated with the corporation's bank should be identified.

Furthermore, the SEC proposed that corporations disclose the standing committees of the board of directors. For example, the SEC wants each corporation not only to disclose the standing committee, such as the nominating committee or audit committee, but also to identify the members of the committees with their affiliations. The objective is to form committees that consist of independent directors.

Moreover, in November 1978, the SEC approved rules with respect to the following disclosure requirements:

1. Relationships that corporate directors have with the company.
2. Whether a corporation has an audit, nominating, or compensation committee.
3. What those committees' functions are.
4. Names of committee members.
5. Report how often the board of directors and the director committees met. The corporation would have to report when a director failed to attend 75 percent of the aggregate number of board and committee meetings he is obligated to attend.
6. Disclose director resignations due to a disagreement concerning the corporation's operations, policies, or practices.[20]

---

[20] Deloitte Haskins & Sells, *The Week in Review,* Pamphlet 78-46 (Washington, D.C.: Deloitte Haskins & Sells, November 1978), p. 7. (See SEC Release No. 34-15384 for further details.)

During the 1980s and early 1990s, the SEC adopted a number of key initiatives related to financial reporting.[21]

- Form 10K signature requirement
- Concept release on Management's Discussion and Analysis (MD&A)
- Disclosure requirements with respect to changes in accounting firm and opinion shopping
- Disclosure related to environmental liabilities and contingencies
- Executive compensation disclosure[22]

Therefore, the SEC has enhanced corporate accountability through the issuance of rules that require more disclosure of the board structure and functions.

In reviewing the historical developments in corporate accountability, we have seen that Congress and the SEC endeavor to maintain corporate accountability through legislation and proposals to eliminate unfair corporate financial reporting. Indeed, within the framework of corporate accountability, corporate management must face laws and rules affecting its accountability to its constituencies. Consequently, the board of directors has turned to the audit committee since it is a viable mechanism to monitor corporate accountability.

Private-Sector Initiatives

National Commission on Fraudulent Financial Reporting (NCFFR)
One of the major guiding conclusions of the NCFFR's recommendations was corporate accountability. The Commission stated:

> When a company raises funds from the public, that company assumes an obligation of public trust and a commensurate level of accountability to the public. If a company wishes access to the public capital and credit markets, it must accept and fulfill certain obligations necessary to protect the public interest. One of the most fundamental obligations of the public company is the full and fair public disclosure of corporate information, including financial results.
>
> The independent public accountant who audits the financial statements of a public company also has a public obligation. As the U.S. Supreme Court has recognized, when the independent public accountant opines on a public company's financial statements, he assumes a public responsibility that transcends the contractual relationship

---

[21] See Chapters 3 and 5 for further discussion.

[22] Korn/Ferry International reported that more than half of the 327 CEOs, in its annual survey believe that the SEC rules are in the best interest of the shareholders. For example, "Seventy-three percent of the CEOs surveyed believe that the SEC's new compensation disclosure and proxy rules will give institutional investors more information and prompt an increase in proxy challenges." See Korn/Ferry International, *Twentieth Annual Board of Directors Study* (New York: 1993).

with his client. The independent public accountant's responsibility extends to the corporation's stockholders, creditors, customers, and the rest of the investing public. The regulations and standards for auditing public companies must be adequate to safeguard that public trust and auditors must adhere to those standards.[23]

To promote corporate accountability, the NCFFR recommended that officers and directors set the tone at the top and focus on the internal control as well as develop and enforce codes of conduct to establish a proper behavioral and ethical environment. Such initiatives can help to strengthen communication and trust, which are needed to guard against fraudulent financial reporting.[24]

American Institute of CPAs (AICPA)   Recognizing the continuing debate over business failure versus audit failure and the general public's misunderstanding of the independent audit process, in April 1988, the Auditing Standards Board (ASB) of the AICPA issued nine Statements on Auditing Standards (SAS) that focus on the "expectation gap":

SAS No. 53	"The Auditor's Responsibility to Detect and Report Errors and Irregularities" (SAS No. 82, "Consideration of Fraud in Financial Statement Audit," supersedes SAS No. 53.)
SAS No. 54	"Illegal Acts by Clients"
SAS No. 55	"Consideration of the Internal Control Structure in a Financial Statement Audit"
SAS No. 56	"Analytical Procedures"
SAS No. 57	"Auditing Accounting Estimates"
SAS No. 58	"Reports on Audited Financial Statements"
SAS No. 59	"The Auditor's Consideration of an Entity's Ability to Continue as a Going Concern"
SAS No. 60	"Communication of Internal Control Structure Related Matters Noted in an Audit"
SAS No. 61	"Communication with Audit Committees"

The aforementioned auditing pronouncements are discussed in Chapter 5; however, it is clearly evident from their titles that the ASB's objective was to enhance and strengthen the communication linkages between independent auditors and the board of directors through its audit committee. In turn, such pronouncements enable both independent auditors and boards to discharge their responsibilities for corporate accountability to the investing public.

[23] National Commission on Fraudulent Financial Reporting, *Report of the National Commission on Fraudulent Financial Reporting* (Washington, D.C.: National Commission on Fraudulent Financial Reporting, 1987), p. 5.
[24] See Appendix H: "COSO, *Internal Control—Integrated Framework* Executive Summary," September 1992.

The Public Oversight Board (POB)   Since 1977, the POB of the AICPA continues to have oversight responsibility for the Peer Review Program, which is administered by the SEC Practice Section. In addition, since 1979, the POB oversees the activities of the Quality Control Inquiry Committee, which is charged to review alleged audit failures. The chief accountant's staff of the SEC periodically reviews and annually reports on the POB's oversight activities related to the SEC Practice Section's programs.

With respect to corporate governance and accountability, the POB points out:

> In most corporations the responsibility for scrutiny of financial statements has been delegated by boards to their audit committees. The experience of the members of the Board indicates that in too many instances the audit committees do not perform their duties adequately and in many cases do not understand their responsibilities.[25]

In response, the POB recommended the following to audit committees and the SEC:

Recommendation V-9:

Audit committees (or the board if there is no audit committee) should assume the following responsibilities relating to an SEC registrant's preparation of annual financial statements: (a) review the annual financial statements; (b) confer with management and the independent auditor about them; (c) receive from the independent auditor all information that the auditor is required to communicate under auditing standards; (d) assess whether the financial statements are complete and consistent with information known to them; and (e) assess whether the financial statements reflect appropriate accounting principles.

Recommendation V-10:

The SEC should require registrants to include in a document containing the annual financial statements a statement by the audit committee (or by the board if there is no audit committee) that describes its responsibilities and tells how they were discharged. This disclosure should state whether the audit committee members (or in the absence of an audit committee, the members of the board) (a) have reviewed the annual financial statements; (b) have conferred with management and the independent auditor about them; (c) have received from the independent auditor all information that the auditor is required to communicate under auditing standards; (d) believe that the financial statements are complete and consistent with information known to them; and (e) believe that the financial statements reflect appropriate accounting principles.[26]

---

[25] Public Oversight Board, *A Special Report by the Public Oversight Board of the SEC Practice Section* (Stamford, Conn.: Public Oversight Board, 1993), p. 50.
[26] Ibid., pp. 51–52.

The Institute of Internal Auditors (IIA)   Also playing an important role in the area of corporate accountability and audit committees is the Institute of Internal Auditors. Recognizing that there must be an agreement in principle on the relationship between the audit committee and the internal audit group, the IIA issued the following positive statement:

Purpose

The Institute of Internal Auditors recognizes that audit committees and internal auditors have common goals. A good working relationship with internal auditors can assist the audit committee in fulfilling its responsibility to the board of directors, shareholders, and other outside parties. This position statement summarizes The Institute's views concerning the appropriate relationship between audit committees and internal auditing. The Institute acknowledges that audit committee responsibilities encompass activities which are beyond the scope of this statement, and in no way intends it to be a comprehensive description of audit committee responsibilities.

Statement

The Institute of Internal Auditors recommends that every public company have an audit committee organized as a standing committee of the board of directors. The Institute also encourages the establishment of audit committees in other organizations, including not-for-profit and governmental bodies. The audit committee should consist solely of outside directors, independent of management.

The primary responsibilities of the audit committee should involve assisting the board of directors in carrying out their responsibilities as they relate to the organization's accounting policies, internal control and financial reporting practices. The audit committee should establish and maintain lines of communication between the board and the company's independent auditors, internal auditors, and financial management.

The audit committee should expect internal auditing to examine and evaluate the adequacy and effectiveness of the organization's system of internal control and the quality of performance in carrying out assigned responsibilities. Internal auditing may be used as a source of information to the audit committee on major frauds or irregularities as well as company compliance with laws and regulations.

To assure that internal auditors carry out their responsibilities, the audit committee should approve and periodically review the internal audit charter, a management-approved document which states internal audit's purpose, authority, and responsibility. The audit committee should review annually the internal audit department's objectives and goals, audit schedules, staffing plans, and financial budgets. The director of internal auditing should inform the audit committee of the results of audits, highlighting significant audit findings and recommendations. The audit committee should also determine whether internal audit activities are being carried out in accordance with the *Standards for the Professional Practice of Internal Auditing,* adopted by The Institute of Internal Auditors.

To help assure independence, the director of internal auditing should have direct communication with the audit committee. The director should attend audit committee meetings and meet privately with the audit committee at least annually. Independence is further enhanced when the audit committee concurs in the appointment or removal of the director of internal auditing.[27]

American Law Institute (ALI)[28] Since 1982, the ALI has issued 12 draft statements on the topic of corporate governance. Such draft statements and recommendations are from the proceedings of the Institute's annual meetings. Over the years, the ALI has strongly supported and endorsed the concept of audit committee. A review of the tentative draft documents and ALI's recommendations for audit committees clearly indicates that the legal profession echoes the position of the accounting profession. Both professions recognize that audit committees have a major role in corporate governance and accountability and in the financial reporting process.

Canada

With respect to public sector initiatives, Canada has mandated the establishment of audit committees for publicly held companies. This direct action was initially required on a provincial basis and, subsequently, on a national basis for federally chartered public companies. For example, the Ontario Business Corporation Act, in Section 182, requires that publicly held companies elect annually an audit committee.[29]

In June 1988, the Commission to Study the Public's Expectation of Audits (the MacDonald Commission) issued its final report. Specifically, the Commission's mission was to investigate as follows:

> Where a gap exists between what the public expects or needs and what auditors can and should reasonably expect to accomplish, the Commission is charged to develop conclusions and recommendations to determine how the disparity should be resolved.[30]

Ultimately, the Commission issued 50 recommendations. With respect to corporate accountability, strengthening the audit environment, and audit committees, the Commission made the following recommendations:

---

[27] The Institute of Internal Auditors, Inc., *Internal Auditing and the Audit Committee: Working Together Toward Common Goals* (Altamonte Springs, Fla.: The Institute of Internal Auditors, 1987), p. 1.
[28] For a good discussion of corporate governance, see American Law Institute, *Principles of Corporate Governance: Analysis and Recommendations* (Philadelphia, Pa.: American Law Institute, 1994).
[29] See Appendix C.
[30] Commission to Study the Public's Expectations of Audits, *Report of the Commission to Study the Public's Expectation of Audits* (Toronto: The Canadian Institute of Chartered Accountants, 1988), p. iii.

R-1   The CICA [Canadian Institute of Charted Accountants] should enlist the support of provincial institutes and other interested bodies in seeking legislative amendments that would require all public companies to have audit committees composed entirely of outside directors.

R-2   The CICA Auditing Standards Committee should provide guidance in the *CICA Handbook* to matters that should be raised by an auditor with an audit committee (or in the absence of an audit committee, with the board of directors) and to actions an auditor should take when not satisfied with the results of such communication. The guidance should stress the need for timeliness in communication.

R-3   The CICA and provincial institutes of chartered accountants should press for changes in the law to require that (1) boards of directors draw up and publish to the shareholders a formal statement of responsibilities assigned to the audit committee, (2) audit committees report annually to the shareholders on the manner in which they have fulfilled their mandate, and that (3) audit committees review both interim financial statements and annual financial statements before publication.[31]

United Kingdom

In the United Kingdom, there are no mandated requirements for audit committees. However, in May 1991, the Financial Reporting Council, the London Stock Exchange, and the accounting profession established the Committee on the Financial Aspects of Corporate Governance (Cadbury Committee). On December 1, 1992, the Committee issued its final report and a Code of Best Practice. The code contains four key areas: board of directors, nonexecutive directors, executive directors, and reporting and controls. Such areas help to engender a high degree of integrity in the financial reporting process and strengthen corporate accountability. The following are excerpts from the code:

> There should be a clearly accepted division of responsibilities at the head of a company, which will ensure a balance of power and authority, such that no one individual has unfettered powers of decision. Where the chairman is also the chief executive, it is essential that there should be a strong and independent element on the board, with a recognized senior member.

> Non-executive directors should bring an independent judgment to bear on issues of strategy, performance, resources, including key appointments, and standards of conduct.

> Directors' service contracts should not exceed three years without shareholders' approval.

---

[31] Ibid., p. 139.

The board should establish an audit committee of at least three non-executive directors with written terms of reference which deal clearly with its authority and duties.[32]

The Committee's central recommendation is that the boards of all listed companies registered in the United Kingdom should comply with the code. The Committee encourages as many other companies as possible to aim at meeting its requirements:

The Committee also recommends:

(a) that listed companies reporting in respect of years ending after 30 June 1993 should make a statement in their report and accounts about their compliance with the Code and identify and give reasons for any areas of non-compliance;

(b) that companies' statements of compliance should be reviewed by the auditors before publication. The review by the auditors should cover only those parts of the compliance statement which relate to provisions of the Code where compliance can be objectively verified.

The publication of a statement of compliance, reviewed by the auditors, is to be made a continuing obligation of listing by the London Stock Exchange.[33]

CORPORATE ACCOUNTABILITY AND THE AUDIT COMMITTEE

The Role of the Audit Committee

The audit committee has a critical role within the framework of corporate accountability since the jurisdiction of the committee is to oversee and monitor the activities of the corporation's financial reporting system and the internal and external audit processes. The audit committee assists the board of directors with the development and maintenance of the corporate accountability framework, because the committee compels the board to be accountable for its stewardship accountability. Thus the audit committee helps create an environment in which the activities of corporate management are subject to scrutiny.

As Harold M. Williams, former chairman of the SEC, asserted:

It should be evident, but perhaps bears repeating, that integrity in reporting financial data is vital both to an efficient and effective securities market and to capital formation. One key to increasing public confidence in that data long advocated by many

---

[32] Committee on the Financial Aspects of Corporate Governance, *The Code of Best Practice* (London, England: Gee [a division of Professional Publishing Ltd.], 1992), pp. 6–7. For further discussion on the successor committee (Hampel Committee) to the Cadbury Committee, see *Accountancy* 120, No. 1249 (September 1997), p. 16, and Appendix F for the Combined Code.

[33] Ibid., p. 3. See Appendix F for the Cadbury Committee's recommendations on audit committees. For a provocative discussion on corporate governance, see Oxford Analytica, *Board Directors and Corporate Governance* (London: August 1992).

segments of the financial community, including public accounting firms, is more direct involvement by boards of directors in the auditing process and the integrity of reported financial information. The vehicle which the Securities and Exchange Commission, the New York Stock Exchange and an increasing number of public corporations have turned to has been the independent audit committee.[34]

As a standing committee appointed by the board of directors, the audit committee is directly accountable for its actions to the board. The audit committee operates in an advisory capacity. Thus the audit committee has limited authority, because a final decision concerning its recommendations is made by the board. The board seeks guidance from the audit committee in formulating or amending the financial accounting policies to service properly the needs of its various constituencies.

With respect to the expectations of the various constituencies, Russell E. Palmer, former managing partner of Touche Ross and Co. (now Deloitte and Touche), stated:

> Every audit committee will be expected to weigh the appropriateness of the corporation's accounting policies as they apply to the corporation and its industry. It seems reasonable that committee members will be expected to assess and be satisfied with the corporation's entire disclosure system—the financial statements, the published stockholders' reports, and even discussions between management and the financial media.[35]

To further illustrate the role of the audit committee, Exhibit 2.1 diagrams the direct relationship between the committee and its constituencies in the internal corporate environment.

Important Surveys

In their survey of audit committees, Joseph F. Castellano, Harper A. Roehm, and Albert A. Vondra found that the corporate community is building a strong case for self-regulation by complying with the recommendation of the Treadway Commission. Such compliance has improved the quality of financial reporting.[36] Their survey results are further supported by Ivan Bull. He found that in a survey of 13 chairpersons of publicly held corporations in Illinois, "most boards were either already following or have since implemented the Treadway Commission rec-

---

[34] Harold M. Williams, "Audit Committees—The Public Sector's View," *Journal of Accountancy* 144, No. 3 (September 1977), p. 71.

[35] Russell E. Palmer, "Audit Committees—Are They Effective? An Auditor's View," *Journal of Accountancy* 144, No. 3 (September 1977), p. 77.

[36] Joseph F. Castellano, Harper A. Roehm, and Albert A. Vondra, "Audit Committee Compliance with the Treadway Commission Report: A Survey," *OHIO CPA Journal* 48, No. 4 (Winter 1989), p. 42.

Exhibit 2.1 The Audit Committee's Accountability Relationship

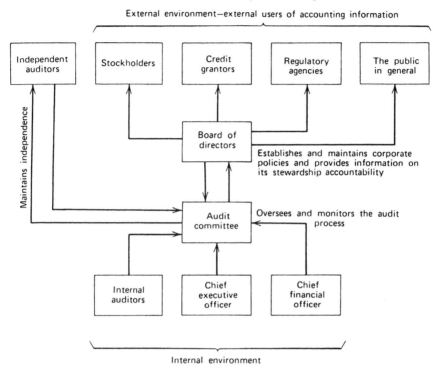

ommendations" to prevent fraudulent misstatements in their financial statements. "Audit committee chairpeople generally believe their committees are 'informed, vigilant, and effective overseers' described in the Treadway report."[37]

In another survey of audit partners, directors of internal auditing, and chief financial officers associated with audit committees of 90 U.S. corporations, Lawrence P. Kalbers and Timothy J. Fogarty investigated the relationship between audit committee effectiveness and the types and extent of the committee's power. They concluded:

> This study suggests that the fundamental types of power needed by audit committees to perform effectively are (1) institutional support, (2) actual authority (written and implied), and (3) diligence. With the possible exception of written mandates (such as audit committee charters), these factors are especially difficult to evaluate

[37] Ivan Bull, "Board of Director Acceptance of Treadway Responsibilities," *Journal of Accountancy* 171, No. 2 (February 1991), p. 67.

with any traditional means of regulation. Perhaps more effective regulation should aim for more substantive reviews of power within the organization.[38]

The Audit Committee and the Chief Executive Officer   The chief executive officer has an obligation not only to the board but also to the standing committees of the board. The chief executive officer (CEO) is primarily responsible for recommending major policy decisions to the board of directors. Since the CEO participates in the decisions concerning the financial accounting policies, he or she should have direct communication with the audit committee.

However, it is essential that the audit committee be totally independent from the CEO because he or she is a "managing director." As a managing director, the CEO participates in the general administration of the corporation as well as assuming ultimate responsibility for the decisions.

Based on a close examination of the audit committees of 13 corporations listed on the New York Stock Exchange, M. L. Lovdal found that:

> Effective audit committees permit the chief executive to attend by invitation only. . . .
> After all, he is the best source concerning questions related to the business and he
> can ensure quick action on committee requests. In achieving the appropriate rela-
> tionship with the chief executive, a key ingredient is the quality of the audit com-
> mittee chairman. He must have both the sensitivity to know when to bring the CEO
> into the group's deliberations and the strength to stand up to him when the commit-
> tee wants to pursue an inquiry or change policy.[39]

In short, the audit committee should determine its own agenda items, which should not be based on the chief executive officer's prerogatives. As Ivan Bull observed:

> Concern about other environmental factors, such as legal liability, also may have in-
> fluenced board agendas and operating practices. The board's practice of allowing

---

[38] Lawrence P. Kalbers and Timothy J. Fogarty, "Audit Committee Effectiveness: An Empirical Investigation of the Contribution of Power," *Auditing: A Journal of Practice & Theory* 12, No. 1 (Spring 1993), p. 45. For additional information, consult Dana Wechsler, "Giving the Watchdog Fangs," *Forbes* 144 (November 13, 1989), p. 130, 132–133; Nelson Luscombe, "More Power to Audit Committees" *CA Magazine* 122, No. 5 (May 1989), pp. 26–37; Dorothy A. McMullen, "Audit Committee Performance: An Investigation of the Consequences Associated with Audit Committees," *Auditing: A Journal of Practice & Theory* 15, No. 1 (Spring 1996), pp. 87–103; Donald J. Kirk and Arthur Siegel, "How Directors and Auditors Can Improve Corporate Governance," *Journal of Accountancy* 181, No. 1 (January 1996), pp. 53–57; Zabihollah Rezaee, "Corporate Governance and Accountability: The Role of Audit Committees," *Internal Auditing* 13, No. 1 (Summer 1997), pp. 27–41; and Michael A. Mackenzie, "The Evolving Board: The Mechanism of Board Oversight," *Canadian Business Law Journal* 26 (1996), pp. 140–144.

[39] Michael L. Lovdal, "Making the Audit Committee Work," *Harvard Business Review* 55 (March–April 1977), p. 110.

and listening to dissent and advice from outside members is healthier than the popular belief that CEOs dominate passive boards.[40]

The Audit Committee and the Chief Financial Officer[41] In most corporations, the chief financial officer (CFO) is responsible for the functions of the controller. In turn, the CFO is accountable to the president for the conduct of the various administrative functions of the controller. Although the controller is responsible for the general administration and supervision of the accounting operations, the CFO has executive responsibility for the financial accounting policies.

Since the audit committee is responsible for assuring that management fulfills its responsibilities in the preparation of the financial statements, the CFO should consult with the committee in order to coordinate the financial accounting activities. Thus the audit committee should have a dialogue with the CFO to consider any questions concerning the financial reporting practices. For example, if the CFO has certain reservations or exceptions to certain accounting policies and practices, the audit committee would recommend the necessary course of action subsequent to its consultation with the independent auditors.

The Audit Committee and the Internal Audit Group The director of internal auditing is essentially responsible for the establishment and maintenance of an effective and efficient system of internal auditing. With respect to the audit committee's involvement with the internal audit group, Lovdal points out:

> The internal audit group can be an avenue for the committee in reaching the source of a variety of problems. One committee I examined uses internal auditors regularly for investigations in such areas as computer security, transfer pricing, and capital budgeting. For these activities, the committee should deal directly with the head of internal audit, rather than solely through other finance or control executives, and should make itself knowledgeable about the organization, staffing, and budgets of the internal audit department.[42]

The reporting responsibility of the internal audit group varies from one organization to the next. For example, the director of internal auditing may report to the controller or chief financial officer and meet with the audit committee on a separate or joint basis. However, the director of internal auditing should have access to the audit committee to provide for a forum whereby the internal audit group can resolve questionable matters between the audit staff and corporate management. (See Chapter 9.)

---

[40] Bull, "Board of Director Acceptance," p. 71. Also see J. Michael Cook, "The CEO and the Audit Committee," *Chief Executive,* No. 76 (April 1993), pp. 44–47.

[41] For further discussion, see Louis Braiotta, Jr., and Jay R. Olson, "Guiding the Audit Committee: A CFO's Concern," *Financial Executive* 51, No. 9 (September 1983), pp. 52–54. See also Chapter 13 for a discussion of the audit committee's review of the quarterly reporting process.

[42] Lovdal, "Making the Audit Committee Work," p. 111.

RECENT DEVELOPMENTS IN CORPORATE GOVERNANCE

During the latter half of the 1990s, several key organizations in both the private and public sectors have issued reports on how boards of directors can improve corporate accountability, responsibility, and governance. The recommendations and/or conclusions of these reports are briefly presented in order to help the audit committee effectively discharge its oversight responsibilities for the audit processes as well as the financial reporting process.

Public Oversight Board

At a January 1994 AICPA conference in Washington, D.C., Walter Schultze, former chief accountant of the Securities and Exchange Commission, indicated his concern for a growing lack of independence and objectivity of the auditing profession. In response, the POB decided to form an Advisory Panel on Auditor Independence, chaired by Donald J. Kirk, former chair of the Financial Accounting Standards Board. In September 13, 1994, the Advisory Panel issued its report entitled *Strengthening the Professionalism of the Independent Auditor*. With respect to the adoption of a corporate governance approach to improve financial reporting, the panel's principal conclusions were:

1. There is no need at this time for additional rules, regulations, or legislation dealing with the conflict-of-interest aspect of auditor independence. There are, however, important steps that should be taken in other ways to strengthen the professionalism of independent auditors.
2. Auditing is different from other services accounting firms render. It imposes special and higher responsibilities. Independent auditing firms, regulators, and overseers of the public accounting profession need to focus on how the audit function can be enhanced and not submerged in large multi-line public accounting/management consulting firms.
3. The Public Oversight Board, the SEC, and others should support proposals to enhance the independence of boards of directors and their accountability to shareholders. Stronger, more accountable corporate boards of directors will strengthen the professionalism of the outside auditor, enhance the value of the independent audit, and serve the investing public.
4. To increase the value of the independent audit, corporate boards of directors and their audit committees must hear independent auditors' views as professional advisors on the appropriateness of the accounting principles used or proposed to be adopted by the company, the clarity of its financial disclosures, and the degree of aggressiveness or conservatism of the company's accounting principles and underlying estimates.
5. The accounting profession should look to the representatives of the shareholders—the board of directors—as the client, not corporate management.

Boards and auditors are, or should be, natural allies in protecting shareholder interests.

6. Auditors must assume the obligation to communicate qualitative judgments about accounting principles, disclosures, and estimates. By doing so, independent auditors can add to the effectiveness of boards of directors in monitoring corporate performance on behalf of shareholders and in assuring that shareholders receive relevant and reliable financial information about company performance and financial condition.

7. By making these suggestions to boards and auditors, the Panel's objective is not to narrow the range of acceptable accounting practices (that may follow in due course) but to give directors a better basis for influencing corporate practices. These suggestions should also enhance the objectivity and strengthen the professionalism of the auditor.

8. Because they share the objective of providing the public with relevant and reliable financial information, the public accounting profession, the standard setters, and the SEC must have more cooperative, less adversarial relationships. CPA firms should be careful in how they communicate their views to the FASB, the SEC, their clients, and the public at large. The SEC should help identify accounting practice problems and look to the private sector standard setters to solve them. It should only be a standard setter of "last resort" and then only after appropriate due process.

9. It is urgent that the SEC take the lead in helping the profession to reduce exposure to unwarranted litigation. There are dangers, not just to the profession but to the investing public, if the current liability situation continues to drift without SEC leadership.

10. While tort reform is necessary, the other suggestions in this report can be considered separately from, and need not await, legislative action on litigation reform.

For the future, the Panel believes that the SEC and the POB should consider devoting resources to stay informed on a continuing basis about developments in the auditing profession and in the market for audit services. As described in this report, some of those developments could materially affect the viability of the independent audit as a private sector activity. By having the facts, the SEC and the POB will be in a position to anticipate and take appropriate steps to strengthen auditor professionalism.[43]

---

[43] Advisory Panel on Auditor Independence, *Strengthening the Professionalism of the Independent Auditor* (Stamford, Conn.: Public Oversight Board, 1994), pp. 30–31. More recently, Chairman Arthur Levitt and Chief Accountant Lynn E. Turner of the Securities and Exchange Commission asked the Public Oversight Board to form a Panel on Audit Effectiveness to review and evaluate current audit methodologies and assess the impact of recent trends on the public interest (see the Public Oversight Board, *Annual Report 1997–1998* (Stamford, Conn.: Public Oversight Board, 1999).

In the fall of 1995, the POB issued a report entitled *Directors, Management, and Auditors—Allies in Protecting Shareholder Interests*. This report was a follow-up to the report of the Advisory Panel on Auditor Independence. To help boards of directors, audit committees, management, and independent auditors achieve a constructive relationship for both the audit and financial reporting processes, the POB recommended the following:

- **Responsibilities of Management** "Financial management should assume an obligation to bring to the attention of both the independent auditor and audit committee the accounting implications of significant new transactions and policies while they are being contemplated, not after the fact or after financial information based on them has been released publicly. This is critical to an effective corporate governance approach to financial reporting."

- **Responsibilities of the Independent Auditor** "The auditor should express his or her views about the appropriateness, not just the acceptability, of the accounting principles and financial disclosure practices used or proposed to be adopted by the company and, particularly, about the degree of aggressiveness or conservatism of its accounting principles and underlying estimates and the relevance and reliability of the resulting information for investment, credit, and similar decisions."

- **Responsibilities of Boards of Directors and Audit Committees** "Boards of directors have a fiduciary responsibility to shareholders and others for reliable financial reports. To meet that responsibility they should be aware of the implications of alternative accounting principles for reporting significant transactions and events as well as the aggressiveness or conservatism of significant estimates. It is vital, therefore, that audit committees function effectively as the board's primary contact with both financial management and the independent auditor."[44]

Additionally, the POB suggested that the following three steps are needed to further improve the credibility of financial reporting:

(1) The board of directors must recognize the primacy of its accountability to shareholders. (2) The auditor must look to the board of directors as the client. (3) The board, and its audit committee, must expect and the auditor must deliver candid communication about the quality of the company's financial reporting.[45]

---

[44] Public Oversight Board, *Directors, Management, and Auditors-Allies in Protecting Shareholder Interests* (Stamford, Conn.: Public Oversight Board, 1995), pp. 3–5. For further discussion, see the recommendations of the Blue Ribbon Committee on Improving the Effectiveness of Corporate Audit Committees as indicated in Chapter 14, Exhibit 14.3.

[45] Ibid., p. 6.

With respect to ways for audit committees to implement these suggestions, the POB prescribed the following steps to ensure that their charter or terms of reference are sufficient and adequate:

- An instruction to the independent auditor that the board of directors, as the shareholders' representative, is the auditor's client.

- An expectation that financial management and the independent auditor perform a timely analysis of significant financial reporting issues and practices.

- An expectation that financial management and the independent auditor discuss with the audit committee their qualitative judgments about the appropriateness, not just the acceptability, of accounting principles and financial disclosure practices used or proposed to be adopted by the company and, particularly, about the degree of aggressiveness or conservatism of its accounting principles and underlying estimates.

- An opportunity for the independent auditor to be available to the full board of directors at least annually to help provide a basis for the board to recommend to shareholders the appointment of the auditor or ratification of the board's selection of the auditor.

The audit committee discussion with the independent auditor about the appropriateness of accounting principles and financial disclosure practices should generally include the following:

- the auditor's independent qualitative judgments about the appropriateness, not just the acceptability, of the accounting principles and the clarity of the financial disclosure practices used or proposed to be adopted by the company

- the auditor's views about whether management's choices of accounting principles are conservative, moderate, or extreme from the perspective of income, asset, and liability recognition, and whether those principles are common practices or are minority practices

- the auditor's reasoning in determining the appropriateness of changes in accounting principles and disclosure practices

- the auditor's reasoning in determining the appropriateness of the accounting principles and disclosure practices adopted by management for new transactions or events

- the auditor's reasoning in accepting or questioning significant estimates made by management

- the auditor's views about how the company's choices of accounting principles and disclosure practices may affect shareholders and public views and attitudes about the company.[46]

---

[46] Ibid., p. 6.

GENERAL ACCOUNTING OFFICE

In September 1996, the General Accounting Office (GAO) issued a report entitled *The Accounting Profession—Major Issues: Progress and Concerns*. While the GAO found that the accounting profession's self-regulation program for strengthening the audit process had responded well to the recommendations by the POB, it identified continuing major issues, such as auditor independence, fraud detection, improvement in audit quality, accounting and auditing standard setting, the financial reporting model, and the impact of growing business complexity on the traditional audit function.

With respect to the subject of corporate governance and auditor independence, the GAO's principal findings are:

> The independence of public accountants—both in fact and appearance—is crucial to the credibility of financial reporting and, in turn, the capital formation process. Various study groups over the past 20 years have considered the independence and objectivity of auditors as questions have arisen from (1) significant litigation involving auditors, (2) the auditor's performance of consulting services for audit clients, (3) "opinion shopping" by clients, and (4) reports of accountants advocating questionable client positions on accounting matters.

> The accounting profession recognizes the importance of auditor independence and has taken various steps to strengthen independence. For example, the profession revised its code of ethics to help ensure auditor independence and objectivity and adopted a code of professional conduct to govern the acceptance of consulting services and/or other activities that may be perceived as creating conflicts of interest. In addition, AICPA members are now required to report annually to the client's audit committee the total fees received for management consulting services during the year under audit and a description of the types of such services rendered. Further, auditing standards require auditors to inform the audit committee of matters such as disagreements with management, consultations with other accountants, and difficulties encountered in performing the audit. The standards also require auditors to report to the audit committee internal control weaknesses that could adversely affect the client's ability to safeguard assets and to produce reliable financial statements.

> Others have also acted to strengthen auditor independence. For example, the SEC requires disclosures when an auditor resigns or is dismissed from an audit in order to discourage the practice of changing auditors to obtain a more favorable accounting treatment. In 1991, the Congress enacted the Federal Deposit Insurance Corporation Improvement Act (FDICIA), which includes requirements for independent audit committees in large banks and savings and loans, such as matters they should discuss with the independent auditor, and also sets audit committee membership requirements for the largest of the institutions. In 1995, the Congress enacted the Private Securities Litigation Reform Act of 1995, which codifies the auditor's responsibility for

reporting illegal acts to audit committees and requires, in certain circumstances, auditors to report illegal acts to regulators.

Despite actions taken by the accounting profession and others to strengthen auditor independence, concerns remain. In 1992 and again in 1994, the SEC Chief Accountant questioned the independence of accounting firms in situations in which they condoned or advocated what he questioned as inappropriate interpretations of accounting standards to benefit their clients. In addition, study groups have expressed concern that the growth of consulting services, relative to a static level of auditing and accounting services, could be perceived as lessening the objectivity of the auditor.

Both the accounting profession and the SEC have been active in examining continuing auditor independence concerns. They have found there is no conclusive evidence that providing traditional management consulting services compromises auditor independence. Further, they believe that such services not only benefit the client, but ultimately benefit investors and other interested parties. GAO believes measures that would limit auditor services or mandate changing auditors at set intervals are outweighed by the value of continuity in conducting audits and the value of traditional consulting services. However, GAO also believes that questions of auditor independence will probably continue as long as the existing auditor/client relationship continues. This concern over auditor independence may become larger as accounting firms move to provide new services that go beyond traditional services. The accounting profession needs to be attentive to the concerns over independence in considering the appropriateness of new services to ensure that independence is not impaired and the auditor's traditional values of being objective and skeptical are not diminished.

GAO supports a recent proposal by the AICPA's Public Oversight Board to bring the independent auditor into a more direct working relationship with the board of directors. The proposal also emphasizes the role of the independent audit committee as an overseer of the company's financial reporting process, a buffer between management and the auditor, and a representative of user interests. Such a change is inherently difficult to accomplish. Further, the change may not happen voluntarily since a GAO survey of Fortune Industrial 500 and Fortune Service 500 companies showed that audit committee chairmen appear satisfied with their present relationship with the independent auditor. The fear of litigation by boards of directors and audit committees is another barrier to voluntarily changing auditor/client relationships and the perceived increase in their responsibilities that may result. Although the recently enacted Private Securities Litigation Reform Act of 1995 provides some liability relief and requires reporting on certain matters that could involve directors and auditors, the Act does not fundamentally address existing working relationships between auditors and boards of directors or audit committees.

As an alternative to voluntary action, the SEC, which has the responsibility and authority under securities laws to ensure that accountants who audit companies registered with the SEC are independent, could more clearly define the roles of boards of directors and audit committees as they relate to the independent auditor. The SEC has been reluctant to exercise authority in matters of corporate governance and may want to seek legislation expressly authorizing the SEC to act in this area. For example, the SEC could seek legislation containing audit committee requirements such as those in FDICIA. Although FDICIA-type requirements do not establish a formal relationship between the auditor and the audit committee, they would be an improvement over the current situation. Such requirements could specify certain audit committee qualifications and basic responsibilities regarding reviewing with the auditors the reports on financial statements, internal controls, and compliance with laws and regulations. An independent and knowledgeable audit committee as envisioned by FDICIA would enhance the effectiveness of having the auditor report directly to the audit committee.

As another alternative, the SEC could work through the major stock exchanges to achieve listing requirements that would more specifically define audit committee duties and responsibilities and their relationships with the independent auditor. The listing agreements of the major stock exchanges already require members to have audit committees, so the basic principle has been established. Such an approach by the stock exchanges, backed by the SEC, would not require legislation.[47]

AICPA SEC PRACTICE SECTION

In addition to the previous POB initiatives and the aforementioned GAO report, in 1997 the Best Practices Task Force of the SEC Practice Section Peer Review Committee of the AICPA issued its report entitled *Best Practices—Accounting Consultations, Communications with Board of Director/Audit Committees, Communications with the SEC Staff*. With respect to the best practices in Communications with Board of Directors/Audit Committees in 1996, the task force conducted a survey of the practices of a sample of peer reviewed firms to address the POB Advisory Panel's recommendations. As a result of the survey, the SEC Practice Section disseminated to all member firms the following recommended guidance:

- Establish policies and procedures within the firm related to communications with boards/audit committees. Discuss such policies and procedures with members of the professional staff to enhance their understanding of the issues and to reemphasize the firm's commitment to client service. The information that follows may be used as a guide in establishing or evaluating the firm's policies and procedures in this area. It also may be useful in strengthening the relationships between firms and their clients' boards/audit committees so that the relationships best serve the needs of those clients and their shareholders.

---

[47] General Accounting Office, *The Accounting Profession—Major Issues: Progress and Concerns* (Washington, D.C.: U.S. Government Printing Office, 1996), pp. 7–9.

- Establish a framework for the development of relationships that stresses open and candid conversation between the auditor and the boards/audit committees and allows the boards to fulfill their responsibilities to their shareholders. These discussions also may serve to facilitate a board's/audit committee's redefinition or determination of their respective roles. Provide a copy of an initiate a discussion with the board/audit committee about the recommendations in the POB Panel's report. Also, providing a copy of and discussing the POB Panel's report with members of senior management reemphasize the auditor's role in facilitating the board's responsibility to their shareholders and serve to enhance the auditor's relationship with management. It may also serve to facilitate a working partnership between the board/audit committee, senior management and the auditor. Providing firm literature to boards/audit committees relative to the role of the board/audit committee also may be useful.

- Discuss with boards/audit committees the appropriateness and acceptability of the accounting principles and the clarity of the Company's financial statement disclosures. Discussions with boards/audit committees would typically include the auditor's judgments regarding the reasonableness of management's estimates included in the Company's financial statements and the auditor's judgments regarding recently issued accounting principles and/or financial statement disclosures. Hold such discussions with management first to ensure that the auditor has a clear and comprehensive understanding of management's rationale for determining the appropriateness of the Company's accounting principles and financial statement disclosures and estimates.

- Consider involving a concurring or second partner and/or a consultation partner in discussions regarding issues relative to the Company before meeting with the audit committee.

- To enhance the efficiency and effectiveness of the audit process, conduct discussions regarding the appropriateness and acceptability of accounting principles, the clarity of financial statement disclosures, and the reasonableness of management's estimates in advance of the Company's year end. A timely discussion allows boards to analyze management's estimates, accounting principles and key financial disclosures along with the auditor's assessment of the acceptability and appropriateness of those estimates, accounting principles and financial statement disclosures and to make appropriate changes to a Company's financial statements before they are finalized. Consider incorporating these discussions into the agenda for the annual audit planning meeting with boards/audit committees. Co-ordinate a final discussion with boards/audit committees at the conclusion of the engagement, in conjunction with communications required under generally accepted auditing standards.

- Establish a regular meeting schedule with boards/audit committees and management to discuss issues relative to a Company, including those noted above. Hold face-to-face discussions with the boards/audit committees at least once a year. Consider communications with the boards/audit committees on a quarterly basis, especially for clients with quarterly reporting requirements. Regular meetings facilitate communication and understanding regarding the expectations of the boards/audit committees of the auditors and an auditor's expectation of boards/audit committees.

- During the proposal process with prospective clients, discuss the POB Panel's report and the firm's commitment to the establishment of a sound working relationship with the board/audit committee.[48]

INDEPENDENCE STANDARDS BOARD

In May 1997, the SEC and the AICPA announced the establishment of the Independence Standards Board (ISB) to set independence standards for auditors of public companies. In February 1998, the SEC formally recognized the ISB. The ISB was established in response to the belief that the accounting profession's AICPA Code of Professional Conduct and the SEC independence regulations were not adequate to deal with auditor independence questions in a rapidly changing business environment along with the independent accounting firms' new service areas. Thus the major objective of this joint effort is to replace the current case-driven system of adopting independence rules with a principles-based system.

The ISB has eight members (four public and four professional) who serve on a part-time basis. In addition, the ISB has a nine-member Independence Issues Committee (IIC). Either the ISB or the IIC may identify and address inquiries related to emerging independence issues. Also, the ISB or the IIC does not alter or replace the AICPA's Code of Professional Conduct.

According to the AICPA's White Paper, which was submitted to the ISB on October 20, 1997, the ISB would adopt the following approach:

> The proposed new conceptual framework is based on the enforced self-regulation model and reflects the economic and other determinants of auditor independence. For purposes of the new framework, independence would be defined as an absence of interests that create an unacceptable risk of bias with respect to the quality or context of information that is the subject of an audit engagement. Consistent with this definition, the ISB would adopt core principles of independence, promulgate guidelines on how those principles would be applied to situations that raise a threat to independence, identify appropriate types of safeguards and require firms to draft independence codes implementing the system, subject to ISB review. The SEC, the AICPA and state boards of accountancy would retain appropriate oversight and enforcement roles.

[48]American Institute of Certified Public Accountants, SEC Practice Section, *Best Practices—Communications with Board of Directors/Audit Committees* (New York: American Institute of Certified Public Accountants, 1997), pp. 24–25.

Under the new framework, the ISB would adopt the following core principles, which reflect a broad consensus of views within the profession regarding the primary considerations bearing on auditor independence:

- Auditors and firms should not be financially dependent upon an audit client;

- Auditors and firms should not have conflicting interests that would impair their objectivity with regard to matters affecting the financial statements; and,

- Auditors and firms should not have relationships with, or engage in activities for, clients that would entail making managerial decisions or otherwise serve to impair an auditor's objectivity.[49]

In May 1998, the ISB had proposed that the AICPA SEC Practice Section adopt a new membership requirement directing auditors to issue an annual independence confirmation under the rules created by the ISB, SEC, and AICPA. Such a report would be issued to the client company's audits committee (or board of directors).[50] In January 1999, ISB issued ISB Standard No. 1, "Independence Discussions with Audit Committees." The new requirement is effective for audits of public companies with fiscal years ending after July 15, 1999, with earlier adoption permitted. (Visit the ISB web site, www.cpaindependence.org)

NATIONAL ASSOCIATION OF CORPORATE DIRECTORS

In September 1996, the National Association of Corporate Directors (NACD) issued the *Report of the NACD Blue Ribbon Commission on Director Professionalism*. Recognizing that the board of directors is the centerpiece of corporate governance, the Commission described and endorsed key elements of professionalism for board members and for boards. The Commission concluded that:

A professional boardroom culture requires that the governance process be collectively determined by individual board members who:

- are independent of management

- are persons of integrity and diligence who make the necessary commitment of time and energy

- recognize that the board has a function independent of management and explicitly agree on that function, and

---

[49]American Institute of Certified Public Accountants, *Serving the Public Interest: A New Conceptual Framework for Auditor Independence* (New York: American Institute of Certified Public Accountants, 1997), pp. 7–8.

[50]For further discussion, see *Invitation to Comment,* "Proposed Recommendation to the Executive Committee of the SEC Practice Section of the American Institute of Certified Public Accountants" (New York: Independence Standards Board, May 29, 1998).

- are capable of performing that function as a group, combining diverse skills, perspectives, and experiences.[51]

To meet the goals of director professionalism, the Commission set forth the following conclusions:

1. *Responsibilities: What Boards Should Do.*   Pursuant to the board's broadly defined powers under state law, each board has the authority to determine its own specific role and responsibilities within the corporation. In consultation with the CEO, the board should clearly define its role, considering both its legal responsibilities to shareholders and the needs of other constituencies, provided shareholders are not disadvantaged.

2. *Processes: How Boards Should Fulfill Their Responsibilities.*   The board is responsible for determining its own governance processes. In determining such processes a board should:

   - establish an independent governance committee
   - create independent leadership roles for directors
   - determine the method for the board's participation in setting board and committee agendas
   - determine the method for selecting and compensating directors and the CEO
   - determine a level and timetable for stock ownership required for each director
   - establish an effective and independent method for periodically evaluating the CEO, the board, and individual directors
   - adopt a policy of holding regular executive sessions without management present, and
   - take a role in selecting advisors to the board, directly retaining those advising the board alone.

3. *Selection: Who Directors Should Be.*   Director selection should be based on the personal qualities sought in all directors and the core competencies the board needs as a whole. Each director should exhibit:

   - integrity and accountability
   - informed judgment
   - financial literacy
   - mature confidence, and
   - high performance standards.

   Areas of core competence that should be represented on the board as a whole include:

   - accounting and finance
   - business judgment
   - management

---

[51] National Association of Corporate Directors, *Report of the NACD Blue Ribbon Commission on Director Professionalism* (Washington, D.C.: NACD, 1996), p. vii. See also the *NACD Board Guidelines* (Washington, D.C.: NACD, 1999).

- crisis response
- industry knowledge
- international markets
- leadership, and
- strategic vision.

Most importantly, the board should:

- have a substantial majority of independent directors
- develop its own definition of independence, and
- seek disclosure of any relationships that would appear to compromise director independence.

In selecting members, the board must assure itself of their commitment to:

- learn the business of the company and the board
- meet the company's stock ownership requirements
- offer to resign on change of employment or professional responsibilities, or under other specified conditions, and
- importantly, devote the necessary time and effort.

In this regard, the board should consider guidelines that limit the number of positions on other boards, subject to individual exceptions—for example, for CEOs and senior executives, one or two; for others fully employed, three or four; and for all others, five or six.

With these characteristics, competencies, and commitments in mind, consideration should also include:

- balance of director contributions
- director diversity, and
- company status.

4. *Evaluation: How Boards and Directors Should Be Judged.* Board effectiveness and credibility depend in part on regular self-evaluation of both the board as a whole and its individual members. The evaluation process should be:

- controlled by the independent directors themselves
- aligned with established evaluation processes and goals
- tailored to meet the needs of the individual company and board
- designed to ensure candor, confidentiality, and trust
- regularly reviewed and improved as necessary, and
- disclosed (process only) to shareholders and the public.

Evaluation of board performance should include consideration of the execution of general board responsibilities as well as:

- delineation of board and management powers
- effective interaction between and among directors, and
- director education and development.

Evaluation of individual director performance should include consideration of the execution of specific board responsibilities as well as:

- personal characteristics, and
- core competencies.

Additional consideration should be given to:

- varying roles for directors, and
- means for removing under-performing directors, if necessary.[52]

THE BUSINESS ROUNDTABLE

In September 1997, the Business Roundtable issued a white paper, *Statement on Corporate Governance*. As previously noted, the Business Roundtable described corporate accountability in its statement on *Corporate Governance and American Competitiveness* (1990). The Business Roundtable summarizes its current views as follows:

> The Business Roundtable wishes to emphasize that the principal objective of a business enterprise is to generate economic returns to its owners. Although the link between the forms of governance and economic performance is debated, The Business Roundtable believes that good corporate governance practices provide an important framework for a timely response by a corporation's board of directors to situations that may directly affect stockholder value. The absence of good corporate governance, even in a corporation that is performing well financially, may imply vulnerability for stockholders because the corporation is not optimally positioned to deal with financial or management challenges that may arise.
>
> Many discussions of corporate governance focus on questions of form and abstract principle: Should a corporation have a non-executive chairman of the board? Should the board have a lead director? Should there be a limit on the number of boards on which a director serves? The Business Roundtable considers such questions important. Indeed, much of this Statement is devoted to discussing them. However, The Business Roundtable wishes to emphasize that the substance of good corporate governance is more important than its form; adoption of a set of rules or principles or of any particular practice or policy is not a substitute for, and does not itself assure, good corporate governance.
>
> Examples of this point abound. A corporation with the best formal policies and processes for board involvement may be at risk if the chief executive officer is not genuinely receptive to relevant board input or if knowledgeable directors hesitate to express their views. A corporation can have excellent corporate governance structures and policies on paper, but if the CEO and the directors are not focused on stockholder value, it may be less likely the corporation will realize that value. Directors can satisfy the most demanding tests for independence, but if they do not

---

[52] Ibid., pp. 21–23.

have the personal stature and self-confidence to stand up to a non-performing CEO, the corporation may not be successful. On the other hand, a corporation that lacks many of the so-called "best practices" for corporate governance, or that does not memorialize its practices in formal documents, may nonetheless perform well if its directors and management are highly able people who are dedicated to advancing the interests of stockholders.

One of the reasons why people focus on the formal, structural aspects of corporate governance is that doing so permits evaluations that appear to be objective and verifiable. Formal attributes of good corporate governance can be tabulated to compare corporate governance practices across the spectrum of companies. Such comparisons do have value, but it would be a mistake to lose sight of their limitations. The "soft," subjective factors in corporate governance—such as the quality of directors and the personalities of CEOs and directors—receive less attention from scholars and journalists but are critical in the real world of corporate behavior. Boards and management should not feel that they have discharged their responsibilities in regard to corporate governance just by putting in place a particular set of structures and formal processes. They must also periodically review these structures and processes to insure that they are achieving good corporate governance in substance.

Corporate governance is not an abstract goal, but exists to serve corporate purposes by providing a structure within which stockholders, directors and management can pursue most effectively the objectives of the corporation. There has been much debate in corporate governance literature about the parties to whom directors owe a duty of loyalty and in whose interest the corporation should be managed. Some say corporations should be managed purely in the interests of stockholders or, more precisely, in the interests of its present and future stockholders over the long-term. Others claim that directors should also take into account the interests of other "stakeholders" such as employees, customers, suppliers, creditors and the community.

The Business Roundtable does not view these two positions as being in conflict, but it sees a need for clarification of the relationship between these two perspectives. It is in the long-term interests of stockholders for a corporation to treat its employees well, to serve its customers well, to encourage its suppliers to continue to supply it, to honor its debts, and to have a reputation for civic responsibility. Thus, to manage the corporation in the long-term interests of the stockholders, management and the board of directors must take into account the interests of the corporation's other stakeholders. Indeed, a number of states have enacted statutes that specifically authorize directors to take into account the interests of constituencies other than stockholders, and a very limited number of state statutes actually require consideration of the interests of other constituencies.

In The Business Roundtable's view, the paramount duty of management and of boards of directors is to the corporation's stockholders; the interests of other stakeholders are relevant as a derivative of the duty to stockholders. The notion that the board must somehow balance the interests of stockholders against the interests of other stakeholders fundamentally misconstrues the role of directors. It is, moreover, an unworkable notion because it would leave the board with no criterion for resolving conflicts between interests of stockholders and of other stakeholders or among different groups of stakeholders.

While The Business Roundtable favors certain broad principles as generally contributing to good corporate governance, not all of these broad principles are necessarily right for all corporations at all times. Good corporate governance is not a "one size fits all" proposition, and a wide diversity of approaches to corporate governance should be expected and is entirely appropriate. Moreover, a corporation's practices will evolve as it adapts to changing situations.[53]

To the extent that the audit committee maintains an independent posture in the corporate environment, the committee will represent a check on the corporate management with respect to its corporate power and stewardship accountability. The primary objective is to foster the accountability relationship between the audit committee and the representatives of management and thereby create an environment in which management will be responsive to its constituencies.

SOURCES AND SUGGESTED READINGS

Advisory Panel on Auditor Independence, *Strengthening the Professionalism of the Independent Auditor* (Stamford, Conn.: Public Oversight Board, 1994).

American Institute of Certified Public Accountants, *Audit Committees, Answers to Typical Questions About Their Organization and Operations* (New York: American Institute of Certified Public Accountants, 1978).

American Institute of Certified Public Accountants, SEC Practice Section, *Best Practices—Accounting Consultations, Communications with Boards of Directors/Audit Committees, Communications with the SEC Staff* (New York: American Institute of Certified Public Accountants, 1997).

American Institute of Certified Public Accountants, *Serving the Public Interest: A New Conceptual Framework for Auditor Independence* (New York: American Institute of Certified Public Accountants, 1997).

American Institute of Certified Public Accountants, *Invitation to Comment,* "Proposed Recommendation to the Executive Committee of the SEC Practice Section of the American Institute of Certified Public Accountants" (New York: American Institute of Certified Public Accountants, 1998).

The American Assembly, *Corporate Governance in America,* Pamphlet 54 (New York: Columbia University, April 1978).

---

[53] The Business Roundtable, *Statement on Corporate Governance* (Washington, D.C.: The Business Roundtable, 1997), pp. 1–4. For additional reading, see *CalPERS Corporate Governance Core Principles and Guidelines: The United States* (Sacramento, CA: California Public Employees' Retirement System, 1998).

American Law Institute, *Principles of Corporate Governance: Analysis and Recommendations* (Philadelphia: American Law Institute, 1994).

Biegler, John C., "Rebuilding Public Trust in Business." *Financial Executive* 45 (June 1977), pp. 23–31.

Braiotta, Louis, and Jay R. Olson, "Guiding the Audit Committee: A CFO's Concern." *Financial Executive* 51, No. 9 (September 1983), pp. 52–54.

Bull, Ivan, "Board of Directors Acceptance of Treadway Responsibilities." *Journal of Accountancy* 171, No. 2 (February 1991), pp. 67–72, 74.

The Business Roundtable, *Corporate Governance and American Competitiveness* (New York: The Business Roundtable, 1990).

The Business Roundtable, *Statement on Corporate Governance* (Washington, D.C.: The Business Roundtable, 1997).

Carmichael, D. R., "The Management Report," *Financial Executive* 46 (November 1978), pp. 46–50.

Castellano, Joseph F., Harper A. Roehm, and Albert A. Vondra, "Audit Committee Compliance with the Treadway Commission Report: A Survey." *Ohio CPA Journal* 48, No. 4 (Winter 1989), pp. 37–42.

Commission to Study the Public's Expectations of Audits, *Report of the Commission to Study the Public's Expectations of Audits* (Toronto, Canada: The Canadian Institute of Chartered Accountants, 1988).

Committee on the Financial Aspects of Corporate Governance, *The Code of Best Practice* (London: Gee [a division of Professional Publishing Ltd.] 1992).

Deloitte Haskins & Sells, *The Week in Review.* Pamphlet 78-46 (Washington, D.C.: Deloitte Haskins & Sells, November 1978).

Estey, John S. and David W. Marston, "Pitfalls (and Loopholes) in the Foreign Bribery Law." *Fortune* (October 1978), pp. 182–188.

General Accounting Office, *The Accounting Profession–Major Issues: Progress and Concerns* (Washington, D.C.: General Accounting Office, 1996).

The Institute of Internal Auditors, Inc. *Internal Auditing and the Audit Committee: Working Together Toward Common Goals* (Altamonte Springs, Fla.: The Institute of Internal Auditors, 1987).

Kalbers, Lawrence P. and Timothy J. Fogarty, "Audit Committee Effectiveness: An Empirical Investigation of the Contribution of Power." *Auditing: A Journal of Practice & Theory* 12, No. 1 (Spring 1993), pp. 24–49.

Korn/Ferry International, *Twentieth Annual Board of Directors Study* (New York: Korn/Ferry International, 1993).

Lovdal, Michael L., "Making the Audit Committee Work," *Harvard Business Review* 55 (March–April 1977), pp. 108–114.

Luscombe, Nelson, "More Power to Audit Committees." *CA Magazine* 122, No. 5 (May 1989), pp. 26–37.

McCauley, Daniel J. and John C. Burton, *Audit Committees,* C.P.S. No. 49 (BNA: 1986).

McCuaig, Bruce W. and Paul G. Makosz, "Is Everything Under Control? A New Approach to Corporate Governance." *Financial Executive* 6, No. 1 (January/February 1990), pp. 24–29.

Miller, Judith, "S.E.C. Sues Aminex and 2 Ex-Officers Under the New Law." *The New York Times* (March 11, 1978), p. 29, Column 3.

Moraglio, Joseph F. and James F. Green, "The FDIC Improvement Act: A Precedent for Expanded CPA Reporting." *Journal of Accountancy* 173, No. 4 (April 1992), pp. 63, 64, 66–68, 71.

O'Malley, Shaun F., "Auditing, Directors, and Management: Promoting Accountability." *Internal Auditing* 5, No. 3 (Winter 1990), pp. 3–9.

National Association of Corporate Directors, *Report of the NACD Blue Ribbon Commission on Director Professionalism* (Washington, D.C.: National Association of Corporate Directors, 1996).

National Commission on Fraudulent Financial Reporting, *Report of the National Commission on Fraudulent Financial Reporting* (Washington, D.C.: National Commission on Fraudulent Financial Reporting, 1987).

Oxford Analytica, *Board Directors and Corporate Governance* (London: August 1992).

Palmer, Russell E., "Audit Committees—Are They Effective? An Auditor's View." *Journal of Accountancy,* 144, No. 3 (September 1977), pp. 76–79.

Public Oversight Board, *A Special Report by the Public Oversight Board of the SEC Practice Section* (Stamford, Conn.: Public Oversight Board, 1993).

Public Oversight Board, *Directors, Management, and Auditors—Allies in Protecting Shareholders' Interests* (Stamford, Conn.: Public Oversight Board, 1995).

Shandor, John, "Audit Committees Take a Broader Role in Corporate Policy." *Corporate Controller* 2 (November/December 1989), pp. 46–48.

Title 1 of Public Law No. 102-242, December 19, 1991.

Title I of Public Law No. 95-213, December 19, 1977.

Wechsler, Dana, "Giving the Watchdog Fangs." *Forbes* 144 (November 13, 1989), pp. 130, 132–133.

Williams, Harold M., "Audit Committees—The Public Sector's View." *Journal of Accountancy,* 144 No. 3 (September 1977), pp. 71–74.

Chapter 3

The External Users of Accounting Information

The objective of this chapter is to provide a broad perspective on the importance of the enterprise's outside constituencies as well as their need for accounting information. In addition, this chapter will examine the role of the audit directors and the ways in which their work is affected by these external groups.

INTRODUCTION

Since the board of directors, through the audit committee, is responsible for assuring that management fulfills its financial reporting obligations, audit directors have an indirect accountability to the external users of accounting information. According to the Financial Accounting Standards Board (FASB):

> Members and potential members of some groups—such as owners, creditors, and employees—have or contemplate having direct economic interests in particular business enterprises. . . . Members of other groups—such as financial analysts and advisors, regulatory authorities, and labor unions—have derived or indirect interests because they advise or represent those who have or contemplate having direct interests.[1]

To respond to the needs of these groups as well as to formulate a basis for financial accounting and reporting standards, the FASB has developed a conceptual framework that consists of five Statements of Financial Accounting Concepts (SFAC) relative to financial reporting for business enterprises:

SFAC No. 1   "Objectives of Financial Reporting by Business Enterprises" (November 1978)

SFAC No. 2   "Qualitative Characteristics of Accounting Information" (May 1980)

---

[1] Financial Accounting Standards Board, *Statement of Financial Accounting Concepts, No. 1* (Stamford, Conn.: Financial Accounting Standards Board, 1978), p. 11.

SFAC No. 3   "Elements of Financial Statements of Business Enterprises" (December 1980)

SFAC No. 5   "Recognition and Measurement in Financial Statements of Business Enterprises" (December 1984)

SFAC No. 6   "Elements of Financial Statements" (December 1985)[2]

The accounting profession has developed and continues to promulgate accounting standards based on a prescribed set of objectives, definitions, and principles, as set forth in the conceptual framework that is discussed in Chapter 5.[3] Notwithstanding the objectives of complete and accurate information in the financial accounting process, it should be noted that both internal accountants and external auditors exercise judgment in the selection of accounting standards for a fair presentation of the financial statements. Thus, if management has presented the financial statements in conformity with generally accepted accounting principles, then such statements are fairly presented.

Moreover, in the absence of more authoritative accounting literature concerning the accounting treatment of a particular item, account, or transaction, practitioners can use the conceptual framework to solve the problem.[4] In an article dealing with the subjects of minority interest, stock issues, and legally enforceable contracts, Steven Rubin indicated how the conceptual framework could be used for the appropriate accounting treatment, and he concluded that:

> Concepts statements can provide helpful guidance in resolving knotty practice problems involving liabilities and other matters. Consult them as you would other sources of established accounting principles. You may be surprised to find that these basic statements will provide the help you need.[5]

One way of classifying the external users is to divide them into groups of investors, credit grantors, regulatory agencies, and other outside constituencies. Such classification is useful from the audit director's point of view, because each constituent has different informational needs and objectives. Thus, the four-way classification of the users is a useful framework for discharging the board of di-

---

[2] SFAC No. 4, "Objectives of Financial Reporting by Nonbusiness Organizations," December 1980. It should be noted that SFACs No. 2 and No. 6 apply to nonbusiness enterprises.

[3] The terms *standards* and *principles* are used interchangeably in practice and throughout this book.

[4] *Statement on Auditing Standards, No. 69*, "The Meaning of Present Fairly in Conformity with Generally Accepted Accounting Principles in the Independent Auditor's Report" (New York: American Institute of Certified Public Accountants, 1992), par. 11.

[5] Steven Rubin, "How Concepts Statements Can Solve Practice Problems," *Journal of Accountancy* 166, No. 4 (October 1988), p. 126. Two authors have developed a flowchart, "An Overview of FASB's Concepts Statements." See Gwen Richardson Pate and Keith G. Stanga, "A Guide to the FASB's Concepts Statements," *Journal of Accountancy* 168, No. 2 (August 1989), pp. 28–31.

rectors' financial accountability. To the extent that the audit committee can monitor the accounting information as well as understand the perceived needs of the
outside constituencies, it can provide a balance in the corporate financial reporting process.

THE INVESTORS

Importance of the Investors

Investors are the largest users of accounting information. As a group, investors include not only potential investors but also the stockholders. As the American Assembly indicates:

> Shareholders are among the major groups in the community to which the corpora-
> tion must respond. As the undisputed owners of the corporation, they possess great
> potential influence. Vocal shareholders, even if a minority, should be heard. Share-
> holders can sensitize management and directors to social as well as economic issues
> and should exercise this power.[6]

The *New York Stock Exchange Fact Book* in 1998 reported that institutional investors held 47.7 percent of $6.2 trillion, which represents the market value of all
New York Stock Exchange (NYSE) listed stock at the end of 1997.[7] In addition,
the *American Stock Exchange Fact Book* reported that institutional activity was
74.7 percent of $162.2 billion, which is the value of all stock listed on the Ameri-
can Stock Exchange (AMEX) in 1997.[8] Although the individual investors held
52.3 percent of the dollar value of the NYSE stock and 25.3 percent of the dollar
value of the AMEX stock for the respective years, the equity investments of the
institutional investors cannot be overlooked because of their market impact on the
volume of trading. These investors represent a dominant force in the daily stock
trading. Their influential role is important, because they can concentrate their investments in large corporations and, thus, increase their market power.

Furthermore, the SEC reported that "the total dollar amount of securities filed
for registration with the SEC during 1992 reached a record of over $700 billion, a

---

[6] The American Assembly, *Corporate Governance in America,* Pamphlet 56 (New York: Columbia University, April 1978), p. 5. The American Assembly convenes annually and has a national session at the
Arden House in Harriman, New York. The Assembly conducts forums on national and multinational issues. See *The American Assembly Report 1991–1992* (New York: Columbia University, 1992).
[7] New York Stock Exchange, *New York Stock Exchange Fact Book* 1998 (New York: New York Stock
Exchange, 1998), p. 63.
[8] American Stock Exchange, *American Stock Exchange Fact Book* 1998 (New York: American Stock
Exchange, 1998), p. 15, and *Security Industry Automation Corporation* database, 1998.

40 percent increase from approximately $500 billion registered last year."[9] Thus, the investing public is of paramount importance to the nation's capital market as well as to the international marketplace, and corporate management must appraise its position regarding the investor's interests.

The Business Roundtable concluded that:

> Corporations are chartered to serve both their shareholders and society as a whole. The interests of the shareholders are primarily measured in terms of economic return over time. The interests of others in society (other stakeholders) are defined by their relationship to the corporation.

> The other stakeholders in the corporation are its employees, customers, suppliers, creditors, the communities where the corporation does business, and society as a whole. The duties and responsibilities of the corporation to the stakeholders are expressed in various laws, regulations, contracts, and custom and practice.[10]

In addition to their significance concerning capital markets, investors have an impact on corporate policies. For example, stockholders can influence corporate policies through their votes at the annual stockholders' meeting. They can vote on such issues as the following:

1. The election and removal of the board of directors
2. Amendments to the corporate charter and bylaws
3. Proposals of the stockholders to corporate management
4. The board of directors' proposals
5. The authorization of a new stock or bond issue
6. Corporate management's conduct with respect to corporate affairs
7. The selection of the independent auditing firm

As a result of the stockholders' voting power, it is essential that the audit directors develop stockholder profiles. For example, they should identify the number of stockholders and their related stockholdings in order to isolate the degree of voting power. Voting power may be concentrated in a family group. Such a group can greatly influence corporate policies due to their percentage of stock ownership. Although the board has other demands from its outside constituencies, the audit committee can aid the board through its understanding and familiarity with investors' interests and investments in the corporation. In short, the primary

---

[9] Securities and Exchange Commission, *1992 Annual Report* (Washington, D.C.: U.S. Government Printing Office, 1992), p. 52. More recently, the SEC reported that "a record $1.4 trillion in securities were filed for registration during the year 1997, a 20 percent increase over the $1.2 trillion in 1996." See SEC *1997 Annual Report* (Washington, D.C.: U.S. Government Printing Office, 1997), p. 73.
[10] The Business Roundtable, *Corporate Governance and American Competitiveness* (New York: The Business Roundtable, 1990), p. 4.

concern of the committee is to give consideration to the stockholders' interests because of their relationship to corporate policy decisions.

In 1992, Richard C. Breeden, former chairman of the SEC, stated in his annual report to Congress:

> The Commission adopted significant revisions of the proxy rules to facilitate effective communications among shareholders and between shareholders and their corporations. The reforms will encourage greater participation by shareholders in corporate governance by removing unnecessary regulatory barriers, reducing the costs of complying with the proxy rules and improving disclosure.
>
> In addition, the Commission revised its rules to ensure that shareholders receive better information about executive compensation. Among other things, the new executive compensation disclosure rules require new tables that will disclose clearly and concisely the compensation received by a corporation's highest paid executives.[11]
>
> The Commission adopted important amendments to its executive compensation disclosure requirements. The amendments are designed to (1) ensure that shareholders receive comprehensible, relevant, and complete information about compensation paid to executives upon which to base their voting and investment decisions; and (2) foster accountability of directors to shareholders by permitting shareholders to vote on the proposals of other shareholders with regard to executive and director compensation, and thereby advise the board of directors of the shareholders' assessment of the compensation policies and practices applied by the board.
>
> After three years of study, two releases for public comment, a two-day public conference, and more than 1,700 public comment letters, the Commission substantially revised its rules governing proxy solicitations. The revisions were adopted to (1) facilitate effective communications among shareholders and between shareholders and their corporations, as well as participation by shareholders in corporate governance, by removing unnecessary regulatory barriers, (2) reduce the costs of complying with the proxy rules, (3) improve disclosures to shareholders, and (4) restore a balance between the free speech rights of shareholders and Congress' concern that solicitation of proxy voting authority be conducted on a fair, honest and informed basis.[12]

Recognizing the significance of the financial reporting process and demands for full disclosure, several investor associations, such as the Investor Responsibility Research Center (IRRC), the National Investor Relations Institute, and the Association for Investment Management and Research, have conducted annual forums dealing with various issues related to the investing public. For example, Maryellen F. Andersen, former chair of the board, and Margaret Carroll, former executive director, of the Investor Responsibility Research Center, note:

---

[11] Securities and Exchange Commission, *1992 Annual Report,* p. viii.
[12] Ibid., p. 53.

Increasing numbers of corporate officers and directors looked to IRRC to help inform their policies and decisions on such diverse questions as assessing environmental liability (through our Environmental Information Service); anticipating questions at annual meetings, challenging shareholder proposals at the SEC, preparing responses for the proxy statement, gauging levels of institutional investor interest in key issues and their likely reaction when those issues are raised (through our Proxy Information Service); and deciding whether or when to enter or re-enter South Africa (through our South Africa Review Package). Corporations in other countries, too, began to look to IRRC for many of the same kinds of information.[13]

The Need for Accounting Information

As the principal constituency of the corporation, investors make decisions based on financial accounting information. Such data is essentially discretionary, since it is predicated on management's judgment. Although regulatory agencies, such as the SEC, can dictate the form and content of their reports, the investors must rely on corporate management. Moreover, investors must not only evaluate the effectiveness of management but also decide whether to increase or decrease their stockholding based on management's financial accounting representations.

More important, because of its stewardship accountability, corporate management must periodically communicate its financial accounting information to its constituencies. The corporate financial statements are the principal reports that are used to communicate accounting data. In November 1978, the Financial Accounting Standards Board released its first statement as part of its conceptual framework project for financial accounting and reporting. As a *Statement of Financial Accounting Concepts,* the board concluded the following on objectives of financial reporting:

> Financial reporting should provide information that is useful to present and potential investors and creditors and other users in making rational investment, credit, and similar decisions. The information should be comprehensible to those who have a reasonable understanding of business and economic activities and are willing to study the information with reasonable diligence.

> Financial reporting should provide information to help present and potential investors and creditors and other users in assessing the amounts, timing, and uncertainty of prospective cash receipts from dividends or interest and the proceeds from the sale, redemption, or maturity of securities or loans. Since investors' and creditors' cash flows are related to enterprise cash flows, financial reporting should provide information to help investors, creditors, and others assess the amounts, timing, and uncertainty of prospective net cash inflows to the related enterprise.

[13] Investor Responsibility Research Center, *Annual Report 1992* (Washington, D.C.: Investor Responsibility Research Center), p. 3.

Financial reporting should provide information about the economic resources of an enterprise, the claims to those resources (obligations of the enterprise to transfer resources to other entities and owners' equity), and the effects of transactions, events, and circumstances that change its resources and claims to those resources.[14]

With respect to the first objective of financial reporting, it is apparent that investors need useful information for investment decisions. However, one must address the usefulness of the financial statements to the users. To resolve this controversy in financial reporting, Most and Chang found that:

The accounting contents of the corporate annual report are regarded as its most important contents, and conversely that the president's letter to the stockholders and the pictorial material presented are viewed as relatively unimportant.[15] . . . The authors believe that the results of their research indicate strongly that investors regard financial statement information as useful for their decisions.[16]

The second objective of financial reporting means that the investors need financial information in order to evaluate their investment objectives. Obviously, investors wish to safeguard the principal amount of their investment and maximize the income and capital appreciation. Furthermore, investors must assess their willingness and ability to accept risk. Similarly, management must effectively use the economic resources of the enterprise in order to generate a monetary return to its investors. Thus, "since an enterprise's ability to generate favorable cash flows affects both its ability to pay dividends and interest and the market prices of its securities, expected cash flows to investors and creditors are related to expected cash flows to the enterprise."[17]

Finally, the third objective of financial reporting relates to the enterprise's financial condition and operating performance. Investors need information on the current and future financial strength of the corporation to appraise the soundness of their investment. Such information is critical. Not only does it indicate the ability of the enterprise to meet its short-term and long-term financial commitments, but it allows investors to evaluate their risk and return on investment. Furthermore, investors need information regarding the uses of economic resources in the operations. Although the enterprise may have an adequate financial position, such a position may deteriorate because of poor operational performance. In short, investors want financial information on the use and disposition of the enterprise's

---

[14]Financial Accounting Standards Board, *Statement of Financial Accounting Concepts, No. 1*, p. viii.
[15]Kenneth S. Most and Lucia S. Chang, "An Empirical Study of Investor Views Concerning Financial Statements and Investment Decisions," *Collected Papers of the American Accounting Association's Annual Meeting* (Sarasota, Fla.: American Accounting Association, August 1978), pp. 245–246.
[16]Ibid., p. 249.
[17]Financial Accounting Standards Board, *Statement on Financial Accounting Concepts, No. 1*, p. 19.

economic resources in order to assess their investment policy.[18] More recent developments regarding investors' need for financial information are discussed later in this chapter.

Role of the Audit Directors

In order to discharge their responsibilities in the area of financial reporting effectively, the audit directors should establish operational objectives.[19] The operational objectives should be based on the investor's need for financial accounting information, which is manifested in the board of directors' stewardship accountability. Such operational objectives should be consistent with the Financial Accounting Standards Board's (FASB's) objectives of financial reporting, because the primary purpose of the committee is to provide assurance regarding the usefulness of the accounting information in the financial statements.

Moreover, in addition to the quantitative representations in the financial statements, the committee should use the following qualitative characteristics in order to assess the financial reporting policies and practices of the corporation:

> The qualitative characteristics of financial statements, like objectives, should be based largely upon the needs of users of the statements. Information is useless unless it is relevant and material to a user's decision. Information should be as free as possible from any biases of the preparer. In making decisions, users should not only understand the information presented, but also should be able to assess its reliability and compare it with information about alternative opportunities and previous experience. In all cases, information is more useful if it stresses economic substance rather than technical form.[20]

The preceding discussions on the operational objectives and the criteria for evaluating the usefulness of the financial statements provide the necessary guidelines for evaluating management's responsibilities in the preparation of the financial statements. In addition, the audit committee should give consideration to the following criteria, which were used by the Financial Analysts Federation in its Awards for Excellence in Corporate Reporting program:

---

[18] For further discussion, see SRI International, *Investor Informational Needs and the Annual Report,* (Morristown, N.J.: Financial Executive Research Foundation, 1987).

[19] For further discussion on the director's role in reviewing financial information and management's statements, see Chapters 10, 13, and 14.

[20] American Institute of Certified Public Accountants, *Report of the Study Group on the Objectives of Financial Statements* (New York: AICPA, 1973), p. 60. For further discussion, see FASB, *Statement of Financial Accounting Concepts No. 2,* "Qualitative Characteristics of Accounting" (May 1980).

1. Responsiveness of management to analysts' and investors' desire for information prerequisite to real understanding of companies and their problems

2. Efforts by companies to supply financial and other information going well beyond the level of disclosure required by the SEC, the exchanges, and the FASB

3. A coordinated and consistent program of personal contact with investors and their representatives—both through provision of experienced and helpful officials in the investor relations function and via regular management presentations to analyst groups, company-sponsored field trips, and so on.

4. A high "candor quotient" in both oral and written communications to the investment community. Too many managements prejudice an otherwise creditable information program by ignoring or glossing over unfavorable developments with a thick patina of corporate optimism.[21]

More recently, the Association for Investment Management and Research issued its *Corporate Information Committee Report* (1995–1996). A checklist of criteria for evaluating financial communications effort stated in part:

Annual Published Information

A. Annual Report
 1. Financial Highlights: Are they clear and unambiguous?
 2. President's Letter Review: Does it hit the highlights of the year in an objective manner? Is it relevant to the company's results and candid in appraising problems? It should include:
  a. Review of the year.
  b. Insights into operating rates, unit production levels, and selling prices.
  c. Acquisitions and divestments, if any.
  d. Government business, if material.
  e. Capital expenditures program; start-up expenses.
  f. Research and development efforts.
  g. Employment costs, labor relations, union contracts.
  h. Energy cost and availability.
  i. Environmental and OSHA costs.
  j. Backlogs.
  k. New products.
  l. Legislative and regulatory developments.
  m. Outlook.
  n. Unusual income or expense.

---

[21] Financial Analysts Federation, "Awards for Excellence in Corporate Reporting," *Financial Analysts Federation News Release* (New York: Financial Analysts Federation, January 1978), p. 1.

3. Officers and Directors:
   a. Age, background, and responsibilities.
   b. Description of company organization.
   c. Outside affiliations of directors.
   d. Principal personnel changes.
4. Statement of Corporate Goals:
   What are the short-term and long-term corporate goals, and how and when does management expect to achieve them? (This section could be included in several areas of the report, but separate treatment is preferred.)
5. Discussions of Divisional and/or Segment Operations:
   a. How complete is the breakdown of sales, materials, costs, overhead, and earnings?
   b. Are the segments logical for analytical purposes? Do they parallel lines of business?
   c. Are unusual developments explained, and do the explanations include management's response?
   d. Comparisons with relevant industry developments should include:
      i. Market size and growth.
      ii. Market penetration.
      iii. Geographical divergencies.
   e. Foreign operations:
      i. Revenues, including export sales.
      ii. Consolidated foreign earnings versus equity interest.
      iii. Market and/or regional trends.
      iv. Tax status.
6. Financial Summary and Footnotes:
   a. Statement of accounting principles, including explanation of changes and their effects.
   b. Adjustments to EPS for dilution.
   c. Affiliates' operating information.
   d. Consolidated finance subsidiary's disclosure of separate balance sheet information and operating results.
   e. Cash flow statement (FAS No. 95).
   f. Tax accounting investment tax credits identified, breakdown of current and deferred taxes for U.S. and non-U.S. tax jurisdictions, reconciliation of effective and statutory tax rates, impact of changes in tax law, early application of FAS No. 96.
   g. Clarity of explanation of currency exchange rate accounting:
      i. Impact on earnings from Balance Sheet translation, if any.
      ii. Indication of "Operating" or Income Statement Effect of exchange rate fluctuations.

    h. Property accounts and depreciation policies:
- i. Methods and asset lives used for tax and for financial reporting.
- ii. Quantification of effect on reported earnings of use of different method and/or asset lives for tax purposes.

    i. Investments: composition and market values disclosed.

    j. Inventories: method of valuation and identifying different methods for various product or geographic segments.

    k. Leases and rentals: terms and liability.

    l. Debt repayment schedules.

    m. Pension funds: costs charged to income, interest rate, and wage-inflation assumptions; amount of any unfunded past service liability; amortization period for unfunded liability (FAS No. 87).

    n. Other postemployment benefits: pay-as-you-go amount, discussion of potential liability, impact of FAS No. 106, including plans to fund or amend, and impact of FAS No. 112.

    o. Capital expenditure programs and forecasts, including costs for environmental purposes.

    p. Acquisitions and divestitures (if material):
- i. Description of activity and operating results.
- ii. Type of financial transaction.
- iii. Effect on reported sales and earnings.
- iv. Quantification of purchase acquisitions or small poolings that do not require restatement of prior years' results. (When restating for pooling, both old and new data are useful for comparison.)

    q. Year-end adjustments.

    r. Restatement of quarterly reports to year-end accounting basis.

    s. Research and development and new products; amount and types of outlays and forecasts.

    t. Contingent liabilities, particularly environmental.

    u. Derivation of number of shares used for calculating primary and fully diluted earnings per share.

    v. Disclosures of the fair values of financial instruments (FAS No. 107).

    w. Goodwill amount being amortized and number of years.

    x. Ten-year statistical summary:
- i. Adequacy of income statement and balance sheet detail.
- ii. Helpfulness of "nonstatement" data (e.g., number of employees, adjusted number of shares, price of stock, capital expenditures, etc.)

B. 10-Ks, 10-Qs, and Other Required Published Information

Quarterly and Other Published Information Not Required

A. Quarterly Reports
   1. Depth of commentary on operating results and developments.
   2. Discussion of new products, management changes, and problem areas.
   3. Degree of detail of profit and loss statement, including divisional or segmental breakdown.
   4. Inclusion of a balance sheet and cash flow statement.
   5. Restatement of all prior- and current-year quarters for major pooling acquisitions and quantification of effect of purchase acquisitions and/or disposals.
   6. Breakout of nonrecurring or exceptional income or expense items, including effects from inventory valuation and foreign currency translation factors.
   7. Explicit statement of accounting principles underlying quarterly statements.
   8. Timeliness of reports.
   9. Separate fourth quarter report.
B. Other Published Material
   1. Availability of proxy statements (even though this is required public information).
   2. Annual meeting report; available with questions and answers and identity of those posing questions.
   3. Addresses to analysts' groups: available with questions and answers.
   4. Statistical supplements and fact books.
   5. Company magazines, newsletters, and explanatory pamphlets.
   6. Press releases: Are they sent to shareholders and analysts? Are they timely? Do they include earnings numbers?
   7. How are documents filed with public agencies (SEC, Federal Trade Commission, Department of Labor, court cases, etc.) made available? Does the company disseminate all material information in 10-K, 10-Q, and similar reports?

Other Aspects

A. Is there a designated and advertised individual (or individuals) for shareholder and analyst contacts?
B. Interviews
   1. Knowledgeability and responsiveness of company contact.
   2. Access to policymakers and operational people.
   3. Candor in discussing negative developments.
C. Presentations to analyst groups: frequency and content
D. Company-sponsored field trips and meetings

E. Annual meetings
   1. Accessibility.
   2. Worthwhile to shareholders and analysts.[22]

Finally, the audit committee should be aware of the independent auditing firm's quality control policies and procedures which provide reasonable assurance that the firm has followed professional standards.[23] The Auditing Standards Board has issued the *Statements on Quality Control Standards,* which identifies five elements of quality control:

- Independence, integrity, and objectivity
- Personnel management
- Acceptance and continuance of clients and engagements
- Engagement performance
- Monitoring

Such quality control standards provide a framework for the firm's quality review program. For example, member firms of the SEC Practice Section are required to rotate engagement partners at least every seven years, and audit engagements are subject to a second-partner review process.

In an article dealing with the subject of quality review by independent auditors, Brian H. MacIver, James Welch, and Priscilla A. Burnaby report that three of the previous nine quality control standards—namely, independence, supervision, and consultation—are misunderstood or inadequately addressed. The authors note, "The most common inadequacies cited by the team captain in review reports included inadequate and deficient financial statement disclosures, inadequate

---

[22] Association for Investment Management and Research, *Corporate Information Committee Report 1995–96* (Charlottesville, Va.: Association for Investment Management and Research, 1997), pp. 75–77. Also see Association for Investment Management and Research, *Financial Reporting in the 1990s and Beyond* (Charlottesville, Va.: Association for Investment Management and Research, 1993).
[23] *Statement on Auditing Standards, No. 25,* "The Relationship of Generally Accepted Auditing Standards to Quality Control Standards" (New York: American Institute of Certified Public Accountants, 1979). For further discussion, see *Statement on Quality Control Standards No. 2,* "System of Quality Control for a CPA Firm's Accounting and Auditing Practice"; *Statement on Quality Control Standards No. 3,* "Monitoring a CPA Firm's Accounting and Auditing Practice"; AICPA Peer Review Board, *Standards for Performing and Reporting on Peer Reviews* (New York: American Institute of Certified Public Accountants, 1996). The audit committee's knowledge and understanding of the independent accounting firm's quality control policies and procedures is important to provide assurance to the full board of directors that the independent auditors are discharging their responsibilities to the client company and the general public.

checklists or failure to prepare checklists properly, and too many hours of continuing professional education in the tax area rather than in the audit area."[24]

CREDIT GRANTORS

Importance of the Credit Grantors

Obviously, credit grantors are a significant group since they are a source of funds to the enterprise. The group consists of both short-term and long-term lenders of credit, such as banks, insurance companies, trade creditors, and bondholders. Short-term creditors are principally concerned with the corporation's ability to maintain an adequate cash position because they expect to be paid in a short period of time. Hence they focus their attention on the working capital position of the enterprise, which represents the relationship between cash and near-cash assets, such as short-term securities, receivables, inventories, and short-term liabilities. Such information is central to this group's decision-making process because the particular assets may be readily converted into cash. Conversely, long-term creditors are concerned not only with the corporation's ability to generate cash but also with its potential profitability. For example, they are interested in the ability of the enterprise to secure a loan with the necessary assets in relationship to its commitments and contingencies, such as a pending lawsuit. Thus credit grantors are primarily interested in the current solvency position of the corporation and its adherence to the loan covenants. In short, the major objective of the creditors is not only to safeguard their claim against the assets of the enterprise but also to obtain assurance with respect to the debt-paying ability of the corporation.

The Need for Accounting Information

Credit grantors need information on the financial and operational conditions of the enterprise. To judge a credit risk or establish a line of credit, they focus their attention on the financial statements as well as other sources of information, such as Dun & Bradstreet or National Credit Office credit reports.

In a study of June 1978, Stanga and Benjamin concluded that:

1. Bankers assign considerable importance to the basic historical financial statements as information sources for making term loan decisions. The comparative income statement is ranked as the most important information item.

2. Bankers attribute a fairly high degree of importance to forecast information. This suggests that accountants should continue striving to improve reporting standards in this area.

---

[24] Brian H. MacIver, James Welch, and Priscilla A. Burnaby, "Quality Review—Observations of a Team Captain," *Ohio CPA Journal* 50, No. 1 (January–April 1991), pp. 54–55.

3. In general, bankers assign a fairly high degree of importance to information regarding executory contracts. This suggests that the accounting profession should concern itself not only with the accounting and reporting problems associated with leases, but also with other types of executory contracts, such as major purchase commitments, labor contracts, and order backlogs.

4. Bankers consider general purchasing power financial statements as relatively unimportant. As noted earlier, other studies have found that security analysts also attribute little, if any, importance to these statements. Given the paramount nature of user needs in financial accounting, it would seem that the FASB should carefully reconsider the usefulness of price-level statements before making this information mandatory in the future.

5. Bankers assign relatively little value to information on corporate social responsibility and to financial breakdowns of amounts relating to human resources. These feelings are present despite the tremendous interest shown by many accountants in these areas in recent years.[25]

Role of the Audit Director

Although the finance committee is responsible for the financial policies and program, the audit committee should give attention to the financial reporting matters concerning the credit lenders. The audit directors are in a unique position because they must monitor the accounting information that is related to the corporation's financial policies. In approaching the financial reporting task, the committee should consult with the chairperson of the finance committee as well as the chief financial officer. For example, the committee's review of the loan agreements and other commitments should be made in view of the preceding discussion of the objectives of financial reporting and the information needs of the credit grantors. Thus the audit directors should be primarily concerned with such matters as:

1. The proper disclosure of the short-term and long-term obligations and any outstanding commitments of the corporation
2. The adherence to the loan covenants regarding the necessary working capital ratios
3. A summary of the sources of creditors' equity and the related cost of debt
4. A forecast of the proposed debt financing activities and repayment schedule and its relationship to the stockholders' equity

As William H. Dougherty, former president of NCNB Corporation, suggests:

[25] Keith G. Stanga and James J. Benjamin, "Information Needs of Bankers," *Management Accounting* 59, No. 12 (June 1978), p. 21. FASB No. 33 was rescinded in 1986 by FASB No. 89, which encourages disclosure on a voluntary basis.

The concern of all involved parties should be with the quality of disclosure—not its quantity, and involved parties should be more vigorous than anyone else in cost/benefit evaluations. . . . The increasing cost of audit and compliance is important because it raises corporate prices.[26]

In addition to the issues already discussed, several Financial Accounting Standards Board Statements are relevant to credit grantors:

SFAS No. 95   "Statement of Cash Flows" (November 1987)
SFAS No. 105   "Disclosure of Information about Financial Instruments with Off-Balance Sheet Risk and Financial Instruments with Concentration of Credit Risk" (March 1990)
SFAS No. 107   "Disclosure About Fair Value of Financial Instruments" (December 1991)
SFAS No. 133   "Accounting for Derivative Instruments and Hedging Activities" (June 1998)

The preceding accounting standards are summarized in the following paragraphs.

Reporting Cash Flows   In November 1987, the FASB issued SFAS No. 95, "Statement of Cash Flows." The Board recognized that a presentation of a company's cash flows is a better measure of liquidity by the users of financial statements. Prior to the issuance of SFAS No. 95, companies could present their funds flow statement on either a working capital or cash basis. Under the new accounting standard, companies are required to classify cash flows as operating, investing, or financial activities.[27] Management is required to provide additional information on cash flows in its presentation of management's discussion and analysis of financial condition and results of operations. Although the FASB has encouraged management to report cash flows from operating activities by the direct method, which consist of classes of cash transactions, the indirect method is commonly used. For example, *Accounting Trends and Techniques—1990* disclosed that in 1989, 583 companies out of 600 used the indirect method.[28] Under this method the net income is reconciled to net cash flow from operating activities by adjusting for deferrals, accrual, and noncash charges.

---

[26]William H. Dougherty, "Financial Reporting—A Banker Looks at the Scene," *Financial Executive* 46, No. 12 (December 1978), p. 53.

[27]Financial Accounting Standards Board, *Statement of Financial Accounting Standards, No. 95*, "Statement of Cash Flows" (Stamford, Conn.: Financial Accounting Standards Board, 1987).

[28]American Institute of Certified Public Accountants, *Accounting Trends and Techniques—1990* (New York: American Institute of Certified Public Accountants, 1990).

Financial Instruments In the late 1980s, the accounting treatment associated with financial instruments and transactions received a great deal of attention because of the lack of financial accounting and disclosure standards. Typically, such financial instruments were treated as off-balance-sheet financing arrangements or unaccrued loss recognition in the financial statements. In March 1990, the FASB issued SFAS No. 105, which deals with disclosures about off-balance-sheet risk, credit risks, interest rates, and current market values of financial instruments.[29] For example, SFAS No. 105 requires companies to disclose concentrations of credit risk from accounts receivable financing arrangements and other financial instruments. In the event that there is nonperformance by the parties to the financing arrangement, management is required to disclose the dollar amount of the loss resulting from credit risk.[30]

Subsequent to the issuance of SFAS No. 105, in December 1991 the FASB issued SFAS No. 107, which requires all financial and nonfinancial institutions to disclose the fair value of financial instruments whether recognized in the balance sheet or not. If management is unable to obtain the quoted market price of a financial instrument, then it may use the quoted market price of a similar instrument or use a valuation technique, such as estimated future cash flows. Fair value disclosure is required for financial instruments such as accounts and notes receivable and payable, investment securities, options, future contracts, and interest rate swaps.[31]

In June 1998, the Financial Accounting Standards Board issued SFAS No. 133, "Accounting for Derivative Instruments and Hedging Activities," which supersedes SFAS No. 105 and 119 and amends SFAS No. 107. In summary, this new accounting standard requires that:

- All derivatives must be measured at fair value and recognized in the balance sheet as assets or liabilities.

- With the exception for derivatives that qualify as hedges (fair-value hedge, cash-flow hedge, and foreign currency hedge), changes in the fair value of derivatives must be recognized in income.

---

[29] Financial Accounting Standards Board, *Statement of Financial Accounting Standards, No. 105,* "Disclosure of Information About Financial Instruments with Off-Balance Sheet Risk and Financial Instruments with Concentrations of Credit Risk" (Norwalk, Conn.: Financial Accounting Standards Board, 1990).

[30] For further review and discussion, see Chad F. Coben, "Implementing SFAS No. 105's Disclosure Requirements," *Journal of Commercial Lending* 74, No. 7 (March 1992), pp. 13–23; and Nathan M. Lubow, "New Disclosures FASB No. 105," *Secured Lender* 48, No. 6 (November/December 1992), pp. 112, 114.

[31] Financial Accounting Standards Board, *Statement of Financial Accounting Standards, No. 107,* "Disclosures About Fair Value of Financial Instruments" (Norwalk, Conn.: Financial Accounting Standards Board, 1991). In October 1994, the FASB issued SFAS No. 119, "Disclosure about Derivative Financial Instruments and Fair Value Instruments."

   With respect to derivatives that qualify as hedges, management may elect to use hedge accounting to defer gains or losses; however, it should be noted that the deferral of such gains or losses depends on the effectiveness of the derivative in offsetting changes in the fair value of the hedged item or changes in future cash flows. In addition, the changes in the fair value of asset, liability, or firm commitment being hedged must be recognized in income to the extent of offsetting gains or losses on the hedged instrument.[32]

   The use of market value accounting and the estimate of fair values may cause positive or negative variability in income because of changes in the market values and inaccurate estimates of fair values of financial instruments.

   The 1992 annual report of a publicly held bank and the 1998 annual report of the largest retailer included the following footnote disclosures.[33]

   The following methods and assumptions were used by the Bank in estimating its fair value disclosures for financial instruments:

   Cash and cash equivalents: The carrying amounts reported in the balance sheet for cash and short-term instruments approximate those assets' fair value.

   Investment and mortgage-backed securities: Fair values for investment and mortgage-backed securities are based on quoted market prices or dealer quotes.

   Loans: Fair values for loans are estimated using discounted cash flow analysis, based on interest rates approximating those currently being offered for loans with similar terms and credit quality. The fair value of accrued interest approximates carrying value.

   Deposits: The fair values disclosed for non-interest bearing accounts and accounts with no stated maturities are, by definition, equal to the amount payable on demand at the reporting date. The fair value of time deposits was estimated by discounting expected monthly maturities at interest rates approximating those currently being offered on time deposits of similar terms. The fair value of accrued interest approximates carrying value.

   Borrowings: The carrying amounts of repurchase agreements and other short-term borrowings approximate their fair values. Fair values of long-term borrowings are estimated using discounted cash flows, based on current market rates for similar borrowings.

   Off-balance sheet instruments: Off-balance sheet financial instruments consist of letters of credit, commitments to extend credit, and interest rate swaps.

---

[32] Financial Accounting Standards Board, *Statement of Financial Accounting Standards No. 133,* "Accounting for Derivatives Instruments and Hedging Activities" (Norwalk, Conn.: Financial Accounting Standards Board, 1998). With respect to the different types of hedges, disclosure, and transition requirements, see SFAS No. 133. This statement is effective for all fiscal quarters of fiscal years beginning after June 15, 1999.

[33] BSB Bancorp, Inc., *1992 Annual Report,* p. 33.

Statement of Financial Accounting Standard No. 107, "Disclosures about Fair Value of Financial Instruments" issued by the Financial Accounting Standards Board, became effective for the Bank for the year ended December 31, 1992. This standard requires disclosure of fair value information about financial instruments, whether or not recognized in the balance sheet, for which it is practicable to estimate that value. In cases where quoted market prices are not available, fair values are based on estimates using present value or other valuation techniques. Those techniques are significantly affected by the assumptions used, including the discount rate and estimates of future cash flows. In that regard, the derived value estimates cannot be substantiated by comparison to independent markets and, in many cases, could not be realized in immediate settlement of the instrument. Accordingly, the aggregate fair value amounts presented do not represent the underlying value of the Bank.

The net carrying amount and fair values of financial instruments as of December 31, 1992 are as follows:

	Carrying Amount	Fair Value
Financial Assets:	(Dollars in Thousands)	
Cash and cash equivalents	$ 27,513	$ 27,513
Investment securities	56,983	57,519
Mortgage-backed securities	152,295	155,610
Loans	765,210	772,886
Allowance for loan losses	(12,916)	
Net loans	752,294	772,886
Other financial assets	8,314	8,314
Total financial assets	$997,399	$1,021,842
Financial liabilities:		
Deposits	$822,115	$ 827,123
Borrowings	99,479	99,791
Total financial liabilities	$921,594	$ 926,914

Financial instruments

The Company uses derivative financial instruments for purposes other than trading to reduce its exposure to fluctuations in foreign currencies and to minimize the risk and cost associated with financial and global operating activities. Settlements of interest rate swaps are accounted for by recording the net interest received or paid as an adjustment to interest expense on a current basis. Gains or losses resulting from market movements are not recognized. Contracts that effectively meet risk reduction and correlation criteria are recorded using hedge accounting. Hedges of firm commitments or anticipated transactions are deferred and recognized when the hedged transaction occurs.

Interest rate instruments

The Company enters into interest rate swaps to minimize the risks and costs associated with its financial activities. The swap agreements are contracts to exchange fixed or variable rates for floating interest rate payments periodically over the life of the instruments. The notional amounts are used to measure interest to be paid or received and do not represent the exposure to credit loss. The rates paid on these swaps range from 3-month Deutschmark LIBOR minus .0676% to 30-day Commercial Paper Non-Financial plus .134%. These instruments are not recorded on the balance sheet, and as of January 31, 1998 and 1997, are as follows:

January 31, 1998

Notional amount (in millions)	Maturity	Rate received	Fair value
$ 585	2006	6.97%	$17
$ 500	2000	5.65%	—
$1,101	2003	30-day commercial paper non-financial	($1)

January 31, 1997

Notional amount (in millions)	Maturity	Rate received
$ 630	2006	6.97%

Foreign exchange instruments

The Company has entered into a foreign currency swap to hedge its investment in Germany. Under the agreement, the Company will pay $1,960 million in German Deutschmarks in 2003 and will receive $1,101 million in United States Dollars. At January 31, 1998, the fair value of this swap was $30 million.

The Company enters routinely into forward currency exchange contracts in the regular course of business to manage its exposure against foreign currency fluctuations on inventory purchases denominated in foreign currencies. These contracts are for short durations (six months or less) and are insignificant to the Company's operations or financial position. (There were approximately $27 million outstanding at January 31, 1998.)

Fair value of financial instruments

Cash and cash equivalents: The carrying amount approximates fair value due to the short maturity of these instruments.

Long-term debt: The fair value of the Company's long-term debt, including current maturities, approximates $8,639 million at January 31, 1998 and is based on the Company's current incremental borrowing rate for similar types of borrowing arrangements.

Interest rate instruments: The fair values are estimated amounts the Company would receive or pay to terminate the agreements as of the reporting dates.

Foreign currency contracts: The fair value of foreign currency contracts are estimated by obtaining quotes from brokers.[34]

REGULATORY AGENCIES

Importance of Regulatory Agencies

In a private enterprise economy, the corporation is a productive resource whereby corporate management is engaged in the ultimate economic decisions regarding the use of the enterprise's economic resources. Such economic decisions are influenced by the various regulatory agencies, such as the Securities and Exchange Commission and the Federal Trade Commission, so that management is not totally independent. Moreover, regulatory agencies provide a comprehensive set of rules and regulations in order to control the enterprise as well as to safeguard the interests of investors and the general public. For example, the objective of the Federal Trade Commission is to prevent monopolistic practices and price discrimination in American industry. Also, several commissions supervise certain industries, such as the utility and transportation industries, as well as the area of labor-management relations. Particularly important is the government's regulation of the securities market and the taxation process. Such regulation is essential to the economy to eliminate financial abuses and unfair practices in the private sector. Thus the audit committee should be concerned with the reporting requirements of the governmental regulatory agencies.

The Need for Accounting Information

In order to formulate sound public policies, the regulatory commissions need accounting information concerning the economic activities of the enterprise. In addition, they need accounting information to monitor the corporation's compliance with the governmental rules and regulations. Although there are many regulatory agencies, of particular importance are the Securities and Exchange Commission and the Federal Trade Commission.

Securities and Exchange Commission (SEC) The principle purpose of the SEC laws is to provide public disclosure of the relevant facts with respect to new securities and securities listed on the stock exchanges.[35] In particular, the

---

[34] Wal∗Mart Stores, Inc., *1998 Annual Report,* pp. 30, 32.

[35] Such rules of law are contained in the Accounting Series Releases, Staff Accounting Bulletins, and Financial Reporting Releases of the SEC.

SEC requires a registration statement which contains background information, such as the size and competitive position of the corporation. Moreover, a prospective investor must be furnished a prospectus, which is a summary of the registration statement. For example, the prospectus will contain such matters as the offering price of the securities, the use of the proceeds by the registrant, and the financial statements.[36] Furthermore, the SEC requires periodic reports from the corporations in order to update its files on each corporation. Such periodic reports include the annual report (10-K) and interim reports (10-Q and 8-K).[37]

The SEC annual Form 10-K report is used to update the information which is included in the registration statement. This report must be filed within 90 days of the end of a registrant's fiscal year. The report contains the following information:

Part I—Item
1. Business
2. Properties
3. Legal proceedings
4. Submission of matters to a note of security holders

Part II—Item
5. Market for the registrant's common stock and related stockholder matters
6. Selected financial data
7. Management's discussion and analysis of financial condition and results of operations
8. Financial statements and supplementary data
9. Changes in and disagreements with accountants on accounting and financial disclosure

Part III—Item
10. Directors and executive officers of the registrant
11. Executive compensation
12. Security ownership of certain beneficial owners and management
13. Certain relationships and related transactions

Part IV—Item
14. Exhibits, financial statement schedules, and reports on Form 8-K Signatures

The SEC quarterly Form 10-Q report is used to report interim changes in the financial position and the results of operating the corporation. This particular re-

---

[36] For a complete description of all the items in the prospectus, see Part I of Form S-1, which is the registration statement.
[37] See Appendix A for further information. For further details and description of all forms, see Regulation S-X and Regulation S-K. Copies may be obtained from the U.S. Government Printing Office.

port must be filed within 45 days after the close of each of the first three quarters. For example, with respect to the financial information, the report contains information on the preparation of financial information, reviews by the independent public accountants, and other financial information. Concerning other information, the report discloses information on such matters as legal proceedings, changes in securities, and other materially important events.

The SEC Form 8-K report is an interim or current report that contains information with respect to certain significant special events. For example, a change in the independent accounting firm must be reported within 15 days subsequent to the change. Other events include such items as a change in control of the registrant or significant legal proceedings. This report is particularly important since it provides timely information regarding the disclosure of material events. Consequently, the SEC needs accounting information not only to monitor management's compliance with its rules but also to protect the investing public.

SEC Topical Developments

The SEC has focused on a number of financial reporting areas that relate to the audit committee's oversight responsibility. The more significant developments in these reporting areas are discussed in the following paragraphs.

Management's Discussion and Analysis The quality of information reported to the SEC concerning Management's Discussion and Analysis (MD&A) of Financial Condition and Results of Operations in the registrant's filings has been of major concern to the investing public and to the SEC. In response, the SEC issued Financial Reporting Release No. 36, which is an interpretive release regarding disclosures required by Item 303 of Regulation S-K with respect to the registrants' filings containing Management's Discussion and Analysis of Financial Condition and Results of Operations.[38] Based on a review project of such filings, the Commission found that several key disclosure matters, namely, prospective information, liquidity and capital resources analysis, material changes in financial statement line items, and business segment analysis, should be considered by registrants in preparing MD&A disclosures. Apparently the SEC determined that interpretive guidance is needed for disclosures concerning the aforementioned matters.

The SEC requires management to discuss favorable or unfavorable trends, significant events, and uncertainties that impact the various reporting areas. Given that MD&A reporting is highly subjective and that management must comply

---

[38] Securities and Exchange Commission, "Management's Discussion and Analysis of Financial Condition and Results of Operations; Interpretive Release," Title 17, *Code of Federal Regulations,* Secs. 211, 231, 241, and 271 (June 1989), pp. 1–44.

with Item 303 of Regulation S-K, the question is frequently asked: Is the objective of the MD&A disclosure requirement being accomplished? Clearly, the MD&A narrative discussion is the appropriate vehicle to provide early warning signals or red flags to the investing public. As a case in point, *Management Accounting* recently observed that the SEC issued an order complaining about a registrant's MD&A reporting, which did not tell investors that nearly 23 percent of its 1989 earnings came from a foreign subsidiary unit—a situation that would not recur. James Adelman of the SEC's Enforcement Division stated, "It will no longer be acceptable for companies to use 'boilerplate' language in MD&As when they know unfolding developments will have an effect on corporate earnings in the future."[39]

In addition to management's involvement with the preparation of MD&A, independent auditors must review this information to ensure that the narrative discussion is not inconsistent with their findings and conclusions regarding their audit report. For example, if management knows of events, trends, or uncertainties that are reasonably likely to occur, then such information should be reported under prospective information. Conversely, if management concludes that events, trends, or uncertainties are not reasonably likely to occur, then no disclosure is required. Thus the reasonably likely standard, and whether management knows of the trends, events, or uncertainties, determines whether such information is disclosed. If management anticipates such trends, events, or uncertainties, then disclosure is optional under prospective information. Professional auditing standards, in particular SAS No. 59, "The Auditor's Consideration of an Entity's Ability to Continue as a Going Concern," dictate that the independent auditors do have the power to issue an unqualified audit report with an explanatory paragraph describing the material uncertainty.[40] This type of audit report gives a warning signal or a red flag to the investing public with respect to the financial condition of the company. Anthony B. Billings and Larry D. Crumbley assert that auditors have a role in signaling a going concern problem. Their role is governed by SAS No. 59, which advances categories of conditions that may arise, including adverse financial ra-

---

[39] Stephen Barlas, "SEC Cracks Down on MD&A Sections," *Management Accounting* 73, No. 12 (June 1992), p. 8. See *Accounting and Auditing Enforcement Release No. 363* (March 31, 1992), 51 SEC Docket 300. Also see *Statement on Standards for Attestation Engagements No. 8*, "Management's Discussion and Analysis" (New York: American Institute of Certified Public Accountants, 1998), which provides guidance to independent accountants engaged to examine or review MD&A as well as the use of agreed-upon procedures; Reva B. Steinberg and Judith Fellner Weiss, "New Rules on Disclosure of Certain Significant Risks and Uncertainties," *CPA Journal* 65, No. 3 (March 1995), pp. 16–20; SEC's interpretation on year 2000 entitled, *Disclosure of Year 2000 Issues and Consequences by Public Companies, Investment Advisers, Investment Companies, and Municipal Securities Issues* (Washington, D.C.: Securities and Exchange Commission, 1998).

[40] *Statement of Auditing Standards, No. 59*, "The Auditor's Consideration of an Entity's Ability to Continue as a Going Concern" (New York: American Institute of Certified Public Accountants, 1988).

tios, negative trends, and loan defaults.[41] Moreover, John E. Ellingsen, Kurt Pany, and Peg Fagan point out that "an auditor may have designed and performed audit procedures—such as analyzing liquidity ratios—to ascertain whether the entity is complying with certain loan covenants. Evaluation of the liquidity ratios not only assists the auditor vis-à-vis the loan covenants but also helps the auditor evaluate whether the ratios raise doubt about the company's ability to continue as a going concern."[42] Of course, the auditor must consider the conditions and events in the aggregate, so that unfavorable liquidity ratios coupled with declining profitability ratios and increased debt-solvency ratios may cause substantial doubt about the entity's going concern ability. Accordingly, SAS No. 59 requires that the independent auditors evaluate, in every audit engagement, whether there is substantial doubt about the entity's ability to continue as a going concern.

Given the continuing debate over business failure versus audit failure and the continued number of lawsuits against well-known publicly held companies and public accounting firms, it is imperative that the audit committee focus its attention on MD&A disclosures in the financial reporting process. The committee should (1) review and discuss the SEC's mandate concerning MD&A reporting and (2) evaluate management's compliance with the SEC's mandated disclosures and its interpretive release. Clearly, one would expect the audit committee to help improve the quality of MD&A disclosures in light of the SEC's interpretive release. This subject is further discussed in Chapter 10.

Disagreements with the Independent Auditors[43]   As noted in Part II, Item 9, of the SEC annual 10-K report, a registrant is required to disclose disagreements on accounting and financial disclosure between managem'nt and the independent auditors. In addition, the SEC requires a registrant to file a Form 8-K and the independent auditors' response with respect to reporting the reasons for changes in independent auditors. This action on the part of the SEC, coupled with Statement on Auditing Standards No. 50, "Reports on the Application of Accounting Principles," is designed to restrict management from audit opinion shopping. Thus, when the principal auditor's client company requests a report on the application of an accounting principle from another accounting firm, the reporting auditor is required to consult with the principal auditor.[44] Such an auditing standard helps ensure the independent auditor's independence.

---

[41] Anthony B. Billings and Larry D. Crumbley, "Financial Difficulties of Governmental Units," *CPA Journal* 58, No. 7 (October 1988), p. 52.
[42] John E. Ellingsen, Kurt Pany, and Peg Fagan, "SAS No. 59: How to Evaluate Going Concern," *Journal of Accountancy* 168, No. 1 (January 1989), p. 27.
[43] See Jerry E. Serlin, "Shopping Around: A Closer Look at Opinion Shopping," *Journal of Accounting, Auditing & Finance* 9, No. 1 (Fall 1985), pp. 74–80.
[44] *Statement on Auditing Standards, No. 50,* "Reports on the Application of Accounting Principles" (New York: American Institute of Certified Public Accountants, 1986), par 1.

Environmental Liabilities[45]   The board of directors has oversight responsibility to determine that management is complying with environmental laws. In some industries with significant environmental exposure, board committees may be appointed to deal with the issue. Whether the full board or a committee is assigned this responsibility, the audit committee should determine that environmental costs and liabilities are properly reflected in the financial statements and related disclosure.

The committee may recommend to the board the establishment and monitoring of an environmental auditing program. See Chapter 10 for further discussion of this subject.

Executive Compensation Disclosure   On October 15, 1992, the SEC adopted amendments to the executive officer and director compensation disclosure requirements applicable to proxy statements, registration statements, and periodic reports (e.g., 10-Qs and 10-K) under the Securities Act of 1933 and the Securities Exchange Act of 1934 (Release Nos. 33-6962, 34-31327, and IC-19032 applicable to Regulation S-K).[46] In sum, executive compensation disclosures for the chief executive officer and the four other highest-paid executives are now required.

Although the compensation committee of the board of directors has oversight responsibility for executive compensation plans, the audit committee should be assured that management has complied with the SEC's new disclosure requirements. The National Association of Corporate Directors has issued the *Report of the NACD Blue Ribbon Commission on Executive Compensation: Guidelines for Corporate Directors*. The disclosure requirements are summarized as follows:

> A summary table containing detailed information on the total compensation for the last three years of the CEO and the four other most highly paid executives (whose annual compensation exceeds $100,000—up from the $60,000 in effect since 1983).

> A compensation committee report describing the factors affecting the committee's decisions regarding executive compensation, and the rationale for CEO compensation.

[45] A National Priority List of potentially responsible parties (PRPs) is issued by the U.S. Environmental Protection Agency on an annual basis. See also the SEC's SAB No. 92, "Accounting and Disclosures Relating to Loss Contingencies," and the AICPA's Accounting Standard Executive Committee, *Statement of Position (SOP) No. 96-1,* "Environmental Remediation Liabilities" (New York: American Institute of Certified Public Accountants, 1996).

[46] Securities and Exchange Commission, "Executive Compensation Disclosure," Title 17, *Code of Federal Regulations,* Parts 228, 299, 240, and 249 (October 1992). In November 1993, the SEC amended its executive compensation disclosure rules to address such matters as executives covered, restricted stock holdings, option valuations, and peer group index. See the *Federal Register* 58, No. 227 (November 29, 1993), pp. 63010 and 63017, for further details.

A performance graph comparing the company's five-year shareholder returns with those of other companies.

Option/SAR tables disclosing various information regarding stock options and stock appreciation rights (SARs) including potential appreciation rates and the unrealized gains on outstanding options.

Other revisions require expanded disclosure of beneficial ownership of a registrant's securities by its executives, incentive stock option repricing, potential lack of independence of compensation committee members, and details of new compensation plans subject to shareholder approval. Required tables and graphs are included in the Appendices of this report.[47]

Federal Trade Commission (FTC) The major objective of the FTC is to police the business community to eliminate unfair methods of competition. Essentially, the FTC is involved with the enforcement of the antitrust laws, such as the Sherman and Clayton Acts. Furthermore, the FTC administers the laws concerning the Robinson-Patman Act. The Robinson-Patman Act prohibits big businesses from exploiting their small competitors through price discrimination and quantity discounts. Thus the FTC needs accounting information regarding distribution costs and related prices to ensure that the corporation is not engaged in unlawful pricing practices.

Role of the Audit Directors

Since the corporate annual report and the SEC annual 10-K report must be examined by the independent public accountants, the audit committee should review these reports with the accountants from a compliance perspective. For example, the audit directors should be concerned with the protection of the corporation's interest against penalties or fines regarding any noncompliance with the laws, such as environmental protection laws. Such penalties can be very costly and reduce the earnings performance of the enterprise. Indeed, there are a myriad of complex laws and regulations affecting the corporation. The members of the committee may not have the necessary legal expertise to determine if the firm is complying with the laws. Accordingly, it may be advisable for the committee to retain the corporation's in-house counsel or outside legal counsel to gain assurance regarding management's compliance. Such assistance will enable the committee to be aware of the effect of certain laws on the corporation and thus avoid expensive or embarrassing fines or penalties. More specifically, the audit directors must make an informed judgment on management's efforts to comply with the laws through a review of the corporation's history of compliance and the necessary

---

[47]National Association of Corporate Directors, *Report of the NACD Blue Ribbon Commission on Executive Compensation: Guidelines for Corporate Directors* (Washington, D.C.: NACD, 1993), p. 21.

managerial corrective actions. Thus the committee can minimize the firm's non-compliance liability based on the above procedures.

OTHER OUTSIDE CONSTITUENCIES

Importance of Other Outside Constituencies

With respect to the significance of the other external users of accounting information, the American Assembly concluded that:

> Employees should be regarded as a crucial part of the constituency of the corporation. Employee interests will be better served by various means, such as collective bargaining, direct communications, and participative management approaches rather than by direct employee representation on boards of directors
>
> Consumers have large roles to play. They act as advance guideposts to the needs and expectations of the marketplace. Corporations which enhance their long-term profitability should build relationships with future customers.[48]

Thus it may be appropriate for corporate management to share the accounting information with the above groups, since such groups not only provide services but also receive the goods and services from the enterprise. Because such groups are vital to the successful operation of the corporation, management should consider sharing its accounting information concerning the economic performance of the enterprise. Although there is no uniform pattern in communicating financial accounting information to employees, it may be desirable to consider a special annual report for employees. Similarly, some managements may consider making available a copy of the annual report to special consumer interest groups.

Through an overview of the importance and the need for accounting information, the audit directors can contribute to improving the effectiveness of the audit function in society. Moreover, the Business Roundtable noted that:

> The central corporate governance point to be made about a corporation's stakeholders beyond the shareholder is that they are vital to the long-term successful economic performance of the corporation. Some argue that only the interests of the shareholders should be considered by directors. The thrust of history and law strongly supports the broader view of the directors' responsibility to carefully weigh the interests of all stakeholders as part of their responsibility to the corporation or to the long-term interests of its shareholders.

[48] The American Assembly, *Corporate Governance in America,* Pamphlet 54, New York: The American Assembly, 1978, p. 6.

Resolving the potentially differing interests of various stakeholders and the best long-term interest of the corporation and its shareholders involves compromises and tradeoffs which often must be made rapidly. It is important that all stakeholder interests be considered, but impossible to assure that all will be satisfied because competing claims may be mutually exclusive.[49]

The Need for Accounting Information

A corporation's stakeholders need accounting information in order to judge management's economic decisions and performance. For example, employees are interested in the solvency position of the corporation since they expect to receive wages in return for their services. Moreover, they are interested in the enterprise's image as a corporate citizen of society. Similarly, consumers need accounting information regarding the present and future economic status of the corporation because they rely on the enterprise to provide the necessary goods and services to the community.

Role of the Audit Directors

To enhance the communication process between the enterprise and stakeholder groups, the committee should consult with the executive in charge of the public relations program. For example, the audit directors should satisfy themselves that the information in any special annual reports to employees is consistent with the financial information in the annual or quarterly reports. In addition, the audit committee should review management's commentary in the special reports in view of the quantitative characteristics of financial reporting. As a participative management approach, the committee may suggest an employee report whereby the financial information is related to each employee. Such reports enhance not only the employee's perception of the organization but also his or her work attitude since both corporate management and the employees are contributing to the organizational goals.

Furthermore, the audit directors should determine that adequate management controls exist with respect to the release of special financial reports to the general public, such as newspaper and other releases, to ensure that such releases are appropriate and consistent with the company's policies and plans. In some instances it may be desirable to clear such distribution of financial information with the audit committee.

---

[49] The Business Roundtable, *Corporate Governance and American Competitiveness,* p. 4.

AICPA Position

The board of directors of the American Institute of Certified Public Accountants reported a strategy for making financial reports more useful:

> Financial decision-makers confront change on a daily basis. The integration of financial markets, the impact of technology, the entry of new competitors, the introduction of new and more complex financial products—all of these have made investing a different business than it was just a few years ago. These innovations automatically bring with them changes in the kind of financial information needed. If the accounting profession is to fulfill its obligation to the public, it must not remain static.
>
> The AICPA has launched an effort to ensure that financial reporting moves with the times. Our Special Committee on Financial Reporting is looking at far-reaching ways to make financial reports more relevant to the realities of today's marketplace by anticipating the financial information needs of the 21st century. This is a wide-ranging and intensive effort. We are ruling out no possibilities as we examine what changes to the existing accounting model should be made to meet user needs in the short and long term. We expect the Special Committee to complete its work within a year.
>
> In the interim, we are taking more immediate steps to improve the utility of financial reports. In this fast-changing economic environment, investors can't afford to look only backwards. They need to anticipate. To serve this need, the AICPA's Accounting Standards Executive Committee, consistent with a recommendation by the POB [Public Oversight Board], has issued a proposal to require management to disclose risks and uncertainties that could significantly affect the company's operations or financial condition. We urge AcSEC [Accounting Standards Executive Committee] to complete its work with all deliberate speed.
>
> To provide further assurance to the investing public, we join the POB in calling for a statement by management, to be included in the annual report, on the effectiveness of the company's internal controls over financial reporting, accompanied by an auditor's report on management's assertions. An assessment by the independent auditor will provide greater assurance to investors as to management's statement. The internal control system is the main line of defense against fraudulent financial reporting. The investing public deserves an independent assessment of that line of defense, and management should benefit from the auditor's perspective and insights. We urge the SEC to establish this requirement.
>
> Finally, the SEC should require audit committees to include a statement in the annual report describing their responsibilities and how these responsibilities were discharged. This will increase the attention that audit committee members give their crucial responsibilities. It will also increase the attention paid to their views by management and other directors.[50]

---

[50] American Institute of Certified Public Accountants, *Meeting the Financial Reporting Needs of the Future: A Public Commitment from the Public Accounting Profession* (New York: AICPA, 1993), pp. 3–4. Also see the AICPA Special Committee on Financial Reporting report, *The Information Needs of Investors and Creditors* (New York: AICPA, 1993).

RECENT DEVELOPMENTS IN BUSINESS REPORTING AND ASSURANCE SERVICES

This section briefly highlights and discusses the findings and conclusions of two major studies conducted by the AICPA Special Committee on Financial Reporting (Jenkins Committee) and the AICPA Special Committee on Assurance Services (Elliott Committee). The major objective of this review discussion is to provide an understanding of the issues and emerging trends impacting the public accounting profession which, in turn, are of particular concern to audit committees in the latter half of the 1990s.

In 1991, a Special Committee on Financial Reporting (Jenkins Committee) was established by the AICPA to study the need for a new financial reporting model in response to the information needs of users. After completing a three-year study of the financial reporting system in the United States, in 1994 the AICPA Special Committee on Financial Reporting issued its final comprehensive report (202 pages) and summary report (20 pages), entitled *Improving Business Reporting—A Customer Focus: Meeting the Information Needs of Investors and Creditors.* As part of the AICPA's broad initiative to improve the value of business information and the public's confidence in the financial reporting process, the study examined the relevance and usefulness of business reporting and the independent auditors' association with that type of reporting. The Committee set forth the following recommendations with respect to four broad categories:

1. Improving the Types of Information in Business Reporting

   Recommendation 1: Standard setters should develop a comprehensive model of business reporting indicating the types and timing of information that users need to value and assess the risk of their investments.

   Recommendation 2: Improve understanding of costs and benefits of business reporting, recognizing that definitive quantification of costs and benefits is not possible.

2. Financial Statements and Related Disclosures

   Recommendation 1: Improve disclosure of business segment information.

   Recommendation 2: Address the disclosures and accounting for innovative financial instruments.

   Recommendation 3: Improve disclosures about the identity, opportunities, and risks of off-balance-sheet financing arrangements and reconsider the accounting for those arrangements.

   Recommendation 4: Report separately the effects of core and non-core activities and events, and measure at fair value non-core assets and liabilities.

   Recommendation 5: Improve disclosures about the uncertainty of measurements of certain assets and liabilities.

Recommendation 6: Improve quarterly reporting by reporting on the fourth quarter separately and including business segment data.

Recommendation 7: Standard setters should search for and eliminate less relevant disclosures.

3. Auditor Association with Business Reporting

Recommendation 1: Allow for flexible auditor association with business reporting, whereby the elements of information on which auditors report and the level of auditor involvement with those elements are decided by agreement between a company and the users of its business reporting.

Recommendation 2: The auditing profession should prepare to be involved with all the information in the comprehensive model, so companies and users can call on it to provide assurance on any of the model's elements.

Recommendation 3: The newly formed AICPA Special Committee on Assurance Services should research and formulate conclusions on analytical commentary in auditors' reports within the context of the Committee's model, focusing on users' needs for information.

Recommendation 4: The profession should continue its projects on other matters related to auditor association with business reporting.

4. Facilitating Change in Business Reporting

Recommendation 1: National and international standard setters and regulators should increase their focus on the information needs of users, and users should be encouraged to work with standard setters to increase the level of their involvement in the standard-setting process.

Recommendation 2: U.S. standard setters and regulators should continue to work with their non-U.S. counterparts and international standard setters to develop international accounting standards, provided the resulting standards meet users' needs for information.

Recommendation 3: Lawmakers, regulators, and standard setters should develop more effective deterrents to unwarranted litigation that discourages companies from disclosing forward-looking information.

Recommendation 4: Companies should be encouraged to experiment voluntarily with ways to improve the usefulness of reporting consistent with the Committee's model. Standard setters and regulators should consider allowing companies that experiment to substitute information specified by the model for information currently required.

Recommendation 5: Standard setters should adopt a longer term focus by developing a vision of the future business environment and users' needs for information in that environment. Standards should be consistent directionally with that long-term vision.

Recommendation 6: Regulators should consider whether there are any alternatives to the current requirement that public companies make all disclosures publicly available.

Recommendation 7: The AICPA should establish a Coordinating Committee charged to ensure that the recommendations in this report are given adequate consideration by those who can act on them.[51]

As a result of the Special Committee's report, standard setters, regulators, professional organizations, professional practitioners, and academicians need to focus their attention on the points of view on the Committee's recommendations. This report has a wealth of information concerning the business reporting model and a comprehensive illustration of the Committee's recommendations. Audit committees should review these recommendations, with particular emphasis on the elements of the Committee's model of business reporting relative to the current model of financial reporting. Additionally, they should discuss the implications for independent auditors.

Recognizing that audit committees have oversight responsibilities for the external audit process, it is desirable to review the Special Committee's form of report that would be issued by the independent auditors. To improve the independent auditors' communications about their role and responsibility, the Committee attempted to articulate an illustrative audit report. This type of report is shown in Exhibit 3.1.

The Committee's proposed audit report is different in several ways from the standard independent auditors' report. First, the introductory paragraph mentions "core earnings" and the audit of the five-year summary of business data and other descriptions. Additionally, the auditors are expressing their opinion on these presentations as opposed to only financial statements. Second, the auditors would be required to substitute the word *presentation* for *financial statement* in the scope paragraph. Finally, the auditors would be required to express two opinions with respect to both financial and nonfinancial data.

Notwithstanding the FASB's current model of financial reporting, the Special Committee has offered 20 recommendations and a comprehensive model of business reporting. In fact, the Committee goes beyond the full disclosure principle with a requirement for disclosure of nonfinancial data. Of course, the major objective is to minimize information overload within the cost-benefit constraint. Moreover, the Committee has broadened the attest function with respect to seven sections of the annual report, as noted in the proposed auditors' report. Regarding flexible auditors' association with business reporting, the Special Committee rec-

---

[51]American Institute of Certified Public Accountants, *Improving Business Reporting—A Customer Focus, Meeting the Information Needs of Investors and Creditors* (New York: AICPA, 1994), 123–127.

Exhibit 3.1   Report of Independent Accountants

This example illustrates the form of report that would be issued if the independent accountant had been engaged to render an opinion on the entire FauxCom annual report, although this may not always be the case.

We have audited the accompanying consolidated balance sheet of FauxCom, Inc. as of December 31, 1993, and 1992, and the related consolidated statements of core earnings and net income, cash flows, and stockholders' equity for each of the two years in the period ended December 31, 1993. We also audited the five-year summary of business data, the description of information about management and shareholders, and the scope and description of the Company's businesses accompanying the financial statements. These financial statements, five-year summary and descriptions are the responsibility of the Company's management. Our responsibility is to express an opinion on these presentations based on our audits.

We conducted our audits in accordance with generally accepted auditing standards. Those standards require that we plan and perform the audit to obtain reasonable assurance about whether the information presented is free of material misstatement. An audit includes examining, on a test basis, evidence supporting the amounts and disclosures presented. An audit also includes assessing the accounting principles used and significant estimates made by management, as well as evaluating the overall presentation. We believe that our audits provide a reasonable basis for our opinion.

In our opinion, the financial statements referred to above present fairly, in all material respects, the financial position of FauxCom, Inc. as of December 31, 1993, and 1992, and the results of its operations and its cash flows for each of the two years in the period ended December 31, 1993, in conformity with generally accepted accounting principles. It is also our opinion that the five-year summary and descriptions referred to above are fairly presented, in all material respects, in conformity with the applicable standards.

As part of the audit, we also performed such audit procedures as we considered necessary to evaluate management's assumptions and analyses and the preparation and presentation of the information in the following sections of the annual report:

• Current year review
• Management's analysis of financial and non-financial data
• Opportunities and risks, including those resulting from key trends
• Management's plans, including critical success factors
• Comparison of actual business performance to previously disclosed forward-looking information
• Broad objectives and strategies
• Impact of industry structure on the Company

In our opinion, the accompanying sections described above are presented in conformity with the respective standards of presentation, and management has a reasonable basis for the underlying assumptions and analyses reflected in the aforementioned sections.

February 15, 1994
Boston, Massachusetts

Source: American Institute of Certified Public Accountants, *Comprehensive Report of the Special Committee on Financial Reporting,* (New York: American Institute of Certified Public Accountants, 1994), p. 184.

ommends that the AICPA Special Committee on Assurance Services and the Auditing Standards Board pursue the subject of alternative levels of assurance within the Committee's reporting framework. In sum, the Committee's report is a significant step in the continuous process of improving financial reporting; however, many preparers of financial statements would argue that the cost of implementing the recommendations would be prohibitive. Moreover, it is reasonable to expect that many nonpublic companies, particularly small companies, would have difficulty with the Committee's proposals.

In 1995, the AICPA established the Financial Reporting Coordinating Committee to coordinate actions taken on the recommendations made by the Jenkins Committee. Although the Coordinating Committee held a symposium (Fall 1996) to continue the discussion of Jenkins Committee's Comprehensive Model for Business Reporting, the debate between the financial statement preparers and users about the aforementioned recommendations continues. However, the Auditing Standards Board has issued a Statement on Standards for Attestation Engagements (SSAE) No. 8, *Management's Discussion and Analysis* (March 1998), in response to the Jenkins Committee's recommendations. Therefore, financial statement preparers and users can engage the accounting profession to provide assurance on the elements of the Comprehensive Model for Business Reporting.[52]

In 1994, a Special Committee on Assurance Services (Elliott Committee) was established by the AICPA to study and report on the current and future assurance needs of all users of both financial statements and nonfinancial information for decision making. After completing a three-year study of the attestation and assurance processes in the United States, this Special Committee completed its work at the end of December 1996. Similar to the previously mentioned Financial Reporting Coordinating Committee, an Assurance Services Committee was formed by the AICPA to follow-up on the findings and conclusions made by the Elliott Committee and communicate new assurance opportunities for AICPA members. The concept of assurance services includes all attestation services with a particular emphasis on enhancing the quality of information through individualized services for decision-making purposes.

As a basis for developing the new concept of assurance services, the Elliott Committee studied such research areas as users' needs for information, megatrends impacting such needs for information, information technology affecting

---

[52]For further discussion regarding an examination, review, or an agreed-upon procedure engagement, see SSAE No. 8. Also see James L. Craig, "The CPA Journal Symposium on Recommendations for Improving Business Reporting," *CPA Journal* 65, No. 1 (January 1995), pp. 18–27; Daniel J. Noll and Jerry J. Weygandt, "Business Reporting: What Comes Next?" *Journal of Accountancy* 183, No. 2 (February 1997), p. 59.

the use of information, and practitioner competencies needed to provide the necessary assurance on the aforementioned information.

Based on the above research areas, the Elliott Committee developed business plans for six initial assurance services, including:

- *Risk Assessment.* This service assures that an entity's profile of business risks is comprehensive and evaluates whether the entity has appropriate systems in place to manage those risks effectively.

- *Business Performance Measurement.* This service evaluates whether an entity's performance measurement system contains relevant and reliable measures for assessing the degree to which the entity's goals and objectives are achieved or how its performance compares to its competitors.

- *Information Systems Reliability.* This service assesses whether an entity's internal information systems (financial and nonfinancial) provide reliable information for operating and financial decisions.

- *Electronic Commerce.* This service assesses whether systems and tools used in electronic commerce provide appropriate data integrity, security, privacy, and reliability.

- *Health Care Performance Measurement.* This service provides assurance about the effectiveness of health care services provided by health maintenance organizations (HMOs), hospitals, doctors, and other providers.

- *Elder Care Plus.* This service assesses whether specified goals regarding care for the elderly are being met by various caregivers.[53]

Finally, audit committee members should be aware that, in September 1997, the AICPA and the Canadian Institute of Chartered Accountants implemented an electronic commerce service called the CPA Web Trust (a seal of assurance for on-line customers that a business adheres to standards for disclosure, transaction integrity, and information protection). See the AICPA website: www.aicpa.org, or the Committee's report, which is available on CD-ROM.[54]

Indeed, there is little doubt that the AICPA's call for action will further impact on the duties and responsibilities of audit committee members.

---

[53]American Institute of Certified Public Accountants, *Special Committee on Assurance Services,* www.aicpa.org, 1996.

[54]Also see Robert K. Elliott, "The Future of Assurance Services: Implications for Academia," *Accounting Horizons* 9, No. 4 (December 1995), pp. 118–127; Robert K. Elliott and Donald M. Pallais, four-part series dealing with the future of Assurance Services, *Journal of Accountancy* 183 Nos. 6, 7, 8, 9 (June, July, August, September 1997).

SOURCES AND SUGGESTED READINGS

The American Assembly, *Corporate Governance in America,* Pamphlet 54 (New York: Columbia University, April 1978).

The American Assembly, *The American Assembly Report 1991–1992* (New York: The American Assembly, 1992).

American Institute of Certified Public Accountants, *Accounting Trends and Techniques—1990* (New York: 1990).

American Institute of Certified Public Accountants, *Report of the Study Group on the Objectives of Financial Statements* (New York: American Institute of Certified Public Accountants, 1973).

American Institute of Certified Public Accountants, *Improving Business Reporting—A Customer Focus, Meeting the Information Needs of Investors and Creditors* (New York: AICPA, 1994).

American Stock Exchange, *American Stock Exchange Fact Book 1991* (New York: 1991).

Association for Investment Management and Research, *Corporate Information Committee Report 1995–1996* (New York: Association for Investment Management and Research, 1997).

Barlas, Stephen, "SEC Cracks Down on MD&A Sections." *Management Accounting* 73, No. 12 (June 1992), p. 8.

Billings, Anthony B., and Larry D. Crumbley, "Financial Difficulties of Governmental Units." *CPA Journal* 58, No. 7 (October 1988), pp. 52–61.

BSB Bancorp, Inc. *1992 Annual Report.*

The Business Roundtable, *Corporate Governance and American Competitiveness* (New York: The Business Roundtable, 1990).

Coben, Chad F., "Implementing SFAS No. 105's Disclosure Requirements." *Journal of Commercial Landing* 74, No. 7 (March 1992), pp. 13–23.

Dougherty, William H., "Financial Reporting—A Banker Looks at the Scene." *Financial Executive,* 46, No. 12 (December 1978), pp. 47–53.

Ellingsen, John E., Kurt Pany, and Peg Fagan, "SAS No. 59: How to Evaluate Going Concern." *Journal of Accountancy* 168, No. 1 (January 1989), p. 27.

Financial Accounting Standards Board, *Statement of Financial Accounting Concepts No. 1* (Stamford, Conn.: Financial Accounting Standards Board, 1978).

Financial Accounting Standards Board, *Statement of Financial Accounting Standards, No. 95,* "Statement of Cash Flows" (Stamford, Conn.: Financial Accounting Standards Board, 1987).

Financial Accounting Standards Board, *Statement of Financial Accounting Standards, No. 105,* "Disclosure of Information About Financial Instruments with Off-Balance Sheet Risk and Financial Instruments with Concentrations of Credit Risk" (Norwalk, Conn.: Financial Accounting Standards Board, 1990).

Financial Accounting Standards Board, *Statement of Financial Accounting Standards No. 107,* "Disclosures About Fair Value of Financial Instruments" (Norwalk, Conn.: Financial Accounting Standards Board, 1991).

Financial Accounting Standards Board, *Statement of Financial Accounting Standards, No. 133,* "Accounting for Derivative Instruments and Hedging Activities" (Norwalk, Conn.: Financial Accounting Standards Board, 1998).

Financial Analysts Federation, "Awards for Excellence in Corporate Reporting," *Financial Analysts Federation News Release* (New York: January 1978).

Investor Responsibility Research Center, *Annual Report 1992* (Washington, D.C. Investor Responsibility Research Center, 1992).

Lubow, Nathan M., "New Disclosures FASB No. 105." *Secured Lender* 48, No. 6 (November/December 1992), pp. 112, 114.

MacIver, Brian H., James Welch, and Priscilla A. Burnaby, "Quality Review—Observations of a Team Captain." *Ohio CPA Journal* 50, No. 1 (January–April 1991), pp. 54–55.

Most, Kenneth S., and Lucia S. Chang, "An Empirical Study of Investor Views Concerning Financial Statements and Investment Decisions," *Collected Papers of the American Accounting Association's Annual Meeting* (Sarasota, Fla.: American Accounting Association, August 20–23, 1978), pp. 241–260.

National Association of Corporate Directors, *Report of the NACD Blue Ribbon Commission on Executive Compensation: Guidelines for Corporate Directors* (Washington, D.C.: National Association of Corporate Directors, 1993).

New York Stock Exchange, *New York Stock Exchange Fact Book 1992* (New York: New York Stock Exchange, 1992).

Pate, Gwen Richardson, and Keith G. Stanga, "A Guide to the FASB's Concepts Statements." *Journal of Accountancy* 168, No. 2 (August 1989), pp. 28–31.

Rubin, Steven, "How Concepts Statements Can Solve Practice Problems." *Journal of Accountancy* 166, No. 4 (October 1988), pp. 123–124, 126.

Securities and Exchange Commission, *1992 Annual Report* (Washington, D.C.: U.S. Government Printing Office, 1992).

Securities and Exchange Commission, *1997 Annual Report* (Washington, D.C.: U.S. Government Printing Office, 1997).

Securities and Exchange Commission, *Accounting and Auditing Enforcement Release No. 363* (March 31, 1992), 51 SEC Docket 300.

Securities and Exchange Commission, "Executive Compensation Disclosure," Title 17 *Code of Federal Regulations,* Parts 228, 229, 240, and 249 (October 1989). See Rules and Regulations, *Federal Register,* 57, No. 204 (October 21, 1992), pp. 48126–48159.

Securities and Exchange Commission, "Management's Discussion and Analysis of Financial Condition and Results of Operations; Interpretive Release," Title 17 *Code of Federal Regulations,* Sec. 211, 231, 241, and 271 (June 1989), pp. 1–44.

Serlin, Jerry E., "Shopping Around: A Closer Look at Opinion Shopping." *Journal Accounting, Auditing & Finance* 9, No. 1 (Fall 1985), pp. 74–80.

SRI International, *Investor Informational Needs and the Annual Report,* Financial Executive Research Foundation (Morristown, N.J.: Financial Executive Institute, 1987).

Stanga, Keith G., and James J. Benjamin, "Information Needs of Bankers." *Management Accounting* 59, No. 12 (June 1978), pp. 17–21.

Statement on Auditing Standards No. 25, "The Relationship of Generally Accepted Auditing Standards to Quality Control Standards" (New York: American Institute of Certified Public Accountants, 1979).

Statement on Auditing Standards No. 50, "Reports on the Application of Accounting Principles" (New York: American Institute of Certified Public Accountants, 1986).

Statement on Auditing Standards No. 59, "The Auditor's Consideration of an Entity's Ability to Continue as a Going Concern" (New York: American Institute of Certified Public Accountants, 1988).

Statement on Auditing Standards No. 69, "The Meaning of Present Fairly in Conformity with Generally Accepted Accounting Principles in the Independent Auditor's Report" (New York: American Institute of Certified Public Accountants, 1992).

Wal∗Mart Stores, Inc., *1998 Annual Report.*

Chapter 4

The Legal Position of the Audit Committee

Although there is no specific body of law that governs the audit committee, the legal obligations of its members are manifested in the state corporation laws and certain federal statutes regarding the directorate responsibilities. The purpose of this chapter is to review the general legal responsibilities of the committee as well as several legal cases involving the committee. In addition, securities litigation (see Exhibit 4.1 on pages 119–124) and the guidelines for minimizing the committee's possible legal liability are presented to put the legal position of the audit directors in proper perspective.[1]

GENERAL LEGAL RESPONSIBILITIES

State Statutes

Although the board of directors has the statutory power to establish standing committees of the board, several state corporation laws limit the board's powers to delegate authority and responsibility. For example, the New York statute provides that:

. . . No such committee shall have authority as to the following matters:

1. The submission to shareholders of any action that needs shareholder's authorization under this chapter

2. The filling of vacancies in the board of directors or in any committee

3. The fixing of compensation of the directors for serving on the board or on any committee

4. The amendment or repeal of the bylaws, or the adoption of new bylaws

[1]Although reference is made to both the federal and state statutes, such references provide only a description of the law. One should have recourse to legal counsel for the appropriate legal interpretation.

5. The amendment or repeal of any resolution of the board which by its terms shall not be so amendable or repealable[2]

Thus the audit committee has limited authority; however, such authority is discretionary because the audit directors can exercise their own judgment in the interest of the board. Moreover, the audit committee, since it is formally constituted, is free to meet in between the board meetings.

More important, each member of the board of directors and the standing committees has a statutory duty of care because of the fiduciary relationship between the directors and the corporation. With respect to the duties of the directors and officers, the New York statute indicates:

> Directors and officers shall discharge the duties of their respective positions in good faith and with that degree of diligence, care and skill which ordinarily prudent men would exercise under similar circumstances in like positions. In discharging their duties, directors and officers, when acting in good faith, may rely upon financial statements of the corporation represented to them to be correct by the president or the officer of the corporation having charge of its books of accounts, or stated in a written report by an independent public or certified public accountant or firm of such accountants fairly to reflect the financial condition of such corporations.[3]

Furthermore, since the directors serve the corporation in a fiduciary capacity, their statutory duty of care cannot be delegated because of the personal nature of the director's relationship with the corporation. Hence although the audit committee can make recommendations to the entire board, the final decisions are made by the board because it has overall responsibility for the committee's actions. In short, the standing committees of the board cannot eliminate each director's duties and obligations because of the fiduciary principle.

Particularly important to the concept of the duty of care is the degree of care. To measure its reasonableness, several state corporation laws provide a business judgment rule. Such a rule protects the directors against personal liability on the presumption that they acted not only in good faith but also exercised reasonable care and prudence regarding their decisions. Thus, in the absence of fraud, bad faith, or negligence, a director cannot be held personally liable concerning matters of corporate policy and business judgment.[4]

Furthermore, the directors may be personally liable for negligence with respect to losses suffered by the corporation.[5] The directors can be held jointly and

---

[2] New York Business Corporation Law, Sec. 712, *McKinney's Consolidated Laws of New York Annotated.* Book 6 (Brooklyn, N.Y.: Edward Thompson Company, 1963).
[3] Ibid., Sec. 717.
[4] Ibid., Sec. 717.
[5] For example, if it can be proven that a director has breached his or her fiduciary duty to the corporation, then the director may be held personally liable for the losses suffered by the corporation.

severally liable to the corporation whereby an injured stockholder or creditor can recover a loss from the individual director, several directors, or the full board. For example, if the directors vote to declare dividends from the corporation's capital rather than from its retained earnings, then they are liable because their actions constitute an unauthorized dividend distribution.[6]

Equally important, directors have a duty of loyalty regarding their activities with the corporation. They cannot exploit the corporation for personal gain because of their fiduciary relationship. For example, if a director has a personal interest in a particular corporate transaction, then he or she should disassociate themselves from the transaction because of the apparent conflict of interest. Thus, each director has an "undivided loyalty and an allegiance" with respect to the interests of the corporation and stockholders.[7]

Moreover, in 1978 the American Bar Association amended Section 35 of its Model Business Corporation Act, which, if adopted as part of the state corporation statutes, increases a director's reliance on the board's standing committees. Specifically, the amendment provides that a director may rely on the information that is presented by a committee although the director is not a member of this group. Such reliance on the board committee is based on the director's confidence in the committee. However, when relying on the committee, the director must adhere to the duty-of-care principle whereby the director should be familiar with the committee's activities. In short, the amendment allows a director to rely on the work of a committee that has an oversight or supervisory responsibility, such as the audit committee. Accordingly, the amendment poses certain questions regarding the legal implications of the committee since it appears that a noncommittee director may be exonerated from any potential liability provided that he or she has exercised his or her duty of care.[8]

The state of Connecticut has enacted legislation that requires companies incorporated with at least 100 stockholders to establish an audit committee. In Sections 33-318(b)(1) and 33-318(b)(2), the statute defines the standard of inde-

---

[6]New York Business Corporation Law, Sec. 719.

[7]Ibid., Sec. 717.

[8]American Bar Association, *Corporate Director's Guidebook* (Chicago: American Bar Association, 1978), p. 42. Also see American Bar Association, *Corporate Director's Guidebook,* 2nd ed. (Chicago: American Bar Association, 1994). Finally, the reader may wish to review the *Escott v. BarChris Construction Corp.* case, 283 F, Supp. 643 (S.D.N.Y. 1968), which deals with the standard of differential liability. In short, the court states that a director with a particular expertise and access to information may be held to a higher standard of liability. Of course, the performance of individual audit committee members is based on their skills and qualifications and access to information. Thus a member with an accounting background would be more aware of the accounting and auditing implications than would be a member without this expertise.

pendence and the functions of the audit committee. See the Connecticut General Statutes Annotated in West 1960 and Supplement 1985 (Eagan, Minn.: West Publishing Corporation) for further details.

In 1984, the American Bar Association adopted a Revised Model Business Corporation Act. In 1998, the American Bar Association adopted the Model Business Corporate Act. Section 8.25 of the act stipulates that a board of directors may create standing committees, such as an audit committee. This stipulation is consistent with the statutory provisions at the state level. In addition, Section 8.3(0), which deals with the standards of conduct for directors, indicates that a director is entitled to rely on information, opinions, reports, or statements—including financial statements—prepared by officers of the corporation and public accountants. A director is also entitled to rely on the opinions of legal counsel as well as on the work of a standing committee of the board of which he or she is not a member. Thus the American Bar Association has reaffirmed its position with respect to good-faith reliance on officers, public accountants, legal counsel, and committee members of the board. (See Appendix G.)

Federal Statutes—Key Sections

In addition to their legal responsibilities at the state level, the directors have a legal liability at the federal level. The federal statutes that are particularly important are summarized as follows:

Securities Act of 1933 Although this particular act provides financial information regarding the public sale of securities, it is needed "to prohibit misrepresentation, deceit, and other fraudulent acts and practices in the sale of securities."[9] In particular, this act provides for civil liability of the directors with respect to fraud in the registration statement. Section 11(a) of the act provides that:

(1) In case any part of the registration statement, when such part became effective, contained an untrue statement of a material fact or omitted to state a material fact required to be stated therein or necessary to make the statement therein not misleading, any person acquiring such security (unless it is proved that at the time of such acquisition he knew of such untruth or omission) may, either at law or in equity, in any court of competent jurisdiction, sue—

(2) Every person who was a director of . . . the issuer at the time of the filing of the part of the registration statement . . .[10]

---

[9] The Securities and Exchange Commission, *The Work of the Securities and Exchange Commission* (Washington, D.C.: U.S. Government Printing Office, 1974), p. 1.
[10] U.S. Cod, Title 15, Sec. 77 k.

In order to avoid any liability, Sections 11(b) and 11(c) of the act provide the following:

Notwithstanding the provisions of subsection (a) of this section no person, other than the issuer, shall be liable as provided therein who shall sustain the burden of proof

(1) that before the effective date of the part of the registration statement with respect to which his liability is asserted (A) he had resigned from or had taken such steps as are permitted by law to resign from, or ceased or refused to act in, every office, capacity, or relationship in which he was described in the registration statement as acting or agreeing to act, and (B) he had advised the Commission and the issuer in writing that he had taken such action and that he would not be responsible for such part of the registration statement; or

(2) that if such part of the registration statement became effective without his knowledge, upon becoming aware of such fact he forthwith acted and advised the Commission, in accordance with paragraph (1) of this subsection, and, in addition, gave reasonable public notice that such part of the registration statement had become effective without his knowledge, or

(3) that (A) as regards any part of the registration statement not purporting to be made on the authority of an expert, and not purporting to be a copy of or extract from a report or valuation of an expert, and not purporting to be made on the authority of a public official document or statement, he had, after reasonable investigation, reasonable ground to believe and did believe, at the time such part of the registration statement became effective, that the statements therein were true and that there was no omission to state a material fact required to be stated therein or necessary to make the statements therein not misleading; and (B) as regards any part of the registration statement purporting to be made upon his authority as an expert or purporting to be a copy of or extract from a report or valuation of himself as an expert, (i) he had, after reasonable investigation, reasonable ground to believe and did believe at the time such part of the registration statement became effective, that the statements therein were true and that there was no omission to state a material fact required to be stated therein or necessary to make the statements therein not misleading, or (ii) such part of the registration statement did not fairly represent his statement as an expert or was not a fair copy of or extract from his report or valuation as an expert; and (C) as regards any part of the registration statement purporting to be made on the authority of an expert (other than himself) or purporting to be a copy of or extract from a report or valuation of an expert (other than himself), he had no reasonable ground to believe and did not believe, at the time such part of the registration statement became effective, that the statements therein were untrue or that there was an omission to state a material fact required to be stated therein or necessary to make the statements therein not misleading, or that such part of the registration statement did not fairly represent the statement of the expert or was

not a fair copy of or extract from the report of valuation of the expert; and (D) as regards any part of the registration statement purporting to be a statement made by an official person or purporting to be a copy of or extract from a public official document, he had no reasonable ground to believe and did not believe, at the time such part of the registration statement became effective, that the statements therein were untrue, or that there was an omission to state a material fact required to be stated therein or necessary to make the statements therein not misleading, or that such part of the registration statement did not fairly represent the statement made by the official person or was not a fair copy of or extract from the public official document.

In determining, for the purpose of paragraph (3) of subsection (b) of this section, what constitutes reasonable investigation and reasonable ground for belief, the standard of reasonableness shall be that required of a prudent man in the management of his property.[11]

Furthermore, Section 12 of the act provides additional liability regarding any transactions that are false or misleading in connection with the issuance of the securities. Thus a director has not only a potential liability with respect to the registration statement but also a liability concerning the written and/or oral representations in the offering prospectus.[12]

Section 13 of the act establishes a limitation in order to enforce a civil action against the wrongdoers.

No action shall be maintained to enforce any liability created under section 77k or 77l (2) of this title unless brought within one year after the discovery of the untrue statement or the omission, or after such discovery should have been made by the exercise of reasonable diligence, or, if the action is to enforce a liability created under section 77l (1) of this title, unless brought within one year after the violation upon which it is based. In no event shall any such action be brought to enforce a liability created under section 77k or 77l (1) of this title more than three years after the security was bona fide offered to the public, or under section 77l (2) of this title more than three years after the sale.[13]

Finally, the following penalties may be assessed under the Securities Act of 1933.

Any person who willfully violates any of the provisions of this subchapter, or the rules and regulations promulgated by the Commission under authority thereof, or any person who willfully, in a registration statement filed under this subchapter, makes any untrue statement of a material fact or omits to state any material fact

---

[11] Ibid., Sec. 77 k.
[12] U.S. Code, Title 15, Sec. 77l.
[13] U.S. Code, Title 15, Sec. 77m.

required to be stated therein or necessary to make the statements therein not misleading, shall upon conviction be fined not more than \$5,000 or imprisoned not more than five years, or both.[14]

Securities Exchange Act of 1934   The primary purpose of this act is to regulate the public sales of the securities through the securities exchanges or brokers after the original sale of the securities. This act also provides the impetus for the Securities and Exchange Commission. More specifically, Section 18 of the act provides the following liability for misleading statements:

(a)   Any person who shall make or cause to be made any statement in any application, report, or document filed pursuant to this chapter or any rule or regulation thereunder or any undertaking contained in a registration statement as provided in subsection (d) of section 78o of this title, which statement was at the time and in the light of the circumstances under which it was made false or misleading with respect to any material fact, shall be liable to any person (not knowing that such statement was false or misleading) who, in reliance upon such statement, shall have purchased or sold a security at a price which was affected by such statement, for damages caused by such reliance, unless the person sued shall prove that he acted in good faith and had no knowledge that such statement was false or misleading. A person seeking to enforce such liability may sue at law or in equity in any court of competent jurisdiction. In any such suit the court may, in its discretion, require an undertaking for the payment of the costs of such suit, and assess reasonable costs, including reasonable attorney's fees, against either party litigant.

(c)   No action shall be maintained to enforce any liability created under this section unless brought within one year after the discovery of the facts constituting the cause of action and within three years after such cause of action accrued.[15]

In contrast to the 1933 act, a plaintiff must prove that he or she relied on a misstatement of fact or omission of fact in the financial statements and as a result suffered a loss.

Furthermore, Section 10 (b) of the act establishes an antifraud provision, which indicates that it is illegal "to use or employ . . . any manipulative or deceptive devices" regarding the security transactions.[16] Equally important, the SEC enacted Rule 10 (b)-5, which provides the following:

It shall be unlawful for any person, directly or indirectly, by the use of any means . . .

(a)   to employ any device, scheme, or artifice to defraud,

[14] U.S. Code, Title 15, Sec. 77x.
[15] U.S. Code, Title 15, Sec. 78r.
[16] U.S. Code, Title 15, Sec. 78j.

(b) to make any untrue statement of a material fact or to omit to state a material fact necessary in order to make the statements made, in the light of the circumstances under which they were made, not misleading, or,

(c) to engage in any act, practice, or course of business which operates or would operate as a fraud or deceit upon any person, in connection with purchase or sale of any security.[17]

Thus Rule 10 (b)-5 can hold directors liable primarily because of clause (b) above. In short, this particular rule increases the director's liability, which did not exist under the provisions of the act.

In addition, the 1934 act provides the following penalties:

(a) Any person who willfully violates any provision of this chapter, or any rule or regulation thereunder the violation of which is made unlawful or the observance of which is required under the terms of this chapter, or any person who willfully and knowingly makes, or causes to be made, any statement in any application, report, or document required to be filed under this chapter or any rule or regulation thereunder or any undertaking contained in a registration statement as provided in subsection (d) of section 78o of this title, which statement was false or misleading with respect to any material fact, shall upon conviction be fined not more than $10,000, or imprisoned not more than two years, or both, except that when such person is an exchange, a fine not exceeding $500,000 may be imposed; but no person shall be subject to imprisonment under this section for the violation of any rule or regulation if he proves that he had no knowledge of such rule or regulation.[18]

Several additional federal acts are briefly set forth below. (See Chapter 2 for other congressional legislation and Appendixes D and E for the Foreign Corrupt Practices Act with amendments and the Federal Deposit Insurance Corporation Improvement Act of 1991.)

The Private Securities Reform Act of 1995

During the latter half of 1995, Congress enacted the Private Securities Litigation Reform Act of 1995 based on House bill 1058 and Senate bill 240. The major objective of this reform legislation was to curb the number of abusive securities class action suits. Of particular interest to audit committees is Section 301, "Fraud Detection and Disclosure" and Section 10A, "Audit Requirements." While Section 10A does not expand the auditors' responsibility to detect fraud or illegal acts, it does require auditors who detect illegal acts to report their findings to the

---

[17] Code of Federal Regulations, Sec. 240, 10(b)-5.
[18] U.S. Code, Title 15, Sec. 78ff.

Securities and Exchange Commission (SEC) if the client company fails to take appropriate remedial action on such acts that have a material effect on the financial statements. If the necessary remedial action has not been taken, the auditors are required to notify the board of directors in writing. Based on these events, the board is required to submit the report to the SEC within one business day. If the board fails to notify the SEC, then the auditors are required to submit their report to the SEC the next business day.[19]

Fraud and False Statements Act

Whoever, in any matter within the jurisdiction of any department or agency of the United States knowingly and willfully falsifies, conceals or covers up by any trick, scheme, or device a material fact, or makes any false, fictitious or fraudulent statements or representations, or makes or uses any false writing or document knowing the same to contain any false, fictitious or fraudulent statement or entry, shall be fined not more than $10,000 or imprisoned not more than five years, or both.[20]

Mail Fraud Act

Whoever, having devised or intending to devise any scheme or artifice to defraud, or for obtaining money or property by means of false or fraudulent pretenses, representations, or promises, or to sell, dispose of, loan, exchange, alter, give away, distribute, supply, or furnish or produce for unlawful use any counterfeit or spurious coin, obligation, security, or other article, or anything represented to be or intimated to or held out to be such counterfeit or spurious articles, for the purpose of executing such scheme or artifice or attempting so to do, places in any post office or authorized depository for mail matter, any matter or thing whatever to be sent or delivered by the Postal Service, or takes or receives therefrom, any such matter or thing, or knowingly causes to be delivered by mail according to the direction thereon, or at the place at which it is directed to be delivered by the person to whom it is addressed, any such matter or thing, shall be fined not more than $1,000 or imprisoned not more than five years, or both.[21]

---

[19] The act is contained in Title 1 of Public Law No. 104-67, December 22, 1995. Sections 301 and 10A are contained in Title 3 of Public Law No. 104-67, December 22, 1995. For further discussion, see the act with respect to such matters as proportionate liability, safe-harbor for forward-looking statements, and loss causation principle. Also see the U.S. Federal Sentencing Commission's Federal Sentencing Guidelines for Organizations (Washington, D.C.: U.S. Federal Sentencing Commission, 1990) for an expanded discussion on encouraging effective programs to prevent and detect violations of law; Edward J. Boyle and Fred N. Knopf, "The Private Securities Litigation Reform Act of 1995, *CPA Journal* 66, No. 4 (April 1996), pp. 44–47; and Daniel L. Goldwasser, "The Private Securities Act of 1995: Impact on Accountants," *CPA Journal* 67, No. 6, (June 1997), pp. 72–75.

[20] U.S. Code, Title 18, Sec. 1001.

[21] U.S. Code, Title 18, Sec. 1341.

Whoever, having devised or intending to devise any scheme or artifice to defraud, or for obtaining money or property by means of false or fraudulent pretenses, representations, or promises, transmits or causes to be transmitted by means of wire, radio, or television communication in interstate or foreign commerce, any writings, signs, signals, pictures, or sounds for the purpose of executing such scheme or artifice, shall be fined not more than $1,000 or imprisoned not more than five years, or both.[22]

Conspiracy Act

If two or more persons conspire to commit any offense against the United States, or to defraud the United States, or any agency thereof in any manner or for any purpose, and one or more of such persons do any act to effect the object of the conspiracy, each shall be fined not more than $10,000 or imprisoned not more than five years, or both.

If, however, the offense, the commission of which is the object of the conspiracy, is a misdemeanor only, the punishment for such conspiracy shall not exceed the maximum punishment provided for such misdemeanor.[23]

Income Taxes[24]
Any person who:

1. *Declaration under penalties of perjury.* Willfully makes and subscribes any return, statement or other document, which contains or is verified by a written declaration that it is made under the penalties of perjury, and which he does not believe to be true and correct as to every material matter; or

2. *Aid or assistance.* Willfully aids or assists in, or procures, counsels or advises the preparation or presentation under, or in connection with any matter arising under, the internal revenue laws, of a return, affidavit, claim or other document, which is fraudulent or is false as to any material matter, whether or not such falsity or fraud is with the knowledge or consent of the person authorized or required to present such return, affidavit, claim or document; or

3. *Fraudulent bonds, permits, and entries.* Simulates or falsely or fraudulently executes or signs any bond, permit, entry, or other document required by the provisions of the internal revenue laws, or by any regulation made in pursuance thereof, or procures the same to be falsely or fraudulently executed or advises, aids in, or connives at such execution thereof; or

4. *Removal or concealment with intent to defraud.* Removes, deposits, or conceals, or is concerned in removing, depositing, or concealing any goods or commodities

---

[22] Ibid., Sec. 1343.

[23] U.S. Code, Title 18, Sec. 371.

[24] It may be advisable to request the outside auditors to remind executives that tax returns must be filed. The audit committee should make certain that the returns were appropriately filed through discussions with the auditors.

for or in respect whereof any tax is or shall be imposed, or any property upon which levy is authorized by section 6331, with intent to evade or defeat the assessment or collection of any tax imposed by this title; or

5. *Compromises and closing agreements.*   In connection with any compromise under section 7122, or offer of such compromise, or in connection with any closing agreement under section 7121, or offer to enter into any such agreement, willfully—

A. *Concealment of property.*   Conceals from any officer or employee of the United States any property belonging to the estate of a taxpayer or other person liable in respect of the tax, or

B. *Withholding, falsifying, and destroying records.*   Receives, withholds, destroys, mutilates, or falsifies any book, document, or record, or makes any false statement, relating to the estate or financial condition of the taxpayer or other person liable in respect of the tax; shall be guilty of a felony and, upon conviction thereof, shall be fined not more than $5,000, or imprisoned not more than 3 years, or both, together with the cost of prosecution.[25]

Any person who willfully delivers or discloses to the Secretary or his delegate any list, return, account, statement, or other document, known by him to be fraudulent or to be false as to any material matter, shall be fined not more than $1,000, or imprisoned not more than 1 year, or both. Any person required pursuant to sections 6047 (b) or (c), 6056, or 6104 (d) to furnish any information to the Secretary or any other person who willfully furnishes to the Secretary or such other person any information known by him to be fraudulent or to be false as to any material matter shall be fined not more than $1,000, or imprisoned not more than 1 year, or both.[26]

LEGAL CASES INVOLVING THE AUDIT COMMITTEE

During the 1970s and 1980s, litigation involving the audit committee exemplified the significance of the audit director's role. The Securities and Exchange Commission's increased enforcement of the provisions of the federal securities laws has imposed greater professional responsibilities on the committee. As one notable conservative columnist and editor stated, "The evolution of the director's responsibility is running ahead of inflation. . . . The contemporary director is supposed to know more about accounting . . . and more about the law."[27] Several legal cases are briefly reviewed in order to demonstrate the philosophy of the courts and the SEC with respect to the audit committee.

[25] Internal Revenue Code, Sec. 7206.
[26] Ibid., Sec. 7207.
[27] "Firing Line," *Time* (February 19, 1979), p. 51.

The Penn Central Case

On August 3, 1972, the SEC released its study with respect to the financial collapse of the Penn Central Company to a Special Subcommittee on Investigations of the House of Representatives. With respect to the role of the directors, the SEC found that the directors had a passive role in company affairs. They avoided confrontation with management on issues that were critical to testing the integrity of management and to providing adequate disclosure to the stockholders. For example, the company's chief financial officer was involved in a lawsuit that claimed improper, unlawful conduct in connection with a subsidiary and a private investment club. Although the board authorized an investigation, it later cancelled the investigation because the chief financial officer threatened to resign. As a result, the financial management was permitted to operate without any effective review of control by the board.[28] In particular, the Commission noted that the directors have a responsibility to obtain from management information that is adequate in both "quantity and quality" in order to discharge their state corporate legal liability. For example, a new director indicated that "lists of new equipment did not particularly help him discharge his responsibilities and thus information regarding the corporate objectives and plans was necessary to do the job."[29] Furthermore, the Commission emphasized the "critical importance" of the director's responsibility as well as "greater utilization of public and independent directors." Such independent directors should be judged on the "reasonableness of their judgment."[30] Thus the Commission's findings and conclusions point toward the need for an advisory committee of outside directors. The audit committee would fulfill this particular purpose.

Lum's, Inc. Case

On April 11, 1974, the SEC obtained a consent injunction from the U.S. District Court against Lum's, Inc. whereby the registrant "agreed not to employ any manipulative scheme to defraud and not to commit any proxy fraud in connection with future acquisitions of businesses or business assets." More specifically, the court ordered that the registrant had to include the following information in its registration or proxy statement:

1. The identity of the individuals who control the acquired business
2. Any material consideration to be paid for the acquiring business in addition to the purchase price

---

[28] Commerce Clearing House, *Federal Securities Law Reporter,* par. 78,931.
[29] Ibid.
[30] Ibid.

3. Any material information known indicating that the earnings of an acquired business were affected by the failure of management to maintain proper accounting records and internal controls

Furthermore, the registrant had to establish a standing audit committee to review the accountant's evaluations of the system of internal controls as well as to review other casino activities in terms of personnel and security. The court required that the audit committee consist of two or more members of the board of directors who are not officers or employees of the company.[31] The Lum's consent injunction is of particular importance because it was the impetus toward the establishment of a standing audit committee through court action.

Mattel, Inc. Case

In the Mattel case of *SEC v. Mattel, Inc.* (October 1, 1974), the Commission sought a consent injunction against the registrant for false financial reporting. The Commission charged not only that the registrant's financial statements for 1971 were overstated by $14 million in sales that were subject to customer cancellation but also that the pretax income was overstated by $10.5 million due to inadequate accounting provisions. As a result, the U.S. District Court ordered Mattel to establish and maintain a financial controls and audit committee whereby three of the four members must be unaffiliated directors. In particular, the court required that the committee have the following five duties and functions:

1. Review the financial controls and accounting procedures and recommend improvements to management.
2. Review the quarterly financial statements to determine whether such reports are in conformity with generally accepted accounting principles.
3. Review all releases and other information to the news media, general public, and stockholders with respect to the financial condition of the company and approve or disapprove such dissemination.
4. Review the results of the independent audit examination of the financial statements.
5. Approve or disapprove any change of the independent auditors.[32]

Thus, through a consent injunction against Mattel, it is clearly evident that the SEC continued to rely more heavily on the independent audit committee to review and monitor the company's financial controls, accounting procedures, and financial statements. Also, this particular legal action provided an initial framework for the duties and functions of the committee. Indeed, the question of what constitutes proper standards and practices for the committee was emerging

---

[31] Commerce Clearing House, *Federal Securities Law Reporter,* par. 94,504.
[32] Ibid., par. 94,807.

through a court settlement; as a consequence the court was dictating the responsibilities of the audit directors. Such an approach is further evidenced by the results of the Killearn Properties case.

Killearn Properties, Inc. Case

In the *SEC v. Killearn Properties, Inc.* case (May 1977), the SEC outlined its directives concerning the audit committee as part of a consent judgment. The defendants were enjoined from directly or indirectly making use of the mails or other communication to transmit any prospectus regarding the stock since the prospectus must meet the requirement of the securities laws. More specifically, the court ordered the defendant to observe the following policies and practices with respect to the audit committee:

B. The Board of Directors shall continue to maintain an Audit Committee ("Committee") of the Board consisting of at least Three (3) persons who shall be members of the Board and outside directors of Killearn. The Committee shall assume, upon the entering of this Order, the following duties, functions and responsibilities:

i. It should review the engagement of the independent accountants, including the scope and general extent of their review, the audit procedures which will be utilized, and the compensation to be paid.

ii. It should review with the independent accountants, and with the company's chief financial officer (as well as with other appropriate company personnel) the general policies and procedures utilized by the company with respect to internal auditing, accounting, and financial controls. The members of the committee should have at least general familiarity with the accounting and reporting principles and practices applied by the company in preparing its financial statements.

iii. It should review with the independent accountants, upon completion of their audit, (a) any report or opinion proposed to be rendered in connection therewith; (b) the independent accountants' perceptions of the company's financial and accounting personnel; (c) the cooperation which the independent accountants received during the course of their review; (d) the extent to which the resources of the company were and should be utilized to minimize time spent by the outside auditors; (e) any significant transactions which are not a normal part of the company's business; (f) any change in accounting principles; (g) all significant adjustments proposed by the auditor; (h) any recommendations which the independent accountants may have with respect to improving internal financial controls, choice of accounting principles, or management reporting systems.

iv. It should inquire of the appropriate company personnel and the independent auditors as to any instances of deviations from established codes of conduct of the company and periodically review such policies.

v. It should meet with the company's financial staff at least twice a year to review and discuss with them the scope of internal accounting and auditing procedures then in effect; and the extent to which recommendations made by the internal staff or by the independent accountants have been implemented.

vi.   It should prepare and present to the company's board of directors a report summarizing its recommendation with respect to the retention (or discharge) of the independent accountants for the ensuing year.

vii.   It should have a power to direct and supervise an investigation into any matter brought to its attention within the scope of its duties (including the power to retain outside counsel in connection with any such investigation).

In addition, the Audit Committee shall have the following special duties, functions and responsibilities:

viii.   review, either by the Committee as a whole or by a designated member, all releases and other information to be disseminated by Killearn to press media, the public, or shareholders of Killearn which concern disclosure of financial conditions of and projections of financial conditions of Killearn and its subsidiaries;

ix.   review of the activities of the officers and directors of Killearn as to their future dealing with the company and take any action the Committee may deem appropriate with regard to such activities;

x.   approve any settlement or disposition of any claims or actions from causes of action arising after the date hereof or any litigation now pending which Killearn may have against any past or present officers, directors, employees or controlling persons.[33]

U.S. Surgical Corporation

In February 1984, the SEC filed an action against U.S. Surgical Corporation and six of its senior executives, alleging numerous improper financial reporting practices from 1979 to 1981. The corporation's pretax earnings were overstated by more than $18 million. This overstatement amounted to 56 percent of the pretax earnings reported during 1979 and 1981. In addition, the improper accounting practices continued during 1982 and 1983. In the final consent order, the corporation agreed to appoint two new independent directors to the audit committee and define new responsibilities of the audit committee. In particular, the committee was required to:

Review for a period of at least five years, prior to release, all earnings reports and the financial statements that accompany the annual audit and quarterly review reports of the external auditors and reports of the internal audit department;

Engage the external auditors to review and report to the committee on accounting policies concerning review recognition, capitalization of certain costs, inventories, R&D expenses, and accruals; and

---

[33] Commerce Clearing House, *Federal Securities Law Reporter,* par. 96,256.

Engage an accounting firm (advisory accountants) for a period of three years to re-view the services performed by the external auditors, and to assist the committee on other matters as requested[34]

This case demonstrated the need for the board of directors through its audit com-mittee to exercise its oversight responsibility for the internal and external auditing processes and financial reporting disclosures.

Based on a review of the court actions, it is apparent that the audit committee has been established to oversee and monitor the conduct of the corporate officials. Although the committee is not directly involved with the day-to-day management affairs, the SEC and the courts forced the registrants to establish committees in order to comply with the requirements of the federal securities laws. Such legal enforcement of the courts has augmented not only the audit directors' legal oblig-ations but also their standard of duty and loyalty to the enterprise.

The critical involvement of audit committees is highlighted by such compa-nies as California Life Corporation, Playboy Enterprises, Inc., and H.J. Heinz Co. Some of the excerpts from *The Wall Street Journal* involving these companies are used to illustrate the audit committee's involvement.

California Life Corporation

When the audit committee learned that Cal Life was late in filing its 1978 annual fi-nancial statements with the SEC, the committee began an investigation. The late fil-ing was the result of a dispute between management and its independent auditors. As Lancaster reported: "Certainly, the committee had some mitigating problems: a new, inexperienced committee chairman, a chief executive who was hard to deal with, and complex and unanticipated accounting issues." With a high expected loss rate on insurance premiums, the auditors lacked confidence that the deferred costs related to new policies could be recovered from future profits. As a result of this dis-agreement, the company reported a $3.2 million loss rather than an anticipated $2.6 million profit. Given the situation at Cal Life, a number of actions were taken to im-prove the financial reporting process. In particular, the senior executives of the firm were replaced and the membership of the audit committee increased to five from three. The committee had convened six times as opposed to two meetings and as-sumed an active role in overseeing the audit processes.[35]

Clearly, this case demonstrated that the audit committee is a viable mecha-nism in helping boards of directors discharge their oversight responsibilities for the financial reporting process. There is little question that the committee has as-sumed greater responsibilities.

---

[34] Commerce Clearing House, *Federal Securities Law Reporter,* par. 105,124.
[35] Hal Lancaster, "Fuss at Cal Life Shows Audit Committee Role Is Critical," *The Wall Street Journal* (March 17, 1980), p. 1.

Playboy Enterprises, Inc.

In the Playboy Enterprises case, the audit committee requested that Hugh Hefner, chief executive officer of Playboy, and four other executives return to the company more than $900,000. The amounts owed by these parties involved perquisites (perks), such as the use of the DC-9 plane and the value of benefits (lodging, meals, valet, etc.) received from the company. As a result, the aforementioned parties repaid their perks and the board also established a compensation committee.[36] Thus the audit committee's close scrutiny of these activities did unearth a significant problem area before it impaired the integrity of the company.

H.J. Heinz

From 1972 to 1979, Heinz was involved in profit-juggling practices at several divisions. More specifically, the audit committee reported that "the practices, designed to give the appearance of smooth profit growth of the divisions, stemmed partly from inadequate internal accounting controls, poor internal communications, the autonomy of division accountants and careless review of division reports by the Heinz corporate staff."[37] To correct these practices, the audit committee recommended more internal auditors, more corporate supervision of division accountants, and a tougher corporate code of conduct. In addition, the audit committee recommended changing the outside auditing firm, and, as a result, another multinational accounting firm is now the auditor. Furthermore, the company hired an outside law firm and another large accounting firm to assist in the special investigation.[38] Clearly, Heinz's audit committee proved to be a very strong and effective operating tool of the company. Its involvement established a high degree of confidence in the quality of the financial reports and disclosures to stockholders, underwriters, and financial analysts. Exhibits 4.1, 4.2, and 4.3 contain a discussion of possible warning signals and "red flags."

As Hugh L. Marsh and Thomas E. Powell assert:

> It would be a misconception to believe the possibility of fraud is the only reason for establishing a chartered audit committee. While the primary role has been to oversee management's financial and reporting responsibilities, the Treadway Commission's investigations indicated that audit committees could serve very effectively to reduce the incidence of fraud.[39]

---

[36] Wall Street Journal Staff Reporter, "Playboy Audit Committee Bares Details of Hefner's High Living on Firm's Tab," *The Wall Street Journal* (April 4, 1980), p. 6.

[37] Thomas Petziner, Jr., "Heinz Senior Officials Didn't Participate in Profit-Juggling Practices, Panel Says," *The Wall Street Journal* (May 9, 1980), p. 2.

[38] Ibid.

[39] Hugh L. Marsh and Thomas E. Powell, "The Audit Committee Charter: Rx for Fraud Prevention," *Journal of Accountancy* 167, No. 2 (February 1989), p. 56.

Exhibit 4.1   Securities Litigation and Preventing Fraudulent Reporting

When Kirschner Medical Corp., a Baltimore-based manufacturer of orthopedic equipment, went public in 1986, President Bruce Hegstad planned to go from $6.5 million to $100 million in revenues. They did indeed skyrocket, reaching $55 million in 1989. Naturally, stock prices soared as well.

But the investors who flocked to Kirschner now claim that the company duped them. During the third quarter of 1989, the company lost $488,000. Despite its assurances of a quick rebound, Kirschner lost $2.5 million in the next quarter and wrote off an additional $13.2 million in losses.

During this time, the company allegedly failed to disclose information about defective products, obsolete inventories and an unprofitable European plant. When the bad news finally came out, stock prices dove $17 a share, causing a lost market value of $35.7 million. Claiming fraudulent financial reporting, over 1,000 investors have filed a class-action suit against Kirschner and three of its executives in the U.S. District Court in Baltimore.

In recent years, corporate boards of directors and their audit committees have faced great vulnerability to such litigation.

According to William R. McLucas, the Security and Exchange Commission's enforcement director, "The agency has a hefty backlog of cases, many focusing on financial fraud and accounting problems."

In 1989, the SEC filed enforcement actions against the officers and directors of 30 public companies and 12 public accounting firms, alleging improper financial reporting practices.[a]

Two years earlier, the National Commission on Fraudulent Financial Reporting, established by accounting associations and chaired by former SEC Commissioner James Treadway, reported that it had "reviewed 119 enforcement actions against public companies and 42 cases against independent public accounting firms by the SEC from 1981–1986."

The commission asserted that "public companies should maintain internal controls that provide reasonable assurance that fraudulent financial reporting will be prevented or subject to early detection."

What is fraudulent financial reporting? The commission defines it "as intentional or reckless conduct, whether act or omission, that results in materially misleading financial statements."

Generally speaking, fraudulent reporting occurs when management intentionally overstates assets and improperly recognizes revenue. These actions clearly differ from unintentional errors.

The irregularities are shown by the misapplication of generally accepted accounting principles, inappropriate valuations, and/or omissions of material information from financial statements. For example, the deliberate distortion of accounting records to overstate inventory, along with falsified transactions to increase sales and overstate earnings, is clearly fraudulent financial reporting.

These activities, often referred to as "cooked books" and "cute accounting," cause management to restate the financial statements, which, in turn, causes a decrease in the market price of the stock. Such misleading representations in the company's annual and quarterly figures can be the basis of a class-action lawsuit.

Exhibit 4.1   (*Continued*)

Typically in this type of litigation, a class of stockholders alleges that the board of directors, the officers and the independent auditing firm have prepared and distributed materially false and misleading financial statements and reports to existing stockholders and potential investors.

Plaintiffs accuse defendants of violating Section 10(b) of the Securities Exchange Act, SEC Rule 10(b)-5 and common law. Relief claims are based on fraud, deceit and negligence by the directors, officers, employees and the independent auditors.

Questions of law and fact commonly arising in these cases are:

- Whether defendants knowingly or recklessly disseminated untrue statements of material fact and/or omitted material facts relating to the sales and earnings during the class period;
- Whether the market prices of securities were artificially inflated by reason of the defendants' conduct, constituting a fraud on the market;
- Whether defendants violated Section 10(b) of the 1934 Act and Rule 10(b)-5 and/or perpetrated common law fraud or negligent misrepresentations upon the members of the class;
- Whether the defendant's SEC Form 10-Q, 10K, annual and quarterly reports, and public announcements of expected earnings and growth during the class period were materially false and misleading.

Failure on the part of the audit committee to review and evaluate the financial statements and related accounting policies in accordance with generally accepted accounting principles is clearly malfeasance.

A case in point is Crazy Eddie Inc., which, like many public companies, had audit committees. According to the SEC, Eddie Antar, founder and former chairman of the East Coast electronics chain, directed activities that resulted in overstating the company's 1985 pretax income by $2 million, or 18.9 percent; by approximately $6.7 million, or 33.8 percent, in 1986; and by "tens of millions of dollars" in 1987.

Peter Martosella, who was brought in to run Crazy Eddie after the fraudulent reporting was discovered, told *Forbes* magazine, "You have to be careful how much you expect of the audit committee. You're talking about people brought in by the CEO, and you're telling them they shouldn't necessarily listen to him. It's not realistic, especially when the chief executive is a charismatic person, a darling of the securities world, like Eddie Antar was."

Antar allegedly made $60 million from the sale of his Crazy Eddie stock; investors allegedly lost $200 million. In 1989 the SEC filed a complaint against Antar and other company officials and employees. Last summer the U.S. District Court for New Jersey entered a $73.5 million judgment against Antar, who is currently a fugitive. (It should be noted that Antar was recently apprehended by the authorities.)

Moreover, a group of about 10,000 shareholders have filed a lawsuit in the federal district court in New York against Crazy Eddie's former officers and directors, as well as its external auditor and several Wall Street brokerage firms.

Exhibit 4.1   (*Continued*)

In another case, Sundstrand Corp. pleaded guilty to a criminal defense procurement fraud of overbilling the Defense Department. Sundstrand agreed to pay a $115 million settlement to the federal government. In addition, the liability insurance carrier for Sundstrand's board of directors and officers agreed to pay $15 million to settle shareholder litigation.

An academic research study found that Sundstrand's audit committee was ineffective since it had too few meetings and too many changes in membership.[b]

As a result of the committee's performance, there were management-imposed scope limitations on the internal audit department, which ultimately caused the company to defraud the federal government.

As the Crazy Eddie and Sundstrand cases demonstrate, merely having an audit committee isn't always enough. So what exactly is this committee supposed to do?

The major impetus for establishing and maintaining audit committees occurred in 1978 when the New York Stock Exchange adopted a policy requiring all of its listed companies to have such a committee, composed solely of independent outside directors. Of course, the NYSE's intent was to increase the investing public's confidence in the quality of financial reporting.

Before the NYSE's mandate, the SEC required companies to establish and maintain independent audit committees.

Thus, a consent injunction and ancillary relief against respondents charged with fraudulent financial reporting issues—for example, in cases against Lum's Inc. and Mattel Inc. in 1974—provided a framework for defining the duties and functions of audit committees.

Lum's agreed not to commit any proxy fraud in connection with future acquisitions of businesses or business assets. Mattel was charged with overstating sales by $14 million. These sales were subject to customer cancellation.

The question of what constitutes proper standards and practices for the audit committee has emerged through settlements, with the courts dictating the audit committee's responsibilities. In particular, the courts in Lum's and Mattel required the following general responsibilities:

- Recommend or approve appointment or independent auditors.
- Review internal accounting control policies and procedures.
- Oversee the duties and results of the internal audit department.
- Review with the independent auditors the proposed scope and general extent of their audit.
- Review, prior to issuance, financial statements and significant press releases concerning financial results.
- Act as a mediator between management and the independent auditors for any disagreements over accounting issues.

Recognizing the SEC enforcement actions, court decisions and the national stock exchange listing requirements for audit committees, the National Commission on Fraudulent

Exhibit 4.1   (*Continued*)

Financial Reporting has fully supported and endorsed implementation of audit committees.

In particular, the commission recommended that "the boards of directors of all public companies should be required by SEC rule to establish audit committees composed solely of independent directors. Such committees should be informed, vigilant, and effective overseers of the financial reporting process and the company's internal controls."

Today, both the American Stock Exchange and the National Association of Securities Dealers have listing requirements for audit committees that are modeled after the NYSE's requirements. The U.S. House of Representatives is currently considering legislation, sponsored by Rep. John Dingell, D-Mich., requiring all public companies to create audit committees.

Given that the audit committee is a part-time operation, the commission's call for vigilance requires committee members to be willing to make a significant commitment of their time.

The audit committee should be informed about the financial and operational aspects of the company and, therefore, should receive sufficient and timely information. If the audit committee meeting is scheduled to coincide with the regular full board meetings, then the committee must receive written information well in advance of the meetings.

To be vigilant, the audit committee should ask probing questions about the propriety of the company's financial reporting process and the quality of its internal controls. This task requires the committee to keep abreast of financial reporting developments affecting the company.

To be an effective independent overseer, the audit committee must be positioned between senior management and the external auditors. This organizational structure allows the audit committee to question management's judgments about financial reporting matters and to suggest improvements in the internal control systems. Finally, the committee should develop a charter that defines its mission, duties and responsibilities; plans its annual agenda; and documents its findings and conclusions.

Through audit committees, boards of directors can meet their oversight responsibilities in the internal and external auditing processes and the financial reporting process.

And, since inhouse legal counsel and outside counsel frequently interact with audit committees, these lawyers are in an excellent position to help the committees develop a constructive relationship between their function and the activities of the full board and, ultimately, minimize the potential for class-action suits by recognizing the warning signals that lead to fraudulent reporting.[c]

For example, corporate legal counsel can assist the audit committees with the following matters:

- Review and approve the standard of independence for the audit committee members as required by the national stock exchanges and the SEC.

Exhibit 4.1 (*Continued*)

- Review the audit committee's charter, which is disclosed in part in the company's annual proxy statement.
- Review significant litigation, claims and assessments with both in-house and outside legal counsel.
- Advise the committee with respect to any pending litigation against the external auditors and any impairment of their independence.
- Advise the committee on proposed investigations and compliance with regulations.

Of course, outside legal counsel may be asked to serve on the audit committee, in which case he or she would address the warning signals directly.

Given the audit committee's critical role in the company's internal control structure, the committee must obtain reasonable assurances from the internal and external auditors that management's assertions in the financial statements are fairly presented. Moreover, the external auditors are required by generally accepted auditing standards to communicate certain matters to the audit committee.

In particular, the auditors are required to report material misstatements in the financial statements or omissions of material information.

It should be emphasized that audit committees should be highly attuned to potential situations of fraudulent financial reporting.

Failure on the part of an audit committee to question management's representations may be the basis for audit committee malfeasance, since the audit committee and the board may be held liable for their failure to know what they were responsible for recognizing.

Source: This discussion is adapted from an article by Louis Braiotta, Jr., "Auditing for Honesty," *American Bar Association Journal* 78, No. 5 (May 1992), pp. 76–79. Copyright © 1992 by Louis Braiotta, Jr.

[a]More recently, the SEC has filed actions against the officers and directors and accounting firms, respectively: 1993 (36, 17); 1994 (78, 31); 1995 (71, 11); 1996 (59, 20); 1997 (90, 22). For additional reading, see a Best Practices Council of the National Association of Corporate Directors report entitled, *Coping with Fraud and Other Illegal Activity* (Washington, D.C.: National Association of Corporate Directors, 1998); Committee of Sponsoring Organizations of the Treadway Commission, *Fraudulent Financial Reporting: 1987–1997 An Analysis of U.S. Public Companies* (New York: Committee of Sponsoring Organizations of the Treadway Commission, 1999). See the SEC *Annual Reports* for further information on enforcement proceedings and related cases and Exhibit 4.3.

[b]For further reading, see Curtis C. Verschoor, "A Case Study of Audit Committee Effectiveness at Sundstrand," *Internal Auditing* 4, No. 4 (Spring 1989), pp. 11–19. Also see Verschoor's article, "Miniscribe: A New Example of Audit Committee Ineffectiveness," *Internal Auditing* 5, No. 4 (Spring 1990), pp. 13–19.

[c]See Exhibit 4.2 for further details.

Exhibit 4.2 Warning Signals of the Possible Existence of Fraudulent Financial Reporting

Symptom	Problem	Solution
I. Industry Matters		
Competitive and economic conditions	Overoptimistic news releases with respect to earnings.	Analyze annual and interim earnings trends to avoid increased opportunities for managing earnings.
	Capital investment in a rapidly changing industry.	
Competitive foreign businesses	Foreign competitors have significant advantages.	Discuss management's strategy as it relates to financial matters.
Government regulations	The industry is subject to new regulations that increase the cost of compliance.	Obtain assurance on the entity's compliance affecting financial matters.
Industry accounting practices	Unusual revenue recognition policies and/or deferred expenses to increase earnings.	Access significant accounting policies that are industry-specific from the NAARS data base, and review and discuss this information with the independent auditors.
II. Entity's Business Matters		
Organizational structure	High turnover in key accounting personnel (e.g., controller). Complex corporate structure that is not warranted.	Determine the reasons for such personnel turnover.
Lines of business and product segments	Rapid expansion of business lines in excess of industry averages.	Investigate the reasons for this rapid expansion.
Lack of security over computer operations	Control procedures over computer are weak.	Inquire of management key security problems.

Accounting policies	Significant changes in accounting practices and estimates by management with an excessive interest in earnings. Unusual year-end transactions that increase earnings. Inconsistencies between financial statements, MDA, and the president's letter.	Compare the entity's policies with the industry norms and determine the reasons for the changes. Raise questions on issues that support these transactions; determine the reasons for the inconsistent disclosures.
Conflict-of-interest	Significant contracts that affect financial statements. Frequent related-party transactions. Failure to enforce the corporate code of conduct.	Determine management intent to disclose such contracts; determine how the company addresses possible conflict-of-interest situations; determine how management monitors compliance with the code.
Frequent change of legal counsel	Disagreements on asserted or unasserted claims and contingencies.	Discuss disclosures with general counsel and outside counsel.
Unexplained significant fluctuations in account balances	Material physical inventory variances.	Focus on the analytical review procedures.

III. External Auditing Matters

Frequent change of auditors	Disagreement on GAAP, which causes opinion shopping.	Investigate the reasons for frequent changes in auditors.
Quantity of lawsuits against the CPA firm	Firm has violated the securities laws.	Review the latest peer review report and the number of lawsuits against the firm.
Nonacceptance of recommendations in the management letter	Breakdowns in the internal control structures.	Obtain assurance from the auditors that management has evaluated the weaknesses and that corrective action has been taken.

IV. Internal Auditing Matters

Departmental organization	The size of the internal audit department is not compatible with the size of the company.	Discuss this matter with chief internal auditor and independent auditor.
Reporting responsibility	Scope restrictions.	Direct access to the audit committee.

125

Exhibit 4.3   Unethical Practices in Financial Reporting

SEC Enforcement Division[a]
Summary of Selected Cases and Alleged Violations—Financial Disclosures
Fiscal Year ended 1989–1997

Date Filed	Release No.	Nature of Alleged Violations
11/1/88	AAER—208	SEC alleged improper accounting practices (e.g., holding quarterly financial records open to record additional sales; preparing invoices for orders that had not been shipped; and delaying the issuance of credit memos for orders that had been returned). The company and seven officers and employees consented to the entry of the Commission's orders against them.
1/9/89	AAER—212	The registrant had overstated earnings and inventory by inflating quantity and cost figures on inventory count sheets and arranged for the supplier to send a false confirmation to the auditors. The company, its officers, its supplier, and the supplier's president all consented to entry of permanent injunctions.
2/8/89	AAER—215	SEC alleged the improper recognition of revenue. The alleged scheme involved failure to record at least $13 million of product returns and the recording of more than $5 million of fictitious revenue from false invoices. Two defendants consented to the entry of injunctions against them.
6/6/89	LR—12119	The company had overstated revenues by prematurely recording a total of 20 transactions as sales even though the sales have not been completed.
9/6/89	AAER—247	SEC filed an action against officers, directors, and employees. Commission alleged the company falsified financial records to overstate pretax income of $20.6 million instead of a loss in 1987. Defendants sold over $60 million of stock that did not reflect the value of the company. Three defendants consented to the entry of injunctions against them.
5/24/90	AAER—258	The registrant recorded unsupported adjustments to revenue. The Commission alleged the company filed materially false and misleading financial statements.
10/11/90	AAER—279	SEC alleged that former officers engaged in improper revenue recognition practices. They are: (1) recorded transactions as sales when customers had not agreed to purchase the equipment and the equipment was not delivered; (2) recorded trials as sales transactions; and (3) removing inventory to simulate delivery of goods sold. The defendants consented to the entry of injunctions.

Exhibit 4.3 (*Continued*)

Date Filed	Release No.	Nature of Alleged Violations
10/26/90	AAER—282	The CEO directed officers and employees to engage in a scheme to inflate accounts receivable and inventory. The perpetration created phony invoices to generate sales. Also, the CEO and two other defendants sold common stock when they knew that the market price was based on materially false representations. Two of the defendants consented to the entry of injunctions.
8/20/91	AAER—311	The corporation used improper revenue recognition practices by recording sales at the time a purchaser agreed verbally to purchase equipment. Also, the client misled the auditors by falsely indicating that certain tractors were loaded for shipment and that risk of loss had passed to the purchaser. The company and two of the individual defendants consented to the entry of injunction.
3/31/92	AAER—363	SEC alleged that the company failed to disclose the importance of its subsidiary's 1989 earnings in the MD&A section of the Form 10-K. The subsidiary accounted for about 23 percent of the parent company's net profit of $497 million. Much of the gain resulted from the country's hyperinflation and a favorable exchange rate. The parent company consented to a cease and desist order.
9/30/93	LR—13813	The Commission alleged that the company made misrepresentations and omissions regarding the deterioration in sales of software and the shipment of $5.2 million of products to certain customers as conditional or fictitious sales. Individual defendants consented to the entry of orders requiring them to disgorge over $2 million and one consented to the entry of a bar from acting as an officer or director of a publicly held company.
3/29/94	EAR—33829	The Commission alleged that, as a result of a fraudulent accounting scheme implemented by three members of the company's senior management, the company reported materially overstated sales, net income, and assets in periodic filings between 1989 and 1992. The inflated sales and earnings enabled the company to falsely report continued growth in revenue and earnings when the company was not profitable. Overall, the company reported nearly $38 million in sales between 1989–1992 that had not taken place.

Exhibit 4.3   *(Continued)*

Date Filed	Release No.	Nature of Alleged Violations
1/4/95	LR—14375	The company improperly recognized revenue on several transactions. The company's false claims of having sold simulators to customers resulted in income statements in which total revenue was inflated by 46 percent to 93 percent.
9/19/96	R—34-37701	The company filed a 10Q that contained financial statements which materially overstated revenue and materially understated losses by improperly recognizing revenue from purported bill and hold transactions.
2/18/97	LR—15260	The company materially overstated earnings and profitability prior to a convertible debt offering. The company consented to entry of an injunction and an order requiring the payment of $3.28 million in disgorgement.

Source: The Securities and Exchange Commission *Annual Reports* (Washington, D.C.: U.S. Government Printing Office, 1990–1997).

GUIDELINES FOR MINIMIZING LEGAL LIABILITY

Obviously, the audit directors wish to avoid potential legal liability. To achieve this objective, the directors should conduct their activities in a manner above reproach. As evidenced by the statutory laws and court cases, their posture is critically important in the corporate environment. Hence they should not only exercise the required standards of care and loyalty in their positions but foster the professionalism regarding their directorship.

To assist the members of the audit committee in minimizing their possible legal liability, the following guidelines are provided. Such guidelines do not purport to be all-inclusive and are not intended to preclude the insertion of additional matters. Also, it should be noted that the guidelines are presented in view of the oversight and advisory capacity of the committee.

Minimizing the Audit Committee's Legal Liability: A Checklist

I. The Independent Auditors
   A. Have we inquired about the qualifications of the personnel whom we engaged in the audit?
      1. Review the backgrounds of the executive partner and auditing personnel.
      2. Inquire about the auditing firm's registration with the SEC practice division of the AICPA.

    3. Inquire about the CPA firm's participation in the voluntary peer review professional practice programs.

B. Have we reviewed their engagement letter?

The auditor's engagement letter sets forth the nature and scope of the audit engagement in order to avoid any misunderstanding between the auditing firm and the client. This letter constitutes a contract regarding the professional services of the CPA firm.

C. Is there evidence that the audit examination was properly planned, supervised, and reviewed?

    1. Inquire about the overall audit plan concerning the scope, conduct, and timing of the audit examination.

    2. Discuss the level of knowledge which is required for the corporation and the industry.

    3. Discuss the ratio of staff assistants to supervisors in connection with the level of responsibilities for the audit.

    4. Review or request an outline of the supervisory review procedures of the staff assistant's work and note any disagreements among the audit personnel.

D. Does the corporate annual report contain a fair and meaningful presentation of the information concerning the financial statements, footnotes, and supplementary information?

Significant changes in the external reporting practices of the corporation should be discussed (e.g., departures from generally accepted accounting principles, exceptions to the consistent application of accounting principles, and the alternative applications of generally accepted accounting principles).

E. Have we reviewed the recommendations made in their management letter to assure the auditors' objectivity?

    1. The management letter contains the auditors' recommendations as a result of their evaluation of the system of internal control. Any matters regarding the material weaknesses in the system of internal control should be discussed as well as full compliance with the provisions of the Foreign Corrupt Practices Act.

    2. Discuss the implementation of the recommendations in the current and prior years' management letters as well as causes of management disagreement with the auditors.

F. Have we reviewed the lawyer's letter concerning litigations, claims, and assessments?

    1. The lawyer's letter contains the opinion of legal counsel with respect to potential litigation, such as a pending lawsuit. Such information is provided to the CPA firms for possible disclosure in the financial statements.

    2. Discuss the accounting treatment concerning the contingency losses and effect on the financial statements.

G. Have we reviewed the letter of management's representation?
The chief financial officer and chief executive officer will furnish a letter to the auditing firm with respect to the corporation's representations concerning the financial position and the results of operations. This letter should be examined in view of the facts in the letter and in the financial statements. This letter is particularly important since it confirms management's responsibilities for the financial statements.

H. Have we reviewed:
    1. Any amendments to the bylaws or corporate charter?
    2. The minutes of the meetings of the board of directors, directors' committees, and stockholders (e.g., compensation committee or finance committees)?

I. Have we reviewed the corporation's compliance with the auditors and legal counsel concerning the:
    1. Securities statutes?
    2. Antitrust laws?
    3. Income tax laws?
    4. Labor laws?
    5. Regulatory laws applicable to the industry?

J. Have we made an evaluation of any material non–arm's-length transactions, such as loans to officers?

K. Have we reviewed:
    1. Results of peer review?
    2. Litigation against the CPA firm?
    3. Adequacy of professional liability insurance?
    4. Independence issues as required by ISB Standard No. 1?
    5. Required disclosures to the audit committee as required by SAS #61?
    6. Extent of management services provided by CPA firm and impact on independence?

II. The Internal Auditors[40]
A. Have we reviewed the qualifications of the internal audit staff?
    1. Review the backgrounds of the director of internal auditing and the internal auditing group.
    2. Inquire about the internal audit staff's participation in the programs of the Institute of Internal Auditors and other professional societies.
    3. Discuss their qualifications with the independent auditing firm.

---

[40]For further reference, see Exhibit 9.4 in Chapter 9, "Vital Checkpoints: Internal Audit Questions for the Audit Committee," prepared by Richard Hickok and Jules Zimmerman.

    B. Have we reviewed their charter or audit plan?

    C. Have we considered the reporting responsibility of the internal audit staff?

    D. Is there evidence that the work of the internal audit staff was properly planned, supervised, and reviewed?

        See item number C under "The Independent Auditors."

    E. Have we reviewed:

       1. Reports on compliance audits?

       2. Reports on operational audits?

       3. Reports on financial audits?

       4. Reports on the system of internal accounting and administrative controls?

         • Have we reviewed the recommendations made in their reports with respect to objectivity?

         • Have we considered the possibility of a long-form report from the Director of Internal Auditing?

    F. Have the internal auditors' recommendations in connection with the prior years' internal audit been implemented?

    G. Have we scrutinized cases of management disagreements with the internal auditors?

    H. Have we reexamined the relationship of the internal audit function to the other departments?

    I. How are activities of the internal audit staff and the independent auditors interrelated?

    J. If the corporation has an electronic data processing installation, have we considered the use of independent EDP consultants to audit the installation?

III. The Representatives of Management (Chief Executive Officer, Chief Financial Officer, Treasurer, and Controller)

    A. Are the qualifications of the representatives of management consistent with the corporate bylaws?

    B. Have we reviewed their administrative functions in relationship to the present financial and accounting policies? (See company's organization chart.)

    C. Have these individuals exercised their authority in accordance with the corporate bylaws?

    D. Have we reviewed the minutes of the meeting of the board of directors concerning their compensation?

    E. Have we reviewed their written reports concerning their responses to the deficiencies noted in the internal audit reports?

F. Are all employees who handle cash, securities, and other valuables bonded?

G. Are the financial and accounting policies and procedures set forth in manuals?

H. Are interim financial reports prepared for submission to management on a timely basis?

I. Is the quality and quantity of information in the interim reports adequate?

J. Have we discussed cases of management disagreements with the auditors?

K. Have we discussed:
1. The engagement letter?
2. The management letter from the independent auditors?
3. The letter of management's representations?
4. The lawyer's letter?

L. Have we discussed the periodic filings with the various regulatory agencies?

Signed by: _____ Date _____

[Should be signed by the chairman of the audit committee][41]

In view of the preceding discussions on the legal position of the audit committee, it is important that the audit directors fully understand the nature and scope of their legal responsibilities concerning the corporation's outside constituencies and the securities markets. However, they should keep their legal obligations in proper perspective. Such obligations should be integrated and balanced with the committee's functions so that the committee's purpose is not defeated. In short, the directors should discharge their responsibilities in a professional manner and not become totally preoccupied with the legal rules and regulations.

SOURCES AND SUGGESTED READINGS

American Bar Association, *Corporate Director's Guidebook* (Chicago: American Bar Association, 1978).

American Bar Association, *Corporate Director's Guidebook* (Chicago: American Bar Association, 1994).

Braiotta, Louis, "Auditing for Honesty." *American Bar Association Journal,* 78, No. 5 (May 1992), pp. 76–79.

---

[41] It is advisable that the audit committee document its activities and have in-house counsel or outside legal counsel review documentation for content and use prior to adoption. Such procedures will help protect the audit committee in cases of possible litigation.

Commerce Clearing House, *Federal Securities Law Reporter* (Chicago: Commerce Clearing House, 1972–73, 1974–75, 1977–78 Transfer binder).

Commerce Clearing House, *Federal Securities Law Reporter* (Chicago: Commerce Clearing House, 1984–1985 Transfer binder).

Committee on Corporate Laws, Section of Corporation, Banking and Business Law of the American Bar Association, *Revised Model Business Corporation Act—Chapter 8: Directors and Officers* (Chicago, Ill.: American Bar Association, 1984).

Committee on Corporate Laws of the Section of Business Law, *Model Business Corporation Act—Chapter 8: Directors and Officers* (Chicago, Ill.: American Bar Association, 1998).

Connecticut General Statutes Annotated, Sections 33-318(b)(1) and (2), West 1960 and Supplement 1985.

"Firing Line," *Time* (February 19, 1979), p. 51.

Internal Revenue Code Chapter 75A, Crimes (1954).

Lancaster, Hal, "Fuss at Cal Life Shows Audit Committee Role is Crucial, Experts Say." *The Wall Street Journal* (March 17, 1980). p. 1.

Marsh, Hugh L., and Thomas E. Powell, "The Audit Committee Charter: Rx for Fraud Prevention." *Journal of Accountancy,* 167, No. 2 (February 1989), pp. 55–57.

New York Business Corporation Law, *McKinney's Consolidated Laws of New York Annotated* (Brooklyn, N.Y.: Edward Thompson Company, 1963, Book 6).

Petziner, Thomas, Jr., "Heinz Senior Officials Didn't Participate in Profit-Juggling Practices, Panel Says." *The Wall Street Journal* (May 9, 1980), p. 2.

Securities and Exchange Commission, 1993, 1994, 1995, 1996, 1997 *Annual Reports* (Washington, D.C.: U.S. Government Printing Office).

Securities Exchange Act Rule 10(b)-5, Title 17, Code of Federal Regulations, Sec. 240 (1974).

Securities and Exchange Commission, *The Work of the Securities and Exchange Commission* (Washington, D.C.: U.S. Government Printing Office, 1974).

United States Code, Titles 15 and 18 (1970).

Verschoor, Curtis C., "Miniscribe: A New Example of Audit Committee Ineffectiveness." *Internal Auditing* 5, No. 4 (Spring 1990), pp. 13–19.

Verschoor, Curtis C., "A Case Study of Audit Committee Effectiveness at Sundstrand," *Internal Auditing* 4, No. 4 (Spring 1989), pp. 11–19.

The Wall Street Journal Staff Reporter, "Playboy Audit Committee Bares Details of Hefner's High Living on Firm's Tab." *The Wall Street Journal* (April 4, 1980), p. 6.

Chapter 5

Rules of the Road— Auditing and Related Accounting Standards

The purpose of this chapter is to introduce the broad framework of generally accepted auditing standards and the integration of such standards with their respective generally accepted financial accounting standards. The integration of auditing and accounting standards will enhance the audit director's understanding of the application of accounting standards in the preparation of the financial statements. Moreover, the audit director will acquire not only a broad perspective on the essential purpose of the audit examination, but also the salient points concerning the auditors' report. In the succeeding chapters, additional financial accounting standards will be discussed in more detail.

AN OVERVIEW OF GENERALLY ACCEPTED AUDITING STANDARDS

Nature of Generally Accepted Auditing Standards

In Chapter 1 reference was made to the auditing standards concerning the scope paragraph of the auditors' report. More specifically, the auditors state,

> We conducted our audit in accordance with generally accepted auditing standards. Those standards require that we plan and perform the audit to obtain reasonable assurance about whether the financial statements are free of material misstatement. An audit includes examining, on a test basis, evidence supporting the amounts and disclosures in the financial statements. An audit also includes assessing the accounting principles used and significant estimates made by management, as well as evaluating the overall financial statement presentation. We believe that our audit provides a reasonable basis for our opinion.

Explicit in the preceding sentence is the auditors' representation that the audit examination has been conducted based not only on authoritative guidelines or rules as established by the American Institute of Certified Public Accountants but also on their professional judgment in the application of auditing procedures. As approved and adopted by the membership of the AICPA, generally accepted auditing standards are as follows:

General Standards

1. The audit is to be performed by a person or persons having adequate technical training and proficiency as an auditor.

2. In all matters relating to the assignment, an independence in mental attitude is to be maintained by the auditor or auditors.

3. Due professional care is to be exercised in the performance of the audit and the preparation of the report.

Standards of Field Work

1. The work is to be adequately planned and assistants, if any, are to be properly supervised.

2. A sufficient understanding of the internal control structure is to be obtained to plan the audit and to determine the nature, timing, and extent of tests to be performed.

3. Sufficient competent evidential matter is to be obtained through inspection, observation, inquiries, and confirmations to afford a reasonable basis for an opinion regarding the financial statements under audit.

Standards of Reporting

1. The report shall state whether the financial statements are presented in accordance with generally accepted accounting principles.

2. The report shall identify those circumstances in which such principles have not been consistently observed in the current period in relation to the preceding period.

3. Informative disclosures in the financial statements are to be regarded as reasonably adequate unless otherwise stated in the report.

4. The report shall either contain an expression of opinion regarding the financial statements taken as a whole or an assertion to the effect that an opinion cannot be expressed. When an overall opinion cannot be expressed, the reasons therefore should be stated. In all cases where an auditor's name is associated with financial

statements, the report should contain a clear-cut indication of the character of the auditor's work, if any, and the degree of responsibility the auditor is taking.[1]

The preceding auditing standards provide a useful framework for measuring the quality of the auditors' professional performance concerning the audit examination and the audit report. Such standards are totally inflexible because the public accountancy profession wishes to maintain high standards and uniformity in the practice of auditing. However, auditing procedures are flexible since the auditors use various methods based upon their professional judgment to perform the audit. Furthermore, the Auditing Standards Board of the AICPA periodically issues pronouncements on auditing matters which represent the board's interpretations of generally accepted auditing standards. These pronouncements provide the auditors with guidance and direction regarding various auditing procedures in a particular auditing situation. (See Appendix M.)

AN ANALYSIS OF THE AUDITING STANDARDS

General Auditing Standards

With respect to the general standards, adequate technical training and proficiency as an auditor implies that the individuals who are performing the audit are professional accountants (certified public accountants). Certified public accountants are requisite to the audit function since their major objective is to express an independent opinion on the financial statements. Their professional opinion is critically important to the users of the financial statements because such users need assurance on corporate management's financial accounting representations. Moreover, the independent auditors have a duty of professional care whereby they must exercise their professional judgment with reasonable care and diligence. (See Appendix J.)

Auditing Standards of Field Work   The first standard of field work centers around the auditors' objectives, plans, and procedures concerning the particular audit engagement. For example, the Auditing Standards Executive Committee points out:

> Audit planning involves developing an overall strategy for the expected conduct and scope of the examination. The nature, extent, and timing of planning vary with the size and complexity of the entity, experience with the entity, and knowledge of the entity's business.[2]

---

[1] American Institute of Certified Public Accountants, *Professional Standards, U.S. Auditing Standards/Attestation Standards,* Vol. 1 (Copyright © 1998 by the American Institute of Certified Public Accountants, Inc.), AU Sec. 150.03.

[2] *Statement on Auditing Standards, No. 22,* "Planning and Supervision" (New York: American Institute of Certified Public Accountants, 1978), par. 3.

Supervision involves directing the efforts of assistants who are involved in accomplishing the objectives of the examination and determining whether those objectives were accomplished.[3]

Thus the first standard of field work requires that the auditors plan their necessary auditing procedures subsequent to their review of such matters as the corporation's accounting policies and procedures and the industry practices of the particular entity. Also, they are required to develop and administer the necessary levels of proper supervision regarding the audit examination.[4]

The second standard of field work requires that the auditors obtain a sufficient understanding of the internal control structure. (See Chapter 8.) Their evaluation of the system of internal control is necessary in order to determine how much reliance can be placed on the entity's financial accounting system. Since the financial statements are the product of the accounting system, the auditors must examine the internal controls and the related recordings of various business transactions. Furthermore, the auditors evaluate the system of internal control to determine the extent of their tests of the accounting records as well as their auditing procedures.

As the third standard of field work, sufficient competent evidential matter means that the auditors must obtain and examine internal and external documentation that supports the financial accounting representations in the financial statements. For example, the auditors will examine not only sales invoices and other documentations but also correspondence from various parties outside the entity, such as banks and customers. The amount of evidential matter to be examined is based on the auditors' professional judgment. Obviously, the auditors' major objective is to examine sufficient evidence to enable them to express their opinion on the fairness of the presentations in the financial statements.

The standards of field work are directly related to the scope of the auditors' examination. The scope of the audit is critically important because the auditors may not express an unqualified opinion on the financial statements if their scope is limited. As the Auditing Standards Executive Committee states:

> Restrictions on the scope of his examination, whether imposed by the client or by circumstances such as the timing of his work, the inability to obtain sufficient competent evidential matter, or an inadequacy in the accounting records, may require him to qualify his opinion or to disclaim an opinion.[5]

---

[3] Ibid., par. 9.

[4] For a complete description of the organizational and operational aspects of a public accounting firm, see any standard auditing textbook.

[5] AICPA, *Professional Standards, U.S. Auditing Standards/Attestation Standards,* Vol. 1, AU Sec. 508.22. See Chapter 13 for a discussion on the various types of auditing reports.

Thus it is imperative that the audit committee examine those situations which may preclude the issuance of an unqualified opinion as a result of a limitation on the auditors' scope. For example, a limitation on the auditors' observation of physical inventories or the confirmation of accounts receivable would be considered a restriction on the scope.[6]

Since the standards of reporting are closely associated with an understanding of generally accepted accounting principles, such standards are discussed in the next section of this chapter.

INTEGRATION OF AUDITING AND RELATED ACCOUNTING STANDARDS

As discussed in Chapter 1, the auditors state in the third paragraph of their report that they are expressing an opinion on the fair presentation of the financial statements. Also, their opinion gives assurance to the users of the statements that management has presented the financial statements in conformity with generally accepted accounting principles.

If there are no exceptions noted by the auditors with respect to the consistent application of generally accepted accounting principles and adequate informative disclosure in the financial statements, then the users can assume that such statements are fairly presented. The following discussion provides an analysis of the four auditing standards of reporting and the opinion paragraph of the auditors' report.

Nature of Generally Accepted Accounting Principles

The first auditing standard of reporting requires the auditors to make a statement in their report on whether the financial statements are presented in accordance with generally accepted accounting principles. In contrast with the 10 generally accepted auditing standards, an authoritative list of generally accepted accounting principles or standards has not been established by any one authoritative source. However, the official pronouncements of several authoritative bodies have been recognized as generally accepted accounting principles. (See Appendix M.) Exhibit 5.1 contains a hierarchy of generally accepted accounting principles.

In addition, several other organizations have influenced modern accounting thought (see Appendixes A and N), such as the following:

* American Accounting Association
* Institute of Management Accountants

---

[6]AICPA, *Professional Standards, U.S. Auditing Standards/Attestation Standards,* Vol. 1, AU Sec. 508.24.

Exhibit 5.1 GAAP Hierarchy Summary

Nongovernmental Entities	State and Local Governments

Established Accounting Principles

10a. FASB Statements and Interpretations, APB Opinions, and AICPA Accounting Research Bulletins

10b. FASB Technical Bulletins, AICPA Industry Audit and Accounting Guides, and AICPA Statements of Position

10c. Consensus positions of the FASB Emerging Issues Task Force and AICPA Practice Bulletins

10d. AICPA accounting interpretations, "Qs and As" published by the FASB staff, as well as industry practices widely recognized and prevalent

12a. GASB Statements and Interpretations, plus AICPA and FASB pronouncements if made applicable to state and local governments by a GASB Statement or Interpretation

12b. GASB Technical Bulletins, and the following pronouncements if specifically made applicable to state and local governments by the AICPA: AICPA Industry Audit and Accounting Guides and AICPA Statements of Position

12c. Consensus positions of the GASB Emerging Issues Task Force† and AICPA Practice Bulletins if specifically made applicable to state and local governments by the AICPA

12d. "Qs and As" published by the GASB staff, as well as industry practices widely recognized and prevalent

Other Accounting Literature

11. Other accounting literature, including FASB Concepts Statements; APB Statements; AICPA Issues Papers; International Accounting Standards Committee Statements; GASB Statements, Interpretations, and Technical Bulletins; pronouncements of other professional associations or regulatory agencies; AICPA *Technical Practice Aids*; and accounting textbooks, handbooks, and articles

13. Other accounting literature, including GASB Concepts Statements; pronouncements in categories (*a*) through (*d*) of the hierarchy for nongovernmental entities when not specifically made applicable to state and local governments; APB Statements; FASB Concepts Statements; AICPA Issues Papers; International Accounting Standards Committee Statements; pronouncements of other professional associations or regulatory agencies: AICPA *Technical Practice Aids*; and accounting textbooks, handbooks, and articles

Source: Statement on Auditing Standards, No. 69, "The Meaning of Present Fairly in Conformity with Generally Accepted Accounting Principles in the Independent Auditor's Report" (New York: American Institute of Certified Public Accountants, 1992), par. 15.

- Financial Executive Institute
- Institute of Internal Auditors
- Cost Accounting Standard Board
- Other regulatory agencies (e.g., Securities and Exchange Commission)

According to the Accounting Principles Board, accounting principles are described as follows:

> Generally accepted accounting principles incorporate the consensus at a particular time as to which economic resources and obligations should be recorded as assets and liabilities by financial accounting. . . .
>
> Generally accepted accounting principles encompass the conventions, rules, and procedures necessary to define accepted accounting practice at a particular time. The standard of generally accepted accounting principles, includes not only broad guidelines of general application, but also detailed practices and procedures.[7]

Since the publication of APB No. 4, the Financial Accounting Standards Board has issued five Statements of Financial Accounting Concepts relative to business organizations and one statement with respect to financial reporting by nonbusiness organizations. In Chapter 3, these statements were identified and their implementation discussed.

Management's selection of accounting principles, methods, or procedures should be based on those principles of accounting that have general acceptance among the public accounting profession. Adoption of such principles is particularly important because it affects the auditors' opinion on the financial statements. If management applies significant accounting principles that lack general acceptance, then the auditors cannot express an unqualified opinion on the statements.[8] Moreover, Rule 203 of the AICPA Rules of Conduct of the Code of Professional Ethics states:

> A member shall not (1) express an opinion or state affirmatively that the financial statements or other financial data of any entity are presented in conformity with generally accepted accounting principles or (2) state that he or she is not aware of any material modifications that should be made to such statements or data in order for them to be in conformity with generally accepted accounting principles, if such statements or data contain any departure from an accounting principle promulgated

---

[7] *Statement of the Accounting Principles Board, No. 4*, "Basic Concepts and Accounting Principles Underlying Financial Statements of Business Enterprises" (New York: American Institute of Certified Public Accountants, 1970), pars. 137–138.

[8] *AICPA Professional Standards, U.S. Auditing Standards/Attestation Standards,* Vol. 1, AU Sec. 508.35.

by bodies designated by Council[9] to establish such principles that have a material effect on the statements or data taken as a whole. If, however, the statements or data contain such a departure and the member can demonstrate that due to unusual circumstances the financial statements or data would otherwise have been misleading, the member can comply with the rule by describing the departure, its approximate effects, if practicable, and the reasons why compliance with the principle would result in a misleading statement.[10]

Thus the auditors may express an unqualified opinion; however, their audit report should be modified to describe the circumstances.

Consistency With respect to the third standard of reporting, the auditors are not required to state in their report whether the accounting principles have been consistently applied in the current and preceding periods. However, as previously mentioned, consistency in the application of accounting principles and adequate informative disclosure in the financial statements can be assumed by the users unless the auditors take exception in their audit report. As the APB pointed out:

> Consistency is an important factor in comparability within a single enterprise. Although financial accounting practices and procedures are largely conventional, consistency in their use permits comparison over time.[11]

The FASB reaffirmed its predecessor's position in SFAC No. 2, which states:

> Information about a particular enterprise gains greatly in usefulness if it can be compared with similar information about other enterprises and with similar information about the same enterprise for some other period or some other point in time. Comparability between enterprises and consistency in the application of methods over time increases the informational value of comparisons of relative economic opportunities or performance. The significance of information, especially quantitative information, depends to a great extent on the user's ability to relate it to some benchmark.[12]

Such a requirement is necessary because management has flexibility in the selection of accounting methods or procedures. In the practice of accounting,

---

[9] See the bodies designated by Council to promulgate technical standards in the *Code of Professional Conduct* (New York: AICPA, 1997), pp. 15–16.

[10] AICPA, *Rules of Conduct of the Code of Professional Conduct* (New York: AICPA, 1997), pp. 11–12. See Appendix J.

[11] *Statement of the Accounting Principles Board, No. 4,* par. 98.

[12] Financial Accounting Standards Board, *Statement of Financial Accounting Concepts, No. 2,* "Qualitative Characteristics of Accounting Information" (Stamford, Conn.: Financial Accounting Standards Board, May 1980), p. 2. See pars. 120–122 for additional emphasis.

several alternative accounting methods are available to management for financial reporting. For example, the annual depreciation charges on the entity's plant and equipment may be computed on the basis of several acceptable depreciation methods. As a result, the auditors must satisfy themselves that management has applied the alternative accounting methods on a consistent basis from period to period in order to enhance the comparability of the financial statements. The comparability of financial statements is essential since the users of the statements make economic decisions and thus need financial accounting information that is meaningful.

However, management can make changes in the application of alternative accounting methods. Changes in the economic conditions that affect a particular enterprise may require a change in the application of an accounting method. For example, a corporation may change its method of pricing inventory items because of the inflationary conditions in the economy and the effects on the financial statements. It is incumbent upon management to justify the change in the accounting methods whereby a particular change enhances a fairer presentation in the financial statements. Such an accounting change should be disclosed in the financial statements in order to indicate the effects of the change upon the statements.[13] Moreover, the auditors are required to point out the change in the application of the accounting methods by modifying their report with an additional paragraph following the opinion paragraph.[14] (See Chapter 10.)

Disclosure   The third reporting standard regarding informative disclosures implies that the information in the financial statements should be relevant to the users of accounting information. The information in the body of the statements, footnotes, and supplementary materials should be pertinent to the informational needs of the users. The accounting principle related to this particular auditing standard is known as the full disclosure principle. Under this principle, management has a reporting responsibility to its constituencies to disclose financial information that is necessary for a proper understanding of the financial statements. Such disclosure of information is based on management's judgment. Furthermore, the auditors have a professional obligation to ensure reasonably adequate informative disclosures in the statements.

The fundamental recognition criteria are set forth by the FASB as follows:

> An item and information about it should meet four fundamental recognition criteria to be recognized and should be recognized when the criteria are met, subject to a cost-benefit constraint and a materiality threshold. Those criteria are:

[13] *Opinions of the Accounting Principles Board, No. 20,* "Accounting Changes" (New York: American Institute of Certified Public Accountants, 1971), par. 17.
[14] AICPA, *Professional Standards, U.S. Auditing Standards/Attestation Standards,* Vol. 1, AU Sec. 508.16.

Definitions—The item meets the definition of an element of financial statements.

Measurability—It has a relevant attribute measurable with sufficient reliability.

Relevance—The information about it is capable of making a difference in user decisions.

Reliability—The information is representationally faithful, verifiable, and neutral.

All four criteria are subject to a pervasive cost-benefit constraint: the expected benefits from recognizing a particular item should justify perceived costs of providing and using the information. Recognition is also subject to a materiality threshold: an item and information about it need not be recognized in a set of financial statements if the item is not large enough to be material and the aggregate of individually immaterial items is not large enough to be material to those financial statements.[15]

However, management may not disclose certain information because such disclosure may injure the entity's competitive position.

Materiality   With respect to materiality, the FASB indicates:

Individual judgments are required to assess materiality in the absence of authoritative criteria or to decide that minimum quantitative criteria are not appropriate in particular situations. The essence of the materiality concept is clear. The omission or misstatement of an item in a financial report is material if, in the light of surrounding circumstances, the magnitude of the item is such that it is probable that the judgment of a reasonable person relying upon the report would have been changed or influenced by the inclusion or correction of the item.[16]

The Auditing Standards Board has reaffirmed the FASB position on materiality as mentioned in SAS No. 47, "Audit Risk and Materiality in Conducting an Audit."

Implicit in the preceding narrative is the pervasive influence of the materiality principle on the financial statements. Although the materiality of a particular financial fact is a matter of professional judgment, consideration should be given to the significance of the information in relationship to the users' information needs. Such consideration may include the effect of the financial item on the entity's net income or financial condition. For example, an inventory loss of $10,000 would be a material item in the financial statements of a small trading or manufacturing concern because such a loss may represent 5 to 10 percent of the company's assets. However, in a large conglomerate enterprise with billions of dollars in assets,

---

[15] Financial Accounting Standards Board, *Statement of Financial Accounting Concepts, No. 5,* "Recognition and Measurement in Financial Statements of Business Enterprises" (Stamford, Conn.: Financial Accounting Standards Board, 1984), par. 63.

[16] Financial Accounting Standards Board, *Statement of Financial Accounting Concepts, No. 2,* par. 132.

inventory loss of $10,000 would be an immaterial item in the financial statements. Thus the nature and size of the financial item and its relative importance to the financial statements determine the materiality of the item. In short, no definitive rules or criteria are used to judge materiality since the circumstances regarding each audit examination vary.

To enhance the usefulness of the financial statements, the APB has adopted a rule with respect to the disclosure of accounting policies. In particular, "the Board believes that the disclosure is particularly useful if given in a separate 'Summary of Significant Accounting Policies' preceding the notes to the financial statements or as the initial note."[17] For example, the disclosures would include, among others, the basis of consolidation, depreciation methods, inventory pricing methods, accounting for research and development costs, and translation of foreign currencies.[18]

The disclosure principle is particularly important because if the auditors do not concur with the adequacy of management's disclosures, then they cannot express an unqualified opinion. Such inadequate disclosures should be stated in their audit report. For further information or additional disclosure matters, see Chapter 10.

Fairness   The fourth auditing standard of reporting requires that the independent auditors express their opinion on the fairness of the financial presentation in the financial statements. However, if the auditors cannot express an opinion, then they are required to acknowledge this fact and the related reasons. Moreover, the auditors are required to disclose the nature of their association and responsibility with the financial statements when their names are associated with the statements. Their professional opinion is based on their informed judgment as a result of the audit. Their opinion should not be construed as an absolute guarantee regarding the accuracy of the financial statements. Furthermore, the Auditing Standards Board points out the following with respect to the term *fairness*:

> The independent auditor's judgment concerning the "fairness" of the overall presentation of financial statements should be applied within the framework of generally accepted accounting principles. Without that framework the auditor would have no uniform standard for judging the presentation of financial position, results of operations, and cash flows in financial statements.[19]

In summary, the auditors should base their judgment on matters such as:

- Whether the accounting principles selected and applied have general acceptance;
- Whether the accounting principles are appropriate in the circumstances;

---

[17] *Opinions of the Accounting Principles Board, No. 22,* "Disclosure of Accounting Policies" (New York: AICPA, 1972), par. 15.

[18] Ibid., par. 13.

[19] *Statement on Auditing Standards, No. 69,* par. 3.

- Whether the financial statements, including the related notes, are informative of matters that may affect their use, understanding, and interpretation;

- Whether the information presented in the financial statements is classified and summarized in a reasonable manner; and

- Whether the financial statements reflect the underlying events and transactions in a manner that presents the statements within limits that are reasonable and practicable to attain in financial statements.[20]

The preceding discussions of an overview of auditing standards and their integration with related accounting standards indicate the need for a framework of acceptable guidelines in order to meet the demand for financial accounting information. Particularly important is the judgment and discretion of management and the independent auditors. Management's involvement in the application of acceptable accounting standards and the auditors' attestation of their financial judgments enhances the usefulness of the financial statements. More important, it is incumbent upon the audit committee to understand the causes or reasons for the auditors' inability to express an unqualified opinion on the financial statements.

Whereas the preceding discussion focuses on the basic framework of auditing standards and the relationship to accounting standards, Exhibit 5.2 is a summary of the more significant auditing standards and related topical areas of interest to audit committees.

ATTESTATION ENGAGEMENTS

In addition to the generally accepted auditing standards associated with the annual audit of financial statements, the Auditing Standards Board and the Accounting and Review Services Committee have issued a codification of four statements on Standards for Attestation Engagements (SSAE) and two SSAEs in response to the banking reform legislation (FDICIA). The basic framework for these standards is shown in Exhibit 5.3. The auditor's responsibility for attestation engagements with respect to special reports, reviews, and agreed-upon procedures is discussed in Chapter 13.

Exhibit 5.4 lists the attestation standards and related topical areas of concern to audit committees. The reader may wish to consult other AICPA statements such as *Statements on Standards for Accounting and Review Services, Statements*

---

[20]Ibid., par. 4. With respect to current Securities and Exchange initiatives dealing with such matters as materiality, revenue recognition, in-process research and development, reserves, and audit adjustments, the reader should visit Chairman Arthur Levitt's speech http://www.sec.gov/news/speeches/spch220.txt.

Exhibit 5.2   Summary of Significant Auditing Standards

Auditing Pronouncements	Topical Area
Statements on Auditing Standards:	
No. 12, "Inquiry of a Client's Lawyer Concerning Litigation, Claims, and Assessments"	Accounting for contingencies (See SFAS No. 5 and Interpretation No. 14)
No. 22, "Planning and Supervision"	Audit plans and execution
No. 31, "Evidential Matter"	Management's assertions
No. 45, "Omnibus Statement on Auditing Standards—1983	Related party disclosures (see SFAS No. 57)
No. 47, "Audit Risk and Materiality in Conducting an Audit"	Inherent and control risks (see SFAC No. 2)
No. 50, "Reports on the Application of Accounting Principles"	Other auditors' opinions
No. 54, "Illegal Acts by Clients"	Violations of laws and regulations that have a material direct effect on financial statements
No. 55, "Consideration of the Internal Control Structure in a Financial Statement Audit"	Quality of the control environment and level of control risk
No. 56, "Analytical Procedures"	Analysis and evaluation of financial statement information
No. 57, "Auditing Accounting Estimates"	Reasonableness of estimates
No. 58, "Reports on Audited Financial Statements"	Types of auditor's reports
No. 59, "The Auditor's Consideration of an Entity's Ability to Continue as a Going Concern"	Violation of the going-concern assumption
No. 60, "Communication of Control-Structure Related Matters Noted in an Audit"	Reportable conditions (deficiencies in the internal control structure) as noted in the management letter
No. 61, "Communication with Audit Committees"	Selection of significant accounting policies and discussion of the auditor's disagreement with management
No. 62, "Special Reports"	Attestation of other historical financial information
No. 65, "The Auditor's Consideration of the Internal Audit Function in an Audit of Financial Statements"	Internal control and the quality of the internal audit function
No. 71, "Interim Financial Information"	Quarterly reports—SEC 10-Q reports (see APB No. 28)
No. 72, "Letters for Underwriters and Certain Other Requesting Parties"	
(See also SAS No. 76 and No. 86 for amendments.)	Comfort letters to investment banking firms

Exhibit 5.2 Summary of Significant Auditing Standards (*Continued*)

Auditing Pronouncements	Topical Area
No. 73, "Using the Work of a Specialist"	Expert opinions (e.g., environmental liabilities)
No. 75, "Engagements to Apply Agreed-upon Procedures to Specified Elements, Accounts, or Items of a Financial Statement"	Specified users agree with the CPAs on the application of agreed-upon procedures to specified elements of financial statements
No. 78, "Consideration of Internal Control in a Financial Statement Audit: An Amendment to SAS No. 55"	Revises the definition and description of internal control
No. 79, "Amendment to SAS No. 58, Reports on Audited Financial Statements"	Eliminated the requirement that auditors modify their reports for a significant uncertainty
No. 82, "Consideration of Fraud in a Financial Statement Audit"	Assessing the risk of material misstatement of the financial statements
No. 83, "Establishing an Understanding with the Client"	Communicates the objectives of the engagement, responsibilities of management and the auditors, and any limitations of the engagement
No. 84, "Communications Between Predecessor and Successor Auditors"	Auditor changes (SEC 8-K Report)
No. 85, "Management Representations"	Audit evidence acknowledging management's responsibility for the financial statements
No. 87, "Restricting the Use of an Auditor's Report"	Auditor's reports intended only for use by certain parties

Note: The Auditing Standards Board has rescinded SAS No. 21 "Segment Information." The Board's Audit Issues Task Force has issued an interpretation "Applying Audit Procedures to Segment Disclosures in Financial Statements" of SAS No. 31, "Evidential Matter." Also see SAS No. 86, "Amendment to SAS No. 72, Letters for Underwriters and Certain Other Requesting Parties."

on Standards for Management Consulting Services, Statements on Quality Control Standards, Standards for Performing and Reporting on Quality Reviews, Statements on Responsibilities in Tax Practices, and *Statements on Standards for Accountants' Services on Prospective Financial Information.*

Exhibit 5.3   Standards for Attestation Engagements

General Standards

1. The engagement shall be performed by a practitioner or practitioners having adequate technical training and proficiency in the attest function.
2. The engagement shall be performed by a practitioner or practitioners having adequate knowledge in the subject matter of the assertion.
3. The practitioner shall perform an engagement only if he or she has reason to believe that the following two conditions exist:
   • The assertion is capable of evaluation against reasonable criteria that either have been established by a recognized body or are stated in the presentation of the assertion in a sufficiently clear and comprehensive manner for a knowledgeable reader to be able to understand them.
   • The assertion is capable of reasonably consistent estimation or measurement using such criteria.
4. In all matters relating to the engagement, an independence in mental attitude shall be maintained by the practitioner or practitioners.
5. Due professional care shall be exercised in the performance of the engagement.

Standards of Fieldwork

1. The work shall be adequately planned and assistants, if any, shall be properly supervised.
2. Sufficient evidence shall be obtained to provide a reasonable basis for the conclusion that is expressed in the report.

Standards of Reporting

1. The report shall identify the assertion being reported on and state the character of the engagement.
2. The report shall state the practitioner's conclusion about whether the assertion is presented in conformity with the established or stated criteria against which it was measured.
3. The report shall state all of the practitioner's significant reservations about the engagement and the presentation of the assertion.
4. The report on an engagement to evaluate an assertion that has been prepared in conformity with agreed-upon criteria or on an engagement to apply agreed-upon procedures should contain a statement limiting its use to the parties who have agreed upon such criteria or procedures.

Source: Statement on Standards for Attestation Engagements, "Attestation Standards" (New York: American Institute of Certified Public Accountants, 1986), pp. 3–4. Reprinted with permission. Copyright 1986 by The American Institute of Certified Public Accountants, Inc.

Exhibit 5.4 Summary of Significant Standards for Attestation Engagements

Statements on Standards for Attestation Engagements:		Topical Area
Codification of SSAE No. 1	"Attestation Standards"	Framework for attestation engagements
Codification of SSAE No. 1	"Attest Services Related to MAS Engagements"	Part of a management advisory services engagement
Codification of SSAE No. 1	"Statements on Standards for Accountants' Services on Prospective Financial Information, Financial Information, Financial Forecasts and Projections"	Financial information about the company's expected financial position, results of operations, and cash flows
Codification of SSAE No. 1	"Reporting on Pro Forma Financial Information"	Pro forma adjustments derived from audited or unaudited historical financial statements
SSAE No. 2	"Reporting on an Entity's Internal Control Structure over Financial Reporting"	Management's assertion about the effectiveness of internal control environment
SSAE No. 3	"Compliance Attestation"	Management's assertion on compliance with specified laws and regulations
SSAE No. 4	"Agreed-upon Procedures Engagements"	Used for engagements other than SAS No. 75 engagements
SSAE No. 5	"Amendment to SSAE No. 1"	Working papers
SSAE No. 6	"Reporting on an Entity's Internal Control Over Financial Reporting: An Amendment to SSAE No. 2"	Internal control
SSAE No. 7	"Establishing an Understanding with the Client"	Communicates the objectives of the engagement
SSAE No. 8	"Management's Discussion and Analysis"	Disclosure and compliance with SEC rules

Exhibit 5.5   International Auditing Pronouncements*

International Standards on Auditing

AU   International Standards on Auditing—Introduction
AU 8000   International Standards on Auditing
           8100—Preface to International Standards on Auditing and Related Services
           8110—Glossary of Terms
           8120—Framework of International Standards on Auditing
           8200—Objective and General Principles Governing on Audit of Financial Statements
           8210—Terms of Audit Engagements
           8220—Quality Control for Audit Work
           8230—Documentation
           8240—Fraud and Error
           8250—Consideration of Laws and Regulations in an Audit of Financial Statements
           8300—Planning
           8310—Knowledge of the Business
           8320—Audit Materiality
           8400—Risk Assessments and Internal Control
           8401—Auditing in a Computer Information Systems Environment
           8402—Audit Considerations Relating to Entities Using Service Organizations
           8500—Audit Evidence
           8501—Audit Evidence—Additional Considerations for Specific Items
           8510—Initial Engagements—Opening Balances
           8520—Analytical Procedures
           8530—Audit Sampling
           8540—Audit of Accounting Estimates
           8550—Related Parties
           8560—Subsequent Events
           8570—Going Concern
           8580—Management Representations
           8600—Using the Work of Another Auditor
           8610—Considering the Work of Internal Auditing
           8620—Using the Work of an Expert
           8700—The Auditor's Report on Financial Statements
           8710—Comparatives
           8720—Other Information in Documents Containing Audited Financial Statements
           8800—The Auditor's Report on Special Purpose Audit Engagements
           8810—The Examination of Prospective Financial Information
           8910—Engagements to Review Financial Statements
           8920—Engagements to Perform Agreed-upon Procedures Regarding Financial Information
           8930—Engagements to Compile Financial Information

International Auditing Practice Statements

AU 10,000   International Auditing Practice Statements

                10,001—Inter-Bank Confirmation Procedures

                10,010—CIS Environments—Stand-Alone Microcomputers

                10,020—CIS Environments—On-Line Computer Systems

                10,030—CIS Environments—Database Systems

                10,040—The Relationship Between Bank Supervisors and External Auditors

                10,050—Particular Considerations in the Audit of Small Businesses

                10,060—The Audit of International Commercial Banks

                10,070—Communications With Management

                10,080—Risk Assessments and Internal Control—CIS Characteristics and Considerations

                10,090—Computer-Assisted Audit Techniques

                10,100—The Consideration of Environmental Matters in the Audit of Financial Statements

Source: Reprinted with permission from the American Institute of Certified Public Accountants, *Professional Standards International Auditing,* Vol. 2 (Copyright © 1998 by the AICPA).

INTERNATIONAL AUDITING STANDARDS

Recognizing that there is a movement toward the "globalization" of the world's securities markets, the International Organization of Securities Commission (IOSCO)[21] has been working with the International Accounting Standards Committee (IASC)[22] and the International Federation of Accountants (IFAC) to develop harmonized accounting and auditing standards. The objective of the initiatives is to enable a company that has complied with these international standards in its equity securities offering documents, to raise capital in a global capital marketplace.

In response to the demand for international auditing standards, the IFAC established an International Auditing Practice Committee (IAPC). This committee has issued a number of pronouncements and related statements, as shown in Exhibit 5.5. Although such standards are adopted on a voluntary basis, the goal of these international organizations and committees is to foster harmonized standards on an international basis. Given the audit committee's oversight responsibility for financial reporting, these standards may have an impact on companies at home and abroad. More recently, the IAPC proposed to issue an International

[21] International Federation of Accountants, *1992 Annual Report,* p. 3.

[22] See American Institute of Certified Public Accountants, *Professional Standards,* Vol. 2, Sec. AC 9000 for the International Accounting Standards, New York, June 1, 1998.

Standard In Auditing (ISA) entitled "Communications to Those Charged with Governance." In short, the IAPC indicated that such an ISA is needed for the following reasons:

> It recognizes the need to provide standards and guidance on the auditor's responsibility to communicate matters of governance interest, arising from the audit of financial statements, to those charged with governance of an entity. Although the structures of governance vary from country to country reflecting cultural and legal background, in many jurisdictions the auditor is required to communicate matters of governance interest, arising from the audit of financial statements, to those charged with governance of an entity. Furthermore, the communication of these matters is part of a mechanism by which the external auditors can add value to the role of those responsible for the governance of the entity.[23]

Thus the IAPC has recognized the benefits of a corporate governance approach to the audit process as a requisite for harmonizing the international accounting and auditing standards. Recall from the discussion in Chapter 2 that the Public Oversight Board has argued that the auditing profession shift its focus from a compliance and rule-oriented audit to a corporate governance approach. (See that Exposure Draft for further discussion of such matters as governance interests, timing of communication, forms of communications, and other matters.)

SOURCES AND SUGGESTED READINGS

American Institute of Certified Public Accountants, *Professional Standards, International Auditing,* Vol. 2 (New York: American Institute of Certified Public Accountants, 1998).

American Institute of Certified Public Accountants, *Professional Standards, U.S. Auditing Standards/Attestation Standards,* Vol. 1 (New York: American Institute of Certified Public Accountants, 1998).

American Institute of Certified Public Accountants, *Rules of Conduct of the Code of Professional Ethics* (New York: American Institute of Certified Public Accountants, 1997).

Financial Accounting Standards Board, *Statement of Financial Accounting Concepts No. 2,* "Qualitative Characteristics of Accounting Information" (Stamford, Conn.: Financial Accounting Standards Board, 1980).

Financial Accounting Standards Board, *Statement of Financial Accounting Concepts No. 5,* "Recognition and Measurement in Financial Statements of Business Enterprises" (Stamford, Conn.: Financial Accounting Standards Board, 1984).

International Auditing Practices Committee, "Communications to Those Charged with Governance," Exposure Draft (New York: International Federation of Accountants, 1998).

---

[23] International Auditing Practices Committee, "Communications to Those Charged with Governance," Exposure Draft (New York: International Federation of Accountants, August 1998), pp. 2–3.

International Federation of Accountants, *1992 Annual Report* (New York: International Federation of Accountants, 1992).

Opinions of the Accounting Principles Board, No. 20, "Accounting Changes" (New York: American Institute of Certified Public Accountants, 1971).

Opinions of Accounting Principles Board No. 22, "Disclosure of Accounting Policies" (New York: American Institute of Certified Public Accountants, 1972.

Statement of the Accounting Principles Board, No. 4, "Basic Concepts and Accounting Principles Underlying Financial Statements of Business Enterprises" (New York: American Institute of Certified Public Accountants, 1970).

Statement on Auditing Standards No. 22, "Planning and Supervision" (New York: American Institute of Certified Public Accountants, 1978).

Statement on Auditing Standards No. 69, "The Meaning of Present Fairly in Conformity with Generally Accepted Accounting Principles in the Independent Auditor's Report" (New York: American Institute of Certified Public Accountants, 1992).

Statement on Standards of Attestation Engagements, "Attestation Standards" (New York: American Institute of Certified Public Accountants, 1986).

Part Two

The Planning Function of the Audit Committee

Chapter 6

An Overview of Audit Planning

The auditing needs and goals of the enterprise are dynamic since they change as the responsibilities of the corporate directors become more complex. Thus the demands on the quality and quantity of auditing services change. To achieve an effective and efficient auditing process, audit planning is essential to meet the fluctuating auditing needs of the enterprise.

Since the audit directors have an oversight responsibility for the overall audit plan, it is essential that they understand not only the purpose of audit planning but also its usefulness in ensuring an effective and efficient auditing process. Although the process of audit planning is an amalgamation of the internal managerial talents as well as the external auditing talents, the audit committee should review the overall audit plan and recommend it to the board of directors for its approval.[1] Therefore, the purpose of this chapter is to introduce the meaning and benefits of audit planning and the broad segments of the overall audit plan. The role of the audit directors in overseeing the entity's audit plan is discussed in Chapter 7.

MEANING OF AUDIT PLANNING

As discussed in the preceding chapter, adequate audit planning is one of the tenets of the generally accepted auditing standards of field work. To indicate its significance, the Auditing Standards Executive Committee's definition is restated:

> Audit planning involves developing an overall strategy for the expected conduct and scope of the examination. The nature, extent, and timing of planning vary with the

---

[1] Such board approval is desirable in order to establish a formal corporate audit policy statement in accordance with the charter for the audit committee.

size and complexity of the entity, experience with the entity, and knowledge of the entity's business.[2]

Furthermore, " 'materiality' and 'audit risk' underlie the application of all the standards, particularly the standards of field work and reporting."[3] Thus implicit in the auditors' planning efforts is their concern with particular financial accounts and locations, such as subsidiaries or divisions that are subject to a high exposure of risk. For example, since "cash transactions are more susceptible to fraud than inventories," the audit work should be "more conclusive."[4] Moreover, the quality of the system of internal control is important because "of the influence on auditing procedures of a greater or lesser degree of misstatement; i.e., the more effective the internal control, the less degree of control risk."[5] The AICPA Control Risk Audit Guide Revision Task Force has summarized some examples of both inherent and control risk attributes that the auditor might consider and the audit decisions that might be affected in Exhibit 6.1. See Chapter 8.

Although the preceding definition of audit planning applies to the independent auditors, it correlates closely with the audit committee's planning efforts. An analysis of the definition will be useful to the audit directors regarding their responsibilities in the audit planning function.

ANALYSIS OF AUDIT PLANNING AND THE COMMITTEE

Overview of the Audit Committee's Strategy[6]

To review the entity's audit plan effectively, the audit directors need their own plan of action. Their plan should be integrated with the annual auditing cycle, which consists of the following: (1) initial planning segment, (2) preaudit segment, and (3) postaudit segment. Thus they will engage in audit planning at several different times during the auditing cycle. The typical steps in the auditing cycle are illustrated in Exhibit 6.2.

---

[2] *Statement on Auditing Standards, No. 22,* "Planning and Supervision" (New York: American Institute of Certified Public Accountants, 1978), par. 3.

[3] American Institute of Certified Public Accountants, Professional Standards, *U.S. Auditing Standards/ Attestation Standards,* Vol. 1 (New York: American Institute of Certified Public Accountants, 1998), AU Sec. 150.03.

[4] Ibid., AU Sec. 150.05.

[5] Ibid., AU Sec. 150.05.

[6] The reader may wish to review the list of auditing pronouncements mentioned in Chapter 5. For example, SAS Nos. 22, 47, 84, and 50 are all relative to the initial planning segment and SAS Nos. 22, 45, 47, 55, 56, 60, 73, and 61 are applicable to the preaudit segment. Of course, the audit committee should review and discuss the engagement letter with the independent auditors.

Exhibit 6.1 Illustration of the Audit Risk Concept

	Example Attributes Considered by the Auditor		Responses by the Auditor
	Inherent Risk	Control Risk	Detection Risk
Matters Pervasive to Many Account Balances or Transaction Classes	• Profitability relative to the industry • Sensitivity of operating results to economic factors • Going concern problems • Nature, cause, and number of known and likely misstatements detected in the prior audit • Management turnover • Management reputation • Management accounting skills	• Business planning, budgeting, and monitoring of performance • Management attitude and actions regarding financial reporting • Management consultation with auditors • Management concern about external influences • Audit committee • Internal audit function • Personnel policies and practices	• Overall audit strategy • Number of locations • Significant balances or transaction classes • Degree of professional skepticism • Staffing • Levels of supervision and review
Matters Pertaining to Specific Account Balances or Transaction Classes	• Difficult to audit accounts or transactions • Contentious or difficult accounting issues • Susceptibility to misappropriation • Complexity of calculations • Extent of judgment related to assertions • Sensitivity of valuations to economic factors • Nature, cause, and number of known and likely misstatements detected in the prior audit	• Effectiveness of the accounting system • Personnel policies and practices • Adequacy of accounting records • Segregation of duties • Adequacy of safeguards over assets and records (including software)	• Substantive analytical procedures and tests of details • Nature of tests • Timing of tests • Extent of tests

Auditors consider the types of factors presented above; however, it is not necessary to categorize such factors by type of risk.

Source: AICPA, *Audit Guide for Consideration of Internal Control in a Financial Statement Audit* (1996), p. 223. Reprinted with permission from the American Institute of Certified Public Accountants, Inc.

Exhibit 6.2 Example: Auditing Cycle

Example: Auditing Cycle (12/31/98 year end)

	Pre-Audit Meeting *(May or June)*	Audit scope
	Interim Audit Meeting *(October or November)*	Audit progress
Completion of field work January 20, 1999	**Post-Audit Meeting** *(early February)*	Review/approve drafts of 10-K annual report
March 15, 1999 Date of annual meeting and proxy statements	**Follow-up Meeting** *(late February or early March)* *(Hold prior to mailing proxy solicitation materials.)*	Recommendations in management letter

For example, during the preaudit segment, James K. Loebbecke, former partner of Touche Ross (now Deloitte & Touche), points out:

> Experience suggests . . . that both auditors and their clients—either management and/or audit committee members—should formally discuss not only the auditor's general methodology but also his specific approach in the client's own situation. This, indeed, should be a regular and early part of every audit examination.[7]

[7]James K. Loebbecke, "Audit Planning and Company Assistance," *CPA Journal* 47, No. 11 (November 1977), p. 34. Also see Douglas R. Carmichael, "The Annual Audit Tune-up," *CPA Journal* 67, No. 12 (December 1997), pp. 24–29. More recently, independent accounting firms have developed a new approach to the annual audit engagement in order to provide more value by identifying performance improvement opportunities for clients. For example, KPMG Peat Marwick (1995) has developed a Business Measurement Process for identifying and assessing the client's business risk through the audit process.

This process has drawn the attention of CEOs and audit committee members. In particular, Kathryn D. Wriston responds to the question of what the board of directors and its audit committee expect and concludes: "The financial vitality of the organization and its long-term strategies to enhance shareholder value includes an assessment of various risks the company faces. Audit involvement in these areas has struck me as being potentially very beneficial to directors" (p. 18). See Kathryn Wriston, "The CPA Journal Symposium on the Future of Assurance Services," *CPA Journal* 66, No. 5 (May 1996), pp. 15–18.

Arthur Andersen (1995) has developed an integrated business risk control strategy to help both audit and nonaudit clients benchmark and evaluate their processes. Auditors explicitly address certain business risks in a financial statement audit. For example, environmental risks, such as legal and regulatory risks, are addressed in the annual audit, whereas competitor and sovereign/political risks are not addressed by the auditors. For further discussion, see KPMG Peat Marwick, *Business Measurement Process* (New York: Montvale, NJ: KPMG Peat Marwick, 1995); Arthur Andersen, *Managing Business Risks* (Chicago, IL: Arthur Andersen, 1995; Pricewaterhouse Coopers, *ABAS Audit Approach Team Asset* (New York: Pricewaterhouse Coopers, 1999).

In SAS No. 61, the Auditing Standards Board stated, "This statement requires the auditor to ensure that the audit committee receives additional information regarding the scope and results of the audit that may assist the audit committee in overseeing the financial reporting and disclosure process for which management is responsible."[8] For example, the independent auditors will discuss such matters as the audit approach and related threshold of materiality and levels of audit risk, anticipated changes in accounting policies and new accounting pronouncements, and special areas that need attention.

With respect to audit risk, the independent auditors attempt to minimize the risk that they have possibly issued an unqualified auditor's report with respect to financial statements that are materially misstated. In addition to following the guidance in SAS No. 47, "Audit Risk and Materiality" in conducting an audit, the auditors have to be aware of intentional misstatements or omissions of information in the financial statements. To assist them in this area of audit risk, the Auditing Standards Board has issued SAS No. 82, "Consideration of Fraud in a Financial Statement Audit." The Board has identified warning signals or "red flags" for the auditors in assessing the risk of materially misstated financial statements due to fraud. The fraud risk factors considered in assessing this type of risk during the planning phase and other conditions that may indicate evidence of fraud during the audit are presented in Exhibits 6.3, 6.4, and 6.5.[9]

In addition to the guidance for the independent auditor's assessment of audit risk, the Auditing Standards Board has issued SAS No. 56, "Analytical Procedures." This statement "requires the use of analytical procedures in the planning and overall review stages of all audits."[10] The Board states that:

> Analytical procedures involve comparisons of recorded amounts, or ratios developed from recorded amounts, to expectations developed by the auditor. The auditor develops such expectations by identifying and using plausible relationships that are reasonably expected to exist based on the auditor's understanding of the client and of the industry in which the client operates. Following are examples of sources of information for developing expectations:
>
>> Financial information for comparable prior period(s) giving consideration to known changes
>>
>> Anticipated results—for example, budgets, or forecasts including extrapolations from interim or annual data

---

[8] *Statement on Auditing Standards, No. 61,* "Communication with Audit Committees" (New York: American Institute of Certified Public Accountants, 1988), par. 2.

[9] For a further discussion of fraud risk factors, see Howard Groveman, "How Auditors Can Detect Financial Statement Misstatement," *Journal of Accountancy* 180, No. 4 (October 1995), pp. 83–86; Vicky B. Heiman-Hoffman, Kimberly P. Morgan, and James M. Patton, "The Warning Signs of Fraudulent Financial Reporting," *Journal of Accounting* 182, No. 10 (October 1996), pp. 75–77.

[10] *Statement on Auditing Standards, No. 56,* "Analytical Procedures" (New York: American Institute of Certified Public Accountants, 1988), par. 1.

Exhibit 6.3   Risk Factors Relating to Misstatements Arising from Fraudulent Financial Reporting

Risk factors that relate to misstatements arising from fraudulent financial reporting may be grouped in the following three categories:

a. *Management's characteristics and influence over the control environment.* These pertain to management's abilities, pressures, style, and attitude relating to internal control and the financial reporting process.

b. *Industry conditions.* These involve the economic and regulatory environment in which the entity operates.

c. *Operating characteristics and financial stability.* These pertain to the nature and complexity of the entity and its transactions, the entity's financial condition, and its profitability.

The following are examples of risk factors relating to misstatements arising from fraudulent financial reporting for each of the three categories described above:

a. *Risk factors relating to management's characteristics and influence over the control environment.* Examples include—
  - A motivation for management to engage in fraudulent financial reporting. Specific indicators might include—
    —A significant portion of management's compensation represented by bonuses, stock options, or other incentives, the value of which is contingent upon the entity achieving unduly aggressive targets for operating results, financial position, or cash flow.
    —An excessive interest by management in maintaining or increasing the entity's stock price or earnings trend through the use of unusually aggressive accounting practices.
    —A practice by management of committing to analysts, creditors, and other third parties to achieve what appear to be unduly aggressive or clearly unrealistic forecasts.
    —An interest by management in pursuing inappropriate means to minimize reported earnings for tax-motivated reasons.
  - A failure by management to display and communicate an appropriate attitude regarding internal control and the financial reporting process. Specific indicators might include—
    —An ineffective means of communicating and supporting the entity's values or ethics, or communication of inappropriate values or ethics.
    —Domination of management by a single person or small group without compensating controls such as effective oversight by the board of directors or audit committee.
    —Inadequate monitoring of significant controls.
    —Management failing to correct known reportable conditions on a timely basis.
    —Management setting unduly aggressive financial targets and expectations for operating personnel.
    —Management displaying a significant disregard for regulatory authorities.

Exhibit 6.3 *(Continued)*

    —Management continuing to employ an ineffective accounting, information technology, or internal auditing staff.

- Nonfinancial management's excessive participation in, or preoccupation with, the selection of accounting principles or the determination of significant estimates.
- High turnover of senior management, counsel, or board members.
- Strained relationship between management and the current or predecessor auditor. Specific indicators might include—
  - —Frequent disputes with the current or predecessor auditor on accounting, auditing, or reporting matters.
  - —Unreasonable demands on the auditor including unreasonable time constraints regarding the completion of the audit or the issuance of the auditor's reports.
  - —Formal or informal restrictions on the auditor that inappropriately limit his or her access to people or information or his or her ability to communicate effectively with the board of directors or the audit committee.
  - —Domineering management behavior in dealing with the auditor, especially involving attempts to influence the scope of the auditor's work.
- Known history of securities law violations or claims against the entity or its senior management alleging fraud or violations of securities laws.

b. *Risk factors relating to industry conditions.* Examples include—
- New accounting, statutory, or regulatory requirements that could impair the financial stability or profitability of the entity.
- High degree of competition or market saturation, accompanied by declining margins.
- Declining industry with increasing business failures and significant declines in customer demand.
- Rapid changes in the industry, such as high vulnerability to rapidly changing technology or rapid product obsolescence.

c. *Risk factors relating to operating characteristics and financial stability.* Examples include—
- Inability to generate cash flows from operations while reporting earnings and earnings growth.
- Significant pressure to obtain additional capital necessary to stay competitive considering the financial position of the entity—including need for funds to finance major research and development or capital expenditures.
- Assets, liabilities, revenues, or expenses based on significant estimates that involve unusually subjective judgments or uncertainties, or that are subject to potential significant change in the near term in a manner that may have a financially disruptive effect on the entity—such as ultimate collectibility of receivables, timing of revenue recognition, realizability of financial instruments based on the highly subjective valuation of collateral or difficult-to-assess repayment sources, or significant deferral of costs.
- Significant related-party transactions not in the ordinary course of business or with related entities not audited or audited by another firm.

Exhibit 6.3 (*Continued*)

- Significant, unusual, or highly complex transactions, especially those close to year end, that pose difficult "substance over form" questions.
- Significant bank accounts or subsidiary or branch operations in tax-haven jurisdictions for which there appears to be no clear business justification.
- Overly complex organizational structure involving numerous or unusual legal entities, managerial lines of authority, or contractual arrangements without apparent business purpose.
- Difficulty in determining the organization or individual(s) that control(s) the entity.
- Unusually rapid growth or profitability, especially compared with that of other companies in the same industry.
- Especially high vulnerability to changes in interest rates.
- Unusually high dependence on debt or marginal ability to meet debt repayment requirements; debt covenants that are difficult to maintain.
- Unrealistically aggressive sales or profitability incentive programs.
- Threat of imminent bankruptcy or foreclosure, or hostile takeover.
- Adverse consequences on significant pending transactions, such as a business combination or contract award, if poor financial results are reported.
- Poor or deteriorating financial position when management has personally guaranteed significant debts of the entity.

Source: Reprinted with permission from *Statement on Auditing Standards No. 82,* "Consideration of Fraud in a Financial Statement Audit" (New York: American Institute of Certified Public Accountants, 1997), pars. 16, 17.

Relationships among elements of financial information within the period

Information regarding the industry in which the client operates—for example, gross margin information

Relationships of financial information with relevant nonfinancial information[11]

Given the accrued benefits from the use of analytical procedures by independent auditors, the results of comparative financial statement balances and financial ratios should alert the audit committee to high-risk areas that may have a significant impact on the financial statements. Recall the discussion in Chapter 4 with respect to "cooked books" and "cute accounting," which produce fraudulent financial statements. For example, the audit committee should be alert to im-

---

[11] Ibid., par. 5. Also see Patrick S. Callahan, Henry R. Jaenicke, and Donald L. Neebes, "SAS 56 and 57: Increasing Audit Effectiveness," *Journal of Accountancy* 165, No. 10 (October 1988), pp. 56–68; and Walter K. Kunitake, Andrew D. Luzi, and William G. Glezen, "Analytical Review in Audit and Review Engagements," *CPA Journal* 55, No. 4, (April 1985), pp. 18–26.

Exhibit 6.4   Risk Factors Relating to Misstatements Arising From Misappropriation of Assets

Risk factors that relate to misstatements arising from misappropriation of assets may be grouped in the two categories below. The extent of the auditor's consideration of the risk factors in category *b* is influenced by the degree to which risk factors in category *a* are present.

a.   *Susceptibility of assets to misappropriation.* These pertain to the nature of an entity's assets and the degree to which they are subject to theft.

b.   *Controls.* These involve the lack of controls designed to prevent or detect misappropriations of assets.

The following are examples of risk factors relating to misstatements arising from misappropriation of assets for each of the two categories described above:

a.   *Risk factors relating to susceptibility of assets to misappropriation*
   • Large amounts of cash on hand or processed
   • Inventory characteristics, such as small size, high value, or high demand
   • Easily convertible assets, such as bearer bonds, diamonds, or computer chips
   • Fixed asset characteristics, such as small size, marketability, or lack of ownership identification

b.   *Risk factors relating to controls*
   • Lack of appropriate management oversight (for example, inadequate supervision or monitoring of remote locations)
   • Lack of job applicant screening procedures relating to employees with access to assets susceptible to misappropriation
   • Inadequate recordkeeping with respect to assets susceptible to misappropriation
   • Lack of appropriate segregation of duties or independent checks
   • Lack of appropriate system of authorization and approval of transactions (for example, in purchasing)
   • Poor physical safeguards over cash, investments, inventory, or fixed assets
   • Lack of timely and appropriate documentation for transactions (for example, credits for merchandise returns)
   • Lack of mandatory vacations for employees performing key control functions

Source: Reprinted with permission from *Statement on Auditing Standards No. 82,* "Consideration of Fraud in a Financial Statement Audit." Copyright © 1997 by The American Institute of Certified Public Accountants, Inc.

proper revenue recognition methods, such as a "bill and hold" arrangement between the company and a customer. Here the company records a sale that increases earnings, but the customer is not obligated to take delivery of the products.[12]

[12] For additional reading, see *SEC v. Barry J. Minkow, Litigation Release* No. 12579 (August 15, 1990), 46 SEC Docket 1777, and *SEC v. Donald D. Sheelen et al., Accounting and Auditing Enforcement Release No. 215* (February 8, 1989), 42 SEC Docket 1562.

Exhibit 6.5   Other Fraud Conditions That May be Identified During the
Audit Engagement

The assessment of the risk of material misstatement due to fraud is a cumulative process
that includes a consideration of risk factors individually and in combination. In addition,
fraud risk factors may be identified while performing procedures relating to acceptance or
continuance of clients and engagements, during engagement planning or while obtaining
an understanding of an entity's internal control, or while conducting fieldwork. Also,
other conditions may be identified during fieldwork that change or support a judgment
regarding the assessment—such as the following:

- *Discrepancies in the accounting records,* including—
  - —Transactions not recorded in a complete or timely manner or improperly recorded
    as to amount, accounting period, classification, or entity policy.
  - —Unsupported or unauthorized balances or transactions.
  - —Last-minute adjustments by the entity that significantly affect financial results.

- *Conflicting or missing evidential matter,* including—
  - —Missing documents.
  - —Unavailability of other than photocopied documents when documents in original
    form are expected to exist.
  - —Significant unexplained items on reconciliations.
  - —Inconsistent, vague, or implausible responses from management or employees
    arising from inquiries or analytical procedures.
  - —Unusual discrepancies between the entity's records and confirmation replies.
  - —Missing inventory or physical assets of significant magnitude.

- *Problematic or unusual relationships between the auditor and client,* including—
  - —Denied access to records, facilities, certain employees, customers, vendors, or
    others from whom audit evidence might be sought.
  - —Undue time pressures imposed by management to resolve complex or contentious
    issues.
  - —Unusual delays by the entity in providing requested information.
  - —Tips or complaints to the auditor about fraud.

Source: Reprinted with permission from *Statement on Auditing Standards, No. 82,* "Consideration of
Fraud in a Financial Statement Audit." Copyright © 1997 by the American Institute of Certified Public Accountants, Inc.

Furthermore, the audit directors will be discussing other aspects of the audit
with the senior management representatives, for example, the chief financial officer and the director of internal auditing. Thus the overall planning strategy of the
directors will be based on their conference with these parties.

More specifically, the following steps provide a framework for the committee's strategy:

1. *Develop an understanding of the entity's business and its industry.*[13] This step is particularly important because the audit committee should understand the external and internal environment within which the entity must operate. Such an understanding of the environmental characteristics will provide all members of the committee with the knowledge to effectively assess the overall audit plan. To accomplish this step, the audit directors should develop a macroapproach supplemented with the suggested professional development course as discussed in Chapter 7.

2. *Review the following with respect to each segment of the corporate audit plan as discussed in the succeeding section of this chapter:*
   a. Purpose and objectives of each audit plan
   b. Resources available for each plan

   Based on their discussions with the independent auditors, the director of internal auditing, and other senior management officers, the audit directors should be familiar with the overall purpose and objectives of each audit segment of the total corporate audit plan. Of particular importance to the committee is assurance of a coordinated plan consistent with the overall auditing goals of the organization. Such assurance may be obtained through a well defined and documented general statement of auditing objectives. Subsequent to the committee's review, the audit objectives and any other relevant information should be formalized into a written corporate document. This corporate document, along with the audit committee's recommendations, should be presented to the board of directors for its approval. Such board approval establishes a formal audit policy.

3. *Based on the audit policy, the internal and external auditing groups should develop appropriate audit plans that are consistent with the entity's auditing goals.* Obviously, the audit directors are not responsible for the preparation of the comprehensive corporate audit plan. However, they must assure themselves that the plan is consistent with the organization's policy. Thus the appropriate internal and external auditing plans will be consolidated into the overall corporate audit plan. Subsequent to the committee's review, the corporate audit plan should be formalized into a written document. This particular document will be used as a reference guide for future audits.

---

[13] The AICPA publishes *Audit and Accounting Guides* and *Industry Risk Alerts*. The audit committee may wish to consult these publications (e.g., *Consideration of the Internal Control Structure in a Financial Statement Audit*) to obtain an orientation to the entity's industry. Also see "Know Your Client's Business," by Robert Walker, *CA Magazine* 124, No. 6 (June 1991), pp. 49–52; John P. McAllister and Mark W. Dirsmith, "How the Client's Business Environment Affects the Audit," *Journal of Accountancy* 59, No. 2 (February 1982), pp. 68–74; Donald N. Wolfe and Gerald Smith, "Planning the Audit in a Distressed Industry," *CPA Journal* 58, No. 10 (October 1988), pp. 46–50; and John W. Hardy and Larry A. Deppe, "Client Acceptance: What to Look For and Why," *CPA Journal* 62, No. 5 (May 1992), pp. 20–27.

4. *Review and appraise the corporate audit policy and plan annually.* In order to guard against obsolescence, the audit committee should review and revise the audit policy and plan on a regular periodic basis.

Chapter 7 discusses the preceding steps along with other aspects of the committee's role.

BENEFITS OF AUDIT PLANNING

Assurance of an Effective Audit Plan

Clearly, the audit committee wishes to obtain maximum auditing services at a reasonable cost. William S. Albrecht observes that one large accounting firm reported that its audit fees have increased "over 50 percent in the last four years" and another firm's increased "40 percent."[14] Consequently, a sound corporate audit plan coupled with the committee's auditing strategy enhances the entity's opportunity to minimize audit costs and maximize on auditing services. Audit planning realizes a number of benefits:

1. It facilitates the effective allocation of resources to the audit function.
2. Inherent in the audit planning process is the psychological benefit of inducing the parties involved to think ahead and thus anticipate potential problems or opportunities.
3. Communication and cooperation among the auditing groups and management is enhanced since the audit committee coordinates their efforts toward the goals of the audit.
4. Since the board of directors expects the audit committee to monitor the audit function, audit planning provides assistance to the committee in accomplishing its task.

---

[14] William S. Albrecht, "Toward Better and More Efficient Audits," *Journal of Accountancy* 144, No. 6 (December 1977), p. 48. With respect to audit costs, "The audit committee should consider whether, and the extent to which, the actual costs of an audit exceed the estimated costs. When cost overruns are significant, the committee should seek satisfactory explanations for the variance. The committee might also wish to consider whether the presently engaged auditors have offered suggestions for management action that can reduce audit costs without diminishing audit effectiveness" (p. A-25). See Daniel J. McCauley and John C. Burton, *Audit Committees* 49 (Washington, D.C.: C.P.S., The Bureau of National Affairs, 1986).

Also see Glenn E. Sumners and Barbara Apostolou, "Preparation Can Cut Audit Fees," *Financial Manager* 3, No. 1 (January/February 1990), pp. 46–49. The reader may wish to consult Chapter 4, which discussed the legal position of the audit committee and fraudulent financial reporting.

5. The audit committee can assess the effectiveness of the audits since the preaudit plan can be compared with the actual results of the audits.
6. Through a review of the audit plan, the committee develops confidence in handling problem areas.

Furthermore, the audit committee's review of the overall plan of the audit provides valuable information, such as the following:

- A summary of the company's financial reporting requirements and the timetable for meeting those requirements
- An understanding of the relationship between the company's system of internal accounting control and the scope of the audit
- The effect of accounting and auditing pronouncements and of SEC and other regulatory requirements on the scope of the audit
- The extent to which the external auditor uses the work of internal auditors in establishing the scope of his or her examination
- Changes in the company's organization, operations, or controls that have caused the external auditor to change the scope of his or her examination
- The degree of audit coverage, such as locations to be visited and the extent of procedures such as inventory observation, receivable confirmation, and so on
- The extent to which auditors other than the principal auditor are used
- Any potential problems that might cause the auditor to qualify his or her opinion
- Accounting principles management has selected for new transactions and the auditor's evaluation of those principles[15]

COMPONENTS OF THE CORPORATE AUDIT PLAN

An Overview

The corporate audit plan should be designed to give consideration to the following factors: (1) financial disclosures, (2) operational efficiency, (3) compliance with corporate policies, and (4) compliance with laws. Thus the overall audit plan should include the following:

1. Statement of the proposed year-end and interim financial audits (see Exhibit 6.6).
2. Statement of the proposed operational audits

---

[15] American Institute of Certified Public Accountants, *Audit Committees, Answers to Typical Questions About Their Organization and Operations* (New York: AICPA, 1978), pp. 15–16.

Exhibit 6.6 Types of Government Audits

Purpose	**2.1** This chapter describes the types of audits that government and nongovernment audit organizations conduct and that organizations arrange to have conducted, of government organizations, programs, activities, functions, and funds. This description is not intended to limit or require the types of audits that may be conducted or arranged. In conducting these types of audits, auditors should follow the applicable standards included and incorporated in the chapters which follow.

2.2 All audits begin with objectives, and those objectives determine the type of audit to be conducted and the audit standards to be followed. The types of audits, as defined by their objectives, are classified in these standards as financial audits or performance audits.

2.3 Audits may have a combination of financial and performance audit objectives or may have objectives limited to only some aspects of one audit type. For example, auditors conduct audits of government contracts and grants with private sector organizations, as well as government and nonprofit organizations, that often include both financial and performance objectives. These are commonly referred to as "contract audits" or "grant audits." Other examples of such audits include audits of specific internal controls, compliance issues, and computer-based systems. Auditors should follow the standards that are applicable to the individual objectives of the audit.

Financial Audits

2.4 Financial audits include financial statement and financial related audits.

a. Financial statement audits provide reasonable assurance about whether the financial statements of an audited entity present fairly the financial position, results of operations, and cash flows in conformity with generally accepted accounting principles. Financial statement audits also include audits of financial statements prepared in conformity with any of several other bases of accounting discussed in auditing standards issued by the American Institute of Certified Public Accountants (AICPA).

b. Financial related audits include determining whether (1) financial information is presented in accordance with established or stated criteria, (2) the entity has adhered to specific financial compliance requirements, or (3) the entity's internal control structure over financial reporting and/or safeguarding assets is suitably designed and implemented to achieve the control objectives.

Exhibit 6.6 (*Continued*)

2.5 Financial related audits may, for example, include audits of the following items:

a. Segments of financial statements; financial information (for example, statement of revenue and expenses, statement of cash receipts and disbursements, statement of fixed assets); budget requests; and variances between estimated and actual financial performance.

b. Internal controls over compliance with laws and regulations, such as those governing the (1) bidding for, (2) accounting for, and (3) reporting on grants and contracts (including proposals, amounts billed, amounts due on termination claims, and so forth).

c. Internal controls over financial reporting and/or safeguarding assets, including controls using computer-based systems.

d. Compliance with laws and regulations and allegations of fraud.

Performance Audits

2.6 A performance audit is an objective and systematic examination of evidence for the purpose of providing an independent assessment of the performance of a government organization, program, activity, or function in order to provide information to improve public accountability and facilitate decision-making by parties with responsibility to oversee or initiate corrective action.

2.7 Performance audits include economy and efficiency and program audits.

a. Economy and efficiency audits include determining (1) whether the entity is acquiring, protecting, and using its resources (such as personnel, property, and space) economically and efficiently, (2) the causes of inefficiencies or uneconomical practices, and (3) whether the entity has complied with laws and regulations on matters of economy and efficiency.

b. Program audits include determining (1) the extent to which the desired results or benefits established by the legislature or other authorizing body are being achieved, (2) the effectiveness of organizations, programs, activities, or functions, and (3) whether the entity has complied with significant laws and regulations applicable to the program.

2.8 Economy and efficiency audits may, for example, consider whether the entity

a. is following sound procurement practices;

b. is acquiring the appropriate type, quality, and amount of resources at an appropriate cost;

Exhibit 6.6 (*Continued*)

c. is properly protecting and maintaining its resources;

d. is avoiding duplication of effort by employees and work that serves little or no purpose;

e. is avoiding idleness and overstaffing;

f. is using efficient operating procedures;

g. is using the optimum amount of resources (staff, equipment, and facilities) in producing or delivering the appropriate quantity and quality of goods or services in a timely manner;

h. is complying with requirements of laws and regulations that could significantly affect the acquisition, protection, and use of the entity's resources;

i. has an adequate management control system for measuring, reporting, and monitoring a program's economy and efficiency; and

j. has reported measures of economy and efficiency that are valid and reliable.

2.9 Program audits may, for example

a. assess whether the objectives of a new, or ongoing program are proper, suitable, or relevant;

b. determine the extent to which a program achieves a desired level of program results;

c. assess the effectiveness of the program and/or of individual program components;

d. identify factors inhibiting satisfactory performance;

e. determine whether management has considered alternatives for carrying out the program that might yield desired results more effectively or at a lower cost;

f. determine whether the program complements, duplicates, overlaps, or conflicts with other related programs;

g. identify ways of making programs work better;

h. assess compliance with laws and regulations applicable to the program;

i. assess the adequacy of the management control system for measuring, reporting, and monitoring a program's effectiveness; and

j. determine whether management has reported measures of program effectiveness that are valid and reliable.

Other Activities of an Audit Organization

2.10 Auditors may perform services other than audits. For example, some auditors may

a. assist a legislative body by developing questions for use at hearings,

b. develop methods and approaches to be applied in evaluating a new or a proposed program,

c. forecast potential program outcomes under various assumptions without evaluating current operations, and

d. perform investigative work.

2.11 The head of the audit organization may wish to establish policies applying standards in this statement to its employees performing these and other types of nonaudit work.

Source: Comptroller General of the United States, *Government Auditing Standards 1994 Revision* (Washington, D.C.: U.S. General Accounting Office, 1994), pars. 2.1 to 2.11.

3. Statement of the proposed internal compliance audits
4. Statement on the status of the external compliance audits

To effectively develop these statements, it is necessary to review the essential segments of the overall audit plan. Such a plan should be comprehensive,[16] and thus the following segments provide a useful framework:

- Financial audit segment
- Operational audit segment
- External compliance audit segment
- Internal compliance audit segment

The following discussion elaborates on each type of nongovernment audit within each auditing segment.

Financial Audits   The financial audit is principally concerned with the audit of the entity's financial statements. Such an audit is conducted by the independent auditors who express their opinion on the fairness of the financial statements. As discussed in Chapter 5, the independent auditors conduct their examination in accordance with generally accepted auditing standards and determine whether the financial statements are presented in conformity with generally accepted account-

---

[16]The General Accounting Office has defined its broad auditing framework as shown in Exhibit 6.6.

ing principles. For example, the external auditors will examine the entity's statement of income, balance sheet, statement of cash flows, and the notes to the financial statements. Moreover, the auditors' examination will include a review of the system of internal controls (tests of controls) and substantive testing of transactions and records based on their professional judgment. The independent auditors must plan their audit engagement and document their audit plan. The audit plan in Exhibit 6.7 is an example. Note that the audit plan will vary from company to company; thus it may require expansion or contraction of certain areas in actual practice.[17]

Although the year-end financial audit is associated with the independent accounting firm, management may request interim financial audits from the internal auditing group. For example, management may request an internal financial audit of the financial statements at the end of a specified period, such as a month or quarter of the year. Internal auditors will conduct their examination and express their opinion on the statements. Such statements will be used within the entity, not distributed to the external users of accounting information. Furthermore, the internal auditors may conduct a review of the system of internal control to determine their effectiveness. Also, they may review management's actions toward the protection and security of the entity's assets. Finally, as a result of their financial audit, the internal auditors may be requested to engage in special assignments, such as the implementation of a fraud prevention program involving various branches or warehouse locations.

Operational Audits   This particular type of audit is usually performed by the internal auditing staff. The primary purpose of such an audit is to review and appraise the activities of a certain function of the enterprise. For example, the internal auditors may review the operating efficiency and the effectiveness of the internal controls of a department. Such a review is essentially a service to management since the auditors generally make recommendations for operational improvements. In addition, the internal auditors may be requested not only to evaluate the managerial performance of the individual managers but to implement fraud prevention measures within the organization. Consequently, the internal auditing group is a critically important auditing resource since such a group can serve management on a company-wide basis.

Although operational auditing is associated with the internal auditors, management may request the services of the management advisory staff of the independent accounting firm. This particular arrangement is known as a management audit. For example, management may request an overall review of a particular function, such as purchasing of materials. Obviously, before such professional

---

[17]Exhibit 6.7 is oversimplified and is intended to stress the time budget aspects of the audit plan.

Time Summary Form

Client: _____

Financial Statement Date: _____

	Budgeted Time					
	Asst.	I/C	Mngr.	Ptnr.	Tot.	Assist.
Planning & administration	___	___	___	___	___	___
Internal control structure	___	___	___	___	___	___
Cash	___	___	___	___	___	___
Investments	___	___	___	___	___	___
Receivables	___	___	___	___	___	___
Inventories	___	___	___	___	___	___
Other assets	___	___	___	___	___	___
Property & equipment	___	___	___	___	___	___
Notes & loans payable	___	___	___	___	___	___
Payables & accruals	___	___	___	___	___	___
Income taxes	___	___	___	___	___	___
Other liabilities	___	___	___	___	___	___
Equity	___	___	___	___	___	___
Revenues	___	___	___	___	___	___
Expenses	___	___	___	___	___	___
Commitments, contingencies, & subsequent events	___	___	___	___	___	___
Related parties	___	___	___	___	___	___
Trial balance & adjustments	___	___	___	___	___	___
Supervision & review	___	___	___	___	___	___
Management letter	___	___	___	___	___	___
Report preparation	___	___	___	___	___	___
Totals	___	___	___	___	___	___

*Attach memorandum explaining significant variances.

Source: George Marthinuss and Larry L. Perry, *Comprehensive Engagement Manual*, Vol. 3, Chapter. 11 (New York: American Institute of Certified Public Accountants, 1992), pp. 11–4. Copyright © 1992 by the American Institute of Certified Public Accountants, Inc. Reprinted with permission.

services are requested, management should weigh the costs against the benefits of the audit.

The operational audit plan may be similar to the financial audit plan, however, the functional units of the entity will be substituted for the financial accounts as shown in Exhibit 6.7. Furthermore, the plan should be modified to include nonfinancial matters, such as conflicts of interests.

Compliance Audits   In contrast to operational audits, compliance audits are oriented primarily not only toward internal adherence to managerial policies but toward the entity's compliance with the various rules and regulations of the regulatory agencies. (See Chapter 4.) For example, the internal auditors may be requested to review the policies and procedures with the traffic and transportation department to determine whether their personnel are adhering to the entity's policies. Conversely, the chief financial officer or legal counsel may be involved with a compliance audit regarding an SEC or internal revenue service review.

The internal compliance audit plan may be structured on the same basis as the operational audit plan. However, the external compliance audit segment should disclose the status of legal compliance matters. Such a status should be a summary of the committee's discussions with the independent auditors and legal counsel. For example, the summary may include abstracts of the lawyer's letter as well as any other correspondence concerning legal compliance. The major objective is to review and inquire about the significance and implications of the entity's legal requirements and contractual obligations.

SOURCES AND SUGGESTED READINGS

Albrecht, William S. "Toward Better and More Efficient Audits." *Journal of Accountancy* 144, No. 6 (December 1977), pp. 48–50.

American Institute of Certified Public Accountants, *Audit Committees, Answers to Typical Questions About Their Organization and Operations* (New York: American Institute of Certified Public Accountants, 1978).

American Institute of Certified Public Accountants, *Professional Standards, U.S. Auditing Standards/Attestation Standards,* Vol. 1 (New York: American Institute of Certified Public Accountants, 1998).

American Institute of Certified Public Accountants, *Audit Guide, Consideration of Internal Control in a Financial Statement Audit* (New York: American Institute of Certified Public Accountants, 1996).

Callahan, Patrick S., Henry R. Jaenicke, and Donald L. Neebes, "SAS 56 and 57: Increasing Audit Effectiveness." *Journal of Accountancy* 165, No. 10 (October 1988), pp. 56–68.

Hardy, John W., and Larry A. Deppe, "Client Acceptance: What to Look For and Why." *CPA Journal* 62, No. 5 (May 1992), pp. 20–27.

Kunitake, Walter K., Andrew D. Luzi, and William G. Glezen, "Analytical Review in Audit and Review Engagements." *CPA Journal* 55, No. 4 (April 1985), pp. 18–26.

Loebbecke, James K., "Audit Planning and Company Assistance." *CPA Journal* 47, No. 11 (November 1977), pp. 31–34.

McAllister, John P., and Mark W. Dirsmith, "How the Client's Business Environment Affects the Audit." *Journal of Accountancy* 59, No. 2 (February 1982), pp. 68–74.

McCauley, Daniel J., and John C. Burton, *Audit Committees* 49 (Washington, D.C.: C.P.S. Bureau of National Affairs, 1986).

Securities and Exchange Commission, *Accounting and Auditing Enforcement Release No. 215,* SEC v. Donald D. Sheelen, et al. (February 8, 1989), 42 SEC Docket 1562.

Securities and Exchange Commission, *Litigation Release No. 12579,* SEC v. Barry J. Minkow (August 15, 1990), 46 SEC Docket 1777.

Statement on Auditing Standards, No. 22, "Planning and Supervision" (New York: American Institute of Certified Public Accountants, 1978).

Statement on Auditing Standards No. 82, "Consideration of Fraud in a Financial Statement Audit" (New York: American Institute of Certified Public Accountants, 1997).

Statement on Auditing Standards No. 56, "Analytical Procedures" (New York: American Institute of Certified Public Accountants, 1988).

Statement on Auditing Standards No. 61, "Communication with Audit Committees" (New York: American Institute of Certified Public Accountants, 1988).

Sumners, Glenn E., and Barbara Apostolou, "Preparation Can Cut Audit Fees." *Financial Manager* 3, No. 1 (January/February 1990), pp. 46–49.

U.S. General Accounting Office, *Government Auditing Standards, Standards for Audit of Government Organizations, Programs, Activities and Functions* (Washington, D.C.: U.S. Government Printing Office, 1988).

Walker, Robert, "Know Your Client's Business." *CA Magazine* 124, No. 6 (June 1991), pp. 49–52.

Wolfe, Donald N., and Gerald Smith, "Planning the Audit in a Distressed Industry." *CPA Journal* 58, No. 10 (October 1988), pp. 46–50.

Videos

American Institute of Certified Public Accountants, *Implementing SAS No. 82 Videocourse* (New York: 1997). Length of video: 100 minutes.

Director's Role in Planning the Audit

Chapter 6 discussed the meaning and benefits of audit planning as well as the overall segments of the corporate audit plan. This chapter will enhance the audit directors' skills and ability to appraise the entity's audit plan effectively. In particular, audit directors will learn the basic steps of planning a strategy toward their review of the audit plan. Such steps will serve as a practical guide to review the coordination of the overall audit plan by the internal and external auditors.

THE COMMITTEE'S PLANNING FUNCTION

Introduction

The planning function of the committee centers on the purpose for which it was organized. The primary purpose of the committee is to provide assurance to the full board of directors that the internal and external resources allocated to the audit function are used effectively to accomplish the goals and objectives of the overall audit plan. To allocate resources to the audit processes effectively, the committee should adopt its own plan of action. In formulating the plan for accomplishing its objective, the committee should consider an integrated approach. Such an approach should be oriented toward the segments of the auditing cycle, which are: (1) initial planning segments, (2) preaudit segment, and (3) postaudit segment. The steps in planning the committee's approach may be summarized as follows[1]:

1. Develop an understanding of the entity's business and its industry.
2. Review the overall purpose, objectives, and resources available for the corporate audit plan and recommend the auditing goals and objectives for approval by the full board of directors.

---

[1] The reader may wish to review the highlights of these steps in Chapter 6. It should be reemphasized that the audit committee is not responsible for the preparation of the comprehensive audit plan, since this is done by the internal and external auditing groups.

3. Review the audit plans of the internal and external auditing groups.
4. Appraise the corporate audit plan annually.

DEVELOPING AN INTEGRATED PLANNING APPROACH

Initial Planning Segment

Although the audit committee is removed from the entity's day-to-day operating activities, it should be oriented primarily toward the qualitative characteristics of the enterprise and its industry through a macroapproach. This approach is designed to give the audit director a sense of the entity's existence and how it must interact with its environment. The underlying rationale for this approach may be stated as follows. If the audit directors have not only a basic understanding of the entity's position in the industry as well as other environmental considerations, such as the economic conditions, but also an understanding of the operational characteristics of the business, then they can discharge their committee responsibilities more effectively. Thus before focusing their attention on the major aspects of the audit plan, the directors should engage in a study and review of the functional aspects of the enterprise. In obtaining this effective overview of the business, the directors should:

> . . . Obtain a knowledge of matters that relate to the nature of the entity's business, its organization, and its operating characteristics. . . . For example, the type of business, type of products and services, capital structure, related parties, locations, and production, distribution, and compensation methods. . . . Also, consider matters affecting the industry in which the entity operates, such as economic conditions, government regulations, and changes in technology. . . . Accounting practices common to the industry, competitive conditions, and, if available, financial trends and ratios should also be considered.[2]

Obviously, their orientation toward the entity is a substantial undertaking since the directors have limited time to contribute. As observed by *The New York Times*:

> Any new member coming into the board of a large corporation today faces a work load of proportions unimagined a decade ago. Texas Instruments, for example, now requires a minimum commitment of 30 days per year by an outside director.[3]

---

[2] *Statement on Auditing Standards, No. 22,* "Planning and Supervision" (New York: American Institute of Certified Public Accountants, 1978), par. 7.

[3] Thomas J. Neff, "Who Will Serve on Tomorrow's Boards?" *The New York Times* (February 25, 1979), Sec. 3, p. 3, cols. 1–4.

Korn/Ferry International reported in its annual survey of 327 companies that 48 percent of the directors in 1992 spent annually 40 to 100 hours on board matters, including review and preparation time, meeting attendance, and travel.[4]

Although the audit directors may be oriented toward the corporation through management presentations and plant visits, it may be advisable to formalize a program for educating them. In light of an action-oriented SEC, the enactment of the Foreign Corrupt Practices Act, litigation against directors, the Treadway report, and the COSO report,[5] such a program is desirable in meeting the dynamic changes in corporate governance and accountability.

To educate the directors effectively so that they can have productive meetings and contribute to the board of directors, they should consider the adoption of the audit director's professional development program shown in Exhibit 7.1. Such a program should be instituted on the basis that it will enhance the audit director's ability to serve effectively on the committee.

Implementation of the program may be coordinated through an executive who is responsible for the corporate human resources or the in-house development and training programs. Clearly, each entity can establish a development program to meet its own needs.

With respect to the adoption of the program, several key points should be noted:

1. The duration of the program will vary since it is contingent on the size and complexity of the entity. The directors should participate in the program for a reasonable period of time each year.
2. Each director should be required to complete a reasonable number of hours of advance preparation.
3. The coordinator of the program should be responsible for the necessary reading materials and conference schedules. Therefore, he or she should consult with the appropriate information sources, such as the internal and external auditing group in order to obtain the necessary literature.
4. The directors should be given an opportunity to critique the program in order to enhance the quality and viability of the conference program.

---

[4] Korn/Ferry International, *Twentieth Annual Board of Directors Study* (New York: Korn/Ferry International, 1993), p. 19. More recently, Korn/Ferry International reported in its survey of 903 companies (1,020 directors) that "The average number of hours required annually to serve on a board continues to run about 150, a serious limit for busy people" (p. 7). See Korn/Ferry International, *25th Annual Board of Directors Study* (New York: Korn/Ferry International, 1998).

[5] See Appendix H.

Exhibit 7.1 Professional Development Program

Description	Presentation (*Estimated*)
I. Industry Matters	One day, group discussion

Discussions with executive management on the external
environmental matters, such as:
1. Competitive and economic conditions
2. Government regulations
3. Foreign operations
4. New technological advancements
5. Industry accounting practices
6. Changes in social attitudes
7. Management's risk assessment process

II. Entity's Business Matters	Two days, group discussion

Discussions with key executives on the internal environmental
matters, such as:
1. Historical perspective of the business
   a. Organizational structure
   b. Lines of business and product segments
2. Company objectives and policies, particularly financial
   accounting policies, controls, and procedures
3. Summary of the entity's principles of operations*
4. Legal obligations of the enterprise
5. Significant documentation, such as the corporate charter and
   bylaws
6. Management's risk assessment process

III. Internal Auditing Matters	One day, presentation and group discussion

Review and discuss with the internal auditing executive such matters
as:
1. The nature and functions of the internal auditing group
2. Organizational characteristics of the staff
3. Representative audit programs and reports
4. The interface between the staff and the independent auditors
5. The monitoring activities of the staff

Exhibit 7.1   (*Continued*)

Description	Presentation (*Estimated*)
IV. External Auditing Matters	One day, presentation and group discussion

Review and discuss with the executive partner matters
such as:

1. The nature and overall purpose of the audit
2. Organizational characteristics of the firm and
   biographical data regarding the auditing personnel
   assigned to the audit, including rotations of staff
3. Prior year's annual reports, Form 10-K report,
   interim financial reports (10Qs), and any 8K reports
4. Key documentation, such as the engagement letter,
   management letter, client representation letter, and
   the lawyer's letter
5. Role of the CPA in matters such as:
   a. Internal controls, audit risk assessment, fraud
      risk assessment, business risk assessment,
      materiality, computer security, and legal com-
      pliance with the Foreign Corrupt Practices Act
   b. Internal auditing evaluation and peer reviews
   c. Financial reporting disclosures, audited and
      unaudited statements (e.g., management's
      discussion and analysis, environmental
      liabilities)
   d. Conflicts of interest advisement
   e. Filings with various regulatory agencies
6. Other services of the firm, such as tax and
   management advisory services

*Tour a selected plant location and/or sales location to understand the cost accounting system.

Phase 1: Preaudit Planning Segment

During this segment of the auditing cycle, the committee should review and appraise: (1) the goals and objectives of the audit function and (2) the resources
available for the audit processes. Subsequent to its review, the committee should
recommend that the goals and objectives developed are in accordance with the
charter for the audit committee, which is approved by the board of directors.[6] The

---

[6]The overall audit plan refers to the charter for the audit committee, which requires full board approval. The annual audit plan does not require full board approval.

major objective of the committee is to gain assurance that the goals and objectives are well defined and explicit. Such a step is necessary because the objectives will become the basis for the conduct of the entity's auditing activities. Thus a general statement of auditing policy will provide a course of action for the parties who are responsible for the entity's audit processes. Moreover, auditing policies not only provide an established framework for the internal and external auditing activities but also identify the type and quality of auditing services to be rendered.

In view of the audit committee's oversight and advisory capacity, the auditing objectives and resource requirements should be defined by the executive auditing personnel. For example, the executive partner of the independent accounting firm will formulate the audit objectives based on his or her discussion with the corporate management accounting executives. Generally speaking, the objectives will relate to the annual financial audit, which includes the annual audit of the financial statements and SEC filings. However, the accounting firm may be requested to render other services, such as tax and management advisory services. The objectives of the external audit ultimately will be spelled out in the independent auditor's engagement letter. Consequently, the audit committee should review and discuss the engagement letter with the executive partner.

Although the financial audit is a major part of the overall audit plan, there are collateral objectives with respect to the operational and compliance audits. Accordingly, the internal auditing executive should define the objectives for the entity's operational and compliance auditing plans. In particular, the broad objectives of such plans should include a provision to maximize the organization's economic resources and minimize the causes of inefficiencies or uneconomical practices.

For example, the objectives may include a provision for performance auditing as well as special purpose audits. Obviously, such objectives vary with the size and complexity of the entity and the professional judgment of the executive internal auditor. Accordingly, the audit committee should request a written general statement of the corporate internal auditing objectives and should review and discuss this corporate document with the internal auditing executive. It is imperative that the objective be documented in order to avoid any misunderstanding among the committee members and the internal auditing group. Furthermore, to achieve an effective review posture, the audit committee should also discuss the corporate auditing goals with the chief financial officer and the controller. The major objective of this interview is to determine that the overall auditing goals satisfy the needs of the organization.

In addition to the preceding approach, the audit committee should give consideration to the following points:

- Are the general auditing objectives for the entity well defined?
- Do the auditing goals appear to be workable or realistic in relation to the auditing resources? For example, is the structure and organization of the internal audit staff conducive to the auditing needs and objectives of the entity?

- Do all the executives who participate in the audit process understand the overall goals and objectives?

- Do the independent auditors and the internal auditors have any conflicting objectives?

- What is the independent auditor's assessment of the objectives of the internal audit staff?

- Do the objectives allow the entity to maximize on the auditing services at a reasonable cost?

Although the audit directors are not accounting and auditing experts, they should challenge the objectives and request possible modifications, if necessary. Subsequent to their review, the general auditing objectives should be recommended to the board of directors in order to establish a formal auditing policy statement. Once approved, the auditing policy will serve as a blueprint of the entity's audit processes.

Phase 2: Preaudit Planning Segment

The major role of the audit directors is to review the corporate audit plan. Since the audit policy has been established, their task is to ensure that the entity's auditing plan is consistent with the audit policy. Thus the planning process of the audit requires the support of the independent auditors, internal auditors, and senior accounting executives. The audit committee essentially reviews the coordination of the plans and schedules from the preceding parties. The parties involved in the planning process should work together to ensure that they are working toward their goals as indicated in the policy statement.

For example, the audit plan of the independent auditors may include such matters as:

- Background information on the client, general information disclosed in the early sections of the SEC form 10-K report (e.g., organization data, business operations and products, audit risk assessment, etc.).

- The purpose and objectives of the audit and the nature, extent, and timing of the audit work, information disclosed in the auditor's engagement letter.

- Assignment and scheduling of audit personnel.

- Preaudit work to be performed by the client's staff. Obviously, the independent auditors will modify their plan, if necessary, during the course of their audit examination.

In view of the working relationship between the work of the independent auditors and the internal auditors, the external auditors may take an active role in formulating the audit plan of the internal auditing group. However, each group has its own auditing goals and responsibilities. The internal auditors cannot assume the role of the external auditors. For example, the internal auditors are concerned primarily with the operational and compliance auditing functions, whereas the independent auditors are concerned with the financial audit activities. According to the Auditing Standards Board:

> Even though the internal auditors' work may affect the auditor's procedures, the auditor should perform procedures to obtain sufficient, competent, evidential matter to support the auditor's report. Evidence obtained through the auditor's direct personal knowledge, including physical examination, observation, computation, and inspection, is generally more persuasive than information obtained indirectly.
>
> The responsibility to report on the financial statements rests solely with the auditor. Unlike the situation in which the auditor uses the work of other independent auditors, this responsibility cannot be shared with the internal auditors. Because the auditor has the ultimate responsibility to express an opinion on the financial statements, judgments about assessments of inherent and control risks, the materiality of misstatements, the sufficiency of tests performed, the evaluation of significant accounting estimates, and other matters affecting the auditor's report should always be those of the auditor.[7]

Moreover, the independent auditor must not only assess the competence and objectivity of the internal auditors but also supervise and test their work if they provide direct assistance in performing the independent auditor's work.[8] Thus based on the independent auditor's judgment, the internal auditing staff may offer valuable assistance during the audit.

In order to appraise the corporate audit plan effectively, the audit committee should give consideration to the following criteria[9]:

- The authority and responsibility for each segment of the corporate audit plan should be clearly defined.
- The chief financial officer should acknowledge his or her general support for the plan to avoid opposition during the course of the internal and external auditing engagements.
- The internal and external resources available for the audit function should be adequate and properly allocated.

---

[7] *Statement on Auditing Standards, No. 65,* "The Auditor's Consideration of the Internal Audit Function in an Audit of Financial Statements" (New York: American Institute of Certified Public Accountants, 1991), pars. 18 and 19.

[8] Ibid., par. 27.

[9] This list of criteria is not all-inclusive and is not intended to preclude the insertion of additional criteria.

- The plan should be realistic against the conditions of the business and its industry.

- The plan should be realistic and consistent with the goals and objectives as expressed in the corporate audit policy statement.

- The scope of the audit plans should be defined and explicit to avoid any duplication of auditing effort.

- The general criteria used to identify areas subject to audit should be explicit (e.g., What is the auditing firm's policy on materiality?).

- The plan should incorporate any applicable resolutions as a result of the board of directors' and stockholders' meetings as well as take into account related matters of the other standing committees, such as the finance committee.

- The extent of auditing work should be reasonable in relationship to the quality of the internal control system. Also, the time associated with each audit plan should be reasonable in relation to the size and complexity of the entity's operations and organizational structure.

- An analysis of the costs and benefits of the auditing resources should be made (e.g., What is the desirability of allocating more financial auditing work to the internal audit staff and reducing the audit time of the independent auditors?).

Postaudit Segment

In the preceding discussion, the committee reviewed and appraised the audit planning activities of the auditors and corporate accounting management officers. Such a review related to the initial planning segment of the auditing cycle. However, this final step should be accomplished during the postaudit segment of the auditing cycle whereby the audit directors should reassess the corporate audit plan. On the basis of their reassessments, the directors should assure themselves that the auditing policy and preaudit plans were effective in order to provide the assurances required by the board of directors.

To provide such assurances to the board, the following general comments are applicable for related auditing and attestation standards (see Chapter 5):

1. The audit committee should inquire into the degree of cooperation received from the entity's personnel who are involved in the auditing process. Also, it should be satisfied that the audit examination was conducted in an impartial and objective manner.

2. Based on a review of the preaudit plan criteria, the committee should assess the results of the audit and inquire into the reasons for any differences (e.g., Are there any problems that preclude the independent auditors from complying with the generally accepted auditing standards?). Such inquiries should be made in relation to the independent auditor's management letter, which dis-

closes their reportable conditions and recommendations for improving the entity's system of internal control. Also, the committee should review progress reports or correspondence regarding the results of the audit (e.g., internal audit reports and financial management correspondence).

3. The committee should inquire into additional matters such as:

   a. The qualitative aspects of the manpower resources allocated to the auditing function (e.g., the quality of the internal auditing group).

   b. The entity's policy and programs concerning general business practices (e.g., corporate conduct, sensitive payments, management perquisites, and conflicts of interest).

   c. The financial reporting disclosure practices of the entity (e.g., accounting policies and SEC disclosure requirements).

RECOMMENDING THE APPOINTMENT OF THE INDEPENDENT AUDITORS

A Synopsis

Based on a review of the independent auditors' report in the annual report, the addressee of their report is ordinarily the board of directors and the shareholders, since the board approves the selection or reappointment and recommends the firm to the shareholders. Selection or reappointment of the auditors is within the province of the audit committee. For example, the Wal-Mart audit committee "monitors the financial condition of Wal-Mart, reviews its financial policies and procedures, its internal accounting controls and the objectivity of its financial reporting and makes recommendations to the Board concerning the engagement of the independent auditors."[10] Furthermore, Lockheed Martin Corporation reports that "The committee recommends the selection and monitors the independence of independent auditors for the Corporation."[11] Recall the discussion in Chapter 2 regarding the Independence Standards Board's requirement that independent auditors issue an annual independence confirmation. Thus the committee should address the following question: What criteria should be used in the selection and reappointment of the independent auditors?

According to the American Institute of Certified Public Accountants, the committee should give consideration to the following points[12]:

[10] Wal-Mart Stores, Inc., *Notice of 1998 Annual Meeting of Shareholders Proxy Statement,* p. 6.

[11] Lockheed Martin Corporation, *Notice of 1998 Annual Meeting and Proxy Statement,* p. 6.

[12] American Institute of Certified Public Accountants, *Audit Committees, Answers to Typical Questions About Their Organization and Operations* (New York: American Institute of Certified Public Accountants, 1978), p. 15. For more information on the relationship between the independent auditors and boards of directors, see the recommendations of the Blue Ribbon Committee on Improving the Effectiveness of Corporate Audit Committees as indicated in Chapter 14, Exhibit 14.3.

1. *Executive auditing personnel*[13]   What has been the company's past experience with the personnel assigned to the audit? Do they convey the impression that they value the company as a client? Do they seem able to work compatibly, but efficiently and independently, with management and the audit committee? Do they demonstrate an understanding of the company's business problems? Do they anticipate problems and advise the company of new accounting tax or SEC developments?

2. *Quality of professional services*   Can the firm supply the professional services the company needs? For example, does the firm have access to individuals skilled in matters affecting the company (such as industry and SEC specialists or specialists in the problems of smaller companies), and are their skills made available to the company? Does the firm have the capability to serve the company efficiently?)

3. *Firm's policies*   What are the firm's quality control policies, including its training policies? What is the firm's policy on rotation of the personnel assigned to the audit? On acceptance of clients? On recruitment of personnel? On growth?[14]

4. *Audit fees*   Has the firm satisfactorily explained significant variances in actual fees from estimate? Have suggestions been made for management actions that might reduce fees?

   With respect to ways for reducing audit fees, management should:

   a. Develop and maintain an accounting policies and procedures manual
   b. Develop an internal auditing group if the costs and potential benefits warrant such a group
   c. Ensure that significant and/or unusual transaction cycles are properly documented and approved
   d. Discuss changes in the system of internal control with the independent auditors prior to implementation to ensure cost-effectiveness
   e. Follow up on the recommendations noted in the independent auditor's management letter to correct deficiencies
   f. Discuss with the auditors significant accounting transactions and their implications during the preaudit planning segment of the auditing cycle (e.g., the impact of new accounting and auditing pronouncements on the audit)
   g. Request a summary of auditing schedules to be prepared by the client's staff
   h. Decide on the desirability of an audit coordinator in order to expedite the audit process[15]

---

[13] See Appendix J.

[14] Cindy H. Nance and William W. Holder, "Planning for the Audit: Logical Steps Towards Cost Containment." *Financial Executive* 45 (May 1977), pp. 48–49.

[15] The audit committee may also wish to consider other matters, such as the independent auditors' professional indemnity insurance and past and pending litigation.

5. *Nonaudit fees* Independent auditing firms of the AICPA/SEC Practice Section are required to report to the audit committee or to the board of directors total fees received for management advisory services and a description of the services rendered during the year.[16] In addition, the National Commission on Fraudulent Financial Reporting recommended that the audit committee "review management's plan to engage the independent public accountant to perform management advisory services during the coming year."[17] Such reporting requirements give assurance to the audit committee and the full board of directors that the independence of the auditing firm is not compromised.

In summary, as Adolph G. Lurie pointed out:

. . . Management should review the company's operations and determine what services it needs from an independent certified public accountant.

In addition to contemplating its needs, management should consider the cost of an auditor's services in relation to its requirements. . . . All things being equal, the lowest fee may not obtain the type and quality of service needed to meet the particular situation.[18]

SOURCES AND SUGGESTED READINGS

American Institute of Certified Public Accountants, *Audit Committees, Answers to Typical Questions About Their Organization and Operations* (New York: American Institute of Certified Public Accountants, 1978).

American Institute of Certified Public Accountants, Membership Requirement Regarding Communication with Audit Committees or Boards of Directors of SEC Clients. In the Division for CPA Firms SEC Practice Section *Peer Review Manual:* Update 3-B (New York: American Institute of Certified Public Accountants, 1987).

Korn/Ferry International, *Twentieth Annual Boards of Directors Study* (New York: Korn/Ferry International, 1993).

Korn/Ferry International, *25th Annual Board of Directors Study* (New York: Korn/Ferry International, 1998).

Lockheed Martin Corporation, *Notice of 1998 Annual Meeting and Proxy Statement.*

---

[16]American Institute of Certified Public Accountants, Membership Requirement Regarding Communications with Audit Committees or Boards of Directors of SEC Clients. In the Division for CPA Firms, SEC Practice Section *Peer Review Manual:* Update 3-B (New York: American Institute of Certified Public Accountants, 1987).

[17]National Commission on Fraudulent Financial Reporting, *Report of the National Commission on Fraudulent Financial Reporting* (Washington, D.C.: National Commission on Fraudulent Financial Reporting, 1987), p. 44.

[18]Adolph G. Lurie, *Working with the Public Accountant* (New York: McGraw-Hill, 1977), pp. 15–16.

Lurie, Adolph G., *Working with the Public Accountant* (New York: McGraw-Hill, 1977).

McKesson Corporation, *1992 Annual Report.*

Nance, Cindy H., and William W. Holder, "Planning for the Audit: Logical Steps Towards Cost Containment." *Financial Executive* 45 (May 1977), pp. 46–50.

National Commission on Fraudulent Financial Reporting, *Report of the National Commission on Fraudulent Financial Reporting* (Washington, D.C.: National Commission on Fraudulent Financial Reporting, 1987).

Neff, Thomas J., "Who Will Serve on Tomorrow's Boards?" *New York Times* (February 25, 1979), Sec. 3, p. 3, cols. 1–4.

Statement on Auditing Standards No. 22, "Planning and Supervision" (New York: American Institute of Certified Public Accountants, 1978).

Statement on Auditing Standards No. 65, "The Auditor's Consideration of the Internal Audit Function of Financial Statements" (New York: American Institute of Certified Public Accountants, 1991).

Wal-Mart Stores, Inc., *Notice of 1998 Annual Meeting of Shareholders Proxy Statement.*

Part Three

The Monitoring and Reviewing Functions of the Audit Committee

Chapter 8

Monitoring the System of Internal Control

In view of legislative action—for example, the Foreign Corrupt Practices Act, the Federal Deposit Insurance Corporation Improvement Act, and private sector initiatives such as the recommendations of the National Commission on Fraudulent Financial Reporting and the Committee of Sponsoring Organizations of the Treadway Commission—the board of directors will rely increasingly on the audit committee for assurance that management is complying with the internal accounting control provisions of the Foreign Corrupt Practices Act. To assist the committee with its task, this chapter will examine the meaning of internal control, the recent developments regarding the responsibilities for such controls, and the role of the audit directors.

MEANING OF INTERNAL CONTROL

Internal Control as Defined by the American Institute of Certified Public Accountants—Historical Perspective

In 1949 the Committee on Auditing Procedures of the AICPA published this definition of internal control:

> Internal control comprises the plan of organization and all of the coordinate methods and measures adopted within a business to safeguard its assets, check the accuracy and reliability of its accounting data, promote operational efficiency, and encourage adherence to prescribed managerial policies. This definition possibly is broader than the meaning sometimes attributed to the term. It recognizes that a "system" of internal control extends beyond those matters which relate directly to the functions of the accounting and financial departments.[1]

[1] American Institute of Certified Public Accountants, *Codification of Statements on Auditing Standards, Nos. 1–21* (New York: American Institute of Certified Public Accountants, 1978), AU Sec. 320.09.

In view of the Institute's broad definition of internal control, the Committee subdivided internal control into the following categories: (1) administrative controls and (2) accounting controls. Such controls were defined as follows:

> Administrative control includes, but is not limited to, the plan of organization and the procedures and records that are concerned with the decision processes leading to management's authorization of transactions. Such authorization is a management function directly associated with the responsibility for achieving the objectives of the organization and is the starting point for establishing accounting control of transactions.
>
> Accounting control comprises the plan of organization and the procedures and records that are concerned with the safeguarding of assets and the reliability of financial records and consequently are designed to provide reasonable assurance that:
>
> a. Transactions are executed in accordance with management's general or specific organization.
>
> b. Transactions are recorded as necessary (1) to permit preparation of financial statements in conformity with generally accepted accounting principles or any other criteria applicable to such statements and (2) to maintain accountability for assets.
>
> c. Access to assets is permitted only in accordance with management's authorization.
>
> d. The recorded accountability for assets is compared with the existing assets at reasonable intervals and appropriate action is taken with respect to any differences.[2]

More specifically, the administrative controls are primarily concerned with the promotion of operational efficiency and the adherence to prescribed managerial policies. Administrative controls relate to the operational and compliance audits as discussed in Chapter 6. Although the internal auditing group is primarily concerned with such controls, the external auditing group may also be concerned with these controls. The definition of the controls are not "mutually exclusive because some procedures and records comprehended in accounting control may be also involved in administrative control."[3] For example, the entity's policy regarding the acquisition of plant and equipment assets may require that such acquisitions be made subsequent to the approval of a capital expenditures committee. Hence the independent auditors may review this administrative control policy to verify the authorization for the additions to the plant and equipment account. Such a review is based on their professional auditing judgment since the "administrative controls

[2] Ibid., AU Sec. 320.27–28.
[3] Ibid., AU Sec. 320.29.

. . . ordinarily relate only indirectly to the financial records and thus would not require evaluation."[4]

Conversely, the accounting controls are principally concerned with safeguarding the entity's assets and providing assurance that the financial statements and the underlying accounting records are reliable. Internal accounting controls relate to the external and internal financial audits as noted in Chapter 6. "The independent auditor is primarily concerned with the accounting controls. Accounting controls . . . generally bear directly and importantly on the reliability of financial records and require evaluation by the auditor."[5] For example, the entity's use of a safe deposit vault to store short-term securities is an accounting control. Management's decision to use the lock box of a bank regarding its cash collection activities is another example of accounting control. Such controls are critically important to the external auditors because they rely on them to determine not only the extensiveness of their auditing work, but also the fairness of the account balances in the financial statements. Also, their study and evaluation of the internal accounting controls serves as a basis for their recommendations in improving the controls whereby such recommendations are communicated to management in their management letter.

Although the meaning of internal control has been defined by the accountancy profession, security analysts do not particularly share the distinctions between the internal controls.[6] As reported by Marilyn V. Brown:

> To the analyst, the term internal control encompasses the entire spectrum of management information systems and procedures. . . . SAS 1-320.27 and 320.28 are inseparable determinants of the soundness and reliability of the financial statements and the future viability and progress of the corporation.[7]

As a result of the inseparability of the administrative and accounting controls, the security analysts advocate "a more comprehensive definition of internal controls would seem appropriate and feasible."[8]

In addition to the security analysts' views, the accountancy profession has been grappling with the internal accounting control provisions of the Foreign Corrupt Practices Act of 1977. (See Chapter 2.) Essentially, the act requires all publicly held enterprises to devise and maintain an adequate system of internal control. However, the act is not specific with respect to the criteria for evaluating the ade-

[4] Ibid., AU Sec. 320.11
[5] Ibid.
[6] For more information on the security analyst's view, see the Cohen Commission's Report on Tentative Conclusions.
[7] Marilyn V. Brown, "Auditors and Internal Controls: An Analyst's View," *CPA Journal* 47, No. 9 (September 1977), p. 30.
[8] Ibid.

quacy of the internal accounting controls. As J. Michael Cook, partner of Deloitte Haskins and Sells (now Deloitte & Touche), and Thomas P. Kelley, the former AICPA managing director-technical, reported:

> . . . there are several areas where views differ, for example, the definition and scope of internal accounting controls and the criteria appropriate for an evaluation of those controls.[9]

Furthermore, at the AICPA Sixth National Conference on SEC Developments held in Washington, D.C., in January 1979, J. Michael Cook pointed out that:

> The AICPA auditing standards board is acting under a mandate from the Institute and is attempting to comply with the SEC requirements to examine the utility and cost-effectiveness of public reporting on internal controls as well as studying the possible effects on privately held companies. Major issues in such a study include the scope of the auditor's study evaluation and compliance tests, forms of representation by management, and the form of the auditor's report.[10]

In October 1987, the National Commission on Fraudulent Financial Reporting concluded that:

> An element within the company of overriding importance in preventing fraudulent financial reporting is the tone set by top management that influences the corporate environment within which financial reporting occurs. To set the right tone, top management must identify and assess the factors that could lead to fraudulent financial reporting; all public companies should maintain internal controls that provide reasonable assurance that fraudulent financial reporting will be prevented or subject to early detection—this is a broader concept than internal accounting controls—and all public companies should develop and enforce effective, written codes of corporate conduct. As a part of its ongoing assessment of the effectiveness of internal controls, a company's audit committee should annually review the program that management establishes to monitor compliance with the code. The Commission also recommends that its sponsoring organizations cooperate in developing additional, integrated guidance on internal controls.[11]

Such recommendations reaffirm the congressional legislation dealing with the internal accounting control provision of the Foreign Corrupt Practices Act, which is designed to reduce the incidence of fraudulent financial reporting.

---

[9] J. Michael Cook and Thomas P. Kelley, "Internal Accounting Control: A Matter of Law," *Journal of Accountancy* 147, No. 1 (January 1979), p. 64.

[10] AICPA Sixth National Conference on SEC Developments, "New Report," *Journal of Accountancy* 147, No. 3 (March 1979), p. 14.

[11] National Commission on Fraudulent Financial Reporting, *Report of the National Commission on Fraudulent Financial Reporting* (Washington, D.C.: National Commission on Fraudulent Financial Reporting, 1987), p. 11.

In April 1988 the Auditing Standards Board of the AICPA published its definition of internal control structure:

> An entity's internal control structure consists of the policies and procedures established to provide reasonable assurance that specific entity objectives will be achieved. Although the internal control structure may include a wide variety of objectives and related policies and procedures, only some of these may be relevant to an audit of the entity's financial statements. Generally, the policies and procedures that are relevant to an audit pertain to the entity's ability to record, process, summarize, and report financial data consistent with the assertions embodied in the financial statements. Other policies and procedures, however, may be relevant if they pertain to data the auditor uses to apply auditing procedures. For example, policies and procedures pertaining to nonfinancial data that the auditor uses in analytical procedures, such as production statistics, may be relevant in an audit.[12]

Furthermore, the Auditing Standards Board stated that an entity's internal control structure consists of the following elements:

- The control environment
- The accounting system
- Control procedures[13]

The Board defined these three elements as follows:

> *Control environment* The collective effect of various factors on establishing, enhancing, or mitigating the effectiveness of specific policies and procedures. Such factors include (1) management philosophy and operating style, (2) organizational structure, (3) the function of the board of directors and its committees, (4) methods of assigning authority and responsibility, (5) management control methods, (6) the internal audit function, (7) personnel policies and practices, and (8) external influences concerning the entity.
>
> *Accounting system* The methods and records established to identify, assemble, analyze, classify, record, and report an entity's transactions and to maintain accountability for the related assets and liabilities.
>
> *Control procedures* The policies and procedures in addition to the control environment and accounting system that management has established to provide reasonable assurance that specific entity objectives will be achieved.[14]

---

[12] *Statement on Auditing Standards, No. 55,* "Consideration of the Internal Control Structure in a Financial Statement Audit" (New York: American Institute of Certified Public Accountants, 1988), par. 6.
[13] Ibid., par. 8.
[14] Ibid., par. 67.

In September 1992, the Committee of Sponsoring Organizations (COSO) of the Treadway Commission issued its final report, *Internal Control-Integrated Framework*. COSO defines and describes internal control as functioning to:

1. Establish a common definition serving the needs of different parties.

2. Provide a standard against which business and other entities—large or small, in the public or private sector, for profit or not—can assess their control systems and determine how to improve them.

Internal control is broadly defined as a process, effected by an entity's board of directors, management and other personnel, designed to provide reasonable assurance regarding the achievement of objectives in the following categories:

Effectiveness and efficiency of operations

Reliability of financial reporting

Compliance with applicable laws and regulations[15]

An executive summary of COSO's four-volume report is presented in Appendix H, which contains the five interrelated components of internal control.

In June 1994 COSO published an addendum, which stated in part: The new addendum "encourages managements that report to external parties on controls over financial reporting to also cover controls over safeguarding of assets against unauthorized acquisition, use or disposition." Those controls, according to the addendum, should be "designed to provide reasonable assurance regarding prevention or timely detection of unauthorized acquisition, use or disposition of the entity's assets that could have a material effect on the financial statements."[16]

COSO provided the illustrative report shown in Exhibit 8.1.

As discussed in Chapter 2, the Federal Deposit Insurance Corporation Improvement Act of 1991 requires that management and the independent auditors re-

---

[15] Committee of Sponsoring Organizations of the Treadway Commission, *Internal Control-Integrated Framework* (New York: American Institute of Certified Public Accountants, 1992), p. 1. For additional reading, see *Statement on Auditing Standards, No. 78,* "Consideration of Internal Control in a Financial Statement Audit: An Amendment to SAS No. 55" (New York: American Institute of Certified Public Accountants, 1995) and copies of the four-volume COSO report, which may be obtained from the American Institute of Certified Public Accountants. Also see Thomas P. Kelley, "The COSO Report: Challenge and Counterchallenge," *Journal of Accountancy* 175, no. 2 (February 1993), pp. 10–18. For a good discussion on internal control, see Wanda A. Wallace, *Handbook of Internal Accounting Controls,* 2nd ed. (Englewood Cliffs, N.J.: Prentice-Hall, 1991); and Michael W. Maher, David W. Wright, and William R. Kinney, Jr., "Assertions-Based Standards for Integrated Internal Control," *Accounting Horizons* 4, No. 4 (December 1990), pp. 1–8.

[16] Committee of Sponsoring Organizations of the Treadway Commission, *Addendum to "Reporting to External Parties"* (New York: American Institute of Certified Public Accountants, 1994), p. 1.

Exhibit 8.1   Illustrative Report: Reporting to External Parties

---

XYZ Company maintains a system of internal control over financial reporting and[a] over safeguarding of assets against unauthorized acquisition, use or disposition which is designed to provide reasonable assurance to the Company's management and board of directors regarding the preparation of reliable published financial statements and such asset safeguarding. The system contains self-monitoring mechanisms, and actions are taken to correct deficiencies as they are identified. Even an effective internal control system, no matter how well designed, has inherent limitations—including the possibility of the circumvention or overriding of controls—and therefore can provide only reasonable assurance with respect to financial statement preparation and such asset safeguarding. Further, because of changes in conditions, internal control system effectiveness may vary over time.

The Company assessed its internal control system as of December 31, 19XX in relation to criteria for effective internal control over financial reporting described in "Internal Control—Integrated Framework" issued by the Committee of Sponsoring Organizations of the Treadway Commission. Based on this assessment, the Company believes that, as of December 31, 19XX, its system of internal control over financial reporting and[a] over safeguarding of assets against unauthorized acquisition, use or disposition met those criteria.

---

[a]In circumstances where all controls over safeguarding of assets against unauthorized acquisition, use or disposition fall within the category of controls over financial reporting, "and" may be changed to "including."

Source: Committee of Sponsoring Organizations of the Treadway Commission, Addendum to "Reporting to External Parties" (New York: American Institute of Certified Public Accountants, 1994), p. 7. Copyright © 1994 by The American Institute of Certified Public Accountants, Inc. Reprinted with permission.

port on the internal control structure over financial reporting and compliance with specified laws and regulations. In response, the Auditing Standards Board has issued two Statements on Standards for Attestation Engagements: SSAE No. 2, "Reporting on an Entity's Internal Control Structure over Financial Reporting," and SSAE No. 3, "Compliance Attestation." More specifically, SSAE No. 2 deals with the independent auditor's report on management's assertion regarding the effectiveness of the entity's internal control structure. When management presents its assertion in a separate report that will accompany the independent auditor's report, the form of report is as shown in Exhibit 8.2.

With respect to SSAE No. 3 and management's assertion in a separate report that will accompany the independent auditor's report, the form of the report is illustrated in Exhibit 8.3.

Exhibit 8.2   Independent Accountant's Report, SSAE No. 2

[*Introductory paragraph*]

We have examined management's assertion [*identify management's assertion, for example, that W Company maintained an effective internal control over financial reporting as of December 31, 19XX*] included in the accompanying [*title of management report*].

[*Scope paragraph*]

Our examination was made in accordance with standards established by the American Institute of Certified Public Accountants and, accordingly, included obtaining an understanding of the internal control over financial reporting, testing, and evaluating the design and operating effectiveness of the internal control and such other procedures as we considered necessary in the circumstances. We believe that our examination provides a reasonable basis for our opinion.

[*Inherent limitations paragraph*]

Because of inherent limitations in any internal control, misstatements due to error or fraud may occur and not be detected. Also, projections of any evaluation of the internal control over financial reporting to future periods are subject to the risk that the internal control may become inadequate because of changes in conditions, or that the degree of compliance with the policies or procedures may deteriorate.

[*Opinion paragraph*]

In our opinion, management's assertion [*identify management's assertion, for example, that W Company maintained an effective internal control over financial reporting as of December 31, 19XX*] is fairly stated, in all material respects, based upon [*identify stated or established criteria*]

Source: Statement on Standards for Attestation Engagements, No. 2, "Reporting on an Entity's Internal Control Structure Over Financial Reporting" (New York: American Institute of Certified Public Accountants, 1993), par. 51. See also *Professional Standards, U.S. Auditing Standards/Attestation Standards,* Vol. 1, AT Sec. 400.46. For further reference, see Joseph Takacs, "Attestation Engagements on Internal Control Structure over Financial Reporting," *CPA Journal* 63, No. 8 (August 1993), pp. 48–53.

RESPONSIBILITY FOR THE SYSTEM OF INTERNAL CONTROL

Management

Although the independent auditors may recommend improvements in the system of internal control, management has the responsibility for the establishment and maintenance of such a system. In order to assist management with its responsibilities, the AICPA formed a Special Advisory Committee on Internal Accounting Control in August 1977. Although the committee was not formed because of the Foreign Corrupt Practices Act, "it is seeking to develop criteria that are sufficiently

Exhibit 8.3 Independent Accountant's Report, SSAE No. 3

[*Introductory paragraph*]

We have examined management's assertion about [*name of entity*]'s compliance with [*list specific compliance requirements*] during the [*period*] ended [*date*] included in the accompanying [*title of management report*]. Management is responsible for [*name of entity*]'s compliance with those requirements. Our responsibility is to express an opinion on management's assertion about the entity's compliance based on our examination.

[*Scope paragraph*]

Our examination was made in accordance with standards established by the American Institute of Certified Public Accountants and, accordingly, included examining, on a test basis, evidence about [*name of entity*]'s compliance with those requirements and performing such other procedures as we considered necessary in the circumstances. We believe that our examination provides a reasonable basis for our opinion. Our examination does not provide a legal determination on [*name of entity*]'s compliance with specified requirements.

[*Opinion paragraph*]

In our opinion, management's assertion [*identify management's assertion—for example, that Z Company complied with the aforementioned requirements for the year ended December 31, 19X1*] is fairly stated in all material respects.

Source: Statement on Standards for Attestation Engagements, No. 3, "Compliance Attestation" (New York: American Institute of Certified Public Accountants, 1993), par. 55. It should be observed that few, if any, companies to date have made such management assertions along with the independent auditors' report thereon.

comprehensive so that their implementation would provide management and boards of directors with reasonable assurance that the broad objectives of internal accounting control are being met."[17] According to the committee, management[18] should be doing the following:

> The committee believes that management should initiate a preliminary assessment of the internal accounting control environment and of the appropriateness and effectiveness of existing accounting control procedures and techniques based on its overall knowledge of the company. On the basis of that preliminary assessment, management should plan the manner, extent, and timing of other procedures deemed appropriate. Those procedures should relate to—

[17] See the "Tentative Report of the Special Advisory Committee on Internal Accounting Control" (New York: American Institute of Certified Public Accountants, 1978), p. 1.

[18] The committee indicates that "the term 'management' as used in this report includes the board of directors and committees thereof, where their involvement would be appropriate." Due to the length and complexity of the report, the information above is a summary of the underlying theme.

a. A reexamination of the accounting control procedures in place and the ongoing process of evaluating them.
b. A consideration of the need for a shift toward more explicit documentation of those control procedures and the process of evaluating them.[19]

For example, Albert S. Martin, former corporate controller of Sun Company, and Kenneth P. Johnson, former vice chairman of Coopers and Lybrand, found that the results of their experiment not only demonstrate compliance with the act but also offer a basis for evaluating the internal accounting controls. They concluded that:

Transactions flows portrayed on flowcharts and internal control questionnaires are an effective communication device for personnel actually running the system.

The development and implementation of educational tools, such as the internal control questionnaire reference manual, assisted local managers in understanding and implementing controls.

The documentation of a system of internal controls enhanced the effectiveness of the internal auditors' work and may reduce the audit fee.[20]

Although the Institute's committee has been primarily concerned with the internal accounting controls, it is argued that, from management's point of view, the criteria for evaluating internal controls should include the administrative controls. As Harvey V. Guttry, former vice president and controller, and Jesse R. Foster, former policy and control manager, both of the Times Mirror Company, assert:

Regardless of where the definitional boundaries of internal accounting controls are placed, it must be emphasized that so-called administrative controls have the most bearing on the success of a business. Management has to avoid the pitfall of over-stressing accounting controls at the expense of administrative or operational controls.[21]

In April, 1979, the Institute's committee issued its final report on internal accounting controls and,[22] it appears that Guttry and Foster have a valid argument as evidenced by the following comments of Leonard M. Savore, former vice president and controller of Clark Equipment Company:

---

[19]"Tentative Report of the Special Advisory Committee on Internal Accounting Control," pp. 5–6.
[20]Albert S. Martin and Kenneth P. Johnson, "Assessing Internal Accounting Control: A Workable Approach," *Financial Executive* 46 (May 1978), p. 35.
[21]Harvey V. Guttry and Jesse R. Foster, "Internal Controls and the Financial Executive," *Financial Executive* 46 (April 1978), 45.
[22]The final recommendations are consistent with the committee's tentative recommendations. Copies of the report are available from the AICPA.

. . . Companies should develop an "action plan" to determine if adequate records are kept and if an adequate system of internal controls is maintained. . . . [He] suggested that, to assure compliance, companies institute special procedures, including annually distributing corporate policy statements and guidelines to all management personnel and authorizing internal auditors and lawyers to investigate and report to the audit committee on violations of the conduct guidelines.[23]

Obviously, the accounting and administrative controls overlap. However, since the external auditors are concerned primarily with the entity's accounting controls and their impact on the financial statements, the criteria for the evaluation should be developed within this context. The development of the criteria is indeed within the province of the AICPA. Since the internal auditors are concerned principally with the administrative controls, it seems logical that the criteria for their evaluation should be developed by the Institute of Internal Auditors. Such an approach is reasonable because both auditing groups have different reporting objectives. As Guttry and Foster point out:

Since the effectiveness of controls, administrative and accounting, is management's responsibility . . . the auditor's role should be limited to reviewing and testing those controls which are pertinent to their examination of the financial statements and using the results of such audit work as a basis for commenting on management's representation.[24]

In April 1988 the Auditing Standards Board reemphasized the overall responsibility and general considerations for the internal control structure. The Board stated:

Establishing and maintaining an internal control structure is an important management responsibility. To provide reasonable assurance that an entity's objectives will be achieved, the internal control structure should be under ongoing supervision by management to determine that it is operating as intended and that it is modified as appropriate for changes in conditions.

The concept of reasonable assurance recognizes that the cost of an entity's internal control structure should not exceed the benefits that are expected to be derived. Although the cost-benefit relationship is a primary criterion that should be considered in designing an internal control structure, the precise measurement of costs and benefits usually is not possible. Accordingly, management makes both quantitative and qualitative estimates and judgments in evaluating the cost-benefit relationship

The potential effectiveness of an entity's internal control structure is subject to inherent limitations. Mistakes in the application of policies and procedures may arise

---

[23] AICPA Sixth National Conference on SEC Developments, "News Report," p. 16.
[24] Guttry and Foster, "Internal Controls," p. 48.

from such causes as misunderstanding of instructions, mistakes in judgment, and personal carelessness, distraction, or fatigue. Furthermore, the policies and procedures that require segregation of duties can be circumvented by collusion among persons both within and outside the entity and by management override of certain policies or procedures.[25]

The Independent Auditors

According to one former executive audit partner, "the independent auditor's external review is an indispensable supplement to a corporate system of internal controls, but it is no substitute for it."[26] As indicated in Chapter 5, the independent auditors are required to study and evaluate the system of internal control. The study and evaluation is performed during their interim-period work, ordinarily a predetermined period prior to the date of the financial statements.

Their major objective is to determine whether the internal control is adequate so that the financial accounting transactions are properly recorded and fairly presented in the financial statements. Furthermore, they must evaluate the controls in order to determine not only how much reliance can be placed on such controls but also the extensiveness of their auditing procedures. Obviously, if the internal control structure is weak, then the assessment of control risk is high; thus the auditors must extend their auditing procedures in order to minimize the risk of errors in the financial statements and limit the level of detection risk. During the audit engagement the auditors test the accounting system through verification tests. For example, tests of controls consist of the auditors' selection of several transactions whereby such transactions are traced through the accounting system. Such tests allow the auditors to determine the degree of reliance they can place on the internal control structure. However, the auditors' examination of the cancelled checks in connection with the bank reconciliation and the examination of the vendors' invoices in support of account balances are substantive tests of transactions.

Since the auditors are required to communicate to senior management and the board of directors or its audit committee reportable conditions in internal control, the following form of report is recommended.[27]

---

[25] *Statement on Auditing Standards, No. 55,* pars. 13–15. For further discussion on the roles and responsibilities for internal control, see the executive summary of COSO's four-volume report in Appendix H.

[26] John C. Biegler, "Rebuilding Public Trust in Business," *Financial Executive* 45 (June 1977), p. 30.

[27] *Statement on Auditing Standards, No. 60,* "Communication of Internal Control Related Matters Noted in an Audit" (New York: American Institute of Certified Public Accountants, 1988), pars. 2 and 12. See also *Professional Standards, U.S. Auditing Standards/Attestation Standards,* Vol. 1, AU Sec. 325.02 and 325.12. A reportable condition may be of such magnitude as to be considered a material weakness in internal control.

In planning and performing our audit of the financial statements of the ABC Corporation for the year ended December 31, 19XX, we considered its internal control in order to determine our auditing procedures for the purpose of expressing our opinion on the financial statements and not to provide assurance on the internal control. However, we noted certain matters involving the internal control and its operation that we consider to be reportable conditions under standards established by the American Institute of Certified Public Accountants. Reportable conditions involve matters coming to our attention relating to significant deficiencies in the design or operation of the internal control that, in our judgment, could adversely affect the organization's ability to record, process, summarize, and report financial data consistent with the assertions of management in the financial statements.

(Include paragraphs to describe the reportable conditions noted.)

This report is intended solely for the information and use of the audit committee (board of directors, board of trustees, or owners in owner-managed enterprises), management, and others within the organization (or specified regulatory agency or other specified third party).[28]

Although the independent auditors may communicate improvements for the system of internal control, Richard H. Benson, partner of Arthur Andersen & Co., reports that his firm "could not provide an opinion on whether the company was in compliance with the new law (Foreign Corrupt Practices Act), because that is a legal matter."[29] Consequently, the independent auditors' report on the internal accounting controls "would not necessarily disclose all weaknesses."[30] In short, although the independent auditors cannot express a legal opinion on the entity's compliance with the act, management should give strong consideration to their recommendations in order to indicate its intent to comply with the law.

The Auditing Standards Board reaffirmed the partners' position in the compliance attestation standard. Specifically, the Board states:

A report issued in accordance with the provisions of this Statement does not provide a legal determination on an entity's compliance with specified requirements. However, such a report may be useful to management, legal counsel, or third parties in making such determinations.[31]

---

[28] The audit committee may wish to discuss the independent auditor's findings and conclusions with respect to their assessment of internal accounting controls at service organizations. Such guidance is contained in *Statement on Auditing Standards, No. 70,* "Reports on the Processing of Transactions by Service Organizations" (New York: American Institute of Certified Public Accountants, 1992). The committee may also wish to consult the AICPA's auditing guide and auditing procedures study, which deals with internal control.

[29] Richard H. Benson, "Changing Demands on the Internal and External Auditors," *Internal Auditor* 36, No. 1 (February 1979), 55.

[30] Ibid.

[31] *Statement on Standards for Attestation Engagements, No. 3,* par. 3.

Another important element of the internal control environment is the internal audit function. As discussed in Chapter 1, the internal auditing group plays a significant part in establishing and maintaining the internal control structure. Although its members are principally engaged in compliance and operational auditing, which deals with the efficiency of the various operating units, they make an important contribution to the financial audit engagements. The independent auditors' consideration and use of the work of internal auditors is discussed in Chapter 9.

THE ROLE OF THE AUDIT DIRECTORS

General Considerations

According to Harold M. Williams, former chairman of the Securities and Exchange Commission, the audit committee should do the following with respect to internal control:

> It should examine the company's internal financial and operational controls and organization. The audit committee should review management letters and controls with both the independent and internal auditors. The committee should determine whether recommendations to management have been adequately considered and appropriately implemented.[32]

Moreover, with respect to the audit committee's involvement, Cook and Kelley point out that:

> . . . Board involvement is appropriate, as a minimum, in establishing the proper internal accounting control environment and in exercising an oversight role over the development, review, evaluation, and monitoring of control procedures and techniques.[33]

The preceding comments have recently been echoed by a number of authoritative sources in both the public and private sectors. As mentioned in the preceding chapters, and in particular, in Chapter 2 on corporate governance and accountability, the audit committee has an important oversight responsibility for the company's internal control. The U.S. Congress, the Securities and Exchange Commission, the courts, the National Commission on Fraudulent Financial Reporting, COSO, and the accounting and legal professions have recognized the ac-

---

[32] Harold M. Williams, "Audit Committee—The Public Sector's View," *Journal of Accountancy* 144 (September 1977), p. 74.
[33] Cook and Kelley, "Internal Accounting Control," p. 62.

crued benefits from the audit committee's overseeing both the auditing processes and financial reporting process.

Although the involvement of the committee is clearly evident, it is obvious that management faces a difficult task of implementing and for monitoring the recommendations as set forth by COSO in its four-volume report. The absence of definitive criteria for evaluating the adequacy of the system of internal control no longer exists. Clearly management has a standard against which it can measure the effectiveness of the company's internal control.

With respect to annual reporting, Charles A. Heimbold, Jr., CEO, and Michael F. Mee, CFO of Bristol-Myers Squibb, state the following in their Report of Management:

> The company maintains a system of internal accounting policies, procedures and controls intended to provide reasonable assurance, given the inherent limitations of all internal control systems, at appropriate costs, that transactions are executed in accordance with company authorization, are properly recorded and reported in the financial statements, and that assets are adequately safeguarded. The company's internal auditors continually evaluate the adequacy and effectiveness of this system of internal accounting policies, procedures and controls, and actions are taken to correct deficiencies as they are identified.[34]

Accordingly, the audit committee should give consideration to the following:

1. Has management devised and implemented a plan of action in order to demonstrate its compliance with applicable legislative action, such as the Foreign Corrupt Practices Act (FCPA) and the Federal Deposit Insurance Corporation Improvement Act (FDICIA)? See Appendixes D and E.
   a. Does management understand the accounting control provisions of the acts? Is such an understanding documented?
   b. Has management documented (e.g., accounting policies and procedures manual) the present system of internal control in view of the COSO report?
2. Based on the independent auditor's management letter, has management implemented its recommendations for improving the system of internal control? (For example, the director of internal auditing may submit a summary report on the follow-up action taken by management.)
3. Have the independent auditors discussed with legal counsel any reportable conditions that are a violation of the act? (The committee should discuss the lawyer's letter and the client's letter of management representations with the independent auditor.)
4. Has the director of internal auditing supplied the necessary special reports regarding the scope of study and evaluation of administrative controls?

---

[34] Bristol-Myers Squibb, *1997 Annual Report,* p. 45.

As recommended by the Public Oversight Board on reporting on internal control:

Recommendation V-12:

The SEC should require registrants to include in a document containing the annual financial statements: (a) a report by management on the effectiveness of the entity's internal control system relating to financial reporting; and (b) a report by the registrant's independent accountant on the entity's internal control system relating to financial reporting.

Recommendation V-13:

The Auditing Standards Board should establish standards that require clear communication of the limits of the assurances being provided to third parties when auditors report on the adequacy of client internal control systems.[35]

SOURCES AND SUGGESTED READINGS

American Institute of Certified Public Accountants, *Codification of Statements on Auditing Standards, Nos. 1–21* (New York: American Institute of Certified Public Accountants, 1978).

American Institute of Certified Public Accountants, *Considerations of the Internal Control Structure in a Computer Environment: A Case Study* (New York: American Institute of Certified Public Accountants, 1991).

American Institute of Certified Public Accountants, *Audit Guide for Consideration of the Internal Control Structure in a Financial Statement Audit* (New York: American Institute of Certified Public Accountants, 1996).

American Institute of Certified Public Accountants, *U.S. Auditing Standards/Attestation Standards,* Vol. 1 (New York: American Institute of Certified Public Accountants, 1998).

AICPA Sixth National Conference on SEC Developments. "News Report," *Journal of Accountancy* 147, No. 3 (March 1979), pp. 13–20.

Benson, Richard H., "Changing Demands on the Internal and External Auditors." *Internal Auditor* 36, No. 1 (February 1979), pp. 53–57.

Biegler, John C., "Rebuilding Public Trust in Business." *Financial Executive* 45, No. 6 (June 1977), pp. 28–31.

Bristol-Myers Squibb, *1997 Annual Report.*

Brown, Marilyn V., "Auditors and Internal Controls: An Analyst's View." *CPA Journal* 47, No. 9 (September 1977), pp. 27–31.

---

[35] Public Oversight Board, *A Special Report by the Public Oversight Board of the SEC Practice Section, AICPA* (Stamford, Conn.: Public Oversight Board, 1993), p. 54. As previously mentioned, the Auditing Standards Board has issued two attestation standards that address the Public Oversight Board's recommendation.

Committee of Sponsoring Organizations of the Treadway Commission, *Internal Control—Integrated Framework* (New York: American Institute of Certified Public Accountants, 1992).

Committee of Sponsoring Organizations of the Treadway Commission, *Addendum to* "Reporting to External Parties" (New York: American Institute of Certified Public Accountants, 1994).

Cook, J. Michael, and Thomas P. Kelley, "Internal Accounting Control: A Matter of Law." *Journal of Accountancy* 47, No. 1 (January 1979), pp. 56–64.

Guttry, Harvey V. and Jesse R. Foster, "Internal Controls and the Financial Executive." *Financial Executive* 46, No. 4 (April 1978), pp. 42–48.

Kelley, Thomas P., "The COSO Report: Challenge and Counterchallenge." *Journal of Accountancy* 175, No. 2 (February 1993), pp. 10–18.

Maher, Michael W., David W. Wright, and William R. Kinney, Jr., "Assertions-Based Standards for Integrated Internal Control." *Accounting Horizons* 4, No. 4 (December 1990), pp. 1–8.

Martin, Albert S., and Kenneth P. Johnson, "Assessing Internal Accounting Control: A Workable Approach." *Financial Executive* 46, No. 5 (May 1978), pp. 24–35.

National Commission on Fraudulent Financial Reporting, *Report of the National Commission on Fraudulent Financial Reporting* (Washington, D.C.: National Commission on Fraudulent Financial Reporting, 1987).

Public Oversight Board, *A Special Report by the Public Oversight Board of the SEC Practice Section, AICPA* (Stamford, CT: Public Oversight Board, 1993).

Statement on Auditing Standards No. 55, "Consideration of the Internal Control Structure in a Financial Statement Audit" (New York: American Institute of Certified Public Accountants, 1988).

Statement on Auditing Standards No. 60, "Communication of Internal Control Structure Related Matters Noted in an Audit" (New York: American Institute of Certified Public Accountants, 1988).

Statement on Auditing Standards No. 70, "Reports on the Processing of Transactions by Service Organizations" (New York: American Institute of Certified Public Accountants, 1992).

Statement on Auditing Standards No. 78, "Consideration of Internal Control in a Financial Statement Audit: An Amendment to SAS No. 55" (New York: American Institute of Certified Public Accountants, 1995).

Statement on Standards for Attestation Engagements No. 2, "Reporting on an Entity's Internal Control Structure Over Financial Reporting" (New York: American Institute of Certified Public Accountants, 1993).

Statement on Standards for Attestation Engagements No. 3, "Compliance Attestation" (New York: American Institute of Certified Public Accountants, 1993).

Takacs, Joseph, "Attestation Engagements on Internal Control Structure over Financial Reporting." *CPA Journal* 63, No. 8 (August 1993), pp. 48–53.

American Institute of Certified Public Accountants, "Tentative Report of the Special Advisory Committee on Internal Accounting Control" (New York: American Institute of Certified Public Accountants, 1978).

Wallace, Wanda, A., *Handbook of Internal Accounting Controls,* 2nd ed. (Englewood Cliffs, N.J.: Prentice Hall, 1991).

Williams, Harold M., "Audit Committees—The Public Sector's View." *Journal of Accountancy* 144, No. 9 (September 1977), pp. 71–74.

Chapter 9

Monitoring the Internal Audit Function

Although references have been made to the internal audit function in the preceding chapters, the major objective of this chapter is to provide guidance for the audit committee's ongoing appraisal of the effectiveness of the entity's corporate auditing staff. In this chapter, the audit director will examine such matters as the structure and organization of the auditing staff, their organizational independence, logistical staff matters, and the quality of personnel and training. In addition, a recapitulation of the salient points concerning the committee's review of this function is provided. Also, the reader should review Appendix K for further information regarding the professional standards and ethics of the internal auditors.

NEED FOR MONITORING THE INTERNAL AUDIT FUNCTION

General Matters

As previously discussed in Chapter 1, the audit directors and the internal auditing group have a logical interface, since both groups have common goals. For example, the audit directors are a service to the board of directors, and the internal auditors are a service to the operating management. Both groups are engaged in an independent assessment of the internal control, as discussed in Chapter 8. Implicit in their ongoing appraisal of the system of internal control is the audit director's monitoring of the internal audit function. This monitoring is extremely beneficial to the board and its operating management for the following reasons. First, the committee's review of the internal auditing staff not only enhances the staff's independence but also strengthens its image in the corporate structure. Second, through the committee's review of the organizational structure and scope of the entity's internal audit function, the external auditing fees can be minimized since the coordination of both auditing activities reduces the potential of either groups to be counterproductive. Third, an effective internal auditing group assists the audit committee in discharging its responsibilities because of its limited time and oversight capacity. Thus it is evident that the committee's oversight responsibility for the internal auditing function is within its province to ensure that such a corporate resource is used effectively and efficiently.

Moreover, the National Commission on Fraudulent Financial Reporting has strongly endorsed the concept of internal auditing to reduce the incidence of fraudulent financial reporting:

> All public companies must have an effective and objective internal audit function. The internal auditor's qualifications, staff, status within the company, reporting lines, and relationship with the audit committee of the board of directors must be adequate to ensure the internal audit function's effectiveness and objectivity. The internal auditor should consider his audit findings in the context of the company's financial statements and should, to the extent appropriate, coordinate his activities with the activities of the independent public accountant.[1]

As the Auditing Standards Board notes:

> Monitoring is a process that assesses the quality of internal control performance over time. It involves assessing the design and operation of controls on a timely basis and taking necessary corrective actions. This process is accomplished through ongoing activities, separate evaluations, or by various combinations of the two. In many entities, internal auditors or personnel performing similar functions contribute to the monitoring of an entity's activities. Monitoring activities may include using information from communications from external parties such as customer complaints and regulator comments that may indicate problems or highlight areas in need of improvement.

> The auditor should obtain sufficient knowledge of the major types of activities the entity uses to monitor internal control over financial reporting, including how those activities are used to initiate corrective actions. When obtaining an understanding of the internal audit function, the auditor should follow the guidance in paragraphs 4 through 8 of SAS No. 65, The Auditor's Consideration of the Internal Audit Function in an Audit of Financial Statements.[2]

In addition, the Internal Auditing Standards Board has issued *Statement on Internal Auditing Standards No. 7,* "Communication with the Board of Directors," now codified into guidelines 110.01, which states in part:

> .01 Internal auditors should have the support of senior management and of the board so that they can gain the cooperation of auditees and perform their work free from interference.

---

[1]*Report of the National Commission on Fraudulent Financial Reporting* (Washington, D.C.: National Commission on Fraudulent Financial Reporting, 1987), pp. 11–12. For further discussion of the internal audit function and chief internal auditor, see pp. 37–39 of the Commission's report.

[2]*Statement on Auditing Standards, No. 78,* "Consideration of Internal Control in a Financial Statement Audit: An Amendment to SAS No. 55" (New York: American Institute of Certified Public Accountants, 1995), par. 38, 39.

.1 The director of the internal auditing department should be responsible to an individual in the organization with sufficient authority to promote independence and to ensure broad audit coverage, adequate consideration of audit reports, and appropriate action on audit recommendations.

.2 The director should have direct communication with the board. Regular communication with the board helps assure independence and provides a means for the board and the director to keep each other informed on matters of mutual interest.

     a. Direct communication occurs when the director regularly attends and participates in those meetings of the board which relate to its oversight responsibilities for auditing, financial reporting, organizational governance and control. The director's attendance at these meetings and the presentation of written and/or oral reports provides for an exchange of information concerning the plans and activities of the internal auditing department. The director of internal auditing should meet privately with the board at least annually.[3]

As Curtis C. Verschoor and Joseph P. Liotta conclude:

Internal auditors should place a high priority on an in-depth review of their relationships with the board of their organization. Internal auditors must not only evaluate whether or not they are in full compliance with the recommendations of *SIAS No. 7*; they should also consider ways of enhancing the quality of their relationships with the board. Copies of *SIAS No. 7* should be furnished to senior management, members of the board, and external auditors, to inform them of the new IIA [Institute of Internal Auditors] reporting guidelines. In view of the trend toward increased communication between external auditors and the board, internal auditors may well wish to reexamine the reporting threshold they use to inform the board of their activities. The public is demanding more effective performance by internal auditors, thereby offering the profession an even greater opportunity for service.[4]

Finally, the Committee of Sponsoring Organizations of the Treadway Commission stated that:

Internal auditors play an important role in evaluating the effectiveness of control systems, and contribute to ongoing effectiveness. Because of organizational position

---

[3] *Standards for the Professional Practice of Internal Auditing,* Section 110.01 (Altamonte Springs, Fla.: Institute of Internal Auditors, 1998), pp. 11–12. For an interesting discussion on the perceptions of audit committee members and chief internal auditors, see Lawrence P. Kalbers, "Audit Committees and Internal Auditors," *Internal Auditor* 49, No. 6 (December 1992), pp. 37–44. See also Jerry Strawser and Barbara Apostolou, "The Role of Internal Auditor Communication with the Audit Committee," *Internal Auditing* 6, No. 2 (Fall 1990), pp. 35–42; and Curtis Verschoor, "Internal Auditing Interactions with the Audit Committee," *Internal Auditing* 7, No. 4 (Spring 1992), pp. 20–23.

[4] Curtis C. Verschoor and Joseph P. Liotta, "Communication with Audit Committees," *Internal Auditor* 47, No. 2 (April 1990), p. 47.

and authority in an entity, an internal audit function often plays a significant monitoring role.[5]

Karen N. Horn, former chairman and CEO of Bank One and a member of several audit committees, summarizes the relationship between the audit committee and internal auditors as follows:

> Our joint responsibilities to our companies are now defined much more broadly. Any type of change this far reaching must become part of the corporate culture. As a senior manager and director, my obligation is to provide you with what the Committee of Sponsoring Organizations calls integrity, ethical values, a control environment, and clear management objectives—in short, to nurture a culture that allows you to do the things described in this article. Internal auditors are then the champions of this new control culture.
>
> The activities are as complex and changing as our organizations; and I believe they have never been more important.[6]

In order to effectively monitor the internal audit function, the agenda for the audit committee should include a review of the following:

1. The objectives, plans, and policy of the corporate internal auditing group (discussed in Chapters 6 and 7 in relation to the planning activities of both the committee and the internal audit group)
2. The organization of the internal auditing group
3. The quality of the auditing personnel and training as well as the use of outside service providers
4. The operational activities of the staff in the context of achieving their goals and objectives (see Chapters 1 and 3)

---

[5]Committee of Sponsoring Organizations of the Treadway Commission, *Internal Control-Integrated Framework* (New York: American Institute of Certified Public Accountants, 1992), p. 5. For additional emphasis, see pp. 84–85 of the "Framework" volume.

[6]Karen N. Horn, "An Audit Committee Member Looks at Internal Auditing," *Internal Auditor* 49, No. 6 (December 1992), p. 36. For an expanded discussion of the relationship between the audit committee and internal auditors, see William E. Chadwick, "Tough Questions, Tough Answers," *Internal Auditor* 52, No. 6 (December 1995), pp. 63–65; Dwight L. Allison, Jr., "Internal Auditors and Audit Committees," *Internal Auditor* 51, No. 1 (February 1994), pp. 50–55; A recent study of chief internal auditors of 72 Canadian manufacturing companies (sales > $50 million), found that "while there were no significant differences with respect to involvement in decisions to dismiss the chief internal auditor, audit committees consisting of solely nonemployee directors were more likely, than audit committees with one or more insiders, to (1) have frequent meetings with the chief internal auditor, and (2) review the internal auditing program and results of internal auditing" (p. 51). See D. Paul Scarbrough, Dasaratha V. Rama, and K. Raghunandan, "Audit Committee Composition and Interaction with Internal Auditing: Canadian Evidence," *Accounting Horizons* 12, No. 1 (March 1998), pp. 51–62.

Such an approach to the monitoring function of the committee enhances its ability to meet the expectations of the board of directors. As discussed in Chapter 2, the audit committee has a critical role in helping the board fulfill its corporate stewardship accountability.

REVIEWING THE ORGANIZATION OF THE CORPORATE AUDIT STAFF

Organizational Structure

Of particular importance to the audit committee is the organizational status of the internal auditing staff in the corporate structure. Structure and organization should be designed to carry out effectively an independent appraisal of management's activities. In view of the Foreign Corrupt Practices Act, an effective and efficient internal auditing staff can assist management with its implementation of a sound system of internal control. Thus it behooves the audit committee to monitor the organizational framework of the corporate auditing group to ensure a comprehensive scope. For example, as George M. Scott and Bart H. Ward point out:

> Without a framework within which to structure their activities, internal auditors regrettably seem likely to remain engrossed with assessing the adequacy of traditional control systems to the exclusion of grappling with the control problems flowing from growth and complexity.[7]

In addition, Michael J. Barrett and P. Tiessen set forth the following proposed recommendations with respect to organizational support for the internal audit group.

Senior Management

Internal audit must be provided with adequate resources and personnel to perform audit examinations with appropriate frequency at all organizational levels, areas, and activities.

Internal audit director's reporting position should be at an administrative level that will ensure independence.

Internal audit director's salary and promotion possibilities should be commensurate with his or her administrative reporting level.

Internal audit director should be free of undue influence to limit the scope of the department's audit scope and audit assignment schedule.

---

[7]George M. Scott and Bart H. Ward, "The Internal Audit—A Tool for Management Control," *Financial Executive* 46, No. 3 (March 1978), p. 33.

All organizational levels, areas, and activities should be subject to internal audit examination. Those performed by senior management should comply with the Corporate Code of Conduct.

Internal audit recommendations should receive strong mandated attention, and there should be appropriate follow-up to better ensure that management has taken appropriate remedial action.

Audit Committee

Audit committee should be composed entirely of external members of the board of directors who are not affiliated with the company in any other capacity.

Director of internal audit should communicate directly and regularly to the audit committee.

Audit committee should play a significant role in concurring with the salary and promotion judgments of senior management for the internal audit director.

Reports or report summaries should be communicated to the audit committee on a regular basis.

Director should meet regularly and privately with the audit committee with no other members of management present.

Requests from the audit committee for special assignments should be considered to be a normal and routine part of the internal audit department's responsibilities.

Director should feel no obligation to immediately report audit committee special assignment requests to senior management.

Director should have the right and responsibility to communicate specific matters directly to the audit committee, and internal audit should be actively encouraged to do so. A communication policy for internal audit should be established to indicate items and reports that should be directly communicated to the audit committee.

A cordial, informal, routine, and trusting relationship should be established and fostered between the director and the audit committee.[8]

Finally, Joseph Castellano, Harper Roehm, and John P. Walker used a "focus-group approach" to explore the relationship between external auditors (EA) and internal auditors (IA). Their objective was to study the implications of the Treadway Commission's recommendation "that the audit committee meet with the external auditors to discuss the performance of the internal auditors and vice versa." They concluded:

While many companies have already implemented this recommendation, this study shows that external and internal auditors do not believe that audit committees give

---

[8] Michael J. Barrett and P. Tiessen, "Organizational Support for Internal Auditing," *Internal Auditing* 5, No. 2 (Fall 1989), pp. 52–53.

their respective inputs equal weight. External auditors tended to be more concerned about what the CFO reported to the committee about their performance than what the internal auditor reported. However, the IA group indicated that they believed the EA input to the audit committee was very important, more so than the CFO's input. These relative differences appear to be related to the audit committee's perceived organizational status of the IA.

The Director of Internal Auditing should be elevated in the organizational hierarchy to a level consistent with the CFO. This would minimize board discounting of IA input, enhance the quality of audits, and meet the spirit of the Treadway recommendation.[9]

Thus it is important to recognize that the framework for the internal auditing function should be established so that it correlates closely with the auditing segments of the corporate audit plan discussed in Chapter 6. This broad framework should also incorporate the nature and scope of the entity's operational activities. For example, it is obvious that if the enterprise is operating on a multinational basis, then the framework for the internal auditing function should be designed to address the auditing needs of the entity in both the domestic and international arenas. Consequently, the organizational structure of this auditing group should be balanced in order to provide assurance to the board that the internal auditing resources are properly allocated.

To ensure that the organizational framework for the internal auditing function is comprehensive and balanced, the audit committee should give consideration to the following points:

1. Corporate auditing philosophy
2. Corporate auditing independence
3. Logistical matters, such as the size and geographic location of staff

Corporate Auditing Philosophy

Continuing developments in corporate accountability and governance necessitate an ongoing appraisal of the entity's auditing philosophy. The audit committee's approach to a reexamination of such a philosophy should be based on its understanding of the auditing group's approaches to the internal auditing function. For example, the auditing approaches may be traditional and therefore not totally conducive to the entity's auditing needs. Such an approach is evidenced by the group's preoccupation with the traditional internal financial auditing activities. Although

[9] Joseph Castellano, Harper Roehm, and John P. Walker, "Status & Quality," *Internal Auditor* 49, No. 3 (June 1992), p. 52. For a more detailed discussion, see the *Standards for the Professional Practice of Internal Auditing* (Altamonte Springs, Fla.: Institute of Internal Auditors, 1998), Section 10, pp. 11–15.

such auditing activities may reduce the outside auditing costs, it is essential that the audit committee review the auditing approaches in the operational and compliance areas. As indicated in Chapter 6, the committee's review of the scope of the entity's internal audit plans should enable it to ensure that adequate coverage is given to the auditing segments of the corporate audit plan. Furthermore, the audit committee should be satisfied that the internal auditing philosophy is supported by modern approaches to the internal auditing function. For example, if the entity has a strong computer environment, then the committee should be satisfied that the internal auditing group has the necessary electronic data processing auditing expertise. Also, since the independent auditors are required to study and evaluate the entity's internal audit function as part of their review of the internal accounting controls, the committee should request a written opinion of their assessment of the internal auditing philosophy and the organizational structure. Obviously, the committee should give strong consideration to the recommendations made by the independent auditors. Many of the salient points discussed in this text will assist the audit committee in its assessment of the entity's internal auditing philosophy.

Corporate Auditing Independence

Fundamental to the structure and organization of the corporate auditing staff is their independence within the corporate framework. While it is obvious that the members of this group are employees of the corporation, their reporting relationship should be established so that the director of internal auditing is responsible to an executive with enough authority to provide the necessary internal auditing coverage. Such a reporting relationship has been advocated by the Institute of Internal Auditors in their "Statement of the Responsibilities of Internal Auditors." (See Chapter 1.) For example, The Conference Board, in a 1978 study on internal auditing, surveyed 274 companies and reported that 76 percent of the internal audit managers report to a vice presidential level or higher, whereas only 40 percent of them reported to such a level in 1963.[10] Moreover, "fifteen percent of the respondents (as against 9 percent in 1963) report to one of the top three officers (chairman, vice chairman, president) or to a board committee."[11]

In 1988 the Conference Board found in a survey of 692 companies that the audit committee has closer ties to internal auditing. The Board reported:

> The survey produced further evidence of the closer working relationship between audit committees and the internal audit function. Just as access to the audit committee by the outside auditing firm has been strengthened, so too has access by the chief

[10]Paul Macchiaverna, *Internal Auditing,* Report No. 748 (New York: The Conference Board, 1978), p. 53.
[11]Ibid., p. 54.

internal auditor. It is more common now for charters to require the committee to meet in private with the internal auditor (with no members of management present), or to state that the committee will be available to the internal auditor when necessary, or both.

Another way companies support the independent status of the internal auditing function is to specify in writing that the audit committee must have a say—or, at a minimum, must be consulted and thoroughly informed—when there is to be a change in internal auditors. Some committees are also charged with monitoring the pay level of the head of internal auditing. These links give the internal auditor an ally in high places and presumably discourage management from trying to undermine or compromise his/her sense of independence.

Another major trend is the increasing extent to which internal auditors formally report to the audit committee. In the 1978 survey, 25 percent of participating firms engaged in this practice. By 1987, this was true of almost *half* (47 percent).[12]

It is apparent that the trend over the years has been to enhance the independence and objectivity of the internal auditing staff. Although some corporate auditing executives are reporting to the chairman of the board or the president, Edward G. Jepsen, former partner of Price Waterhouse & Company (now Pricewaterhouse-Coopers), points out:

> As a practical matter, such a person (chairman or president) may not be able to give the department the attention it needs—and thus there is a danger that it would become isolated from top management. A common organizational structure is for the department to report directly on a day-to-day basis to the company's senior financial officer and have a dotted-line relationship (implying less frequent contact but clear access) to the chairman or president.[13]

Also, Jepsen states that a "logical development" of the formation of the audit committee is having the corporate auditing executive meet periodically with the committee to discuss the corporate auditing function.[14] For example, the Conference Board's "survey shows that more than seven out of ten auditing staffs are meeting regularly with their committees (audit) to discuss auditing affairs."[15] More specifically, of the 258 internal auditing staffs surveyed, 55 percent discuss the internal auditing organization.[16] It is clearly evident that the internal audit staff must be "free of organizational pressures" that restrict their independence and objectivity

[12] Jeremy Bacon, *The Audit Committee: A Broader Mandate,* Report No. 914 (New York: The Conference Board, 1988), pp. 20–21.
[13] Edward G. Jepsen, "Internal Auditors Move into the Spotlight," *Internal Auditor* 36, No. 2 (April 1979), pp. 27–28.
[14] Ibid.
[15] Macchiaverna, *Internal Auditing,* p. 55.
[16] Ibid., p. 57.

in "selecting areas to be examined or in evaluating those areas."[17] Also, as discussed in Chapter 1, the director of internal auditing must be able to meet regularly with the audit committee.

Logistical Matters

Depending on the nature, size, and complexity of the entity, management will have different corporate auditing needs. Thus the particular circumstances of the entity will govern the organizational structure of the internal auditing staff. For example, the Conference Board reports that "corporate audit staffs are either centralized at corporate headquarters or are decentralized, with some members permanently located at various subsidiaries or divisions."[18] Furthermore, the Board's study disclosed a number of internal auditing staffs have made changes in their organizational structure. They are:

> Reporting of subsidiary and divisional audit staffs in some companies has been centralized. These units now report to corporate auditing, instead of to subsidiary or division management. Typically, this has been due to bolster the independence of resident audit staffs, and to increase corporate control over decentralized operations.
>
> Decentralizing audit operations on a geographical basis—moving auditors formerly based at corporate headquarters to other company locations. This has been done so that auditing can better cover far-flung company operations. It also reduces the amount of travel required of auditors—a major cause of dissatisfaction which can result in high staff turnover.
>
> Creating special sections—to focus on individual corporate functions, or specialist groups, which assist the main audit group. For example, most EDP audit sections perform specialized data processing audits, as well as assist financial or operational auditors in their duties.[19]

In addition to the preceding logistical considerations, the audit committee should give consideration to the cost-benefit factor regarding the size and location of the audit staff. The cost of the corporate auditing resources should be weighed against the potential benefits from such resources. For example, Richard H. Benson of Arthur Andersen & Co. asserts that the travel costs associated with sending auditors to other countries from the United States can be "minimized by internal auditors working with locally based external auditors as a team."[20] Moreover, Jepsen notes that although there is no definitive criterion for relating the size of the

[17] Jepsen, "Internal Auditors," p. 27.

[18] Macchiaverna, *Internal Auditing,* p. 68.

[19] Ibid., pp. 68–69.

[20] Richard H. Benson, "Changing Demands on Internal and External Auditors," *Internal Auditor* 36, No. 1 (February 1979), pp. 56–67.

staff with "corporate sales or total assets," consideration should be given to the quality of the system of internal control.[21] Clearly, the size and location of the internal auditing staff should be a function of the adequacy of the internal accounting and administrative controls. Thus the committee should assess the potential opportunity cost and related degree of risk management is willing to assume. For example, the committee should discuss with both the internal and independent auditing executives the potential opportunity cost of not auditing specific locations in light of the internal control conditions. One large corporation reported that "15 major locations are audited once a year, while the remaining 185 minor locations are scheduled for visits once every two years."[22] The selection of the major areas is ordinarily based on the concept of materiality and relative risk (discussed in Chapter 5) for the financial audit. Conversely, in connection with the operational audits, "it should be possible to develop some estimates of the profit contribution resulting from the operational audits compared to the related audit costs."[23] Consequently, the committee should review the budget of the internal auditing staff as well as the outside auditing fees in relation to the entity's auditing needs and potential auditing benefits. Obviously, if the system of internal control is strong, based on the opinions of both the independent and internal auditors, then the high costs of such auditing services should be curtailed.

Equally important, the committee should review the organization chart of the internal auditing function to determine that it is balanced in accordance with the corporate audit plan. An illustrative organization chart in Exhibit 9.1 shows how the internal audit function might be organized on a centralized basis for a multinational enterprise. Because the chart is oversimplified, the organizational arrangements will vary and contain more detail in actual practice. The major objective is to show the reporting and functional relationships of the internal auditing function. Moreover, the scope of the international auditing operations will also involve financial, operational, and compliance audits at the resident audit staff level. For example, the Conference Board found that the organizational arrangements regarding the international auditing operations vary whereby "some companies base their international auditors at corporate headquarters in the U.S.," and others are centrally located overseas.[24] If the enterprise is highly diversified, it may decide to decentralize its internal auditing function for such reasons as "increased travel costs," increased "staff dissatisfaction" with traveling, and "more frequent audit coverage."[25] In short, the organizational arrangement should be designed to maximize the corporate auditing services and minimize the economic cost of such services without sacrificing the quality of the auditing work.

[21] Jepsen, "Internal Auditors," p. 28.
[22] Macchiaverna, *Internal Auditing*, p. 71.
[23] Jepsen, "Internal Auditors," p. 31.
[24] Macchiaverna, *Internal Auditing*, p. 71.
[25] Ibid., pp. 72–73.

Exhibit 9.1   Sample Organization Chart of an Internal Audit Operation

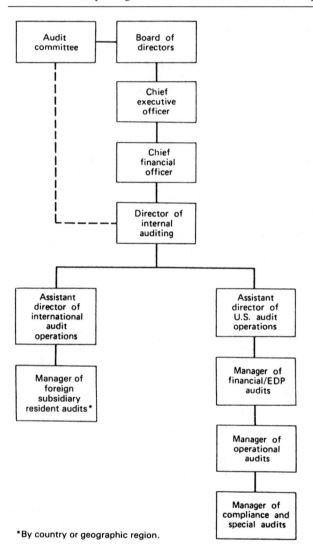

*By country or geographic region.

APPRAISING THE QUALITY OF THE AUDITING STAFF

The Corporate Auditing Staff

The quality of the auditing personnel and training has an important influence on the performance of the staff. If the auditing personnel's training, skills, and education are not compatible to their broadened responsibilities, they become preoccupied with the routine checking of the accounting transactions and records. As a result, management becomes more susceptible to unfavorable developments, such as deficiencies in the system of internal control and potential fraudulent practices. According to Myles L. Mace, CBS, Inc. reorganized their internal audit function subsequent to their discovery of management fraud in one of their operating divisions. Mace found that:

> The internal audit function required multi- and nontraditional skills. More people with skills related to an audit examination were recruited. They included generalists with operational backgrounds, who could provide insight into operational auditing in contrast to straight financial auditing. Persons with computer science backgrounds were added . . . and the company enlisted help in security and protective science.[26]

It is imperative that the audit committee review the selection process for the corporate auditing personnel. In reviewing the selection process, the committee should seek assistance from the independent auditors. For example, outside auditors, in their review of the internal audit function, are required to review the competence of the internal audit staff. They inquire about their qualifications, including the entity's "practices for hiring, training, and supervising the internal audit staff."[27] Although the weaknesses in the internal audit function may be disclosed in the independent auditor's management letter concerning the system of internal control, it is desirable to request their comprehensive evaluation of the function. Although such an evaluation may require a special assignment for the independent accounting firm, it is beneficial to the entity in the long run. Obviously, independent auditors can perform an effective evaluation because of their requisite auditing knowledge and objectivity. The audit committee should request a written opinion from the independent auditors concerning the overall effectiveness of the corporate auditing staff.

More recently, a number of companies have outsourced a portion or all of the internal audit function. In 1997, the Internal Auditing Standards Board issued

---

[26] Myles L. Mace, "Strengthening the Functions of Internal Auditors," *Harvard Business Review* 55, No. 4 (July–August 1977), p. 46.

[27] *Statement on Auditing Standards, No. 65,* "The Auditor's Consideration of the Internal Audit Function in an Audit of Financial Statements" (New York: American Institute of Certified Public Accountants, 1991), par. 9.

SIAS No. 18, "Use of Outside Service Providers" (now codified into Guidelines 220.02, sub-subsections 1–13.). With respect to the selection of outside service providers by senior management or the board, the Board stated:

> When the director of internal auditing intends to use and rely on the work of an outside service provider, the director should assess the competence, independence, and objectivity of the outside service provider as it relates to the particular assignment to be performed. This assessment should also be made when the outside service provider is selected by senior management or the board, and the director intends to use and rely on the outside service provider's work. When the selection is made by others and the assessment determines that the director should not use and rely on the work of an outside service provider, then the results of the assessment should be communicated to senior management or the board, as appropriate.[28]

While the debate continues over the circumstances in which the independent auditing firm performs a portion of an audit client's internal audit function, the Board concluded:

> In assessing the independence and objectivity of the outside service provider, the director of internal auditing should consider:
>
> a. The financial interest the provider may have in the organization.
>
> b. The personal or professional affiliation the provider may have to the board, senior management, or others within the organization.
>
> c. The relationship the provider may have had with the organization or the activities being reviewed.
>
> d. The extent of other ongoing services the provider may be performing for the organization.
>
> e. Compensation or other incentives that the provider may have.[29]

In order to facilitate discussion, the audit committee should review the independent auditor's comments regarding the quality of auditing personnel in relation to the following considerations:

1. The professional qualifications and educational backgrounds of the staff. For example, The Conference Board found that audit managers are attempting to "elevate the professionalism" of the internal audit staff by employing "more CPA's, certified internal auditors or MBA's."[30]

---

[28] *Standards for the Professional Practice of Internal Auditing,* Sec. 220.02.3.

[29] Ibid., 220.02.6. For a more detailed discussion of outsourcing internal audit activities, see Anthony J. Ridley and Lew Burnham, "Where Are the Auditors? *Directors and Boards* 22, No. 2 (Winter 1998), pp. 61–63.

[30] Macchiaverna, *Internal Auditing,* p. 75.

2. Professional training and development programs for the corporate audit staff are available through several professional accounting societies and especially the Institute of Internal Auditors. Also, in-house professional development programs of the independent accounting firm may be a possible source of training. For example, to increase the professionalism of the internal audit staff, the Institute of Internal Auditors sponsors the Certified Internal Auditor (CIA) Program. As John D. Marquardt and John F. Bussman report, "The number of candidates sitting for the CIA Exam has increased from 654 in 1974, the year it was first offered, to 2,091 in 1978."[31] More recently, according to the Certification Department of The Institute of Internal Auditors, as of November 1992, the number of certified internal auditors has increased to 19,264. Clearly, the trend is toward professionalizing the internal audit staff in order to enhance their professional auditing integrity and objectivity in the corporate structure.

3. The performance appraisal and evaluation system. "These typically evaluate: (1) an auditor's technical knowledge; (2) compliance with audit policies and procedures; (3) administrative skills and work habits; and (4) effectiveness in interpersonal relationships."[32]

The audit committee's appraisal of the quality and training of the corporate auditing staff provides assurance to the board of directors that the internal auditing function is adequately staffed. Such assurance to the board indicates that this auditing staff is used wisely and responsibly in the interests of the board's outside constituencies.

As previously noted, the Auditing Standards Board has issued SAS No. 65, "The Auditor's Consideration of the Internal Audit Function in an Audit of Financial Statements." This auditing standard is designed to provide expanded guidance to independent auditors when considering the work performed by internal auditors. Recognizing that both the audit committee and the independent auditors have cross-purposes in understanding and assessing the internal audit functions, Exhibits 9.2 and 9.3 compare the SAS No. 65 requirements with a model response from the director of internal auditing. These responses are not intended to be all-inclusive. However, such model responses will enable the audit committee to gain reasonable assurance on the effective interaction between the internal audit group and the independent auditors.

In addition to the model responses in Exhibits 9.2 and 9.3, the reader may wish to review Exhibit 9.4, which contains a list of questions dealing with internal auditing activities.

---

[31] John D. Marquardt and John F. Bussman, "The CIA Examination: A Topical Profile and Index Update," *The Internal Auditor* 36, No. 2 (April 1979), p. 41.
[32] Macchiaverna, *Internal Auditing,* p. 89.

Exhibit 9.2   Representative Responses for Understanding the Internal Audit Function

SAS No. 65 Requirements	Internal Auditors' Documented Response
• Organizational status with the entity	• Presentation and discussion of a written charter or mission statement of the internal audit function and free access to the entity's audit committee.
• Application of professional standards	• Adherence to high professional standards as promulgated by the IIA's *Standards for the Professional Practice of Internal Auditing,* official pronouncements, and *Code of Ethics.*
• Audit plans	• Discussion, coordination, and implementation of the planned external and internal audit scope and related joint planning memos relative to audit risk assessment (e.g., small divisions and subsidiaries that have undergone recent management changes or other material changes in their business activities may need additional audit work).
	• Discussion of proposed scope of any special investigations relative to the potential impact on the financial statements and the opinion of general counsel.
	• Review on the follow-up of the external auditor's management letter and nonaudit services.
• Access to records and any scope limitations on activities	• Review of unrestricted access to records and departments as disclosed in the written charter of the internal audit function and approved by the audit committee.

Source: Louis Braiotta, Jr., and Hugh L. Marsh, "Developing a Constructive Relationship Under the Guidance of SAS No. 65," *Internal Auditing* 8, No. 2 (Fall 1992), p. 7. Reprinted with permission from *Internal Auditing,* copyright © 1992, Warren Gorham Lamont, 31 St. James Avenue, Boston, MA 02116. All rights reserved.

While each audit committee may develop its own approach to monitoring the activities of the corporate auditing staff, the following recapitulation of the salient points should be helpful.[33]

---

[33] The reader should review the questions in the checklist in Chapter 3. It should be reemphasized that the audit directors are reviewing and assessing this function in their oversight and advisory capacity. They are *not* assuming the day-to-day operations of this particular group. For additional discussion, see Joseph Mchugh and K. Raghunandan, "Hiring & Firing the Chief Internal Auditor," *Internal Auditor* 54, No. 4 (August 1994), pp. 34–39; Wanda A. Wallace and G. Thomas White, "Reporting on Internal Control," *Internal Auditor* 51, No. 4 (August 1994), pp. 40–42.

Exhibit 9.3 Representative Responses for Assessing Competency and Objectivity of the
Internal Auditors

SAS No. 65 Requirements	Internal Auditors' Documented Response
• Educational level and professional experience of internal auditors	• Presentation and discussion of the current vitas of the internal audit group and their organization and composition (e.g., generalists with operational backgrounds versus financial auditing personnel). Demonstrate a mix of auditing skills and education.
• Professional certification and continuing education	• Advisement of the number of CIAs, MBAs, CPAs, CMAs, and CISAs on the staff • Advisement of the number of professional training and development opportunities for the staff and the budgeted dollar amount.
• Audit policies, programs, and procedures	• Presentation of audit policies and procedures relative to financial, operational, and compliance audits, including quality control, rotation practices, and corporate conduct.
• Practices regarding assignment of internal auditors	• Discussion of work schedules, time budgets, and costs.
• Supervision and review of internal auditors' activities	• Discussion of the level of knowledge required for the entity and the industry. • Review of the ratio of staff assistants to supervisors relative to the scope and responsibilities for the audit. • Discussion of supervisory review procedures of staff assistants' work and note disagreements. • Review of audit risk assessment methodologies.
• Quality of working-paper documentation, reports, and recommendations	• Review of the reports issued with a response from the auditee and reasons for management disagreements, including the timeliness of both. • Review of the timetable for implementing recommendations.
• Evaluation of internal auditors' performance relative to SAS No. 65 requirements	• Discussion of the most recent peer review reports on the internal audit function. • Discussion of prior year's review of the internal audit function by the external auditors and any response or changes made as a result.

Source: Louis Braiotta, Jr., and Hugh L. Marsh, "Developing a Constructive Relationship Under the Guidance of SAS No. 65," *Internal Auditing* 8, No. 2 (Fall 1992), p. 9. Reprinted with permission from *Internal Auditing*, Copyright © 1992, Warren Gorham & Lamont, 31 St. James Avenue, Boston, MA 02116. All rights reserved.

Exhibit 9.4 Vital Checkpoints: Internal Audit Questions for the Audit Committee

---

Mission Statement. Each company should develop and disseminate an annual policy statement re the objectives of internal audit.

- ✓ Does a mission statement exist for the internal audit function?
- ✓ Is this mission statement approved by the chief executive officer or senior management?
- ✓ Are the internal audit objectives known and understood by all levels of management?

Annual Internal Audit Plan. The senior internal auditor should prepare an annual plan setting forth goals and objectives such as:

- Planned level of audit coverage
- Staffing
- Areas of audit risk
- Degree of coordination with external audit function
- Special projects
- Annual cost
- Compliance with corporate codes of conduct

- ✓ Is this plan reviewed and approved by appropriate levels of management?
- ✓ Was this plan reviewed with the external auditors?
- ✓ Were their comments and/or recommendations incorporated in the plan?
- ✓ Did they note any deficiencies in the plan that were not incorporated in the final plan?
- ✓ Has management placed any scope restrictions on the extent of audit coverage?
- ✓ Does the plan provide coverage of the Company's computer control functions?
- ✓ Do you have the necessary human resources in terms of trained experienced staff to achieve the annual plan?

Progress Reports. The internal auditor should report annually on progress in meeting the previously approved annual plan:

- ✓ Has management adequately addressed the comments and recommendations set forth in your reports?
- ✓ Who receives copies of your reports?
- ✓ Are copies of your recent reports made available to the external auditor?
- ✓ Do they receive appropriate management support?
- ✓ Were there any significant recommendations relating to control weaknesses or company policy that have not been adequately addressed and corrected?
- ✓ Do you monitor that the necessary corrective action has in fact been implemented?
- ✓ Did your audit procedures uncover any instances of employee fraud, questionable or illegal payments, or violations of laws or regulations? (Follow-up questions, as appropriate).
- ✓ Were any limitations placed on the phase of your audit plan during this period?
- ✓ Did you receive appropriate management support and cooperation?
- ✓ In connection with the audit functions completed during this period, did you review all the related computer control functions? Were they deemed adequate?

Exhibit 9.4   *(Continued)*

✓ Is the computer security system reviewed in connection with these audit procedures? Are they adequate?

✓ Does each computer system reviewed have an adequate backup system and disaster contingency plan?

Other Areas. Additional areas can be covered in private meetings with internal auditors as appropriate:

✓ Are you satisfied with the adequacy and competence of financial management in the areas subject to audit review?

✓ Does the internal audit function receive the appropriate level of support from senior management and operating management?

✓ Are you satisfied with the level of cooperation and support from the external auditors?

✓ Are the internal and external audit functions coordinated to maximize the effectiveness of both groups and to minimize any unnecessary duplication of effort?

✓ Have there been any material changes in the internal audit staff that would adversely impact your ability to complete your objective for the current period?

✓ To what extent, if any, have you been assigned special projects that have adversely impacted your ability to achieve your goals?

✓ Are you satisfied that the "tone at the top" is appropriate?

✓ Has the company taken the appropriate action with respect to management comments submitted by the external auditors?

Further Questions. Additional internal auditing questions can be addressed privately to financial personnel, senior management, or the external auditor, as appropriate:

✓ Are you satisfied with respect to the level of performance of the internal audit function?

✓ Do the internal auditors perform their duties and responsibilities objectively and professionally?

✓ Do they perform their audits effectively?

✓ Are they considered constructive and effective by operating management?

✓ Do they receive the appropriate level of management support and cooperation?

✓ Does an appropriate degree of mutual respect exist between the internal and external auditors?

✓ Is there an effective working relationship between the internal and external auditors to maximize effectiveness and minimize cost?

Source: Richard S. Hickok and Jules Zimmerman, *Vital Checkpoints: Internal Audit Questions for the Audit Committee* (New York: Hickok Associates, Inc., 1990). Copyright © 1990 by Hickok Associates, Inc. Reprinted with permission.

1. Assist in the overall internal auditing policy determination, and approve such policies to ensure that the staff has authority commensurate with their responsibilities.
2. Review the scope of the internal and external auditing plans to maximize on the resources allocated to the audit function and minimize the outside auditing fees.
3. Review copies of the internal auditing reports and critically evaluate the findings, recommendations, management's response, and courses of action taken. Also, review the disposition of the recommendations in the independent auditor's management letter.
4. Review and appraise the staff's organization regarding their auditing philosophy, independence, and logistical operations.
5. Assess the quality of the auditing personnel and training to ensure that the internal auditing function is adequately staffed. Also, the auditing work should be properly planned, supervised, and reviewed.
6. Assure the director of internal auditing that the committee supports his or her function in the corporate structure and the director has access to the committee and the functional areas within the entity. Also, obtain assurance that the staff is receiving the proper cooperation from management.
7. Determine the need for special assignments, such as investigating computer security and other methods for the protection of the assets (e.g., cases of management disagreements with the auditors).

It is evident that the internal audit function is extremely important in the corporate structure because it assists corporate management, including the board and its audit committee, in fulfilling its responsibilities for corporate accountability. The audit directors have a critical role in monitoring the activities of the internal auditing staff as well as preserving its independence in the corporate auditing process.

SOURCES AND SUGGESTED READINGS

Bacon, Jeremy, *The Audit Committee: A Broader Mandate,* Report No. 914 (New York: The Conference Board, Inc., 1988).

Barrett, Michael J., and P. Tiessen, "Organizational Support for Internal Auditing." *Internal Auditor* 5, No. 2 (Fall 1989), pp. 39–53.

Benson, Richard H., "Changing Demands on Internal and External Auditors." *Internal Auditor* 36, No. 1 (February 1979), pp. 53–57.

Braiotta, Louis, Jr., and Hugh L. Marsh, "Developing a Constructive Relationship Under the Guidance of SAS No. 65." *Internal Auditing* 8, No. 2 (Fall 1992), pp. 3–11.

Castellano, Joseph, Harper Roehm, and John P. Walker, "Status & Quality." *Internal Auditor* 49, No. 3 (June 1992), pp. 49–52.

Committee of Sponsoring Organizations of the Treadway Commission, *Internal Control-Integrated Framework* (New York: American Institute of Certified Public Accountants, 1992).

Horn, Karen N., "An Audit Committee Member Looks at Internal Auditing." *Internal Auditor* 49, No. 6 (December 1992), pp. 32–36.

Jepsen, Edward G., "Internal Auditors Move into the Spotlight." *Internal Auditor* 36, No. 2 (April 1979), pp. 26–32.

Kalbers, Lawrence P., "Audit Committees and Internal Auditors." *Internal Auditor* 49, No. 6 (December 1992), pp. 37–44.

Macchiaverna, Paul, *Internal Auditing,* Report No. 748 (New York: The Conference Board, Inc., 1978).

Mace, Myles L., "Strengthening the Functions of Internal Auditors." *Harvard Business Review* 55, No. 4 (July–August 1977), pp. 46–47.

Marquardt, John D., and John F. Bussman, "The CIA Examination: A Topical Profile and Index Update." *Internal Auditor* 36, No. 2 (April 1979), pp. 41–47.

National Commission on Fraudulent Financial Reporting, *Report of the National Commission on Fraudulent Financial Reporting* (Washington, D.C.: National Commission on Fraudulent Financial Reporting, 1987).

Scott, George M., and Bart H. Ward, "The Internal Audit—A Tool for Management Control." *Financial Executive* 46, No. 3 (March 1978), pp. 32–37.

Standards for the Professional Practice of Internal Auditing (Altamonte Springs, Fla.: Institute of Internal Auditors, 1998).

Statement on Auditing Standards No. 55, "Consideration of the Internal Control Structure in a Financial Statement Audit" (New York: American Institute of Certified Public Accountants, 1988).

Statement on Auditing Standards No. 65, "The Auditor's Consideration of the Internal Audit Function in an Audit of Financial Statements" (New York: American Institute of Certified Public Accountants, 1991).

Strawser, Jerry, and Barbara Apostolou, "The Role of Internal Auditor Communication with the Audit Committee." *Internal Auditing* 6, No. 2 (Fall 1990), pp. 35–42.

Verschoor, Curtis, "Internal Auditing Interactions with the Audit Committee." *Internal Auditing* 7, No. 4 (Spring 1992), pp. 29–23.

Verschoor, Curtis, and Joseph P. Liotta, "Communication with Audit Committees." *Internal Auditor* 47, No. 2 (April 1990), pp. 42–47.

Chapter 10

Reviewing Accounting Policy Disclosures

The purpose of this chapter is to introduce accounting policy disclosures in the financial statements. Through a review of the significant accounting policies, the audit committee can obtain assurance on behalf of the board of directors that management is fulfilling its financial accounting reporting responsibilities. Such a review will be conducted with the independent public accountants in order to determine the integrity and objectivity of the financial statements based on management's formulation and implementation of the corporate accounting policies. Although this chapter will discuss accounting pronouncements concerning accounting disclosures (APB No. 22) and accounting changes (APB No. 20), it makes no attempt to discuss in detail the technical pronouncements applicable to APB No. 22 since such a discussion is beyond the scope of the text. As indicated in Chapter 1, the purpose of the audit committee is to oversee and monitor the accounting and auditing processes; technical accounting matters are management's responsibility. The reader may wish to consult any standard accounting text for detailed information regarding the technical subjects as outlined in APB No. 22.

AUDIT COMMITTEE'S REVIEW OBJECTIVE

An Overview

As indicated in Chapters 2 and 3, the audit committee has a critical role in reviewing the disclosures in the financial statements. The committee represents an independent check on corporate management with respect to its responsibilities for reporting its stewardship accountability to the outside constituencies. In particular, the audit committee is responsible for assuring that management has prepared the financial statements in conformity with generally accepted accounting principles. Thus it must assess not only management's judgment regarding the application of accounting principles but also the adequacy of the disclosures in the financial statements.[1] According to the American Institute of Certified Public Accountants, the committee's review objective may be summarized as follows:

> The audit committee should meet with management and the external auditor to review the financial statements and the audit results. This is an especially important function of the audit committee.

> Some audit committees confine their review of the financial statements to major or critical items, while others examine the statements in considerable detail. The scope of the review is something each audit committee must set forth for itself, bearing in mind that at the conclusion of the meeting the members should have a comprehensive understanding of any major financial reporting problems encountered, how they were resolved, and whether the resolution is satisfactory. Factors affecting the extent of the review include the committee's confidence in management, the system of internal accounting control, and the external auditor; the existence of any unresolved differences between the auditor and management; the extent of adjustments or additional disclosures, if any, proposed by the auditor; and any unusual occurrences during the year. The committee's major concern throughout the review should be whether the financial statements fairly present the company's financial results in conformity with generally accepted accounting principles.[2]

In addition, it is important that audit committee members be aware that the Public Oversight Board has issued the following recommendations with respect to determination of accounting treatment in the financial reporting process:

> Recommendation V-6:

> The following recommendation of the Macdonald Commission should be adopted by the Auditing Standards Board in the United States:

>> When new accounting policies are adopted in response to new types of transactions or new kinds of assets or obligations, the auditor should be satisfied that the accounting policies adopted properly reflect the economic substance of the transaction, asset, or liability in accordance with the broad theory governing present-day financial reporting and the established concept of conservatism in the face of uncertainty.

> Recommendation V-7:

> Peer reviewers should evaluate the consultation process by which specific accounting conclusions are reached, as they do now, and should also inquire whether that process leads to accounting that is appropriate in the circumstances. In testing com-

---

[1] For a more detailed discussion of accounting principles, see Chapter 5.
[2] American Institute of Certified Public Accountants, Audit Committees, Answers to Typical Questions About Their Organization and Operations (New York: American Institute of Certified Public Accountants, 1978), pp. 16–17.

pliance with the consultation policies and procedures in a firm, the peer review team should evaluate the quality of the conclusions reached.

Recommendation V-8:

The concurring partner, whose participation in an audit is a membership requirement of the SEC Practice Section, should be responsible for assuring that those consulted on accounting matters are aware of all of the relevant facts and circumstances, including an understanding of the financial statements in whose context the accounting policy is being considered. The concurring and consulting partners should know enough about the client to ensure that all of the relevant facts and circumstances are marshalled, and also possess the increased detachment that comes from not having to face the client on an ongoing basis. The concurring partner should have the responsibility to conclude whether the accounting treatment applied is consistent with the objectives of Recommendation V-6.[3]

The American Institute of Certified Public Accountants has set forth the following to further ensure the independent auditor's integrity and objectivity in the financial reporting process:

The credibility of the independent audit is essential to public trust, the keystone of the financial reporting system. The accounting profession prides itself on the integrity and objectivity of its members. The future of our profession, not to mention our livelihood, rests on this reputation.

A few recent high-profile financial scandals have, however, called auditors' independence into question. Neither the accounting profession nor the financial markets can afford an erosion of public confidence. For that reason, auditors must scrupulously preserve their objectivity, in reality and appearance. We therefore call on the SEC and other regulatory bodies to prohibit public companies and other organizations with public accountability from hiring the partner responsible for their audit for one year after the partner ceases to serve that client.

Additional steps can be taken, with the support of the business community, to secure public confidence in the independent audit and the financial reporting system. SEC registrants and other publicly accountable organizations should be required to have audit committees composed entirely of independent directors whenever practicable. The audit committee members should be charged with specific responsibilities, including overseeing the financial reporting process, and recommending appointment of the entity's auditors.[4]

---

[3] Public Oversight Board, A Special Report by the Public Oversight Board of the SEC Practice Section, AICPA (Stamford, Conn.: Public Oversight Board, 1993), pp. 48–49.

[4] American Institute of Certified Public Accountants, Meeting the Financial Reporting Needs of the Future: A Public Commitment from the Public Accounting Profession (New York: American Institute of Certified Public Accountants, 1993), p. 4.

The reader may wish to revisit Chapter 2 and Chapter 3 to review the key discussion points made by several key organizations about the financial reporting process. While the preceding review objective is broad based, it is important to reemphasize the audit committee's position regarding such review activities. As John J. Schornack, former partner of Arthur Young & Co. (now Ernst & Young), points out:

> Audit committee members are not omniscient. . . . Matters of compliance with professional reporting standards and technical disclosures are the responsibilities of corporate management and the professional experts such as the outside auditor and legal counsel. . . . The primary purpose of the audit committee is oversight of the financial reporting.[5]

James Gerson et al., partners of Coopers & Lybrand (now PricewaterhouseCoopers), note that "to effectively review financial statements, the audit committee must understand the company's business and industry, and the attendant risks. The committee should be satisfied that the key financial systems and the procedures and controls that support them will generate information necessary to manage and properly report on the operations of the company."[6] The authors further state:

> Typically, the committee meets with management and the independent auditors to review the financial statements for the year and the results of the annual audit. The nature of this review depends on the complexity of the company, its industry, and the committee's confidence in company management. When performing this review, the committee should pay particular attention to judgmental areas, such as those involving valuation of assets and liabilities. The committee should be sensitive to areas where different assumptions and judgments could have a significant effect on the statements. These areas could include accounting and disclosure for obsolete or slow-moving inventory; the allowance for doubtful accounts; warranty, product liability and litigation reserves; and commitments and contingencies.[7]

Such oversight responsibility of the audit committee is evidenced in Ameritech's annual report, as presented in Exhibit 10.1 and Exhibit 10.1A.

---

[5] John J. Schornack, "The Audit Committee—A Public Accountant's View," Journal of Accountancy 147, No. 4 (April 1979), p. 74.

[6] James S. Gerson, J. Robert Mooney, Donald F. Moran, and Robert K. Waters, "Oversight of the Financial Reporting Process—Part I," CPAS Journal 59, No. 7 (July 1989), p. 28.

[7] James S. Gerson, J. Robert Mooney, Donald F. Moran, and Robert K. Waters, "Oversight of the Financial Reporting Process—Part II," CPA Journal 59, No. 8 (August 1989), p. 40. A recent study on the association between audit committee formation and the quality of accounting earnings found "a significant increase in the market's reaction to earnings reports subsequent to the formation of the audit committee" (p. 1). See John J. Wild, "The Audit Committee and Earnings Quality," *Journal of Accounting, Auditing & Finance* 11, No. 2 (Spring 1996), pp. 247–276.

Exhibit 10.1.   Illustrative Management Report and Audit Committee Report

---

Report of Management

FINANCIAL STATEMENTS

Management of Ameritech Corporation and its subsidiaries (the company) has the responsibility for preparing the accompanying consolidated financial statements and for the integrity and objectivity of the statements. The statements were prepared in accordance with generally accepted accounting principles and, in management's opinion, are fairly presented. The consolidated financial statements include amounts that are based on management's best estimates and judgments. Management also prepared the other information in the annual report, and is responsible for its accuracy and consistency with the consolidated financial statements.

The company's consolidated financial statements have been audited by Arthur Andersen & Co., independent public accountants. Management has made available to Arthur Andersen & Co. all the company's financial records and related data, as well as the minutes of meetings of shareowners and directors. Furthermore, management believes that all representations made to Arthur Andersen & Co. during their audit were valid and appropriate.

INTERNAL CONTROL SYSTEM

The company maintains a system of internal control over the preparation of its published financial statements. The system is designed to provide reasonable assurance as to the integrity and reliability of the consolidated financial statements, the protection of assets from unauthorized use or disposition, and the prevention and detection of fraudulent financial reporting. The internal control system provides for appropriate division of responsibility and is documented by written policies and procedures that are communicated to employees and updated as necessary. Management also recognizes its responsibility for fostering a strong ethical climate so that the company's affairs are conducted according to the highest standards of personal and corporate conduct. An effective internal control system, no matter how well designed, can provide only reasonable assurance with respect to the preparation of reliable financial statements. Also, because of changes in conditions, the effectiveness of an internal control system may vary over time. However, management through its internal audit process, continuously monitors the internal control system in place to minimize this risk.

The company maintains a strong internal auditing program to independently assess the effectiveness of the internal controls and to recommend possible improvements. In addition, as part of their audit of the company's consolidated financial statements, Arthur Andersen & Co. considered the internal control system in order to establish a basis for reliance thereon in determining the nature, timing and extent of audit tests to be applied. Management has considered the recommendations of its internal auditors and Arthur Andersen & Co. concerning the company's system of internal control, and has responded appropriately to these recommendations.

Exhibit 10.1. *(Continued)*

Management assessed the company's internal control system in relation to criteria for effective internal control over financial reporting described in "Internal Control—Integrated Framework" issued by the Committee of Sponsoring Organizations of the Treadway Commission. Those criteria consist of five interrelated internal control components, which are: control environment, risk assessment, control activities, information and communication, and monitoring. Based on its assessment, management believes that, as of December 31, 1992, its system of internal control over financial reporting has met those criteria.

William L. Weiss
Chairman and Chief Executive Officer

Betty F. Elliott
Vice President and Comptroller

February 5, 1993

Report of Audit Committee Chairman

The audit committee (the committee) of the Board of Directors is composed of three independent directors who are not officers or employees of the company. The committee, which held three meetings during 1992, oversees the company's financial reporting process on behalf of the Board of Directors.

In fulfilling its responsibility, the committee recommended to the Board of Directors, subject to shareowner ratification, the selection of the company's independent public accountants. The committee discussed with the internal auditors and the independent public accountants the overall scope and specific plans for their respective audits. The committee also discussed the company's consolidated financial statements and the adequacy of the company's system of internal control. The committee met regularly with the company's internal auditors and independent public accountants, without management present, to discuss the results of their audits, their evaluation of the system of internal control and the overall quality of the company's financial reporting. The meetings also were designed to facilitate any private communications with the committee desired by the internal auditors or the independent public accountants.

Hal C. Kuehl
Chairman, Audit Committee

February 5, 1993

Source: Ameritech Corporation, *1992 Annual Report*, p. 28.

Exhibit 10.1A   Illustrative Management Report and Audit Committee Report

Report of Management

SHAREOWNERS, AMERITECH CORPORATION

The consolidated financial statements were prepared in accordance with generally accepted accounting principles, which required the use of estimates and judgment. Management prepared these statements and other information in the annual report and is responsible for their integrity and objectivity.

Our consolidated financial statements have been audited by Arthur Andersen LLP. Management has made available to Arthur Andersen LLP all of our financial records and related data, as well as the minutes of meetings of shareowners and directors. We believe that all representations made to Arthur Andersen LLP were valid and appropriate.

Management maintains a system of internal control over the preparation of our published financial statements that provides reasonable assurance as to the integrity and reliability of the consolidated financial statements, the protection of assets from unauthorized use or disposition, and the prevention and detection of fraudulent financial reporting. The internal control system provides appropriate division of responsibility, and written policies and procedures are communicated to employees and updated as necessary. Management is responsible for proactively fostering a strong ethical climate so that the company's affairs are conducted according to the highest standards of personal and corporate conduct.

The company maintains a strong internal auditing program to assess the effectiveness of internal controls and recommend possible improvements. As part of their audit of the consolidated financial statements, Arthur Andersen LLP considered the internal control system to determine the nature, timing and extent of necessary audit tests. Management has considered the recommendations of our internal auditors and Arthur Andersen LLP concerning the company's system of internal control, and has responded appropriately.

Management assessed the company's internal control system in relation to criteria for effective internal control. These criteria consist of five interrelated components, which are: control environment, risk assessment, control activities, information and communication and monitoring. Based on its assessment, management believes that, as of December 31, 1997, our system of internal control has met these criteria.

The board of directors, through its audit committee which consists solely of outside directors, serves in an oversight capacity to assure the integrity and objectivity of the financial reporting process. The role of the committee includes monitoring accounting and financial controls and assuring the independence of Arthur Andersen LLP. Both the internal auditors and the independent public accountants have complete access to the committee and periodically meet with the committee, with and without management present.

Sincerely,

Richard C. Notebaert   *Oren G. Shaffer*

Richard C. Notebaert   Oren G. Shaffer
Chairman and Chief Executive Officer   Executive Vice President and
January 13, 1998   Chief Financial Officer

Source: Ameritech Corporation, 1998 Annual Report, p. 34.

Thus, in order to discharge its oversight responsibility concerning financial reporting, the committee's agenda should include a review of the significant accounting policies and their related disclosure requirements. Such a review will enable the committee to obtain assurance that management is fulfilling its financial accounting and reporting responsibilities. Furthermore, since the board of directors is primarily concerned with corporate policies, the committee can ensure that major changes in accounting policies are brought before the board in a timely manner. Therefore, the remainder of this chapter will discuss the committee's role in reviewing accounting policy disclosures.[8]

ACCOUNTING POLICY DISCLOSURES

Accounting Policies

As noted in Chapter 4, the Securities and Exchange Commission in the Killearn Properties case indicated that the audit committee should have at least general familiarity with accounting and reporting principles and practices in preparing its financial statements. Thus the committee members should have a broad overview of the significant accounting policies. Such a task is a critical undertaking since it requires the committee to judge management's formulation and implementation of such policies. The committee will look to the independent public accountants' professional assessment of the entity's accounting policies in accordance with the disclosure requirements, discussed in Chapter 5. For example, the audit committee's understanding of the information in the financial statement and significant accounting policies is evidenced by the data included in both the Report of Management and the Report of Audit Committee Chairman, as illustrated by Ameritech Corporation in Exhibit 10.1.

The independent auditors must be satisfied that management is complying with the disclosure requirements as outlined by the Accounting Principles Board.[9] For example, management must present a summary of the significant accounting policies as part of the financial statements in the annual report. Such disclosure of significant accounting policies sets forth the accounting principles and methods used to prepare the financial statements. A summary of significant accounting policies frequently includes[10]:

[8] For a more detailed discussion of reporting publicly on internal control, see Curtis C. Verschoor, "Reporting on Internal Control: An Analysis of Empirical Evidence," *Internal Auditing* 12, No. 1 (Summer 1996), pp. 43–45; Frank R. Urbanic, "A Content Analysis of Audit Committee Reports," *Internal Auditing* 12, No. 1 (Summer 1996), pp. 36–42; and Chapter 8 of this book.

[9] See Opinions of the Accounting Principles Board, No. 22, "Disclosure of Accounting Policies" (New York: AICPA, 1972), par. 15.

[10] As previously noted, the reader may wish to consult a standard accounting text. Also see Appendix M for further reference information.

- Basis of consolidation and use of estimates and assumptions
- Depreciation methods
- Financial instruments
- Inventory pricing methods
- Accounting for research and development costs
- Basis for foreign currency translation
- Accounting treatment for:
  Pension plans
  Intangible assets, such as goodwill
  Income taxes and investment credits
  Revenue recognition on long-term construction contracts
- Accounting changes

A summary of significant accounting policies of Wal-Mart Stores, Inc., and Lockheed Martin Corporation is illustrated in Exhibit 10.2.

Obviously, the disclosure of the key accounting policies will vary from company to company; however, it is incumbent upon the independent auditors to concur with management on the adequacy of such policy disclosures. If management's disclosures are inadequate, the independent auditors cannot express an unqualified opinion on the financial statements.

Therefore, as part of its financial review responsibilities, the committee should discuss "any significant disagreement between management and the independent accountants and whether such disagreement has been resolved to the satisfaction of both."[11] Concerning the resolution of such disagreements, the committee should stress the overall objectives of financial reporting as discussed in Chapter 3.

Accounting Changes

Of particular importance to the audit committee are the changes in accounting during the fiscal period. According to the Accounting Principles Board:

> A change in accounting by a reporting entity may significantly affect the presentation of both financial position and results of operations for an accounting period and the trends shown in comparative financial statements and historical summaries. The change should therefore be reported in a manner which will facilitate analysis and understanding of the financial statements.[12]

---

[11] Schornack, "The Audit Committee," p. 76.
[12] Opinions of the Accounting Principles Board, No. 20, "Accounting Changes" (New York: AICPA, 1971), par. 1.

Exhibit 10.2 Significant Accounting Policies

Wal-Mart Stores, Inc.

SUMMARY OF SIGNIFICANT ACCOUNTING POLICIES

Consolidation

The consolidated financial statements include the accounts of subsidiaries. Significant intercompany transactions have been eliminated in consolidation.

Cash and cash equivalents

The Company considers investments with a maturity of three months or less when purchased to be cash equivalents.

Inventories

The Company uses the retail last-in, first-out (LIFO) method for domestic Wal-Mart discount stores and Supercenters and cost LIFO for SAM's Clubs. International inventories are on other cost methods. Inventories are not in excess of market value.

Pre-opening costs

Costs associated with the opening of stores are expensed during the first full month of operations. The costs are carried as prepaid expenses prior to the store opening. If the Company had expensed these costs as incurred, net income would have been reduced by $2 million, $9 million and $2 million in fiscal 1998, 1997 and 1996, respectively.

Interest during construction

In order that interest costs properly reflect only that portion relating to current operations, interest on borrowed funds during the construction of property, plant and equipment is capitalized. Interest costs capitalized were $33 million, $44 million and $50 million in 1998, 1997 and 1996, respectively.

Financial instruments

The Company uses derivative financial instruments for purposes other than trading to reduce its exposure to fluctuations in foreign currencies and to minimize the risk and cost associated with financial and global operating activities. Settlements of interest rate swaps are accounted for by recording the net interest received or paid as an adjustment to interest expense on a current basis. Gains or losses resulting from market movements are not recognized. Contracts that effectively meet risk reduction and correlation criteria are recorded using hedge accounting. Hedges of firm commitments or anticipated transactions are deferred and recognized when the hedged transaction occurs.

Advertising costs

Advertising costs are expensed as incurred and were $292 million, $249 million and $219 million in 1998, 1997 and 1996, respectively.

Exhibit 10.2 *(Continued)*

Operating, selling and general and administrative expenses

Buying, warehousing and occupancy costs are included in operating, selling and general and administrative expenses.

Depreciation and amortization

Depreciation and amortization for financial statement purposes are provided on the straight-line method over the estimated useful lives of the various assets. For income tax purposes, accelerated methods are used with recognition of deferred income taxes for the resulting temporary differences. Estimated useful lives are as follows:

Building and improvements	5–33 years
Fixtures and equipment	5–12 years
Transportation equipment	2–5 years
Goodwill	20–40 years

Long-lived assets

In fiscal 1997, the Company adopted Statement of Financial Accounting Standards No. 121, Accounting for the Impairment of Long-Lived Assets and for Long-Lived Assets to be Disposed Of. The statement requires entities to review long-lived assets and certain intangible assets in certain circumstances, and if the value of the assets is impaired, an impairment loss shall be recognized. Due to the Company's previous accounting policies, this pronouncement had no material effect on the Company's financial position or results of operations.

Comprehensive income

In June 1997, the Financial Accounting Standards Board (FASB) issued Statement No. 130, "Reporting Comprehensive Income," which is effective for fiscal years beginning after December 15, 1997. This statement establishes standards for reporting and display of comprehensive income and its components. The Company anticipates adopting this Statement in fiscal 1999. Since this Statement requires only additional disclosure, there will be no effect on the Company's results of operations or financial position.

Net income per share

In fiscal 1998, the Company adopted Statement of Financial Accounting Standards No. 128, Earnings Per Share. Statement 128 replaces primary and fully dilutive earnings per share with basic and dilutive earnings per share. Unlike primary earnings per share, basic earnings per share excludes any dilutive effect of options. Basic earnings per share for all periods presented are the same as previously reported. Basic net income per share is based on the weighted average outstanding common shares. Dilutive net income per share is based on the weighted average outstanding shares reduced by the effect of stock options.

Exhibit 10.2 *(Continued)*

The shares used in the computations for basic and dilutive net income per share are as follows (in millions):

	1998	1997	1997
Basic	2,258	2,292	2,296
Dilutive	2,267	2,296	2,299

Foreign currency translation

The assets and liabilities of most foreign subsidiaries are translated at current exchange rates and any related translation adjustments are recorded in Consolidated Shareholders' Equity. Operations in Brazil and Mexico operate in highly inflationary economies and certain assets are translated at historical exchange rates and all translation adjustments are reflected in the Consolidated Income Statements.

Estimates and assumptions

The preparation of consolidated financial statements in conformity with generally accepted accounting principles requires management to make estimates and assumptions. These estimates and assumptions affect the reported amounts of assets and liabilities and disclosure of contingent assets and liabilities at the date of the consolidated financial statements and the reported amounts of revenues and expenses during the reporting period. Actual results could differ from those estimates.

Reclassifications

Certain reclassifications have been made to prior periods to conform to current presentation.

Lockheed Martin Corporation

SUMMARY OF SIGNIFICANT ACCOUNTING POLICIES

Organization—Lockheed Martin Corporation (Lockheed Martin or the Corporation) is engaged in the design, manufacture, integration and operation of a broad array of products and services ranging from aircraft, spacecraft and launch vehicles to missiles, electronics, information systems and energy management. The Corporation serves customers in both domestic and international defense and civilian markets, with its principal customers being agencies of the U.S. Government.

Basis of consolidation and use of estimates—The consolidated financial statements include the accounts of wholly-owned and majority-owned subsidiaries. Material intercompany balances and transactions have been eliminated in consolidation. The preparation of consolidated financial statements in conformity with generally accepted accounting principles requires management to make estimates and assumptions, in particular estimates of anticipated contract costs and revenues utilized in the earnings recognition process, that affect the reported amounts in the financial statements and accompanying notes. Actual results could differ from those estimates.

Exhibit 10.2 *(Continued)*

Classifications—Receivables and inventories are primarily attributable to long-term contracts or programs in progress for which the related operating cycles are longer than one year. In accordance with industry practice, these items are included in current assets. Book overdrafts, which are immaterial, are included in current liabilities. Certain amounts for the prior years have been reclassified to conform with the 1997 presentation.

Inventories—Inventories are stated at the lower of cost or estimated net realizable value. Costs on long-term contracts and programs in progress represent recoverable costs incurred for production, allocable operating overhead, and, where appropriate, research and development and general and administrative expenses. Pursuant to contract provisions, agencies of the U.S. Government and other customers have title to, or a security interest in, certain inventories as a result of progress payments and advances. General and administrative expenses related to commercial products and services provided essentially under commercial terms and conditions are expensed as incurred. Costs of other product and supply inventories are principally determined by the first-in, first-out or average cost methods.

Property, plant and equipment—Property, plant and equipment are carried principally at cost. Depreciation is provided on plant and equipment generally using accelerated methods of depreciation during the first half of the estimated useful lives of the assets; thereafter, straight-line depreciation generally is used. Estimated useful lives generally range from 8 years to 40 years for buildings and 2 years to 20 years for machinery and equipment.

Intangible assets—Intangible assets related to contracts and programs acquired are amortized over the estimated periods of benefit (15 years or less) and are displayed on the consolidated balance sheet net of accumulated amortization of $651 million and $505 million at December 31, 1997 and 1996, respectively. Cost in excess of net assets acquired (goodwill) is amortized ratably over appropriate periods, primarily 40 years, and is displayed on the consolidated balance sheet net of accumulated amortization of $881 million and $617 million at December 31, 1997 and 1996, respectively. The carrying values of intangible assets are reviewed if the facts and circumstances indicate potential impairment of their carrying value, and any impairment determined is recorded in the current period. Impairment is measured by comparing the undiscounted cash flows of the related business operations to the appropriate carrying values.

Environmental matters—The Corporation records a liability for environmental matters when it is probable that a liability has been incurred and the amount can be reasonably estimated. A substantial portion of these costs are expected to be reflected in sales and cost of sales pursuant to U.S. Government agreement or regulation. At the time a liability is recorded for future environmental costs, an asset is recorded for estimated future recovery considered probable through the pricing of products and services to agencies of the U.S. Government. The portion of those costs expected to be allocated to commercial business is reflected in costs and expenses at the time the liability is established.

Sales and earnings—Sales and anticipated profits under long-term fixed-price production contracts are recorded on a percentage of completion basis, generally using units of delivery as the measurement basis for effort accomplished. Estimated contract profits are taken into earnings in proportion to recorded sales. Sales under certain long-term fixed-price

Exhibit 10.2 *(Continued)*

contracts which, among other things, provide for the delivery of minimal quantities or require a significant amount of development effort in relation to total contract value, are recorded upon achievement of performance milestones or using the cost-to-cost method of accounting where sales and profits are recorded based on the ratio of costs incurred to estimated total costs at completion.

Sales under cost-reimbursement-type contracts are recorded as costs are incurred. Applicable estimated profits are included in earnings in the proportion that incurred costs bear to total estimated costs. Sales of products and services provided essentially under commercial terms and conditions are recorded upon shipment or completion of specified tasks.

Amounts representing contract change orders, claims or other items are included in sales only when they can be reliably estimated and realization is probable. Incentives or penalties and awards applicable to performance on contracts are considered in estimating sales and profit rates, and are recorded when there is sufficient information to assess anticipated contract performance. Incentive provisions which increase or decrease earnings based solely on a single significant event are generally not recognized until the event occurs.

When adjustments in contract value or estimated costs are determined, any changes from prior estimates are reflected in earnings in the current period. Anticipated losses on contracts or programs in progress are charged to earnings when identified.

Research and development and similar costs—Corporation-sponsored research and development costs primarily include research and development and bid and proposal efforts related to government products and services. Except for certain arrangements described below, these costs are generally included as part of the general and administrative costs that are allocated among all contracts and programs in progress under U.S. Government contractual arrangements. Corporation-sponsored product development costs not otherwise allocable are charged to expense when incurred. Under certain arrangements in which a customer shares in product development costs, the Corporation's portion of such unreimbursed costs is expensed as incurred. Customer-sponsored research and development costs incurred pursuant to contracts are accounted for as contract costs.

Derivative financial instruments—The Corporation may use derivative financial instruments to manage its exposure to fluctuations in interest rates and foreign exchange rates. The Corporation designates interest rate swap agreements as hedges of specific debt instruments and recognizes the interest differentials as adjustments to interest expense over the terms of the related debt obligations. There were no interest rate swap agreements outstanding at December 31, 1997. Forward exchange contracts are also designated as qualifying hedges of firm commitments or specific anticipated transactions. Gains and losses on these contracts are recognized in income when the hedged transactions occur. At December 31, 1997, the amounts of forward exchange contracts outstanding, as well as the amounts of gains and losses recorded during the year, were not material. The Corporation does not hold or issue financial instruments for trading purposes.

Accounting changes—Effective December 31, 1997, the Corporation adopted Statement of Financial Accounting Standards (SFAS) No. 128, "Earnings Per Share", which established

Exhibit 10.2   *(Continued)*

new standards for computing and disclosing earnings per share. The Statement requires dual presentation of "basic" and "diluted" earnings per share, each as defined therein, which replace primary and fully diluted earnings per share, respectively, required under previous guidance. In accordance with SFAS No. 128, all earnings per share amounts included in this annual report have been restated to conform to the provisions of the new standard and required disclosures have been made (see Note 6).

Effective January 1, 1997, the Corporation adopted the American Institute of Certified Public Accountants' Statement of Position (SOP) No. 96-1, "Environmental Remediation Liabilities." SOP No. 96-1 provides authoritative guidance on certain accounting issues relative to the recognition, measurement, display and disclosure of environmental remediation liabilities. The impact of the adoption of this SOP was not material to the Corporation's consolidated results of operations, financial position or disclosures.

Effective January 1, 1996, the Corporation adopted SFAS No. 121, "Accounting for the Impairment of Long-Lived Assets and for Long-Lived Assets to Be Disposed Of." SFAS No. 121 requires that certain long-lived assets to be held and used be reviewed for impairment whenever events or changes in circumstances indicate that the carrying amount of an asset may not be recoverable. Additionally, SFAS No. 121 requires that certain long-lived assets to be disposed of be reported at the lower of carrying amount or fair value less costs to sell. The impact of the adoption of this standard was not material to the Corporation's consolidated results of operations or financial position.

Also in 1996, the Corporation adopted SFAS No. 123, "Accounting for Stock-Based Compensation." SFAS No. 123 allows companies to continue to measure compensation cost for stock-based employee compensation plans using the intrinsic value method of accounting as prescribed in Accounting Principles Board (APB) Opinion No. 25, "Accounting for Stock Issued to Employees," and related interpretations. The Corporation has elected to continue its APB Opinion No. 25 accounting treatment for stock-based compensation, and has adopted the provisions of SFAS No. 123 requiring disclosure of the pro forma effect on net earnings and earnings per share as if compensation cost had been recognized based upon the estimated fair value at the date of grant for options awarded.

Recently issued accounting pronouncements—In June 1997, the Financial Accounting Standards Board issued SFAS No. 131, "Disclosures about Segments of an Enterprise and Related Information." SFAS No. 131 establishes standards for the way in which publicly-held companies report financial and descriptive information about their operating segments in financial statements for both interim and annual periods, and requires additional disclosures with respect to products and services, geographic areas of operation and major customers. The Statement is effective for fiscal years beginning after December 15, 1997; however, application is not required for interim periods in 1998. The adoption of SFAS No. 131 will have no impact on the number or composition of the Corporation's reported business segments, or on its consolidated results of operations or financial position, but is expected to increase the level of disclosure of segment information.

Sources: Wal-Mart Stores, Inc., *1998 Annual Report*, pp. 30–31. Lockheed Martin Corporation, *1997 Annual Report*, pp. 31–32.

In order to familiarize the committee with the accounting changes, the types of changes are briefly set forth at this point.

Change in Accounting Principle A change in accounting principle results from the adoption of a generally accepted accounting principle different from the one used previously for reporting purposes. For example, a change in the method of inventory pricing is a common change in accounting principles. Although there is a presumption that an accounting principle, once adopted, should not be changed, management may overcome this presumption if it justifies the use of an alternative acceptable accounting principle. For example, management may justify the change in accounting principle on the basis of the issuance of a new FASB accounting standard. Moreover, management may justify the change on the basis that such a change in accounting method enhances the fairness in the presentation of the financial statements.

With respect to the disclosure of a change in accounting principle, the Board stated:

> The nature of and justification for a change in accounting principle and its effect on income should be disclosed in the financial statements of the period in which the change is made. The justification for the change should explain clearly why the newly adopted accounting principle is preferable.[13]

An example of a change in accounting principle is disclosed in the 1992 annual report of Exxon Corporation, presented in Exhibit 10.3.

Change in Accounting Estimate Certain accounting actions are based on management's judgment regarding the use of estimates. Accounting estimates are required because of the matching principle of accounting that revenues and their related costs must be properly matched in the same accounting period to determine a fair measurement of the net income or loss of the entity. Thus as management acquires additional information and more experience concerning such matters as the economic life of plant and equipment assets and probable uncollectible receivables, a change in accounting estimate may occur.

Concerning the disclosure of changes in accounting estimates, Ford Motor Company reported:

> Depreciation and Amortization—Automotive. Depreciation is computed using an accelerated method that results in accumulated depreciation of approximately two-thirds of asset cost during the first half of the asset's estimated useful life. On aver-

---

[13] Ibid., par. 17. Additional reporting matters should be discussed with the chief financial officer and/or the external auditor.

Exhibit 10.3   Illustrative Accounting Changes

ACCOUNTING CHANGES

Statement of Financial Accounting Standards No. 106, "Employers' Accounting for Postre-tirement Benefits Other Than Pensions," and No. 109, "Accounting for Income Taxes," were implemented in the fourth quarter of 1992, effective as of January 1, 1992. The cumu-lative effect of these accounting changes on years prior to 1992, as shown below, has been reflected in the first quarter of 1992.

	(millions of dollars)
SFAS No. 106 (net of S408 million income tax effect)	$(800)
SFAS No. 109	760
Net charge	$(40)

The cumulative effect per share was $(0.64) and $0.61 for SFAS No. 106 and No. 109, respectively, resulting in a net charge of $(0.03).

Neither standard had a material effect on 1992 income before the cumulative effect of the accounting changes.

Source: Exxon Corporation, 1992 Annual Report, p. F12.

age, buildings and land improvements are depreciated based on a 30-year life; auto-motive machinery and equipment are depreciated based on a $14\frac{1}{2}$-year life.

It is the company's policy to review periodically fixed asset lives. A study completed during 1990 indicated that actual lives for certain asset categories generally were longer than the useful lives used for depreciation purposes in the company's finan-cial statements. Therefore, during the third quarter of 1990, the company revised the estimated useful lives of certain categories of property, retroactive to January 1, 1990. The effect of this change in estimate was to reduce 1990 depreciation expense by $211 million and increase 1990 net income, principally in the U.S., by $135 mil-lion or $0.29 per share.

When plant and equipment are retired, the general policy is to charge the cost of such assets, reduced by net salvage proceeds, to accumulated depreciation. All main-tenance, repairs and rearrangement expenses are expensed as incurred. Expenditures that increase the value or productive capacity of assets are capitalized. The cost of special tools is amortized over periods of time representing the productive use of such tools. Preproduction costs incurred in connection with new facilities are expensed as incurred.[14]

[14] Ford Motor Company, 1990 Annual Report, p. 26.

Change in the Reporting Entity   This particular change occurs when the reporting entity changes its reporting as a result of a change in its composition, such as a merger. As the Board points out:

> One special type of change in accounting principle results in financial statements which, in effect, are those of a different reporting entity. This type is limited mainly to (a) presenting consolidated or combined statements in place of statements of individual companies, (b) changing specific subsidiaries comprising the group of companies for which consolidated financial statements are presented, and (c) changing the companies included in combined financial statements. A different group of companies comprise the reporting entity after each change. A business combination accounted for by the pooling of interests method also results in a different reporting entity.[15]

For example, Bristol-Myers Squibb reported:

Business Combination

On October 4, 1989, Squibb Corporation merged with a subsidiary of Bristol-Myers Company, and Bristol-Myers Company changed its name to Bristol-Myers Squibb Company. As a result, 97.4 million shares of Squibb common stock became entitled to be exchanged at a ratio of one share of Squibb for 2.4 Bristol-Myers Squibb shares, and 9.8 million shares of Squibb common stock owned by Squibb as treasury stock were retired. The merger has been accounted for as a pooling-of-interests.

In connection with the merger, a charge of $740 million was recorded in the fourth quarter of 1989 to integrate the operations of Bristol-Myers and Squibb and to organize its businesses on a global basis. The fourth quarter of 1989 also included an additional $115 million charge for the costs of professional fees and other expenses related to the merger. The after-tax effect of both charges was $693 million, or $1.32 per share.[16]

   Thus it is apparent that management has "choices among accounting principles or procedures" and that such choices affect "the major areas in the financial statements requiring subjective determinations."[17] Hence the major objective of the committee is to review management's choices of accounting principles and methods with the external auditor in order to obtain assurance that its choices are not only in compliance with the current accounting standards but also are properly disclosed.

---

[15] Opinions of the Accounting Principles Board, No. 20, par. 12.
[16] Bristol-Myers Squibb Company, 1990 Annual Report, p. 56.
[17] Schornack, "The Audit Committee," pp. 75–76.

GUIDELINES FOR REVIEWING ACCOUNTING POLICY DISCLOSURES

General Approach

In reviewing the accounting policy disclosures, the audit committee should adopt a systematic review approach. Such an approach should include the following:

1. *Preliminary review*   Before meeting with management and the external auditors, the committee should be familiar with such matters as:
   a. The nature of the accounting practices of the business and its industry. It should request a summary of the entity's financial reporting requirements. If necessary the committee may wish to review the accounting policies and procedures manual and other documented information regarding the relationship between the accounting system and internal accounting controls. Are such accounting practices in line with the industry practices?
   b. A summary of the minutes of the meetings of the stockholders, board of directors, and other standing committees of the board, particularly the finance committee. The accounting policies should reflect the board's authorization regarding the financial accounting affairs of the entity.
   c. The prior year's financial statements and audit reports and a summary of the effect of accounting pronouncements of the FASB, AICPA, and SEC on the statements. Are there any trends that have a disproportionate effect on the financial status of the entity?
   d. The impact of accounting changes and the rationale for such changes in the previous accounting periods.
   e. The prior years' government reports, such as the SEC and IRS report filings. The committee may wish to engage the services of tax counsel or legal counsel concerning such matters.

   In addition to the preceding matters, the committee should request a written summary of an annual review of the accounting policy disclosures from the chief financial officer, executive audit partner, and executive internal auditor. Such a summary review will enable the committee to identify major financial reporting problems that affect the accounting policies. Obviously, the committee can expedite its review through the use of such summaries and thus maximize its review time. Much of the preliminary review activities can occur during the initial and preaudit segments of the auditing cycle, as discussed in Chapters 6 and 7.

2. *Postaudit review*   During the committee's review of the drafts of the financial statements, it should give consideration to the following matters with the aforementioned parties:

Exhibit 10.4   Illustrative Disclosure of Management's Financial Reporting Responsibility

---

STATEMENT OF MANAGEMENT'S RESPONSIBILITY

Management is responsible for the preparation and accuracy of the consolidated financial statements and other information included in this report. The financial statements have been prepared in conformity with generally accepted accounting principles using, where appropriate, management's best estimates and judgments.

In meeting its responsibility for the reliability of the financial statements, management has developed and relies on the Company's system of internal accounting control. The system is designed to provide reasonable assurance that assets are safeguarded and that transactions are executed as authorized and are properly recorded. The system is augmented by written policies and procedures and an internal audit department.

The Board of Directors reviews the financial statements and reporting practices of the Company through its Audit Committee, which is composed entirely of directors who are not officers or employees of the Company. The committee meets regularly with the independent auditors, internal auditors and management to discuss audit scope and results and to consider internal control and financial reporting matters. Both the independent and internal auditors have direct unrestricted access to the Audit Committee. The entire Board of Directors reviews the Company's financial performance and financial plan.

Mark A. Pulido

Mark A. Pulido

President and Chief Executive Officer

Richard H. Hawkins

Richard H. Hawkins

Vice President and Chief Financial Officer

Source: McKesson Corporation, *1998 Annual Report*, p. 21.

a. Proposed management changes in accounting policies, such as a change in the inventory pricing methods and the external auditor's concurrence. Also, proposed changes in such policies concerning the new reporting requirements of the FASB, SEC, and other regulatory agencies.[18]

b. Changes in the entity's operations, such as a merger with an acquisition of another entity and the related effects on the existing accounting policies. Certain accounting standards govern the accounting treatment for the basis of valuing such investments (e.g., equity versus cost method of accounting). In view of the recommendations of the other standing committees and the approval of the board, the accounting policies should reflect such resolutions. An example of the committee's involvement and a change in accounting policy is reflected in the McKesson Corporation's Summary Annual Report and the SEC Form 10-K Report, shown in Exhibits 10.4 and 10.5.

---

[18] SEC matters regarding proxy materials should be discussed at this point, particularly compliance with the rules of the AICPA's SEC Practice Section. See Chapter 7.

Exhibit 10.5   Illustrative Change in Accounting Policy

Accounting Change.   In fiscal 1998, the Company adopted SFAS No. 128 "Earnings per Share," which requires a dual presentation of basic and diluted earnings per share ("EPS"). Basic EPS excludes dilution and is computed by dividing net income available to common stockholders by the weighted average number of common shares outstanding for the period. Diluted EPS reflects the potential dilution that would occur if securities or other contracts to issue common stock were exercised or converted into common stock. All share and per share amounts have been restated in accordance with the provisions of SFAS No. 128.

New Accounting Pronouncements.   In fiscal 1998, the Financial Accounting Standards Board issued SFAS No. 130 "Reporting Comprehensive Income," which requires that an enterprise report, by major components and as a single total, the change in its net assets during the period from nonowner sources; SFAS No. 131 "Disclosures about Segments of an Enterprise and Related Information," which establishes annual and interim reporting standards for an enterprise's operating segments and related disclosures about its products, services, geographic areas, and major customers; and SFAS No. 132 "Employers' Disclosures about Pension and Other Postretirement Benefits," which standardizes the disclosure requirements for pensions and other postretirement benefits and expands disclosures on changes in benefit obligations and fair values of plan assets. The Company plans to implement these statements in fiscal 1999. Adoption of these statements will not impact the Company's consolidated financial position, results of operations or cash flows, and any effect will be limited to the form and content of its disclosures.

Source: McKesson Corporation, *1998 Annual Report*, pp. 32–31.

c. The committee should judge the existing accounting policies in light of the objectives of financial reporting discussed in Chapter 3. Such financial reporting objectives serve as a criterion for judging management's selection of accounting methods.[19]

d. Since many independent accounting firms engaged in auditing publicly held corporations implement quality control review programs, the committee should ask the external auditor to review the disclosure check list items applicable to the significant accounting policies. As a basis for discussion, the committee can use the auditor's summary review memo, previously requested, in order to reconcile significant disclosure matters. Moreover, the committee may wish to request a copy of the accounting firm's disclosure check list concerning the financial statements. Such disclosure check lists are usually cross-referenced to the disclosure requirements in the accounting

---

[19] The reader should review in Chapter 5 such concepts as consistency, full disclosure, materiality, and fairness in financial statement presentation.

Exhibit 10.6   Accounting Policy Disclosures: A Check List

	Yes	No	Remarks
1. Summary of the significant accounting policies reviewed by the external auditor, chief financial officer, and internal auditor. Summaries obtained.	_____	_____	
2. Accounting policies are consistent in relationship to the industry practices (conservative or liberal).	_____	_____	
3. Current reporting requirements are reflected in the accounting policies.	_____	_____	
4. Accounting changes reviewed and the external auditor's concurrence obtained.	_____	_____	
5. Disclosure of significant accounting policies is adequate to support the auditor's unqualified opinion.	_____	_____	
6. Major financial reporting problems resolved satisfactorily.	_____	_____	
7. Unresolved differences between the auditor and management reviewed.	_____	_____	
8. Additional disclosures reviewed.	_____	_____	
9. Unusual occurrences during the year, such as a disposal of a segment of the business properly disclosed in the financial statements.	_____	_____	
10. Accounting policies are consistent with a fair presentation of the financial statement in conformity with generally accepted accounting principles.	_____	_____	
11. Accounting policies reflect the board's authorization regarding financial and accounting matters.	_____	_____	

Signed by: _____   Date _____

(Should be signed by the chairman of the audit committee)*

*See Chapter 4, Minimizing the Audit Committee's Legal Liability: A Check List, with respect to procedures to document audit committee activities.

pronouncements. An illustrative accounting policy disclosure check list in Exhibit 10.6 shows how the audit committee might document its review.[20]

In summary, as Russell E. Palmer, former managing partner of Touche Ross and Co. (now Deloitte & Touche), points out, "Committee members need not be auditors, or even accountants, but they must understand the financial reporting process."[21] Thus while each member of the committee may not possess the requisite accounting knowledge, they should approach their review task with imagination, perceptiveness, and resourcefulness in order to assure themselves that the policies are reasonable and consistent with the financial reporting requirements of the FASB, AICPA, SEC, and other regulatory agencies. Furthermore, the committee should exercise judgment regarding the need for the use of specialists in areas of complex accounting, tax, and legal matters. For example, several independent consultants, who are retired partners of CPA firms, sit on the corporate audit committee to assist the committee with complex accounting issues.[22] In short, the primary objective of the committee's review should be to scrutinize management's judgment in selecting the accounting principles and methods used in the preparation of the financial statements and to recommend the statements for the approval of the board of directors.

SOURCES AND SUGGESTED READINGS

American Institute of Certified Public Accountants, Audit Committees, Answers to Typical Question About Their Organization and Operations (New York: American Institute of Certified Public Accountants, 1978).

American Institute of Certified Public Accountants, Meeting the Financial Reporting Needs of the Future: A Public Commitment from the Public Accounting Profession (New York: American Institute of Certified Public Accountants, 1993).

Ameritech Corporation, *1992 Annual Report.*

Ameritech Corporation, *1998 Annual Report.*

Exxon Corporation, *1992 Annual Report.*

Bristol-Myers Squibb Company, *1990 Annual Report.*

Ford Motor Company, *1990 Annual Report.*

---

[20] This check list is not all-inclusive; and additional matters may be inserted based on the committee's judgment.

[21] Russell E. Palmer, "Audit Committees—Are They Effective? An Auditor's View," *Journal of Accountancy* 144, No. 3 (September 1977), p. 78.

[22] Obviously, a retired partner would not sit on the audit committee of a corporation that is a client of his or her former firm.

Gerson, James S., J. Robert Mooney, Donald F. Moran, and Robert K. Waters, "Oversight of the Financial Reporting Process—Part I." *CPA Journal* 59, No. 7 (July 1989), pp. 22–28.

Gerson, James S., J. Robert Mooney, Donald F. Moran, and Robert K. Waters, "Oversight of the Financial Reporting Process—Part II." *CPA Journal* 59, No. 8 (August 1989), pp. 40, 42–47.

Lockheed Martin Corporation, *1997 Annual Report.*

McKesson Corporation, *1998 Annual Report.*

Opinions of the Accounting Principles Board, No. 20. "Accounting Changes" (New York: American Institute of Certified Public Accountants, 1971).

Opinions of the Accounting Principles Board, No. 22, "Disclosure of Accounting Policies" (New York: American Institute of Certified Public Accountants, 1972).

Palmer, Russell, E., "Audit Committees—Are They Effective? An Auditor's View," *Journal of Accountancy* 144, No. 3 (September 1977), pp. 76–79.

Public Oversight Board, *A Special Report by the Public Oversight Board of the SEC Practice Section,* AICPA (Stamford, Conn.: Public Oversight Board, 1993).

Schornack, John J., "The Audit Committee—A Public Accountant's View," *Journal of Accountancy* 147, No. 4 (April 1979), pp. 73–77.

Wal-Mart Stores, Inc., *1998 Annual Report.*

Chapter 11

A Perspective on Fraud and the Auditor

In view of the general misconception concerning the auditor's responsibility for the detection of fraud, the purpose of this chapter is to examine the implications of management fraud as it relates to the external auditor and the audit committee. Moreover, the audit director will not only examine the meaning and rationale for management fraud but also explore ways to safeguard the entity against such fraud. The committee's monitoring of certain general business practices, such as conflicts of interest, will be discussed in Chapter 12.

MEANING OF FRAUD IN A FINANCIAL STATEMENT AUDIT

According to the Auditing Standards Board of the AICPA, fraud and its characteristics are described as follows:

> Although fraud is a broad legal concept, the auditor's interest specifically relates to fraudulent acts that cause a material misstatement of financial statements. The primary factor that distinguishes fraud from error is whether the underlying action that results in the misstatement in financial statements is intentional or unintentional. Two types of misstatements are relevant to the auditor's consideration of fraud in a financial statement audit—misstatements arising from fraudulent financial reporting and misstatements arising from misappropriation of assets.[1]

The types of aforementioned misstatements are described by the Board as follows:

> *Misstatements arising from fraudulent financial reporting* are intentional misstatements or omissions of amounts or disclosures in financial statements to deceive financial statement users. Fraudulent financial reporting may involve acts such as the following:

[1] *Statement on Auditing Standards, No. 82,* "Consideration of Fraud in a Financial Statement Audit" (New York: American Institute of Certified Public Accountants, 1997), par. 3.

- Manipulation, falsification, or alteration of accounting records or supporting documents from which financial statements are prepared

- Misrepresentation in, or intentional omission from, the financial statements of events, transactions, or other significant information

- Intentional misapplication of accounting principles relating to amounts, classification, manner of presentation, or disclosure

Misstatements arising from misappropriation of assets (sometimes referred to as defalcation) involve the theft of an entity's assets where the effect of the theft causes the financial statements not to be presented in conformity with generally accepted accounting principles. Misappropriation can be accomplished in various ways, including embezzling receipts, stealing assets, or causing an entity to pay for goods or services not received. Misappropriation of assets may be accompanied by false or misleading records or documents and may involve one or more individuals among management, employees, or third parties.[2]

In addition, the Internal Auditing Standards Board of the Institute of Internal Auditors states that:

Fraud encompasses an array of irregularities and illegal acts characterized by intentional deception. It can be perpetrated for the benefit of or to the detriment of the organization and by persons outside as well as inside the organization.[3]

With respect to fraudulent financial reporting, the National Commission on Fraudulent Financial Reporting defined such reporting as:

. . . intentional or reckless conduct, whether act or omission, that results in materially misleading financial statements. Fraudulent financial reporting can involve many factors and take many forms. It may entail gross and deliberate distortion of corporate records, such as inventory count tags, or falsified transactions, such as fictitious sales or orders. It may entail the misapplication of accounting principles. Company employees at any level may be involved, from top to middle management to lower-level personnel. If the conduct is intentional, or so reckless that it is the legal equivalent of intentional conduct, and results in fraudulent financial statements, it comes within the Commission's operating definition of the term *fraudulent financial reporting*.

Fraudulent financial reporting differs from other causes of materially misleading financial statements, such as unintentional errors. The Commission also distinguished fraudulent financial reporting from other corporate improprieties, such as employee embezzlements, violations of environmental or product safety regulations,

---

[2] Ibid., pars. 4, 5.
[3] *Standards for the Professional Practice of Internal Auditing* (Altamonte Springs, Fla.: Institute of Internal Auditors, 1998), Section 280.01.1.

and tax fraud, which do not necessarily cause the financial statements to be materially inaccurate.[4]

Although there is a distinction between fraudulent financial reporting and misappropriation of assets, this chapter addresses both types of fraud.

Although both the private sector and public sector have initiated action, particularly the Foreign Corrupt Practices Act of 1977 (discussed in Chapter 2), to protect the business community against management fraud, it is apparent that such positive actions will not completely eliminate this corporate problem. Since the passage of the act, management fraud cases continue to be discussed in the news media. The cost of management fraud to the business community is indeterminable, primarily because many cases are not revealed or not discovered. Furthermore, the cost of compliance to safeguard the entity from management fraud is increasing. For example, see the reports by the Association of Certified Fraud Examiners in Exhibits 11.1 and 11.2.[5]

Consequently, the cost in money and time to businesses and consumers to reform corporate behavior, as well as the cost of liability insurance, is constantly increasing.

In October 1997, Ernst & Young's Fraud Investigative Group in the United Kingdom surveyed senior executives in 11,000 major organizations in 32 countries. Based on 1,205 responses, Ernst & Young reported the following findings:

- The experience of organisations participating in our surveys shows that the curse of fraud continues. More than half had been defrauded in the last 12 months. 30% had suffered more than five frauds in the last five years.

- 84% of the worst frauds were committed by employees, nearly half of whom had been with the organisation for over 5 years.

- Most of the worst frauds were committed by management.

- 87% of respondents thought the incidence of fraud would increase, or at best remain static, over the next 5 years. Yet less than half of these organisations had done as much as they cost effectively could to protect their business against fraud.

- Only 13% of fraud losses had been recovered—including insurance recoveries.

---

[4]National Commission on Fraudulent Financial Reporting, *Report of the National Commission on Fraudulent Financial Reporting* (Washington, D.C.: National Commission on Fraudulent Financial Reporting, 1987), p. 2.

[5]In an article entitled "Six Common Myths About Fraud," Joseph T. Wells, chairman of the Association of Certified Fraud Examiners, identifies such myths as: (1) Most people will not commit fraud; (2) Fraud is not material; (3) Most fraud goes undetected; (4) Fraud is usually well concealed; (5) The auditor can't do a better job in detecting fraud; and (6) Prosecuting fraud perpetrators deters others. For further discussion, see *Journal of Accountancy* 169, No. 2 (February 1990), pp. 82–88.

Exhibit 11.1 Fraud Statistics

Fraud Costs the American Economy $186–310 Billion Annually

No national white-collar crime statistics are maintained in the United States. However, the Association of Certified Fraud Examiners, citing estimates by various experts, projects the annual cost of fraud to be between two and five percent of our nation's Gross Domestic Product.

90% of Americans Have Been Victims of Fraud

Taking into account the proliferation of phony mail sweepstakes, telephone boiler-room operations, fraudulent auto repair scams, and all other forms of fraud, it is estimated that 90% of all Americans have been victims of fraud at least once. Consumers lose a minimum of $1 billion to investment scams alone. Three quarters of these frauds are estimated to have been perpetrated by telephone. (*Your Money* [April 3, 1993], Cable News Network, Transcript #155-6)

Employee Theft Occurs in 95% of American Companies

Corporate fraud experts estimate that 95% of all corporations are experiencing—or have experienced—theft by employees. Some experts hold that less than 10% of these matters are ever uncovered. (*The Montreal Gazette* [June 22, 1992], "This Week in Business," Philip Levi)

Telecommunications Fraud Costs Consumers $15 Billion a Year

According to *U.S. West,* businesses and consumers lose at least $15 billion annually to telephone and telecommunications fraud. Telecommunication Advisors, Inc. estimates that one business in eighteen has a chance of being "hacked." ("Predicasts," a division of ZFF Communications Co.; *Common Carrier Week* [February 24, 1992], Warren Publishing Inc.)

80% of All Employees Have Pilfered in the Work Force

Eighty percent of 9,000 employees surveyed admitted that they had "stolen" small items on the job, e.g., personal long-distance calls, stationery, postage stamps, office supplies, and related items. (*Theft by Employees,* Hollinger and Clark)

33% of All Employees Have Stolen Money or Merchandise on the Job

While 80% of the work force has admitted to taking small items from employers, one third of all employees have stolen money or merchandise at least once during their employment. (*Theft by Employees,* Hollinger and Clark)

Credit Card Fraud Costs $3 Billion Annually

On a nationwide basis, credit card fraud alone costs at least $3 billion per year, and is on the increase. (*Business Wire*; Business Wire, Inc., December 10, 1992)

Telephone Scams Cost the Public $2 Billion a Year

The U.S. Secret Service estimates that boiler-room operations, phony sweepstakes, advance fee swindles, and other telephone scams cost approximately $2 billion a year. (*The San Francisco Chronicle* [September 14, 1992], Bill Wallaue)

Exhibit 11.1 *(Continued)*

Computer Hackers Cost Consumers $2.2 Billion per Year

The U.S. Secret Service estimates that hackers cost the economy at least $2.23 billion per year. (*The Los Angeles Times* [April 8, 1993], Timothy Chou)

Mail Fraud Costs Americans $15–40 Billion per Year

Mail fraud can take many forms, from phony sweepstakes to overvalued merchandise to chain letter referral schemes. Fraud experts estimate that Americans lose $15 to $40 billion annually to mail fraud schemes. (*The Buffalo News* [February 26, 1993], Richard Schroeder)

Insurance Fraud Costs Americans $20 Billion per Year

As of 1992, false and fraudulent insurance claims have cost insurance companies and their policyholders as much as $20 billion per year. ("Predicasts," a division of ZFF Communications Co.; *Common Carrier Week* [January 9, 1992]; Warren Publishing Inc.) Some industry experts estimate that the cost of fraudulent claims may be as much as 25% of each premium dollar paid. (*National Underwriter, Property & Casualty Risk & Benefits Management,* Edition 7/29/91, Gary Black)

Approximately 10% of Health Care Claims Involve Fraud and Abuse

According to the General Accounting Office, approximately 10% of the nation's health care expenditures are being skimmed by unscrupulous health care providers involved in every aspect of the industry. (*Healthline* [July 30, 1992], American Political Network, Inc.)

Source: Association of Certified Fraud Examiners, *Fraud Statistics Fact Sheet* (Austin, Tex.: Association of Certified Fraud Examiners, 1993). More recently, the Association of Certified Fraud Examiners (CFE) disclosed in its *Report to the Nation on Occupational Fraud and Abuse* that "fraud and abuse costs U.S. organizations more than $400 billion annually" (p. 13). For an expanded discussion of this survey of 2,608 CFEs, see *Report to the Nation on Occupational Fraud and Abuse* (Austin, Tex.: 1996). In addition, in early 1998, the Association conducted a survey of 600 CFEs and released the preliminary results at the Ninth Annual Fraud Conferences in New Orleans. The Association indicated that the purpose of the survey was to gather statistical information on the effects of occupational fraud; not only what it costs but also how its victims react. Are fraudsters prosecuted? What are the conviction rates? Are fraudsters sued in civil courts? Who usually wins? What success do companies have in collecting judgments against occupational fraudsters? When a company declines to take legal action, what are the reasons? Overall, the general observations of the respondents were as follows: The attitudes of CFEs in the 1998 survey were generally downbeat about the levels of fraud and the ways in which victim organizations and the courts deal with white-collar crime. When asked if fraud is worse than it was five years ago, 390 of 594 respondents (66 percent) said that it was. Another 130 respondents (22 percent) said the level of fraud is the same as it was five years ago. Only 41 respondents (7 percent) thought that fraud levels diminished over that period. About two-thirds of the respondents indicated company managers lack the desire to prosecute the perpetrators.

Exhibit 11.2   Minimizing the Cost of Occupational Fraud and Abuse

Occupational fraud and abuse cannot be eliminated in the workforce, but its costs can be reduced. Doing so requires preventative action, starting with a basic understanding of the nature of these offenses.

Generally, occupational fraud and abuse starts small and continues to grow, sometimes threatening the very existence of the organization. Because of fraud's clandestine nature, employers often are reluctant to believe it exists. This is especially true in small organizations.

It is equally true, however, that trust is the cornerstone of occupational fraud and abuse. As a result, the organization must seek a balance between trusting its employees too much and too little. While some occupational fraud is well hidden, most is not. And most can be prevented and detected with common sense and inexpensive solutions.

Consult a Certified Fraud Examiner

Certified Fraud Examiners have special knowledge concerning fraud detection and deterrence. Regular audits are not designed specifically for fraud and abuse. A Certified Fraud Examiner can assess your organization's unique fraud risks and design programs to cost-effectively reduce exposures. Of course, Certified Fraud Examiners can also help resolve suspected fraud and abuse matters.

Set the Tone at the Top

Employees who view their leaders as honest people are more inclined to emulate that behavior. The opposite is also true. Don't give employees an excuse to be dishonest.

Have a Written Code of Ethics

A written code of ethics sets forth what the organization expects from its employees. Although many larger organizations are implementing written codes, the same cannot be said of smaller ones. And that's where the risk to occupational fraud and abuse is highest.

Check Employee References

Some occupational offenders chronically abuse their positions and are simply discharged. These persons usually go on to other organizations where they continue their patterns of fraud and abuse. They often purposely select organizations where they know pre-screening is nonexistent.

Examine the Bank Statements

The organization's unopened bank statement should be reviewed at the highest possible level. Since most occupational fraud involves skimming cash and false disbursements, a responsible person unconnected to the bank reconciliations should look for unusual patterns, dual endorsements, unfamiliar vendors, and unfamiliar financial trends.

Have a Hotline

In this study, the majority of occupational fraud and abuse cases were discovered through tips and complaints by fellow employees. Employees are often in a position to observe improper conduct but frequently have no way to report it without fear of retribution. Some companies use a subscriber service while others maintain an internal hotline.

Exhibit 11.2   *(Continued)*

Create a Positive Work Environment

Employees frequently commit occupational fraud and abuse as a way of "getting back" at the organization for perceived workplace injustices. By creating a positive and open work environment, the employing organization can often reduce the motivation for its employees to commit fraud and abuse.

Source: Association of Certified Fraud Examiners, *Report to the Nation on Occupational Fraud Abuse* (Austin, Tex.: Association of Certified Fraud Examiners, 1996, pp. 33–38).

- Respondents' replies indicated that the better the directors understanding of the business as a whole, the lower the incidence of fraud they suffered.

- However, less than half the respondents believed that their directors had a good understanding of areas outside their core business, including remote and overseas operations.

- Less than a quarter of the respondents believed their directors had a good understanding of electronic communication or information technology.

- With the millennium approaching fast, three in four organisations had failed to include within their Year 2000 projects an assessment of the vulnerability of their computer systems to fraud.

- The proportion of organisations with fraud reporting policies was higher than in our last survey, but communication of these to the workforce was still poor.[6]

As David Sherwin, head of Ernst & Young's Fraud Investigation Group, asserts:

Companies need to act positively to prevent fraud from happening in the first place. They should ensure all the simple steps are conscientiously applied.

Areas of neglect include:

- *Lack of knowledge of the workings of remote sites and overseas operations.* Senior management reveals that it still doesn't make regular visits to remote locations in order to ensure that adequate controls are in place—placing too much reliance, instead, on local management.

- *Poor understanding by directors of electronic communications and IT.* Although computer systems are being widely reviewed to eliminate "millennium bomb" problems, the vulnerability of these systems to fraud was checked by only one in four companies surveyed.

[6] Ernst & Young, *Fraud: The Unmanaged Risk, An International Survey of the Effect of Fraud on Business* (London: Ernst & Young, 1998), p. 1.

- *Inadequate fraud-reporting policies for staff.* While most companies are developing such policies, communication remains poor. Over half the companies said they were opposed to hotlines to enable staff to report fraud. Such opposition was lowest in the U.S. and greatest in continental Europe.[7]

Intentional Distortions of Financial Statements

Concerning management's deliberate misrepresentations in the entity's financial position and results of operations, L. B. Sawyer, A. A. Murphy, and M. Crossley report:

> Management fraud has been found in overstatements of inventory to show healthy assets which are, in truth, sickly . . . the acceptance of inferior goods to conceal a tottering cash position . . . delayed key expenditures to increase current profits to the detriment of the long-range survival of the company . . . overstatements of receivables to puff both assets and sales . . . fictitious sales which construct a facade of vigorous business volume . . . and understatements of liabilities to gloss over the financial picture.[8]

With respect to legal cases concerning management fraud and the audit committee, the reader should review several cases in Chapter 4. Such a review indicates that the SEC and the courts have ruled on the establishment of the audit committee by the registrant in order to comply with the provisions of the federal securities laws. As a result, the legal obligations of the audit directors have intensified because their standard duty of care and loyalty to the entity has increased in light of the management fraud activities. Consequently, the audit committee will look to the internal and external auditing executives as well as legal counsel for assistance in preventing management fraud. In short, since management fraud is perpetrated by the top executives of the entity, it is ordinarily conducted on a sophisticated basis and thus requires the professional expertise of auditors, legal counsel, or special investigators.

The rationale for management fraud is essentially attributable to "different pressures" that force management into deliberate misrepresentations of accounting information as well as the misappropriations of assets.[9] Sawyer, Murphy, and Crossley summarize the reasons as follows:

- "Executives sometimes take rash steps from which they cannot retreat," such as setting unattainable objectives regarding the earnings per share figure. Such

---

[7] Ernst & Young, *Ernst's & Young's Business Upshot* (Cleveland, Ohio) (July/August 1998), p. 3.
[8] Lawrence B. Sawyer, Albert A. Murphy, and Michael Crossley, "Management Fraud: The Insidious Specter," *Internal Auditor* 36, No. 2 (April 1979), pp. 12–13.
[9] Ibid., p. 17.

rash actions may involve actually lying to the external auditors in order to inflate the bottom line of the entity.

- "Profit centers may distort facts to hold off divestments," whereby management of a subsidiary will deliberately manipulate transactions and alter documents and records to falsify its profitability performance.

- "Incompetent managers may deceive in order to survive," based on their actual performance versus their reported results.

- "Performance may be distorted to warrant larger bonuses," through the manipulation of the reported figures regarding the company's incentive plans.

- "The need to succeed can turn managers to deception," whereby such individuals place personal gains and self-interest before their stewardship accountability to their constituencies (discussed in Chapter 2).

- "Unscrupulous managers may serve interests which conflict," as discussed in Chapter 4 in relation to the state and federal statutory laws covering the directors and officers. Such laws provide a standard duty of care and loyalty to the entity.

- "Profits may be inflated to obtain advantages in the marketplace," whereby the perpetrators are confident that "their own abilities transcend any fear of detection."

- "People who control both the assets and their records are in a perfect position to falsify the latter." Thus a sound system of internal control, discussed in Chapter 8, is essential.[10]

Expanding on the aforementioned rationale and motivation for fraudulent financial reporting, the National Commission on Fraudulent Financial Reporting characterized various situations and opportunities:

> Fraudulent financial reporting usually occurs as the result of certain environmental, institutional, or individual forces and opportunities. These forces and opportunities add pressures and incentives that encourage individuals and companies to engage in fraudulent financial reporting and are present to some degree in all companies. If the right combustible mixture of forces and opportunities is present, fraudulent financial reporting may occur.

> A frequent incentive for fraudulent financial reporting that improves the company's financial appearance is the desire to obtain a higher price from a stock or debt offering or to meet the expectations of investors. Another incentive may be the desire to postpone dealing with financial difficulties and thus avoid, for example, violating a restrictive debt covenant. Other times the incentive is personal gain: additional compensation, promotion, or escape from penalty for poor performance.

[10]Ibid., pp. 17–19.

Situational pressures on the company or an individual manager also may lead to fraudulent financial reporting. Examples of these situational pressures include:

Sudden decreases in revenue or market share. A single company or an entire industry can experience these decreases.

Unrealistic budget pressures, particularly for short-term results. These pressures may occur when headquarters arbitrarily determines profit objectives and budgets without taking actual conditions into account.

Financial pressure resulting from bonus plans that depend on short-term economic performance. This pressure is particularly acute when the bonus is a significant component of the individual's total compensation.

Opportunities for fraudulent financial reporting are present when the fraud is easier to commit and when detection is less likely. Frequently these opportunities arise from:

The absence of a board of directors or audit committee that vigilantly oversees the financial reporting process.

Weak or nonexistent internal accounting controls. This situation can occur, for example, when a company's revenue system is overloaded from a rapid expansion of sales, an acquisition of a new division, or the entry into a new, unfamiliar line of business.

Unusual or complex transactions. Examples include the consolidation of two companies, the divestiture or closing of a specific operation, and agreements to buy or sell government securities under a repurchase agreement.

Accounting estimates requiring significant subjective judgment by company management. Examples include reserves for loan losses and the yearly provision for warranty expense.

Ineffective internal audit staffs. This situation may result from inadequate staff size and severely limited audit scope.

A weak corporate ethical climate exacerbates these situations. Opportunities for fraudulent financial reporting also increase dramatically when the accounting principles for transactions are nonexistent, evolving, or subject to varying interpretations.[11]

---

[11] National Commission on Fraudulent Financial Reporting, *Report of the National Commission on Fraudulent Financial Reporting,* pp. 23–24. For a good discussion, see James D. Stice, W. Steve Albrecht, and Leslie M. Brown, "Lessons to be Learned—ZZZZ Best, Regina, and Lincoln Savings," *CPA Journal* 61, No. 4 (April 1991), pp. 52–53. A recent study of 75 fraud and 75 no-fraud firms noted that no-fraud firms with outside members on the board of directors significantly reduce the likelihood of financial statement fraud. See Mark S. Beasley, "An Empirical Analysis of the Relation Between the Board of Director Composition and Financial Statement Fraud," *Accounting Review* 71, No. 4 (October 1996), pp. 443–465. For additional reading, see a Best Practices Council of the National Association of Corporate Directors report, *Coping with Fraud and Other Illegal Activity* (Washington, D.C.: National Association of Corporate Directors, 1998); Mark S. Beasley, Joseph V. Carcello, and Dana R. Hermanson, *Fraudulent Financial Reporting: 1987–1997 An Analysis of U.S. Public Companies* (New York: Committee of Sponsoring Organizations of the Treadway Commission, 1999).

The rationale for management fraud is based on the various pressures that emanate from the internal and external environment of the corporation. Moreover, such frauds are augmented by the economic motives of the perpetrator as well as the organizational structure of the entity.

Computer Fraud

In addition to management fraud, computer fraud has been a major constant problem of the business community. As Marshall Romney points out:

> In 1974 alone an estimated 339 computer-related frauds occurred with an average loss of over $500,000 and a total of over $200 million. This frightening sum reflects the escalating use of computers: from approximately 60,000 in 1970 to more than 200,000 today (1977). Four out of five are being used to keep financial records. This proliferation of computer usage made the task of finding material misstatement of financial statements increasingly difficult.[12]

In 1987 the National Commission on Fraudulent Financial Reporting concluded:

> The increasing power and sophistication of computers and computer-based information systems may contribute even more to the changing nature of fraudulent financial reporting. The last decade has seen the decentralization and the proliferation of computers and information systems into almost every part of the company. This development has enabled management to make decisions more quickly and on the basis of more timely and accurate information. Yet by doing what they do best—placing vast quantities of data within easy reach—computers multiply the potential for misusing or manipulating information, increasing the risk of fraudulent financial reporting.[13]

As defined by Brandt Allen:

> Computer fraud is . . . any defalcation or embezzlement accomplished by tampering with computer programs, data files, operations, equipment or media and resulting in losses sustained by the organization whose computer system was manipulated.[14]

---

[12] Marshall Romney, "Detection and Deterrence: A Double Barreled Attack on Computer Fraud," *Financial Executive* 45, No. 7 (July 1977), p. 36.

[13] National Commission on Fraudulent Financial Reporting, *Report of the National Commission on Fraudulent Financial Reporting,* p. 28. The reader may wish to review the Equity Funding Corporation of America case, which illustrates the use of computers to create fictitious insurance policies and, in turn, overstate assets by more than $120 million and overstate the corporation's earnings. See *United States v. Weiner,* 578 F. 2d 757 (9th Cir.), cert. denied, 439 U.S. 981 (1978).

[14] Brandt Allen, "The Biggest Computer Frauds: Lessons for CPA's," *Journal of Accountancy* 143, No. 5 (May 1977), 52.

Through an analysis of 150 major publicly documented computer fraud cases, Allen was able "to determine the major control lapses that seem to invite" computer fraud schemes.[15] As a result of his survey, he selected 15 of the "biggest" computer frauds (illustrated in Exhibit 11.3).

From this summary of the long-running computer frauds, it is interesting to note some general observations:

1. The number of perpetrators, ordinarily one, indicates a violation of the basic principle of internal control, which states that no one individual should handle a transaction from the time of origination to the point of final disposition. According to the Auditing Standards Board, a major component of internal control is control activities. The Board stated:

   Control activities are the policies and procedures that help ensure that management directives are carried out. They help ensure that necessary actions are taken to address risks to achievement of the entity's objectives. Control activities have various objectives and are applied at various organizational and functional levels. Generally, control activities that may be relevant to an audit may be categorized as policies and procedures that pertain to the following:

   - Performance reviews
   - Information processing
   - Physical controls
   - Segregation of duties

   Generally, control activities that may be relevant to an audit may be categorized as policies and procedures that pertain to the following.

   - *Performance reviews.* These control activities include reviews of actual performance versus budgets, forecasts, and prior period performance; relating different sets of data—operating or financial—to one another, together with analyses of the relationships and investigative and corrective actions; and review of functional or activity performance, such as a bank's consumer loan manager's review of reports by branch, region, and loan type for loan approvals and collections.

   - *Information processing.* A variety of controls are performed to check accuracy, completeness, and authorization of transactions. The two broad groupings of information systems control activities are general controls and application controls. General controls commonly include controls over data center operations, system software acquisition and maintenance, access security, and application system development and maintenance. These controls apply to mainframe, minicomputer, and end-user environments. Application controls apply to the processing of individual applications. These controls help ensure that transactions are valid, properly authorized, and completely and accurately processed.

---

[15] Ibid.

Exhibit 11.3 Long-Running Computer Frauds

Case	Summary	Amount (thousands)	Time Frame (years)	Type of Scheme	Computer Manipulation	Fraudulent Debit	Job Position of Primary Perpetrator	Number of Perpetrators Inside/Outside	Means of Detection
1.	Accountant at West Coast department store set up phony vendors, purchases, and vouchers.	$ 100	1.3	Disbursements	Unauthorized transactions	Inventory	Accountant	1/–	Suspicious bank employee
2.	Claims reviewer at insurance company prepared false claims payable to friends in a manner that would be paid automatically by the computer.	$ 128	4	Fraudulent claims paid	Unauthorized transactions added	Expense	Claims clerk	1/22	Error made by greedy associate
3.	Clerk at storage facility entered false information to computerized inventory system to mask theft of inventory. Shipments then made without billing.	$4,000	6	Inventory/ billing	Input transactions altered	Inventory	Computer terminal operator	1/13	Physical inventory shortage detected in audit
4.	Warehouse employees manipulated computerized inventory system through unauthorized terminal entries to mask inventory thefts.	$ 200	1.5	Inventory	Unauthorized terminal entries	None (inventory records changed as to location)	Warehouse employee(s)	"Several"	Suspicious wife of store manager

268

5.	Accountant at metal fabricating company padded payroll, thereby extracting funds for own use.	$ 100	3	Payroll	Unknown	Expense	Accountant	1/–	IRS investigation
6.	Officer of London bank stole funds from inactive customer accounts.	$ 290	5	Account transfers	Unauthorized addition and alteration of transactions	Customer accounts (liability)	Computer liaison officer	1/–	Unknown
7.	Bank employee misused on-line banking system to perpetrate large lapping fraud, including unrecorded transactions, altered transactions, and unauthorized account transfers.	$1,400	3	Lapping	Transactions altered, added, and withheld	Customer accounts (liability)	Teller supervisor	1/–	Gambling activities uncovered by police raid
8.	Manufacturing company manager who had designed and installed automated accounting system used it to steal.	$1,000	2	Disbursements (also billings fraud)	Transactions altered (also unauthorized transactions)	Inventory (also expense)	Operations manager	1/1	Suspicious associate
9.	Customer representatives of large public utility, together with outside associate, erased customer receivables using computer error correction codes; received kickback from customer.	$ 25 (probable loss much greater)	2	Accounts receivable— collections	Unauthorized transactions	Expense (adjusting entry)	Customer service representative	2/1	Suspicious bank employee together with expanded type of scheme

Exhibit 11.3 *(Continued)*

Case	Summary	Amount (thousands)	Time Frame (years)	Type of Scheme	Computer Manipulation	Fraudulent Debit	Job Position of Primary Perpetrator	Number of Perpetrators Inside/Outside	Means of Detection
10.	Clerk in department store established phony purchases and vouchers paid to friend's company.	$ 120	3	Disbursements	Unauthorized transactions	Inventory	Accounts clerk	1/1	Suspicious associate
11.	Organized crime ring operated check-kiting fraud between two banks, using computer room employees who altered deposit memos to record check deposits as available for immediate withdrawal.	$ 900	4	Kiting (float fraud)	Transactions altered	(Timing)	VP— computer systems (also assistant branch manager)	2/3	Bank messenger failed to deliver checks on time
12.	Accountant at large wholesaler established phony vendors through computerized accounting system that he operated.	$1,000	4	Disbursements	Unauthorized transactions	Inventory	Controller	1/–	Gave up
13.	Officer of brokerage house misappropriated company funds through computer system that he controlled.	$ 277	3	Account transfer	Unauthorized transactions	Revenue account (interest earned)	VP- computer systems	1/–	Unknown

14.	Partner at brokerage house transferred funds from firm's accounts to his own.	$ 81	3	Account transfers	Unauthorized transactions	Expense (via adjusting entry)	Partner head of computer system	1/–	Unknown
15.	Director of publishing subsidiary manipulated computer system to add false sales and block recording of accounts payable—all to improve operating results, thereby securing a position on board of directors.	$11,500	"Several years"	Padded sales (also unrecorded expense)	Program alterations (also file changes)	Receivables	Director of subsidiary	5/–	Unknown

Source: Allen, "The Biggest Computer Frauds: Lessons for CPA's," *Journal of Accountancy* 143, No. 5 (May 1977), p. 61.

- *Physical controls.* These activities encompass the physical security of assets, including adequate safeguards, such as secured facilities, over access to assets and records; authorization for access to computer programs and data files; and periodic counting and comparison with amounts shown on control records. The extent to which physical controls intended to prevent theft of assets are relevant to the reliability of financial statement preparation, and therefore the audit, depends on the circumstances such as when assets are highly susceptible to misappropriation. For example, these controls would ordinarily not be relevant when any inventory losses would be detected pursuant to periodic physical inspection and recorded in the financial statements. However, if for financial reporting purposes management relies solely on perpetual inventory records, the physical security controls would be relevant to the audit.

- *Segregation of duties.* Assigning different people the responsibilities of authorizing transactions, recording transactions, and maintaining custody of assets is intended to reduce the opportunities to allow any person to be in a position to both perpetrate and conceal errors or irregularities in the normal course of his or her duties.[16]

For example, the duties of the employees who have custody over cash should be separated from the duties of the employees who handle the accounting records.

2. Sixty percent of the computer manipulations were caused by unauthorized transactions. Such unauthorized transactions and access to terminals can be controlled through a sound system of internal control over the electronic data processing system.

3. Unauthorized disbursements can be contained through a countersigning approach whereby various signatures are required in accordance with predetermined dollar limits. Also, the person who is authorized to sign the checks should not authorize the check payments. The audit committee should have assurance that management has established a sound system of internal control over the computer system in order to comply with the internal accounting control provision of the Foreign Corrupt Practices Act discussed in Chapter 8. Moreover, Romney indicates that "the EDP internal audit head would report directly to them," and as the internal audit staff is given "more freedom and power" to investigate management fraud, such actions represent a "strong deterrent force" against fraud.[17]

---

[16] *Statement on Auditing Standards, No. 78,* "Consideration of the Internal Control in a Financial Statement Audit: An Amendment to SAS No. 55" (New York: American Institute of Certified Public Accountants, 1995), pars. 32, 9 (appendix).

[17] Romney, "Detection and Deterrence," p. 39. See Chapter 8 regarding the cost/benefit analysis of the system of internal control. For further reference, see Belden Menkus, "Eight Factors Contributing to Computer Fraud," *Internal Auditor* 47, No. 5 (October 1990), pp. 71–73.

THE EXTERNAL AUDITOR'S RESPONSIBILITY

An Overview[18]

As previously discussed in Chapter 6 dealing with audit planning, the Auditing Standards Board of the AICPA issued a standard that requires independent auditors to assess the risk of materially misstated financial statements due to fraud. According to the Board:

> The auditor should specifically assess the risk of material misstatement of the financial statements due to fraud and should consider that assessment in designing the audit procedures to be performed. In making this assessment, the auditor should consider fraud risk factors that relate to both (a) misstatements arising from fraudulent financial reporting and (b) misstatements arising from misappropriation of assets in each of the related categories presented in paragraphs 16 and 18. While such risk factors do not necessarily indicate the existence of fraud, they often have been observed in circumstances where frauds have occurred.

> As part of the risk assessment, the auditor also should inquire of management (a) to obtain management's understanding regarding the risk of fraud in the entity and (b) to determine whether they have knowledge of fraud that has been perpetrated on or within the entity. Information from these inquiries could identify fraud risk factors that may affect the auditor's assessment and related response. Some examples of matters that might be discussed as part of the inquiry are (a) whether there are particular subsidiary locations, business segments, types of transactions, account balances, or financial statement categories where fraud risk factors exist or may be more likely to exist and (b) how management may be addressing such risks.[19]

The fraud audit risk factors for potentially materially misstated financial statements are presented in Chapter 6.

With respect to the effect of fraud on the auditor's report, the Board states:

> A risk of material misstatement due to fraud is always present to some degree. The auditor's response to the foregoing assessment is influenced by the nature and significance of the risk factors identified as being present. In some cases, even though fraud risk factors have been identified as being present, the auditor's judgment may be that audit procedures otherwise planned are sufficient to respond to the risk factors. In other circumstances, the auditor may conclude that the conditions indicate a

---

[18] In addition to the external auditor's role and responsibility for detecting fraud and illegal acts, the reader may wish to consult other auditing standards with respect to the internal auditor, fraud examiner, and government auditors. See the bibliography for the applicable reference.

[19] *Statement on Auditing Standards No. 82,* "Consideration of Fraud in a Financial Statement Audit," pars. 12, 13. For further reference, see Douglas R. Carmichael, "The Auditor's New Guide to Errors, Irregularities and Illegal Acts," *Journal of Accountancy* 166, No. 3 (September 1988), pp. 40–48.

need to modify procedures. In these circumstances, the auditor should consider whether the assessment of the risk of material misstatement due to fraud calls for an overall response, one that is specific to a particular account balance, class of transactions or assertion, or both. The auditor also may conclude that it is not practicable to modify the procedures that are planned for the audit of the financial statements sufficiently to address the risk. In that case withdrawal from the engagement with communication to the appropriate parties may be an appropriate course of action.[20]

Finally, the external auditor has a responsibility to communicate fraud to the audit committee or board of directors. More specifically:

> The auditor's consideration of the risk of material misstatement due to fraud and the results of audit tests may indicate such a significant risk of fraud that the auditor should consider withdrawing from the engagement and communicating the reasons for withdrawal to the audit committee or others with equivalent authority and responsibility (hereafter referred to as the audit committee). Whether the auditor concludes that withdrawal from the engagement is appropriate may depend on the diligence and cooperation of senior management or the board of directors in investigating the circumstances and taking appropriate action. Because of the variety of circumstances that may arise, it is not possible to describe definitively when withdrawal is appropriate. The auditor may wish to consult with his or her legal counsel when considering withdrawal from an engagement.
>
> Whenever the auditor has determined that there is evidence that fraud may exist, that matter should be brought to the attention of an appropriate level of management. This is generally appropriate even if the matter might be considered inconsequential, such as a minor defalcation by an employee at a low level in the entity's organization. Fraud involving senior management and fraud (whether caused by senior management or other employees) that causes a material misstatement of the financial statements should be reported directly to the audit committee. In addition, the auditor should reach an understanding with the audit committee regarding the expected nature and extent of communications about misappropriations perpetrated by lower-level employees.
>
> When the auditor, as a result of the assessment of the risk of material misstatement due to fraud, has identified risk factors that have continuing control implications (whether or not transactions or adjustments that could be the result of fraud have been detected), the auditor should consider whether these risk factors represent reportable conditions relating to the entity's internal control that should be communicated to senior management and the audit committee. (See SAS No. 60, *Communication of Internal Control Related Matters Noted in an Audit* [AICPA, *Professional Standards,* vol. 1, AU sec. 325].) The auditor also may wish to communicate other risk factors identified when actions can be reasonably taken by the entity to address the risk.

[20] Ibid., par. 26.

The disclosure of possible fraud to parties other than the client's senior management and its audit committee ordinarily is not part of the auditor's responsibility and ordinarily would be precluded by the auditor's ethical or legal obligations of confidentiality unless the matter is reflected in the auditor's report. The auditor should recognize, however, that in the following circumstances a duty to disclose outside the entity may exist:

a. To comply with certain legal and regulatory requirements[a]

b. To a successor auditor when the successor makes inquiries in accordance with SAS No. 84, *Communications Between Predecessor and Successor Auditors*[b]

c. In response to a subpoena

d. To a funding agency or other specified agency in accordance with requirements for the audits of entities that receive governmental financial assistance

Because potential conflicts with the auditor's ethical and legal obligations for confidentiality may be complex, the auditor may wish to consult with legal counsel before discussing matters covered by paragraphs 38 through 40 with parties outside the client.

[a] These requirements include reports in connection with the termination of the engagement, such as when the entity reports an auditor change under the appropriate securities law on Form 8-K and the fraud or related risk factors constitute a "reportable event" or is the source of a "disagreement," as these terms are defined in Item 304 of Regulation S-K. These requirements also include reports that may be required, under certain circumstances, pursuant to the Private Securities Litigation Reform Act of 1995 (codified in section 10A(b)1 of the Securities Exchange Act of 1934) relating to an illegal act that has a material effect on the financial statements.
[b] In accordance with SAS No. 84, communication between predecessor and successor auditors requires the specific permission of the client.[21]

In addition to fraud in a financial statement audit, the external auditor has a responsibility for detecting illegal acts by client companies. As defined by the Auditing Standards Board:

The term *illegal acts,* for purposes of this Statement, refers to violations of laws or governmental regulations. Illegal acts by clients are acts attributable to the entity whose financial statements are under audit or acts by management or employees acting on behalf of the entity. Illegal acts by clients do not include personal misconduct by the entity's personnel unrelated to their business activities.[22]

Although the external auditor may recognize that the client has committed an illegal act, the determination of whether the act is illegal is dependent on legal judg-

---

[21] Ibid., pars. 36, 38–40.
[22] *Statement on Auditing Standards, No. 54,* "Illegal Acts by Clients" (New York: American Institute of Certified Public Accountants, 1988), par. 2. For further discussion, see Donald L. Neebes, Dan M. Guy, and O. Ray Whittington, "Illegal Acts: What Are the Auditor's Responsibilities?" *Journal of Accountancy* 171, No. 1 (January 1991), pp. 82–84, 86, 88, 90–93.

ment. Therefore, the auditor would consult with legal counsel or await a court ruling, depending on the circumstances.

In view of the fact that illegal acts vary in their relation to the financial statements, the Auditing Standards Board makes the following distinction between direct and indirect effects:

> The auditor considers laws and regulations that are generally recognized by auditors to have a direct and material effect on the determination of financial statement amounts. For example, tax laws affect accruals and the amount recognized as expense in the accounting period; applicable laws and regulations may affect the amount of revenue accrued under government contracts. However, the auditor considers such laws or regulations from the perspective of their known relation to audit objectives derived from financial statement assertions rather than from the perspective of legality *per se*. The auditor's responsibility to detect and report misstatements resulting from illegal acts having a direct and material effect on the determination of financial statement amounts is the same as that for fraud as described in SAS No. 82, "Consideration of Fraud in a Financial Statement Audit."

> Entities may be affected by many other laws or regulations, including those related to securities trading, occupational safety and health, food and drug administration, environmental protection, equal employment, and price-fixing or other antitrust violations. Generally, these laws and regulations relate more to an entity's operating aspects than to its financial and accounting aspects, and their financial statement effect is indirect. An auditor ordinarily does not have sufficient basis for recognizing possible violations of such laws and regulations. Their indirect effect is normally the result of the need to disclose a contingent liability because of the allegation or determination of illegality. For example, securities may be purchased or sold based on inside information. While the direct effects of the purchase or sale may be recorded appropriately, their indirect effect, the possible contingent liability for violating securities laws, may not be appropriately disclosed. Even when violations of such laws and regulations can have consequences material to the financial statements, the auditor may not become aware of the existence of the illegal act unless he is informed by the client, or there is evidence of a governmental agency investigation or enforcement proceeding in the records, documents, or other information normally inspected in an audit of financial statements.[23]

Warning signals for possible illegal acts are presented in Exhibit 11.4.

Finally, the auditor is required to communicate with the audit committee as follows:

> The auditor should assure himself that the audit committee, or others with equivalent authority and responsibility, is adequately informed with respect to illegal acts that come to the auditor's attention. The auditor need not communicate matters that are

---

[23] Ibid., pars. 5, 6.

Exhibit 11.4   Warning Signals of Possible Illegal Acts

- Unauthorized transactions, improperly recorded transactions, or transactions not recorded in a complete or timely manner in order to maintain accountability for assets

- Investigation by a governmental agency, an enforcement proceeding, or payment of unusual fines or penalties

- Violations of laws or regulations cited in reports of examinations by regulatory agencies that have been made available to the auditor

- Large payments for unspecified services to consultants, affiliates, or employees

- Sales commissions or agents' fees that appear excessive in relation to those normally paid by the client or to the services actually received

- Unusually large payments in cash, purchases of bank cashiers' checks in large amounts payable to bearer, transfers to numbered bank accounts, or similar transactions

- Unexplained payments made to government officials of employees

- Failure to file tax returns or pay government duties or similar fees that are common to the entity's industry or the nature of its business

Source: *Statement on Auditing Standards, No. 54,* "Illegal Acts by Clients," par. 9.

clearly inconsequential and may reach agreement in advance with the audit committee on the nature of such matters to be communicated. The communication should describe the act, the circumstances of its occurrence, and the effect on the financial statements. Senior management may wish to have its remedial actions communicated to the audit committee simultaneously. Possible remedial actions include disciplinary action against involved personnel, seeking restitution, adoption of preventive or corrective company policies, and modifications of specific control procedures. If senior management is involved in an illegal act, the auditor should communicate directly with the audit committee. The communication may be oral or written. If the communication is oral, the auditor should document it.[24]

With respect to detection of management fraud and reporting illegal acts, the Public Oversight Board set forth the following recommendations.

Recommendation V-1:

Accounting firms should assure that auditors more consistently implement, and be more sensitive to the need to exercise the professional skepticism required by, the auditing standard that provides guidance on the auditor's responsibility to detect and report errors and irregularities.

[24] *Statement on Auditing Standards, No. 54,* "Illegal Acts by Clients," par. 17.

Recommendation V-2:

The Auditing Standards Board, the Executive Committee of the SEC Practice Section or some other appropriate body should develop guidelines to assist auditors in assessing the likelihood that management fraud which may affect financial information may be occurring and to specify additional auditing procedures when there is a heightened likelihood of management fraud.[25]

Recommendation V-14:

The accounting profession should support carefully drafted legislation requiring auditors to report to the appropriate authorities, including the SEC, suspected illegalities discovered by the auditor in the course of an audit if the client's management or board of directors fails to take necessary action with respect to such suspected illegalities and the auditor believes that they are or may be significant to the entity. The profession should seek adequate guidance as to the types of illegalities that would be encompassed by this requirement.[26]

It is reemphasized that the auditor's purpose is to express an objective opinion on the fairness of the presentation in the financial statements. A review of the scope paragraph of the external auditor's standard report explicitly indicates that he or she should plan and perform the audit to obtain reasonable assurance about whether the financial statements are free of material misstatement. Such a statement is also acknowledged to the client company in the engagement letter, whereby the auditor explicitly states that the audit may not detect all material irregularities. Accordingly, if the auditor conducts his or her examination in accordance with generally accepted auditing standards, then he or she is not responsible for the detection of fraud. It should be recognized that the auditor's examination in full compliance with the promulgated auditing standards is not a guarantee that fraud is totally nonexistent. As noted in the preceding discussion on computer fraud, a sophisticated scheme along with collusion may go undetected by the independent auditor. As a result, it is incumbent on the audit committee to obtain reasonable assurance from the external auditors that management has taken the necessary actions to protect the assets of the entity. Such assurance is obtained through the committee's review of the auditor's management letter regarding management's responsibility for the financial accounting system and the related internal controls as well as appropriate fidelity bond insurance coverage.

In view of the nature and complex problems of management fraud, the AICPA's standing committee on methods, perpetration, and detection of fraud has provided a preliminary list of warning signals of the possible existence of fraud. (See Exhibit 11.5.)

---

[25] Public Oversight Board, *A Special Report by the Public Oversight Board of the SEC Practice Section, AICPA* (Stamford, Conn.: Public Oversight Board, 1993), p. 43.

[26] Ibid., p. 55. (See the proposed Financial Fraud Detection and Disclosures Act for further reference.)

Exhibit 11.5 Warning Signals of the Possible Existence of Fraud

---

1. Highly domineering senior management and one or more of the following, or similar, conditions are present:
   - An ineffective board of directors and/or audit committee.
   - Indications of management override of significant internal accounting controls.
   - Compensation or significant stock options tied to reported performance or to a specific transaction over which senior management has actual or implied control.
   - Indications of personal financial difficulties of senior management.
   - Proxy contests involving control of the company or senior management's continuance, compensation, or status.

2. Deterioration of quality of earnings evidenced by:
   - Decline in the volume or quality of sales (e.g., increased credit risk or sales at or below cost).
   - Significant changes in business practices.
   - Excessive interest by senior management in the earnings per share effect of accounting alternatives.

3. Business conditions that may create unusual pressures:
   - Inadequate working capital.
   - Little flexibility in debt restrictions such as working capital ratios and limitations on additional borrowings.
   - Rapid expansion of a product or business line markedly in excess of industry averages.
   - A major investment of the company's resources in an industry noted for rapid change, such as a high technology industry.

4. A complex corporate structure where the complexity does not appear to be warranted by the company's operations or size.

5. Widely dispersed business locations accompanied by highly decentralized management with inadequate responsibility reporting system.

6. Understaffing which appears to require certain employees to work unusual hours, to forego vacations, and/or to put in substantial overtime.

7. High turnover rate in key financial positions such as treasurer or controller.

8. Frequent change of auditors or legal counsel.

9. Known material weaknesses in internal control which could practically be corrected but remain uncorrected, such as:
   - Access to computer equipment or electronic data entry devices is not adequately controlled.
   - Incompatible duties remain combined.

10. Material transactions with related parties exist or there are transactions that may involve conflicts of interest.

11. Premature announcements of operating results or future (positive) expectations.

Exhibit 11.5 *(Continued)*

---

12. Analytical review procedures disclosing significant fluctuations which cannot be reasonably explained, for example:

    - Material account balances.
    - Financial or operational interrelationships.
    - Physical inventory variances.
    - Inventory turnover rates.

13. Large or unusual transactions, particularly at year-end, with material effect on earnings.

14. Unusually large payments in relation to services provided in the ordinary course of business by lawyers, consultants, agents, and others (including employees).

15. Difficulty in obtaining audit evidence with respect to:

    - Unusual or unexplained entries.
    - Incomplete or missing documentation and/or authorization.
    - Alterations in documentation or accounts.

16. In the performance of an examination of financial statements unforeseen problems are encountered, for instance:

    - Client pressures to complete audit in an unusually short time or under difficult conditions.
    - Sudden delay situations.
    - Evasive or unreasonable responses of management to audit inquiries.

Source: American Institute of Certified Public Accountants, *CPA Letter* 59, No. 5 (March 12, 1979), p. 4.

This check list of warning signals is particularly important as a guide to the audit committee in its inquiries of the audit partner to identify the auditor's alertness to the possibility of fraud. For example, the committee may wish to correlate the check list of warning signals with the auditor's management letter in order to identify potential problem areas. The major objective is to determine whether the auditor is taking a fresh look at the current year's audit examination as opposed to merely rolling over previous years' examinations. Furthermore, the committee's review of the check list will enable it to create an environment "that fosters morality and high business ethics."[27] "The systems should provide checks and balances and reports that cause flares to streak across the corporate sky if improprieties are practiced."[28]

---

[27] Sawyer, Murphy, and Crossley, "Management Fraud," p. 24.
[28] Ibid.

INVESTIGATING KNOWN FRAUD[29]

Summary Guidelines

As previously noted, the annual audit examination does not guarantee the nonexistence of fraud. However, through a sound system of internal control, adequate fidelity bond insurance, and effective internal and external audits, the entity is afforded reasonable protection against fraud. Nevertheless, on the discovery of fraud, it is essential that the board of directors call for a careful and competent investigation of the situation. While such an investigation is a burden on the entity, "corporate heads, including the boards of directors, should regard the occurrence as a business problem, not a legal problem."[30] Hence the board, through its audit committee, should demonstrate that it has taken the necessary course of action to properly uncover the fraud in order to maximize on its recovery from the fidelity bond insurance company.

Although the approach to an investigation may vary, Sawyer, Murphy, and Crossley point out that "an executive should be assigned to coordinate . . . the investigation."[31] Ordinarily the executive is the director of internal auditing. However, the audit committee may wish to engage special investigators and/or external auditors whereby both groups will coordinate their efforts with the internal auditors. Moreover, the surety company usually makes its own investigation because it must attest to the validity of the entity's claim. However, it is important to recognize that such an investigation should not be made solely by the surety company because its objective is to minimize the claim for the loss. Thus the audit committee should ensure that the investigation is properly coordinated with the auditors or the special investigators and the surety company. In particular, the committee should be assured that: (1) the suspect has not been notified of the present investigation; (2) the investigation has been properly planned in advance and will be conducted expeditiously to prevent covering up the evidence; (3) all corporate transactions involving the suspect and the methods used to perpetrate the fraud have been properly investigated and documented; (4) the existence of possible collusion has been carefully considered; (5) the dollar amount of the defalcation has been properly ascertained and the amount of the funds recovered; and (6) any legal action, if appropriate, has been taken against the perpetrator(s). Such assurance is obtained through the committee's review of the reports from the auditors, legal counsel, and the surety company as well as its consultation with the external audit partner regarding disclosure matters in the financial statements.

---

[29] For further reference, see Denzil Y. Causey, "The CPA Guide to Whistle Blowing," *CPA Journal* 58, No. 8 (August 1988), pp. 26–37; Timothy L. Williams and W. Steve Albrecht, "Understanding Reactions to Fraud," *Internal Auditor* 47, No. 4 (August 1990), pp. 45–51.

[30] Sawyer, Murphy, and Crossley, "Management Fraud," p. 20.

[31] Ibid.

From the preceding discussion, it is evident that the audit committee should recognize not only the primary purpose of the annual audit examination but also the implications of the auditor's responsibility for the detection of fraud. The committee will look primarily to the internal and external auditors for assistance concerning the necessary measures for the prevention of fraud. For example, it may request a periodic survey of the fraud prevention measures within the entity. Such a survey may be done by the internal audit group to determine the soundness of the system of internal control. Consequently, during its review of the audit plans discussed in Chapters 6 and 7, the committee should address the need for a survey of the fraud prevention measures. When such a survey is conducted, the committee should review the internal auditor's report with the outside audit partner to obtain the partner's assessment of the entity's fraud prevention activities. The committee should be satisfied that there is adequate follow-up regarding the internal auditor's recommendations so that if and when fraud should occur, it can be confident that the cause of the fraud was not related to recommendations that were overlooked. Such an oversight on the part of the committee may be a cause for an unrecovered insurance claim. It is obvious that the audit committee must be alert not only to the possibility of fraud but also to the steps necessary to safeguard the entity from such fraud.

As Hugh L. Marsh and Thomas E. Powell conclude:

> It would be a misconception to believe the possibility of fraud is the only reason for establishing a chartered audit committee. While the primary role has been to oversee management's financial and reporting responsibilities, it is only one task. Nevertheless, the Treadway Commission's investigations indicated that audit committees could serve very effectively to reduce the incidence of fraud. When fraudulent financial reporting did occur despite the existence of an audit committee, the following important points in the audit committee's charter often had been omitted:
>
> *Authorization for resources.* As noted by the Treadway Commission, only in unusual circumstances would an audit committee need a separate staff, but the means for accomplishing this should be addressed.
>
> *Issues related to CPAs' independence.* The press has made much ado about the practice of some CPAs of using audit services as a "loss leader" for management advisory services. Strong opinions have been expressed on both sides of this issue, but it would seem prudent for the audit committee to oversee management's judgments about the independence of its CPAs.
>
> *Seeking a second opinion.* Some observers speak of it disparagingly as "opinion shopping"; others refer to it as seeking a technically correct opinion. But any time a second opinion is sought, the audit committee should know what the issues were and how they were resolved.
>
> *Preservation of internal auditor independence.* Internal auditors occupy the unique position of "independent" staff members. This independence is strengthened and

ensured through audit committee action. Direct and unrestricted access to records is essential and the audit committee should concur with the appointment and discharge of the director of internal audit.[32]

SOURCES AND SUGGESTED READINGS

Allen Brandt, "The Biggest Computer Frauds: Lesson for CPA's," *Journal of Accountancy* 143, No. 5 (May 1977), pp. 52–62.

Association of Certified Fraud Examiners, *Fraud Statistics Fact Sheet* (Austin, Tex.: Association of Certified Fraud Examiners, 1993).

Association of Certified Fraud Examiners, *Report to the Nation on Occupational Fraud Abuse* (Austin, Tex.: Association of Certified Fraud Examiners, 1996).

Beasley, Mark S., "An Empirical Analysis of the Relation Between the Board of Director Composition and Financial Statement Fraud," *Accounting Review* 71, No. 4 (October 1996), pp. 443–465.

Carmichael, Douglas R., "The Auditor's New Guide to Errors, Irregularities and Illegal Acts," *Journal of Accountancy* 166, No. 3 (September 1988), pp. 40–48.

Causey, Denzil Y., "The CPA Guide to Whistle Blowing." *CPA Journal* 58, No. 8 (August 1988), pp. 26–37.

The CPA Letter 59, No. 5, American Institute of Certified Public Accountants (March 12, 1979), pp. 1–6.

Ernst & Young, *Fraud: The Unmanaged Risk, An International Survey of the Effect of Fraud on Business* (London: Ernst & Young, 1998).

Marsh, Hugh L., and Thomas E. Powell, "The Audit Committee Charter: Rx for Fraud Prevention." *Journal of Accountancy* 167, No. 2 (February 1989), pp. 55–57.

Menkus, Belden, "Eight Factors Contributing to Computer Fraud." *Internal Auditor* 47, No. 5 (October 1990), pp. 71–73.

National Commission on Fraudulent Financial Reporting, *Report of the National Commission on Fraudulent Financial Reporting* (Washington, D.C.: National Commission on Fraudulent Financial Reporting, 1987).

Neebes, Donald L., Dan M. Guy, and O. Ray Whittington, "Illegal Acts: What Are the Auditor's Responsibilities?" *Journal of Accountancy* 171, No. 1 (January 1991), pp. 82–84, 86, 88, 90–93.

Public Oversight Board, *A Special Report by the Public Oversight Board of the SEC Practice Section, AICPA* (Stamford, Conn.: Public Oversight Board, 1993).

Romney, Marshall, "Detection and Deterrence: A Double Barrel Attack on Computer Fraud." *Financial Executive* 45, No. 7 (July 1977), pp. 36–41.

[32] Hugh L. Marsh and Thomas E. Powell, "The Audit Committee Charter: Rx for Fraud Prevention." *Journal of Accountancy* 167, No. 2 (February 1989), pp. 55–57.

Sawyer, Lawrence B., Albert A. Murphy, and Michael Crossley, "Management Fraud: The Insidious Specter." *Internal Auditor,* 36, No. 2 (April 1979), pp. 11–25.

Statement on Auditing Standards No. 54, "Illegal Acts by Clients" (New York: American Institute of Certified Public Accountants, 1988).

Statement on Auditing Standards No. 55, "Consideration of the Internal Control Structure in a Financial Statement Audit" (New York: American Institute of Certified Public Accountants, 1988).

Statement on Auditing Standards No. 82, "Consideration of Fraud in a Financial Statement Audit" (New York: American Institute of Certified Public Accountants, 1997).

Stice, James D., W. Steve Albrecht, and Leslie M. Brown, "Lessons to be Learned—ZZZZ Best, Regina, and Lincoln Savings." *CPA Journal* 61, No. 4 (April 1991), pp. 52–53.

United States v. Weiner, 578 F. 2d 757 (9th Cir), cert. denied, 439 U.S. 981 (1978).

Wells, Joseph T., "Six Common Myths About Fraud." *Journal of Accountancy* 169, No. 2 (February 1990), pp. 82–88.

Williams, Timothy L., and W. Steve Albrecht, "Understanding Reactions to Fraud." *Internal Auditor,* No. 4 (August 1990), pp. 45–51.

Additional Suggested Readings

Albrecht, W. S., M. B. Romney, D. J. Cherrington, I. R. Payne, and A. J. Roe, *How to Detect and Prevent Business Fraud* (Englewood Cliffs, N.J.: Prentice-Hall, 1982).

American Institute of Certified Public Accountants, "Legal Scene." *Journal of Accountancy.* New York: AICPA (published monthly).

Association of Certified Fraud Examiners, *Professional Standards and Practices for Certified Fraud Examiners* (Austin, Tex.: Association of Certified Fraud Examiners, 1979).

Association of Certified Fraud Examiners, *The White Paper* (Austin, Tex.: Association of Certified Fraud Examiners) (published bimonthly).

Bloom Becker, Buck, *Spectacular Computer Crimes* (New York: Dow Jones Irwin, 1990).

Bologna, G. Jack, and Robert J. Lindquist, *Fraud Auditing and Forensic Accounting* (New York: John Wiley & Sons, 1987).

Bologna, G. Jack, Robert J. Lindquist, and Joseph Wells, *The Accountant's Handbook of Fraud & Commercial Crime* (New York: John Wiley & Sons, 1992).

Davia, Howard R., Patrick C. Coggins, John C. Wildeman, and Joseph T. Kastantin, *Management Accountants' Guide to Fraud Discovery and Control* (New York: John Wiley & Sons, Inc., 1992).

Domanick, Joe, *Faking It in America* (Chicago: Contemporary Books, 1989).

Elliott, Robert K., and John J. Willingham, *Management Fraud: Detection and Deterrence* (New York: Petrocelli Books, 1980).

Glover, Hubert D., and James C. Flagg, *Effective Fraud Detection and Prevention Techniques* (Altamonte Springs, Fla.: Institute of Internal Auditors, 1993).

Institute of Internal Auditors, "Fraud Findings." *Internal Auditor* (Altamonte Springs, Fla.:) (published monthly).

Jacobson, Alan, *How to Detect Fraud Through Auditing* (Altamonte Springs: Fla.: Institute of Internal Auditors, 1990).

Kellogg, Irving, *Fraud, Window Dressing, and Negligence in Financial Statements* (New York: McGraw-Hill, 1991).

Levy, Marvin M., *Computer Fraud: A Basic Course for Auditors* (New York: American Institute of Certified Public Accountants, 1990).

Levy, Marvin M., *Detection of Errors, Fraud, and Illegal Acts* (New York: American Institute of Certified Public Accountants, 1990).

Merchant, Kenneth A., *Fraudulent and Questionable Financial Reporting* (Morristown, N.J.: Financial Executive Research Foundation, 1987).

Standards for the Professional Practice of Internal Auditing (Altamonte Springs, Fla.: Institute of Internal Auditors, 1998).

U.S. General Accounting Office, *Government Auditing Standards, Standards for Audit of Governmental Organizations, Programs, Activities, and Functions* (Washington, D.C.: U.S. Government Printing Office, 1988).

White, Richard, and William G. Bishop, "The Role of the Internal Auditor in the Deterrence, Detection, and Reporting of Fraudulent Financial Reporting," *The Institute of Internal Auditors Reports on Fraud* (Altamonte Springs, Fla.: Institute of Internal Auditors, 1986).

Videos

Association of Certified Fraud Examiners, *Cooking the Books: What Every Accountant Should Know About Fraud* (1991); *The Corporate Con: Internal Fraud and the Auditor* (1992); and *Beyond the Numbers: Professional Interview Techniques* (1994) Austin, Tex.; length of videos: 50 minutes.

Institute of Internal Auditors, *A New Look at Ethics and Fraud*. Altamonte Springs, Fla., 1988; length of video: 60 minutes.

Chapter 12

Reviewing Certain General Business Practices

In Chapter 2 it was established that corporate boards of directors and their audit committees have a major role in establishing and maintaining corporate accountability and governance. In addition, it was noted that the boards and their committees have encountered increasing pressure from the SEC and Congress as evidenced particularly by the passage of the Foreign Corrupt Practices Act. Such pressures have created an environment whereby the audit committee should review and monitor certain corporate policies and practices regarding sensitive payment areas. The purpose of this chapter is to examine those areas, such as questionable foreign payments, conflicts of interest, corporate perquisites, and corporate contributions. This chapter will discuss the nature of these sensitive matters and identify ways to assist the committee with its review.

QUESTIONABLE FOREIGN PAYMENTS

Nature of Questionable Foreign Payments

In view of the Foreign Corrupt Practices Act, many accounting practitioners and corporate executives have been studying the legal and ethical implications of the foreign bribery provision.[1] Their examination of this provision includes not only a definitional analysis of the questionable foreign payments but also corporate policy and compliance matters. As discussed in Chapter 2, the primary purpose of the bribery provision is to prohibit all U.S. companies, both private and public, foreign

---

[1] With respect to the antibribery section of the act, the Criminal Division of the Justice Department has adopted review procedures to assist management. In short, the Justice Department will review the proposed transactions only upon written request, and it will issue a review letter to determine whether disclosure is required. This matter should be discussed with the executive audit partner, the chief financial officer, and legal counsel. For further reference, see the Department of Justice's "Foreign Corrupt Practices Act Option Procedure," *Code of Federal Regulations,* Sec. 28, Part 77.

companies registered with the SEC, and directors, officers, stockholders, employees, and agents to bribe foreign government officials. Furthermore, the act states that any direct or indirect payment or offer intended to promote business constitutes foreign bribery. Equally important, the act prohibits the use of mails or any means or instrumentalities of interstate commerce to make corrupt payments or authorization of the payments regarding "anything of value" to the following:

1. Any foreign official,
2. Any foreign political party or official thereof, or
3. Any person, while knowing or having reason to know that all or a portion of the payment will be offered to any of the preceding groups or any candidate for foreign political office.[2]

Moreover, it should be noted that certain payments called "facilitating" or "grease" payments are not covered under the act because such payments are ministerial or clerical. However, with respect to disclosure of such payments, the SEC indicates that:

> These so-called facilitating payments have been deemed to be material where the payments to particular persons are large in amount or the aggregate amounts are large, or where corporate management has taken steps to conceal them through false entries in corporate books and records.[3]

Thus it is management's responsibility to identify and determine whether payments for customs documents or minor permits, which are essentially facilitating payments, should be disclosed.

As mentioned in Chapter 2, the Foreign Corrupt Practices Act was amended in August 1988. The amendments not only limited criminal penalties to individuals who knowingly failed to comply with the internal accounting control provision but also clarified the term *bribery* and increased penalties.[4] As Judith L. Roberts reports, the amendments' clarification and restriction of criminal penalties should substantially reduce the compliance burden and anticompetitive impact of the Foreign Corrupt Practices Act.[5] In addition, Marlene C. Piturro observed that since the enactment of the Act, the FBI has uncovered "400 cases of misconduct and

---

[2] The act is contained in Title I of Public Law No. 95-213. (See Appendix D.)

[3] Securities and Exchange Commission, "Report of the Securities and Exchange Commission on Questionable and Illegal Corporate Payments and Practices," submitted to the Senate Banking, Housing and Urban Affairs Committee, May 12, 1976, p. 27.

[4] The amendments are contained in The Omnibus Trade and Competitiveness Act, in Title V of Public Law No. 100-418, August 23, 1988. (See Appendix D.)

[5] Judith L. Roberts, "Revision of the Foreign Corrupt Practices Act by the 1988 Omnibus Trade Bill: Will It Reduce the Compliance Burdens and Anticompetitive Impact?" *Brigham Young University Law Review,* No. 2 (1989), p. 506.

recouped $300 million in illegal payments."[6] See Chapter 2 for further discussion of the act.

Triton Energy Corporation, for example, disclosed the following in its annual report to stockholders:

Federal Securities Lawsuits—From May 27, 1992, through June 15, 1992, six separate suits were filed in federal district court in Dallas, Texas, by alleged shareholders against the Company and various present and former directors and officers of the Company. Plaintiffs in all of these cases seek to represent alleged classes of persons and/or entities who purchased the Company's securities. The plaintiffs in five of the six suits allege violations of the Securities Exchange Act of 1934 (the "1934 Act") and Rule 10b-5 promulgated thereunder, common law fraud and statutory fraud and negligent misrepresentation. Among other allegations, the plaintiffs base their claims upon alleged disclosure deficiencies in the Company's reports filed under the 1934 Act with respect to the financial condition of the Company, the Janacek litigation, the Company's Indonesian operations, including certain alleged bribes, violations of Indonesian law and falsified accounting records, and related arbitration and litigation matters. Plaintiffs in these cases seek, among other relief, to recover both actual and exemplary monetary damages in unspecified amounts. The parties to these five lawsuits have agreed, subject to the Court's approval, to consolidate these cases into a single lawsuit. The parties in a sixth lawsuit have not yet agreed to consolidation with the other federal securities lawsuits. Plaintiffs in the sixth case allege violations of Sections 10(b) and 20(a) of the 1934 Act and Rule 10b-5 promulgated thereunder. Among other allegations, the plaintiffs assert claims based upon an alleged conspiracy among the defendants in the case to manipulate the price of the Company's securities and alleged insider trading. Plaintiffs in this case also allege disclosure deficiencies, including failure to disclose material facts about the Company's financial condition. In addition, the plaintiffs in the sixth case have asserted certain claims against the Company's independent auditors. Plaintiffs in this case seek, among other relief, to recover actual and exemplary monetary damages in unspecified amounts and to force the individual defendants to disgorge alleged profits made in certain securities transactions.

These federal securities lawsuits are at a very preliminary stage. Due to the various uncertainties inherent in litigation, no assurance can be given as to the ultimate outcome of this litigation or any effect the litigation may ultimately have on the Company's consolidated financial condition. The Company intends to vigorously defend these lawsuits. Based on knowledge of the facts to date and consultation with its legal advisors, including in-house counsel to the Company, the Company currently believes that the Company's liabilities, if any, with respect to these lawsuits should not have a material adverse effect on the Company's consolidated financial condition.[7]

---

[6]Marlene C. Piturro, "Just Say . . . Maybe," *World Trade* 5, No. 5 (June 1992), p. 86.
[7]Triton Energy Corporation, *1992 Annual Report,* p. 34.

On May 20, 1993, *The Wall Street Journal* observed:

> Triton Energy Corp. acknowledged that the Justice Department is investigating whether the company violated federal law and is most likely focusing on the Foreign Corrupt Practices Act related to Triton's Indonesian operations. The SEC is conducting a similar inquiry and the company is cooperating.[8]

More recently, the Organization of Economic Cooperation and Development (OECD) reached an accord with its member countries to address the problem of bribery in international business. As Donald J. Johnston, secretary-general of the OECD, points out:

> The Convention on Combating Bribery of Foreign Public Officials in International Business Transactions is an instrument which will permit OECD and other countries to move in a co-ordinated manner to adopt national legislation to make it a crime to bribe foreign public officials. The Convention sets a high standard for national laws. It includes a broad, clear definition of bribery; it requires dissuasive penalties; it sets a strong standard for enforcement; and it provides for mutual legal assistance. The entry into force provisions are designed to encourage signatories to act quickly and in concert.[9]

The Convention contains 17 articles. Article 8 includes an accounting provision that states:

> 1.   In order to combat bribery of foreign public officials effectively, each Party shall take such measures as may be necessary, within the framework of its laws and regulations regarding the maintenance of books and records, financial statement disclosures, and accounting and auditing standards, to prohibit the establishment of off-the-books accounts, the making of off-the-books or inadequately identified transactions, the recording of non-existent expenditures, the entry of liabilities with incorrect identification of their object, as well as the use of false documents, by companies subject to those laws and regulations, for the purpose of bribing foreign public officials or of hiding such bribery.
>
> 2.   Each Party shall provide effective, proportionate and dissuasive civil, administrative or criminal penalties for such omissions and falsifications in respect of the books, records, accounts and financial statements of such companies.[10]

---

[8] "Triton Energy Corp.: Justice Department Probing for Possible Law Violations," *The Wall Street Journal* (May 20, 1993), Sec. A, p. 7, col. 3. See also Andy Zipser, "Crude Grab? How a Tiny Producer Lost Its Indonesian Stake," *Barron's* 72, No. 21 (May 25, 1992), pp. 12–15, and "Triton to Settle SEC's Indonesia Bribery Charges," *Oil and Gas Journal* 95, No. 10 (March 10, 1997), p. 27.
[9] Organization of Economic Cooperation and Development, *Convention on Combating Bribery of Foreign Public Officials in International Business Transactions* (Paris: OECD, 1997), p. 3.
[10] Ibid., p. 8.

Obviously, the negotiated convention by the OECD with its member nations is a major step toward solving the problem of bribery in international business. Presumably the OECD's convention will be adopted by the individual governments of the member countries.

Summary Guidelines: Historical Perspective

To monitor questionable foreign payments effectively, the audit committee should review the corporate policy and other documentation that supports management's compliance with such policy. Concerning corporate policy, the American Assembly's recommendations regarding the standards of corporate conduct are useful in formulating policy guidelines:

> Although American corporations operating overseas should give due regard to the ethical judgments of other societies, each U.S. corporation can maintain only one set of universal principles that must not be compromised in foreign subsidiaries. Some U.S. practices of a less important nature may be adjusted to custom, practice, and law; such cases should be evaluated before the fact and stated publicly.

> American corporations should proscribe bribery and kickbacks everywhere. . . . American corporations operating in foreign lands should not be prohibited by American law from contributing to political parties when such contributions are legal under that country's laws, expected as part of good corporate responsibility, and are disclosed.[11]

Such a corporate policy is essential as evidenced by a Conference Board study whereby the Board surveyed 35 firms on their approaches to the improper payments problem and found that "a handful" of companies did not have problems because of their existing corporate policies and practices.[12] Such companies "simply enjoin company employees from any illegal activity or conflicts of interest."[13] However, "many companies reported sharp divisions in their management ranks regarding the types of payments that should be enjoined."[14] Thus it is necessary to define clearly the proper and improper payments within the context of the Foreign Corrupt Practices Act to avoid any misunderstanding among the employees. Furthermore, the justification for such a corporate policy is supportable, as the *Journal of Accountancy* observed in a study of 109 large corporations, which disclosed that:

---

[11] The American Assembly, *The Ethics of Corporate Conduct,* Pamphlet 52 (New York: Columbia University, April 1977), pp. 6–7.
[12] James Greene, "Assuming Ethical Conduct Abroad," *Conference Board Information Bulletin No. 12* (November 1976), p. 1.
[13] Ibid., p. 3.
[14] Ibid.

... Dozens of corporations maintained more than $63.1 million in off-book bank accounts that were not part of the official corporate books. ... $14.2 million in sensitive payments was financial through overbilling, and $3.3 million was through ... phony invoices ... $2 million was funneled through closely guarded cost funds ... known to just a few top company executives. Inflated expense accounts generated almost $500,000 more—typically for personal political contributions by key management personnel.[15]

Moreover, "such payments are usually concealed by schemes that would be undetectable by auditors, no matter how thorough the audit."[16] Such findings and conclusions totally agree with the discussion in Chapter 11.

Consequently, as Walter E. Hanson, former chairman of Peat, Marwick, Mitchell & Co. (now KPMG Peat Marwick) points out, senior management should establish "clear and unequivocal statements of policy and codes of conduct as well as 'mechanisms,' such as the audit committee, to monitor corporate management's behavior."[17] In short, "self-policing by business is the only alternative ... to increasing government regulation and eventual government takeover."[18] See Appendix I for further discussion on business conduct.

With respect to monitoring the improper foreign payments area, former partner Dennis R. Beresford and James D. Bond of Ernst and Whinney (now Ernst & Young) conclude:

A key element in preventing and detecting illegal foreign bribes is proper supervision of employees in sensitive positions. A formal code of conduct that is appropriately communicated and monitored is a most important step in exercising this proper care.[19]

Specifically, the Conference Board found that "a heavy majority" of the companies enforce compliance with their policies through a "periodic (usually annual) statement from their managers."[20] An example of such a statement is the following:

Representing my organization, I warrant that, to the best of the my knowledge, none of our employees is in violation of the company's policies and practices with regard to business ethics, offering or accepting gifts and gratuities, contributions, conflict of interest, safeguarding company assets, community and governmental participation,

---

[15] See "An Examination of Questionable Payments and Practices," Charles E. Simon and Company, Washington, D.C. 1978, *Journal of Accountancy* 145, No. 4 (May 1978), p. 7.

[16] Ibid.

[17] Walter E. Hanson, "A Blueprint for Ethical Conduct," Statement in Quotes, *Journal of Accountancy* 145, No. 6 (June 1978), p. 80.

[18] Ibid., p. 82.

[19] Dennis R. Beresford and James D. Bond, "The Foreign Corrupt Practices Act—Its Implications to Financial Management," *Financial Executive* 46, No. 8 (August 1978), p. 32.

[20] Greene, "Assuring Ethical Conduct," p. 17.

and sales agents, consultants and other professional services, and that these policies and practices are reviewed with key employees annually.[21]

Moreover, several public accounting firms request such statements.[22]

John C. Taylor, partner of Paul, Weiss, Rifkind, Wharton, and Garrison, suggests that the prevention of improper payments can be controlled through proper internal controls as follows:

> The policy must require that every payment and every transaction with outside parties is reflected on the books of the corporation promptly, accurately and in the normal financial reporting channels.

> The policy must absolutely prohibit bribes, payments for illegal acts, and legally proscribe political contributions.

> The policy must be specific and intelligible to people in the field who will have to operate within its bounds.[23]

Hence the policy must define what are "proper and improper payments at a high corporate level directly responsible to the board.[24]

For example, the policy should include predetermined fixed levels of responsibility regarding the decisions in the sensitive payments area. Thus it is essential that the policy identify those executives in charge of the acceptable arrangements for proper payments as well as their reporting responsibility to the audit committee or the board of directors.[25]

With respect to enforcing such a policy, Taylor indicates that "normal auditing techniques are the best means of uncovering departures from the policy."[26] Such techniques should be coupled with the following procedures:

> . . . review of all professional and consulting fees. . . . use of annual representation letters from all personnel in sensitive positions . . . constant review of signatories on all bank accounts world wide. . . . obtain letters from outside professionals, agents, and joint ventures certifying that they are not using corporate funds . . . for improper purposes.[27]

Hugh L. Marsh, former general manager of internal auditing for the Aluminum Company of America, points out the compliance of Alcoa with the Foreign Corrupt Practices Act. Such compliance includes:

[21] Ibid.
[22] Ibid.
[23] John C. Taylor III, "Preventing Improper Payments Through Internal Controls," *Conference Board Record* 13, No. 8 (August 1976), pp. 17–18.
[24] Ibid., p. 18.
[25] Ibid.
[26] Ibid.
[27] Ibid.

Policy guidelines for business conduct

Representation letters of compliance with company policy

Conflict of interest surveys at the request of the board of directors

Monitoring and auditing procedures to ensure compliance with company policy and reports to the Audit Committee

Maintaining a corporate Security Department

Circulating a summary of the Foreign Corrupt Practices Act by the chief executive officer to all managers worldwide[28]

Moreover, Marsh continues:

> ... I urge you to sit down with your chief financial officer and legal counsel and obtain a thorough understanding of the implications of this law. I urge you to involve these people as well as your external auditors in assessing the risk within your own business and developing an inventory of control practices. . . . I urge that you consider development of a policy statement for standards of conduct of your business and develop monitoring procedures that are appropriate.[29]

Additional Summary Guidelines

As James S. Gerson et al. point out:

> The committee should be aware that the Foreign Corrupt Practices Act (FCPA) requires public companies to keep reasonably detailed records of all transactions and to maintain internal accounting controls that provide reasonable assurance that those transactions are properly authorized and recorded.[30]

With respect to boards of directors and their compliance with applicable laws and regulations, the Business Roundtable states:

> Law compliance is a fundamental requirement of both private and corporate persons. Boards of directors participate in a number of different ways. The audit committee of the board of directors, actions of other board committees, the approval and review policies of the board, review by the corporate general counsel, and, where necessary, by outside counsel retained by the general counsel or appointed by the board are all procedures that can be used in fulfilling this function.

---

[28] Hugh L. Marsh, "The Foreign Corrupt Practices Act: A Corporate Plan for Compliance," *Internal Auditor* 36, No. 2 (April 1979), pp. 73–74.

[29] Ibid., p. 76.

[30] James S. Gerson, J. Robert Mooney, Donald F. Moran, Robert K. Waters, "Oversight of the Financial Reporting Process—Part I," *CPA Journal* 59, No. 7 (July 1989), p. 28.

Legislation and regulation affecting the corporation change frequently. The general counsel of the corporation should regularly brief the board on significant changes in applicable laws, including legal developments affecting the corporation or their duties as directors.[31]

Finally, in an article dealing with compliance with the amended act, Sandra G. Gustavson and Jere W. Morehead suggest the following to help coordinate a company's compliance efforts and loss control program:

- Develop clear, specific policy statements
- Establish and maintain a written code of conduct
- Implement formal approval procedures for payments[32]

The External Auditor's Responsibility

As noted in Chapter 11, the external audit examination cannot guarantee that irregularities or illegal acts are nonexistent. According to the Auditing Standards Board:

Certain illegal acts have a direct and material effect on the determination of financial statement amounts. Other illegal acts, such as those described,[33] may, in particular circumstances, be regarded as having material but indirect effects on financial statements. The auditor's responsibility with respect to detecting, considering the financial statements effects of, and reporting these other illegal acts is described in this Statement. These other illegal acts are hereinafter referred to simply as *illegal acts*. The auditor should be aware of the possibility that such illegal acts may have occurred. If specific information comes to the auditor's attention that provides evidence concerning the existence of possible illegal acts that could have a material indirect effect on the financial statements, the auditor should apply audit procedures, specifically directed to ascertaining whether an illegal act has occurred. However, because of the characteristics of illegal acts as explained above, an audit made in accordance with generally accepted auditing standards provides no assurance that illegal acts will be detected or that any contingent liabilities that may result will be disclosed.[34]

---

[31] The Business Roundtable, *Corporate Governance and American Competitiveness* (New York, 1990), p. 10.

[32] Sandra G. Gustavson and Jere W. Morehead, "Complying with the Amended Foreign Corrupt Practices Act," *Risk Management* 37, No. 4 (April 1990), p. 5.

[33] See Chapter 11 for additional emphasis.

[34] *Statement on Auditing Standards, No. 54,* "Illegal Acts By Clients" (New York: American Institute of Certified Public Accountants, 1988), par. 7.

As a case in point, "When something has come to a director's attention in the area of commercial bribery, what can the auditors do to help directors find out if there is a problem: for example, in a department where there may be a suspicion of a kickback?"[35] According to David L. James, former partner of Arthur Young and Co. (now Ernst & Young), the board member should discuss this matter with "a member of the audit committee, preferably the chairman." Furthermore, James points out:

> When we get into the area of irregularities, e.g., fraud, questionable conduct, and the like, we sit down with the audit committee, indicate that this question has been raised, glean as much information from the director as possible, and then figure out how to attack the particular problem.[36]

While the external auditors can assist the audit committee in the sensitive payments area, it is important to recognize that:

> With respect to high level executive conflicts of interest, the Board of Directors has the obligation, in selecting such executives, to make exhaustive background checks of prospective candidates such as are now being followed in filling high U.S. Government posts.[37]

Such investigations of the candidates will not only help curtail the problem of improper payments and conflicts of interest but will also strengthen the board's image in the business community. As a result, the major objective is to review the corporate policy and internal monitoring procedures, as discussed in this chapter and the preceding chapter, with the external auditors.

In short, as Grover R. Heyler, partner of Latham and Watkins, concludes, ". . . directors need to go beyond what the auditors might be able to do."[38] In addition to the annual questionnaires regarding sensitive areas, Heyler suggests the following:

- A conflict of interest committee can be established.

- The board can require reports on trading in the company's stock.

- Controls on the disclosure of inside information and press releases can be initiated.

[35] Gerald F. Boltz, Grover R. Heyler, David L. James, and Francis M. Wheat, "Corporate Directors' Responsibilities," *Financial Executive* 45, No. 1 (January 1977), p. 21.

[36] Ibid.

[37] Herbert Robinson and J. Karl Fishbach, "Commercial Bribery—The Corporation as Victim," *Financial Executive* 47, No. 4 (April 1979), p. 16.

[38] Boltz, Heyler, James, and Wheat, "Corporate Directors' Responsibilities," p. 20.

- Provisions can be made for some independent review of relationships between the company and firms affiliated with insiders.[39]

CORPORATE PERQUISITES

Meaning of Corporate Perquisites

During the latter part of the 1970s, the SEC scrutinized the area of perquisites, or "perks," as evidenced by several SEC releases. For example, SEC Release No. 33-5758, issued in November 1976, stated:

> . . . it has been suggested that disclosure should be required of the numerous emerging forms of indirect compensation or "perquisites" now given to management personnel.

Furthermore, in April 1977 the SEC asked, in Securities Exchange Act Release No. 13482, "Should the Commission amend its proxy rules . . . to provide for more detailed or comprehensive disclosure of management remuneration?" Finally, in August 1977, the SEC issued Interpretative Release No. 33-5856, "Disclosure of Management Remuneration," whereby it pointed out that the securities acts require not only the disclosure of direct remuneration paid to directors and officers but also personal benefits ". . . sometimes referred to as 'perquisites.' " The Commission believed that certain personal benefits received by management from the corporation should be reported as remuneration:

> Among the benefits received by management which the Commission believes should be reported as remuneration are payments made by registrants for the following purposes: (1) home repairs and improvements; (2) housing and other living expenses (including domestic service) provided at principal and/or vacation residences of management personnel; (3) the personal use of company property such as automobiles, planes, yachts, apartments, hunting lodges, or company vacation houses; (4) personal travel expenses; (5) personal entertainment and related expenses; and (6) legal, accounting, and other professional fees for matters unrelated to the business of the registrant. Other personal benefits which may be forms of remuneration are the following: the ability of management to obtain benefits from third parties, because the corporation compensates, directly or indirectly, the bank or supplier for providing the loan or services to management; and the use of the corporate staff for personal purposes.

> Certain incidental personal benefits which are directly related to job performance may be omitted from aggregate reported remuneration provided they are authorized

---

[39] Ibid.

and properly accounted for by the company. Parking places, meals at company facilities, and office space and furnishings at company-maintained offices are a few examples of personal benefits directly related to job performance.

In addition, certain incidental benefits received by management which are ordinary and necessary to the conduct of company business may not be forms of remuneration. These job-related benefits are benefits which are available to management employees generally, which do not relieve the individual of expenditures normally considered to be of a personal nature and which are extended to management solely for the purposes of attracting and maintaining qualified personnel, facilitating their conduct of company business, or improving their efficiency in job performance. While itemized expense accounts may be considered job-related benefits whose value would be excluded from the aggregate remuneration reported, some may be forms of remuneration if they are excessive in amount or conferred too frequently. In any case, management is usually in the best position to determine whether a certain benefit should be viewed as a form of remuneration based on the facts and circumstances involved in each situation.

The value of all forms of remuneration should be included within the appropriate item(s) of disclosure. Nonmonetary forms of remuneration must be valued as accurately as possible. The appropriate valuation may be based upon appraisals, the value of the benefit to the recipient, the valuation assigned for tax purposes, or some other appropriate standard.

Although the preceding SEC release attempted to resolve the disclosure problem of perquisites, many accounting practitioners and corporate executives raised questions regarding the disclosure of certain items. In an attempt to resolve the issues, the SEC issued a second Interpretive Release, No. 33-5904, which contained questions and interpretative responses of the Commission's Division of Corporation Finance. In particular, the questions related to (a) the use of company property; (b) membership in clubs and professional association; (c) medical, insurance, and other reimbursement plans; (d) payments for living and related expenses; (e) use of corporate staff; (f) benefits from third parties; (g) company products; and (h) business expenses. Specifically, the Commission asserted[40]:

Corporations make a great variety of expenditures which relate to management, many of which result in benefits to executives. Whether these constitute remuneration usually depends upon the facts and circumstances involved in each situation. In general, expenditures which simply assist an executive in doing his job effectively or which reimburse him for expenses incurred in the performance of his functions are not remuneration, while expenditures made for his personal benefit or for purposes unrelated to the business of the company would constitute remuneration. In some

---

[40] In addition to the SEC releases cited, the reader should review Release No. 33-5950, "Proposed Amendments to Disclosure Forms Regulations" (July 1978) with the independent auditors.

instances, expenditures may serve both purposes, and if neither is predominant, allocation to the extent reasonably feasible may be called for.

In determining whether the value of specific benefits should be included in aggregate remuneration, registrants should keep in mind that full disclosure of the remuneration received by officers and directors is important to informed voting and investment decisions. In particular, remuneration information is necessary for an informed assessment of management and is significant in maintaining public confidence in the corporate system. Of course, accurate and sufficiently detailed books and records are prerequisites to the appropriate disclosure of remuneration information.[41]

Of particular importance to the Audit Committee is SEC Release No. 33-6003 issued in December 1978 to amend Regulation S-K. This release affects not only item 4 of the S-K but also proxy materials and other filing forms. For example, this release increases all remuneration paid to or accrued by the corporation's five highest paid officers or directors whose total remuneration exceeds $50,000 annually.[42]

As mentioned in Chapter 3, in October 1992 the SEC adopted amendments to the executive officer and director compensation disclosure requirements. With respect to perquisites, Release Nos. 33-6962, 34-31327, and 1C-19032 pertaining to Regulation S-K set forth the following:

Perquisites. Several commenters suggested that, to reflect inflation, the perquisites and other personal benefits reporting threshold should be raised from the lesser of $25,000 or 10% of reported salary and bonus, and that the requirement to itemize each perquisite or benefit in a footnote be eliminated. Given the effect of inflation since the last revision of Item 402 in 1983, which has been taken into account in the Commission's upward adjustment of the dollar benchmark for designating the named executives, the Commission similarly has increased the perks/personal benefits threshold in the final rule to call for disclosure only when the aggregate value of these items exceeds the lesser of either $50,000 or 10% of total salary and bonus disclosed in the Summary Compensation Table.

As proposed, the registrant would have been required to identify each perquisite included in the amount reported in a footnote to the Other Annual Compensation column. The Item has been revised to require footnote or textual narrative disclosure of the nature and value of any particular perquisite or benefit only for those perks values at more than 25% of the sum of all perquisites reported as Other Annual Compensation for that executive.[43]

---

[41] Although the SEC has stated that perquisites of less than $10,000 per individual may be excluded in the aggregate renumeration, such exclusion should be disclosed in the registrant's transmittal letter.

[42] As of October 21, 1992, this amount was increased to $100,000, as discussed in Chapter 3. For further reference, see Kathleen T. McGahran, "SEC Disclosure Regulation and Management Perquisites," *The Accounting Review* 63, No. 1 (January 1988), pp. 23–41; and Coopers & Lybrand, "Executive Perquisites Study Release: An Overview of the Findings," *Executive Briefing* (May 1992), pp. 1–3.

[43] Securities and Exchange Commission, "Executive Compensation Disclosure," *Federal Register* 57, No. 204 (October 21, 1992), p. 48131.

In view of these new disclosure requirements in the company's annual proxy statement, the audit committee should ascertain that the compensation committee and management are complying with the compensation and perquisite disclosure requirement. Such information should be reviewed by general counsel and the independent auditors.

Summary Guidelines

In monitoring corporate perquisites, the audit committee should give consideration to the following matters.

1. All perquisites should be formally approved by the board of directors as recommended by the compensation or audit committee. Such approval should be duly noted in the minutes of the board's meetings and the committee's meetings.
2. The perquisites should be clearly defined in view of the SEC releases regarding the nature of such payments or reimbursements. As discussed in this chapter, such SEC releases provide guidance to the auditors and management in connection with the entity's compliance with the securities laws. Such perks should not be excessive or unusual in light of the rulings.
3. The committee should request a report from the internal auditors concerning the status of the entity's perquisites.[44] In reviewing the audit report, the committee should obtain assurance in writing that the internal accounting and administrative controls (discussed in Chapter 8) are effective. Also, the committee should inquire about management's method of valuation of personal benefits and related tax consequences. Thus it is desirable to discuss the tax implications with the corporate tax specialist or outside tax advisor in order to coordinate the income tax and SEC reporting requirements.

CORPORATE CONTRIBUTIONS

In addition to the usual practice of monitoring certain business practices, such as compliance with the Foreign Corrupt Practices Act in regard to perquisites and

---

[44] It may be advisable to retain the outside auditors to review the travel and entertainment expenses for several of the senior executives each year. It is imperative that the company have an appropriate approval system of expense accounts. In its 1987 report, the National Commission on Fraudulent Financial Reporting recommended that "the committee should review in-house policies and procedures for regular review of officers' expenses and perquisites, including any use of corporate assets, inquire as to the results of the review, and, if appropriate, review a summarization of the expenses and perquisites of the period under review" (Washington, D.C.: National Commission on Fraudulent Financial Reporting, 1987), p. 180.

travel and entertainment, audit committees may also be requested by the board of directors to review other business practices, such as corporate contributions, to ensure compliance with corporate policy.

Nature of Corporate Contributions

According to R. A. Schwartz, corporate contributions or philanthropy may be defined as "a philanthropic transfer of wealth to be a one way flow of resources from a donor to a donee, a flow voluntarily generated by the donor though based on no expectation that a return flow, or economic quid pro quo, will reward the act."[45] Furthermore, as reported by C. Lowell Harriss:

> The interests and kinds of involvement differ enormously from firm to firm, as do the dollar outlays in corporate giving. Deductions on corporate tax returns of contributions have been rising, from $252 million in 1950 to $1,350 million in 1976. But such contributions represent less than 1 percent of profits and less than 5 percent of the community's total philanthropy.[46]

Corporate contributions also consist of nonmonetary giving which includes:

- Employees' personal time in nonprofit activities
- Company property, such as the firm's auditorium
- Loans at concessionary rates
- Job training for the disadvantaged and disabled.[47]

As Harriss observes in a Conference Board study by James F. Harris and Anne Klepper, "If a price tag were put on all such nonmonetary or indirect aid in 1974, the estimate of corporate contributions would double (to well over $2 billion)."[48]

Business Week observed that "total corporate giving has remained flat at $6.1 billion since 1990." Typically, "corporation donations are usually 1% to 2% of pretax domestic income." For example, more companies have developed a strategic plan and target charities more directly related to their operations.[49]

---

[45] R. A. Schwartz, *Corporate Philanthropic Contributions,* Pamphlet 72 (New York: New York University, 1968), p. 480.

[46] C. Lowell Harriss, "Corporate Giving: Rationale and Issues," *Two Essays on Corporate Philanthropy and Economic Education* (Los Angeles: International Institute for Economic Research, October 1978), p. 2.

[47] Ibid., p. 3.

[48] See James F. Harris and Anne Klepper, "Corporate Philanthropic Public Service Activities" (New York: The Conference Board, 1976).

[49] Lois Therrien, "Corporate Generosity Is Greatly Depreciated," *Business Week* (November 2, 1992), pp. 118–120.

Concerning the justification of corporate contributions, Schwartz notes that:

- Gifts that will enhance the public image of a corporation can advantageously shift the demand curve for corporation's product.

- The compatibility of corporate giving with monetary profit maximization is further suggested by the benefits a firm can derive from "farming out" research programs to educational institutions, while reaping both the gains of subsequent technological advances and the beneficial publicity with the gift.[50]

Although the Foreign Corrupt Practices Act covers illegal contributions abroad, it is also illegal to make political contribution through the use of corporate funds in U.S. federal elections. As noted by Roderick M. Hills, former chairman of the SEC: "The 'chance' of 'Watergate' gave us the opportunity for better government, and began a series of corporate investigations that already have improved our vision and raised corporate behavioral standards."[51] Thus it is necessary "to create an internal reporting system that will place these rather difficult payment questions squarely before the independent directors, outside auditors, and outside counsel."[52]

Summary Guidelines

Ferdinand K. Levy and Gloria M. Shatto summarize four evaluative principles regarding corporate contributions programs:

- If the gift is not legal or if it is questionable, don't make it.

- The contribution should represent the corporation and should not be a personal gift or whim of one executive.

- Contributions "in kind" or well specified are generally preferable to unrestricted gifts.

- Each contribution should stand alone and be capable of being justified on the basis of some type of cost-benefit analysis.[53]

---

[50] Schwartz, *Corporate Philanthropic Contributions,* p. 480. For further reference, see Harry L. Freeman, "Corporate Strategic Philanthropy," *Vital Speeches* 58, No. 8 (February 1, 1992), pp. 246–250; Betty S. Coffee and Jia Wang, "Board Composition and Corporate Philanthropy," *Journal of Business Ethics* 11, No. 10 (October 1992), pp. 771–778.

[51] Roderick M. Hills, "Views on How Corporations Should Behave," *Financial Executive* 44, No. 11 (November 1976), p. 34.

[52] Ibid., p. 32.

[53] Ferdinand K. Levy and Gloria M. Shatto, "A Common Sense Approach to Corporate Corporations," *Financial Executive* 46, No. 8 (September 1978), p. 37.

Moreover, "the entire corporate giving program . . . must be open to the public and should be capable of both an internal and external audit."[54] Thus it is evident that the audit committee should review the corporation's policy concerning its contributions and adhere to the monitoring practices discussed earlier in this chapter.

James A. Joseph notes that foundations need to:

- Clarify what is private and what is public;
- Reaffirm the moral authority of the traditional notion of public trust;
- Examine whether the enthusiasm with which foundations portray nonprofit voluntary activities as a distinctive sector may contribute to the tendency of critics and supporters to overlook the diversity within that sector;
- Demonstrate to the public that responsible governance and efficient management are all part of the public trust; and
- Reflect, retain, and reaffirm principles and practices that are fundamental to effectiveness in philanthropy.[55]

The following financial statement disclosure regarding this subject is presented to inform the reader of management's representations to the stockholders.

Schering-Plough—Through corporate giving, the Schering-Plough Foundation and employee voluntarism—contributed much in 1992 to the communities where it operates; to health care, educational and arts organizations; and to those in need. The Foundation made grants totalling $2.8 million in 1992, complementing corporate contributions of $1.9 million.[56]

In recent years, audit committees have increasingly assumed additional responsibilities such as those discussed in this chapter. Perhaps the most challenging are directing and monitoring special investigations related to management fraud and fraudulent financial reporting, as discussed in Chapters 4 and 11. Based on the ever-increasing duties and responsibilities of the audit committee, the role of monitoring business practices will continue to expand into additional areas in the future.

SOURCES AND SUGGESTED READINGS

The American Assembly, *The Ethics of Corporate Conduct*. Pamphlet 52 (New York: Columbia University, April 1977), pp. 1–11.

---

[54] Ibid., p. 38.
[55] James A. Joseph, "Reaffirming Our Public Accountability," *Foundation News* 33, No. 4 (July/August 1992), pp. 44–45.
[56] Schering-Plough, *1992 Annual Report,* p. 4

Beresford, Dennis R., and James D. Bond, "Foreign Corrupt Practices Act—Its Implications to Financial Management." *Financial Executive* 46, No. 8 (August 1978), pp. 26–32.

Boltz, Gerald E., Grover R. Heyler, David L. James, and Francis M. Wheat, "Corporate Directors' Responsibilities." *Financial Executive* 45, No. 1 (January 1977), pp. 12–21.

The Business Roundtable, *Corporate Governance and American Competitiveness* (New York: The Business Roundtable, 1990).

Charles E. Simon and Company, "An Examination of Questionable Payments and Practices" (Washington, D.C.: 1978).

Coffee, Betty S., and Jia Wang, "Board Composition and Corporate Philanthropy." *Journal of Business Ethics* 11, No. 10 (October 1992), pp. 771–778.

Coopers & Lybrand, "Executive Perquisites Study Release: An Overview of the Findings." *Executive Briefing* (May 1992).

Department of Justice, "Foreign Corrupt Practices Act Option Procedure." *Code of Federal Regulations,* Sec. 28, Part 77, 1978.

Foreign Corrupt Practices Act, Title I of Public Law No. 95-213, December 19, 1977.

Freeman, Harry L., "Corporate Strategic Philanthropy." *Vital Speeches* 58, No. 8 (February 1, 1992), pp. 246–250.

Gerson, James S., J. Robert Mooney, Donald F. Moran, and Robert K. Waters, "Oversight of the Financial Reporting Process—Part I." *CPA Journal* 59, No. 7 (July 1989), pp. 22–28.

Greene, James, "Assuring Ethical Conduct Abroad." *The Conference Board Information Bulletin No. 2* (November 1976), pp. 1–18.

Gustavson, Sandra G., and Jere W. Morehead. "Complying with the Amended Foreign Corrupt Practices Act." *Risk Management* 37, No. 4 (April 1990), pp. 76–82.

Hanson, Walter E., "A Blueprint for Ethical Conduct." Statement in "Quotes," *Journal of Accountancy* 145, No. 6 (June 1978), pp. 80–84.

Harris, James F., and Anne Klepper, "Corporate Philanthropic Public Service Activities" (New York: The Conference Board, 1976).

Harriss, C. Lowell, "Corporate Giving: Rationale and Issues." *Two Essays on Corporate Philanthropy and Economic Education* (Los Angeles, Calif.: International Institute for Economic Research, October 1978), pp. 1–13.

Hills, Roderick M., "Views on How Corporations Should Behave." *Financial Executive* 44, No. 11 (November 1976), pp. 32–34.

Joseph, James A., "Reaffirming Our Public Accountability." *Foundation News* 33, No. 4 (July/August 1992), pp. 44–45.

Levy, Ferdinand K., and Gloria M. Shatto, "A Common Sense Approach to Corporate Contributions." *Financial Executive* 46, No. 9 (September 1978), pp. 36–40.

Marsh, Hugh L., "The Foreign Corrupt Practices Act: A Corporate Plan for Compliance." *Internal Auditor* 36, No. 2 (April 1979), pp. 72–76.

McGrahan, Kathleen T., "SEC Disclosure Regulation and Management Perquisites." *Accounting Review* 63, No. 1 (January 1988), pp. 23–41.

National Commission on Fraudulent Financial Reporting, *Report of the National Commission on Fraudulent Financial Reporting* (Washington, D.C.: National Commission on Fraudulent Financial Reporting, 1987).

The Omnibus Trade and Competitiveness Act, Title V of Public Law No. 100-418. August 23, 1988.

Organization of Economic Cooperation and Development, *Convention on Combating Bribery of Foreign Public Officials in International Business Transactions* (Paris: OECD, 1997).

Piturro, Marlene C., "Just Say . . . Maybe," *World Trade* 5, No. 5 (June 1992), pp. 86–91.

Roberts, Judith L., "Revision of the Foreign Corrupt Practices Act by the 1988 Omnibus Trade Bill: Will It Reduce the Compliance Burdens and Anticompetitive Impact?" *Brigham Young University Law Review,* No. 2 (1989), pp. 491–506.

Robinson, Herbert, and J. Karl Fishbach, "Commercial Bribery—The Corporation as Victim." *Financial Executive* 47, No. 4 (April 1979), pp. 16–19 and 50–51.

Schering-Plough, *1992 Annual Report.*

Schwartz, R. A. *Corporate Philanthropic Contributions.* Pamphlet 72 (New York: New York University, June 1968), pp. 479–497.

Securities and Exchange Commission, "Report of the Securities and Exchange Commission on Questionable and Illegal Corporate Payments and Practices" (Washington, D.C.: May 12, 1976).

Securities and Exchange Commission, "Executive Compensation Disclosure." *Federal Register* 57, No. 204 (October 21, 1992), pp. 48126–48159.

Statement on Auditing Standards, No. 17. "Illegal Acts by Clients" (New York: American Institute of Certified Public Accountants, 1977).

Statement on Auditing Standards, No. 54, "Illegal Acts by Clients" (New York: American Institute of Certified Public Accountants, 1988).

Taylor, John C. III, "Preventing Improper Payments Through Internal Controls." *The Conference Board Record* 13, No. 8 (August 1976), pp. 17–19.

Therrien, Lois, "Corporate Generosity Is Greatly Depreciated." *Business Week* (November 2, 1992), pp. 118–120.

Triton Energy Corporation, *1992 Annual Report.*

The Wall Street Journal, "Triton Energy Corp.: Justice Department Probing for Possible Law Violations" (May 20, 1993), sec. A, p. 7, col. 3.

Zipser, Andy, "Crude Grab? How a Tiny Producer Lost Its Indonesian Stake." *Barron's* 72, No. 21 (May 25, 1992), pp. 12–15.

Part Four

The Reporting Function and the Audit Committee

Chapter 13

Independent Auditors' Reports

The independent auditors' report is the expression of their professional opinion on the financial statements. As discussed in Chapter 1, although the financial statements are management's responsibility, the independent auditors have a responsibility to attest to the fairness of management's representations in the statements through their audit report.

The purpose of this chapter is to familiarize the audit directors with the different types of audit opinions as well as other audit reports regarding matters such as interim financial information and special reports.[1] An understanding of the audit opinions and other audit reports provides an important opportunity for each audit director to obtain additional insight into the nature and importance of the independent auditors' reporting responsibility.

THE AUDITORS' REPORTS ON AUDITED FINANCIAL STATEMENTS

As discussed in Chapters 1 and 5, the independent auditors or accountants report their objective opinion on the fairness of the representations in the financial statements. Such an expression of their opinion is required in accordance with generally accepted auditing standards as promulgated by the Auditing Standards Board (previously Auditing Standards Executive Committee of the AICPA). Moreover, it was indicated that corporate management has full responsibility for the fairness of the representations in the financial statements. Such a distinction concerning the responsibility for the financial statements is particularly important because if the independent auditors do not concur with the fairness of management's representations, then they are required to inform the users of the financial statements of their exceptions. In particular, the fourth auditing standard of reporting is restated for additional emphasis.

---

[1]Attestation engagements with respect to other information, such as reports on internal control and compliance with specified laws and regulations, were discussed in Chapter 5.

The Standard Auditors' Report (Unqualified Opinion)

> The report shall either contain an expression of opinion regarding the financial statements, taken as a whole,[2] or an assertion to the effect that an opinion cannot be expressed. When an overall opinion cannot be expressed, the reasons therefor should be stated. In all cases where an auditor's name is associated with financial statements, the report should contain a clear-cut indication of the character of the auditor's work, if any, and the degree of responsibility the auditor is taking.[3]

A particular report, the Standard Auditors' Report (Unqualified Opinion), is used by the auditors when they have no exceptions regarding management's representations in the financial statements. In practice, such a report is often described as a "clean opinion." An example of this report was illustrated and discussed in Chapter 1. Explicit in the auditors' unqualified report is that their examination has been performed within the general auditing guidelines or standards as set forth by the AICPA. Moreover, their unqualified opinion informs the users of the financial statements that such statements have been prepared by management in conformity with generally accepted accounting principles applied on a consistent basis. Such an unqualified opinion is based not only on their examination of the financial statements but also on tests of the accounting records that underlie such statements.

While the auditors' report is not explicit with respect to the system of internal control, it implies that the entity's internal control structure is adequate. However, since the inception of the Foreign Corrupt Practices Act, this audit report has been reevaluated in terms of its content because it is argued that the auditors should make their report explicit with respect to management's adherence to the accounting provision in the act. For example, in April 1979, the SEC in its Release No. 34-15772 announced its proposed rules for requiring a statement of management on internal accounting control in the annual reports of all publicly held corporations. Such a statement should disclose management's compliance with the internal accounting control provision of the Foreign Corrupt Practices Act as well as uncorrected material weaknesses in the controls as reported by the independent auditors. Furthermore, the Commission's proposal requires the independent auditors to modify their audit report to disclose management's inaction in disclosing or correcting such material weaknesses. While this proposal is applicable to fiscal years that end between December 16, 1979, and December 15, 1980, the Commission also proposes that the auditors express an opinion on management's re-

---

[2]According to the Auditing Standards Board, the phrase "taken as a whole" with respect to the financial statements applies to the statements of both the current period and one or more prior periods presented on a comparative basis. See *Statement on Auditing Standards, No. 58* "Reports on Audited Financial Statements" (New York: American Institute of Certified Public Accountants, 1988), par. 04.
[3]The reader may wish to review Chapter 5 at this point.

port on the system of internal accounting control for fiscal years that end after December 15, 1980.[4] Thus it is evident that the users of the financial statements rely on the auditors' report to determine whether the statements are fairly presented. As a result, the auditors' report must be clear and concise with respect to the findings and results of the audit examination. To achieve this objective, the Auditing Standards Board has developed audit reports or opinions, which are summarized as follows:

- *Unqualified opinion.* An unqualified opinion states that the financial statements present fairly, in all material respects, the financial position, results of operations, and cash flows of the entity in conformity with generally accepted accounting principles. This is the opinion expressed in the standard report.

- *Explanatory language added to the auditor's standard report.* Certain circumstances, while not affecting the auditor's unqualified opinion on the financial statements, may require that the auditor add an explanatory paragraph (or other explanatory language) to his report.

- *Qualified opinion.* A qualified opinion states that, except for the effects of the matter(s) to which the qualification relates, the financial statements present fairly, in all material respects, the financial position, results of operations, and cash flows of the entity in conformity with generally accepted accounting principles.

- *Adverse opinion.* An adverse opinion states that the financial statements do not present fairly the financial position, results of operations, or cash flows of the entity in conformity with generally accepted accounting principles.

- *Disclaimer of opinion.* A disclaimer of opinion states that the auditor does not express an opinion on the financial statements.[5]

As discussed in Chapter 8, the Auditing Standards Board has issued *Statement on Standards for Attestation Engagements, No. 2,* "Reporting on the Entity's Internal Control Structure over Financial Reporting." Given the demand from the investing public for management's assertions about the effectiveness of the entity's internal control, it is reasonable to expect that the audit committee may give consideration to this type of attestation engagement. Thus it is important for the audit committee to review closely and discuss the recommendations in the annual management letter from the independent auditors.

---

[4]In May 1980 the SEC decided to withdraw this proposed rule; however, it will continue to monitor private-sector initiatives and reconsider the need for new rules over the next three years.

[5]*Statement on Auditing Standards, No. 58,* "Reports on Audited Financial Statements" (New York: American Institute of Certified Public Accountants, 1988), par. 10. For additional reference, see Robert S. Roussey, Ernest L. Ten Eyck, and Mimi Blanco-Best, "Three New SASs: Closing the Communication Gap," *Journal of Accountancy* 166, No. 6 (December 1988), pp. 44–52.

Explanatory Language with the Auditor's Standard Report

The Auditing Standards Board requires independent auditors to modify their standard audit report under certain circumstances. Such a modification may require the addition of an explanatory paragraph or other explanatory language. More specifically, the circumstances include instances when:

    a. The auditor's opinion is based in part on the report of another auditor.

    b. To prevent the financial statements from being misleading because of unusual circumstances, the financial statements contain a departure from an accounting principle promulgated by a body designated by the AICPA Council to establish such principles.*

    c. There is substantial doubt about the entity's ability to continue as a going concern.

    d. There has been a material change between periods in accounting principles or in the method of their application.

    e. Certain circumstances relating to reports on comparative financial statements exist.

    f. Selected quarterly financial data required by SEC Regulation S-K has been omitted or has not been reviewed.

    g. Supplementary information required by the Financial Accounting Standards Board (FASB) or the Governmental Accounting Standards Board (GASB) has been omitted, the presentation of such information departs materially from FASB or GASB guidelines, the auditor is unable to complete prescribed procedures with respect to such information, or the auditor is unable to remove substantial doubts about whether the supplementary information conforms to FASB or GASB guidelines.

    h. Other information in a document containing audited financial statements is materially inconsistent with information appearing in the financial statements.[6]

Certain circumstances may arise, for example, when the auditors must rely on the report of another auditor or the auditors may not be independent. With respect to the former, the auditors' reporting obligations are based on their decisions whether to make reference to the other auditors' report. Therefore, if the auditors decide "to make reference to the report of another auditor as a basis, in part," for

---

*For further reference, see "Departures from the New Standard Auditor's Report on Financial Statements of Business Enterprises: A Survey of the Application of *Statement on Auditing Standards, No. 58*," *Financial Report Survey* (New York: American Institute of Certified Public Accountants, 1990).

[6]American Institute of Certified Public Accountants, *Professional Standards, U.S. Auditing Standards/Attestation Standards,* Vol. 1 (New York: American Institute of Certified Public Accountants, 1998), AU Sec. 508.11.

their opinion, their report should disclose this fact.[7] When auditors decide to make no reference to the report of another auditor because of their acceptance of the auditor's independence and reputation, the standard short-form unqualified report is acceptable.

However, when the auditors are not independent, for example, there is a conflict of interest between the public accounting firm and the client, they should "disclaim an opinion with respect to the financial statements and should state specifically" that they are not independent.[8] Such an action is necessary on the part of the auditors, because of the auditing standard of independence discussed in Chapter 5.

Furthermore, in addition to their expression of an unqualified opinion, the auditors may wish to emphasize certain matters regarding the financial statements. For example, they may wish to indicate that the corporation has had "significant transactions with related parties," such as transactions between the entity and the officers or directors.[9] In addition, they may wish to disclose "an unusually important subsequent event" that occurred after the date of the financial statements. Obviously, such matters are disclosed based on the professional judgment of the auditors. However, while the auditors may wish to emphasize certain matters, they can express an unqualified opinion.

To familiarize the audit committee with various examples of the wording in the auditors' modified unqualified report, a model report is presented in Exhibit 13.1.

OTHER AUDITING OPINIONS

The Qualified Opinion

According to the Auditing Standards Board, the auditors may express a qualified opinion that " 'except for' the effects of the matter to which the qualification relates, the financial statements" are presented fairly.[10] Concerning the "exceptions" noted by the auditors, the Board delineated the following circumstances:

> There is a lack of sufficient competent evidential matter or there are restrictions on the scope of the audit that have led the auditor to conclude that he cannot express an unqualified opinion and he has concluded not to disclaim an opinion.

---

[7]American Institute of Certified Public Accountants, *Professional Standards, U.S. Auditing Standards/Attestation Standards,* Vol. 1 (New York: American Institute of Certified Public Accountants, 1998), AU Sec. 508.12.
[8]Ibid., AU Sec. 504.09.
[9]Ibid., AU Sec. 508.19.
[10]Ibid., AU Sec. 508.20.

Exhibit 13.1   Independent Auditor's Report: Example 1

Opinion Based in Part on Report of Another Auditor

We have audited the consolidated balance sheets of ABC Company as of December 31, 19X2 and 19X1, and the related consolidated statements of income, retained earnings, and cash flows for the years then ended. These financial statements are the responsibility of the Company's management. Our responsibility is to express an opinion on these financial statements based on our audits. We did not audit the financial statements of B Company, a wholly-owned subsidiary, which statements reflect total assets of \$_____ and \$_____ as of December 31, 19X2 and 19X1, respectively, and total revenues of \$_____ and \$_____ for the years then ended. Those statements were audited by other auditors whose report has been furnished to us, and our opinion, insofar as it relates to the amounts included for B Company, is based solely on the report of the other auditors.

We conducted our audits in accordance with generally accepted auditing standards. Those standards require that we plan and perform the audit to obtain reasonable assurance about whether the financial statements are free of material misstatement. An audit includes examining, on a test basis, evidence supporting the amounts and disclosures in the financial statements. An audit also includes assessing the accounting principles used and significant estimates made by management, as well as evaluating the overall financial statement presentation. We believe that our audits and the report of other auditors provide a reasonable basis for our opinion.

In our opinion, based on our audits and the report of other auditors, the consolidated financial statements referred to above present fairly, in all material respects, the financial position of ABC Company as of December 31, 19X2 and 19X1, and the results of its operations and its cash flows for the years then ended in conformity with generally accepted accounting principles.[a]

Lack of Consistency

As discussed in Note X to the financial statements, the Company changed its method of computing depreciation in 19X2.[b]

An Entity's Ability to Continue as a Going Concern

The accompanying financial statements have been prepared assuming that the Company will continue as a going concern. As discussed in Note X to the financial statements, the Company has suffered recurring losses from operations and has a net capital deficiency that raises substantial doubt about its ability to continue as a going concern. Management's plans in regard to these matters are also described in Note X. The financial statements do not include any adjustments that might result from the outcome of this uncertainty.[c]

---

[a]*Statement on Auditing Standards, No. 58,* par. 13.

[b]*Professional Standards, U.S. Auditing Standards/Attestation Standards,* Vol. 1, AU Sec. 508.17.

[c]*Statement on Auditing Standards, No. 59,* "The Auditor's Consideration of an Entity's Ability to Continue as a Going Concern" (New York: American Institute of Certified Public Accountants, 1988), par. 13. For further discussion, see John E. Ellingsen, Kurt Pany, and Peg Fagan, "SAS No. 59: How to Evaluate Going Concern," *Journal of Accountancy* 168, No. 1 (January 1989), 24–31.

The auditor believes, on the basis of his audit, that the financial statements contain a departure from generally accepted accounting principles, the effect of which is material, and he has concluded not to express an adverse opinion.[11]

With respect to the aforementioned circumstances, an example of the auditors' report is illustrated in Exhibit 13.2.

The Adverse Opinion

The adverse opinion is expressed by the auditors when, in their judgment, "the financial statements taken as a whole are not presented fairly in conformity with generally accepted accounting principles."[12] The adverse opinion is appropriate where the auditors' exceptions are so material that the statements as a whole are not fairly presented. Thus the distinction between the adverse opinion and qualified opinion is predicated on the concept of materiality discussed in Chapter 5. When the auditors express an adverse opinion, their audit report should disclose "all the substantive reasons" for the opinion as well as "the principal effects of the subject matter" on the financial statements, "if reasonably determinable."[13] "If the effects are not reasonably determinable, the report should so state."[14] If management applies accounting principles that are not in conformity with acceptable principles (discussed in Chapter 5), then the auditors are required to render an adverse opinion. For example, if management refuses to disclose material information in the notes to the statements, such inaction constitutes a violation of the disclosure principle. Thus an adverse opinion is appropriate. Such a violation of the disclosure principle would materially distort the financial statements taken as a whole. However, the expression of an adverse opinion is infrequent in practice because management opts for an unqualified opinion and as a result makes the necessary adjustments.

An example of an adverse opinion is shown in Exhibit 13.3.

Disclaimer of Opinion

When the auditors lack sufficient information to form an opinion regarding the financial statements, their report should indicate that they are unable to express an opinion. For example, it is appropriate to express a disclaimer of opinion when the auditors have not conducted "an examination sufficient in scope" to warrant the expression of an opinion on the statements taken as a whole.[15] In contrast to

---

[11] Ibid., AU Sec. 20.
[12] Ibid., AU Sec. 58.
[13] Ibid., AU Sec. 59.
[14] Ibid., AU Sec. 59.
[15] Ibid., AU Sec. 62.

Exhibit 13.2   Independent Auditor's Report: Example 2

Scope Limitations

[*Same first paragraph as the standard report*]
Except as discussed in the following paragraph, we conducted our audits in accordance with generally accepted auditing standards. Those standards require that we plan and perform the audit to obtain reasonable assurance about whether the financial statements are free of material misstatement. An audit includes examining, on a test basis, evidence supporting the amounts and disclosures in the financial statements. An audit also includes assessing the accounting principles used and significant estimates made by management, as well as evaluating the overall financial statement presentation. We believe that our audits provide a reasonable basis for our opinion.

We were unable to obtain audited financial statements supporting the Company's investment in a foreign affiliate stated at $_____ and $_____ at December 31, 19X2 and 19X1, respectively, or its equity in earnings of that affiliate of $_____ and $_____, which is included in net income for the years then ended as described in Note X to the financial statements; nor were we able to satisfy ourselves as to the carrying value of the investment in the foreign affiliate or the equity in its earnings by other auditing procedures. In our opinion, except for the effects of such adjustments, if any, as might have been determined to be necessary had we been able to examine evidence regarding the foreign affiliate investment and earnings, the financial statements referred to in the first paragraph above present fairly, in all material respects, the financial position of X Company as of December 31, 19X2 and 19X1, and the results of its operations and its cash flows for the years then ended in conformity with generally accepted accounting principles.[a]

Departure from a Generally Accepted Accounting Principle

[*Same first and second paragraphs as the standard report*]
The Company has excluded, from property and debt in the accompanying balance sheets, certain lease obligations that, in our opinion, should be capitalized in order to conform with generally accepted accounting principles. If these lease obligations were capitalized, property would be increased by $_____ and $_____, long-term debt by $_____ and $_____, and retained earnings by $_____ and $_____ as of December 31, 19X2 and 19X1, respectively. Additionally, net income would be increased (decreased) by $_____ and $_____ and earnings per share would be increased (decreased) by $_____ and $_____, respectively, for the years then ended.

In our opinion, except for the effects of not capitalizing certain lease obligations as discussed in the preceding paragraph, the financial statements referred to above present fairly, in all material respects, the financial position of X Company as of December 31, 19X2 and 19X1, and the results of its operations and its cash flows for the years then ended in conformity with generally accepted accounting principles.[b]

Inadequate Disclosure

[*Same first and second paragraphs as the standard report*]
The Company's financial statements do not disclose [*describe the nature of the omitted*

Exhibit 13.2 (*Continued*)

disclosures]. In our opinion, disclosure of this information is required by generally accepted accounting principles.

In our opinion, except for the omission of the information discussed in the preceding paragraph, . . .*c*

---

*a*Professional Standards, U.S. Auditing Standards/Attestation Standards, Vol. 1, AU Sec. 26 (New York: American Institute of Certified Public Accountants, 1998).
*b*Ibid., AU Sec. 39.
*c*Ibid., AU Sec. 42. For further reference, see Jack C. Robertson, "Analysts' Reactions to Auditors' Messages in Qualified Reports," *Accounting Horizons* 2, No. 2 (June 1988), pp. 82–89.

Exhibit 13.3 Independent Auditor's Report: Example 3

Adverse Opinion

[*Same first and second paragraphs as the standard report*]
As discussed in Note X to the financial statements, the Company carries its property, plant, and equipment accounts at appraisal values, and provides depreciation on the basis of such values. Further, the Company does not provide for income taxes with respect to differences between financial income and taxable income arising because of the use, for income tax purposes, of the installment method of reporting gross profit from certain types of sales. Generally accepted accounting principles require that property, plant, and equipment be stated at an amount not in excess of cost, reduced by depreciation based on such amount, and that deferred income taxes be provided.

Because of the departures from generally accepted accounting principles identified above, as of December 31, 19X2 and 19X1, inventories have been increased $_____ and $_____ by inclusion in manufacturing overhead of depreciation in excess of that based on cost; property, plant, and equipment, less accumulated depreciation, is carried at $_____ and $_____ in excess of an amount based on the cost to the Company; and deferred income taxes of $_____ and $_____ have not been recorded; resulting in an increase of $_____ and $_____ in retained earnings and in appraisal surplus of $_____ and $_____, respectively. For the years ended December 31, 19X2 and 19X1, cost of goods sold has been increased $_____ and $_____, respectively, because of the effects of the depreciation accounting referred to above and deferred income taxes of $_____ and $_____ have not been provided, resulting in an increase in net income of $_____ and $_____, respectively.

In our opinion, because of the effects of the matters discussed in the preceding paragraphs, the financial statements referred to above do not present fairly, in conformity with generally accepted accounting principles, the financial position of X Company as of December 31, 19X2 and 19X1, or the results of its operations or its cash flows for the years then ended.

Source: Professional Standards, U.S. Auditing Standards/Attestation Standards, Vol. 1 (New York: American Institute of Certified Public Accountants, 1998), AU Sec. 60.

the qualified opinion, the disclaimer of opinion means that the auditors do not have sufficient knowledge about the fairness of management's representations in the financial statements. Furthermore, the auditors should indicate the reason for the disclaimer of opinion in their report. Thus, although the circumstances regarding the issuance of the qualified opinion may be the same for a disclaimer of opinion, the distinction between the former and the latter is based on the degree of materiality with respect to each circumstance. Such a distinction is contingent upon the auditors' professional judgment. Accordingly, the audit committee should inquire about the public accounting firm's criteria for judging materiality as it relates to the financial statements.

An example of a disclaimer of opinion is shown in Exhibit 13.4.

OTHER REPORTS OF THE AUDITORS

Report on Interim Financial Statements

In addition to the auditors' opinion on the annual financial statements, they may be requested to review the interim or quarterly financial information submitted to the stockholders. For example, the SEC (Accounting Series Release No. 177) requires that certain registrants have the independent auditors review certain data contained in the Form 10-Q in an unaudited note to the financial statements. This requirement is necessary for those large corporations whose shares are traded publicly. Concerning their position on the auditors' review of interim financial information:

> The Commission believes that all registrants would find it useful and prudent to have independent public accountants review quarterly financial data on a timely basis during the year prior to the filing of Form 10-Q and it encourages registrants to have such a review made. While such a review does not represent an audit and cannot be relied upon to detect all errors and omissions that might be discovered in a full audit of quarterly data, it will bring the reporting, accounting and analytical expertise of independent professional accountants to bear on financial reports included in Form 10-Q and therefore should increase the quality and the reliability of the data therein in a cost-effective way.[16]

With respect to the auditors' objective of a review of interim financial statements, *Statement on Auditing Standards, No. 71* issued by the Auditing Standards Board in May 1992 states:

---

[16]The SEC does not require reports on interim financial information from the independent auditors; however, if the registrant requests a report on reviewed interim financial information presented in a quarterly report, then the auditors must comply with *Statement on Auditing Standards, No. 71*.

Exhibit 13.4   Independent Auditor's Report: Example 4

Disclaimer of Opinion

We were engaged to audit the accompanying balance sheets of X Company as of December 31, 19X2 and 19X1, and the related statements of income, retained earnings, and cash flows for the years then ended. These financial statements are the responsibility of the Company's management.

[Second paragraph of standard report should be omitted]
The Company did not make a count of its physical inventory in 19X2 or 19X1, stated in the accompanying financial statements at $_____ as of December 31, 19X2, and at $_____ as of December 31, 19X1. Further, evidence supporting the cost of property and equipment acquired prior to December 31, 19X1, is no longer available. The Company's records do not permit the application of other auditing procedures to inventories or property and equipment.

   Since the Company did not take physical inventories and we were not able to apply other auditing procedures to satisfy ourselves as to inventory quantities and the cost of property and equipment, the scope of our work was not sufficient to enable us to express, and we do not express, an opinion on these financial statements.

Source: Professional Standards, U.S. Auditing Standards and Attestation Standards, Vol. 1 (New York: American Institute of Certified Public Accountants, 1998), AU Sec. 63.

The objective of a review of interim financial information is to provide the accountant, based on applying his or her knowledge of financial reporting practices to significant accounting matters of which he or she becomes aware through inquiries and analytical procedures, with a basis for reporting whether material modifications should be made for such information to conform with generally accepted accounting principles. The objective of a review of interim financial information differs significantly from the objective of an audit of financial statements in accordance with generally accepted auditing standards. The objective of an audit is to provide a reasonable basis for expressing an opinion regarding the financial statements taken as a whole. A review of interim financial information does not provide a basis for the expression of such an opinion, because the review does not contemplate (*a*) tests of accounting records through inspection, observation, or confirmation, (*b*) obtaining corroborating evidential matter in response to inquiries, or (*c*) the application of certain other procedures ordinarily performed during an audit. A review may bring to the accountant's attention significant matters affecting the interim financial information, but it does not provide assurance that the accountant will become aware of all significant matters that would be disclosed in an audit.[17]

   To achieve their review objective, auditors apply procedures that "consist primarily of inquiries and analytical review procedures concerning significant

---

[17]*Statement on Auditing Standards, No. 71,* "Interim Financial Information" (New York: American Institute of Certified Public Accountants, 1992), par. 9.

accounting matters relating to the financial information to be reported."[18] For example, they should apply the following procedures:

- Inquiry concerning: (1) the internal control structure, including the control environment, the accounting system, and, to the extent appropriate, control procedures, for both annual and interim financial information; and (2) any significant changes in the internal control structure since the most recent financial statement audit or review of interim financial information to ascertain the potential effect of (1) and (2) on the preparation of interim financial information.

- Application of analytical procedures to interim financial information to identify and provide a basis for inquiry about relationships and individual items that appear to be unusual. (Emphasis added—financial ratios, comparative analysis, etc.)

- Reading the minutes of meetings of stockholders, the board of directors, and committees of the board of directors to identify actions that may affect the interim financial information.

- Reading the interim financial information to consider whether, on the basis of information coming to the accountant's attention, the information to be reported conforms with generally accepted accounting principles.

- Obtaining reports from other accountants, if any, who have been engaged to make a review of the interim financial information of significant components of the reporting entity, its subsidiaries, or its other investees.

- Inquiry of officers and other executives having responsibility for financial and accounting matters concerning (1) whether the interim financial information has been prepared in conformity with generally accepted accounting principles consistently applied, (2) changes in the entity's accounting practices, (3) changes in the entity's business activities, (4) matters about which questions have arisen in the course of applying the foregoing procedures, and (5) events subsequent to the date of the interim financial information that would have a material effect on the presentation of such information.

- Obtaining written representations from management concerning its responsibility for the financial information, completeness of minutes, subsequent events, and other matters about which the accountant believes written representations are appropriate in the circumstances.[19]

The audit committee's review of the reports of the independent auditors' limited reviews of the interim financial statements is an important task, because it

---

[18] Ibid., par. 6.
[19] Ibid., par. 13.

can alert the board of directors to possible changes in accounting policies in a timely manner and thus minimize unanticipated financial reporting implications at the end of the year.[20]

With respect to communication with audit committees, the Auditing Standards Board requires that when independent auditors "become aware of matters that cause them to believe that interim financial information filed or to be filed with a specified regulatory agency is probably materially misstated as a result of a departure from generally accepted accounting principles,"[21] they should apply the following procedures:

- If, in the accountant's judgment, management does not respond appropriately to the accountant's communication within a reasonable period of time, the accountant should inform the audit committee, or others with equivalent authority and responsibility (hereafter referred to as the audit committee), of the matter as soon as practicable. This communication may be oral or written. If information is communicated orally, the accountant should document the communication in appropriate memoranda or notations in the working papers.[22]

- If, in the accountant's judgment, the audit committee does not respond appropriately to the accountant's communication within a reasonable period of time, the accountant should evaluate (*a*) whether to resign from the engagement related to the interim financial information, and (*b*) whether to remain as the entity's auditor or stand for reelection to audit the entity's financial statements. The accountant may wish to consult with his or her attorney when making these evaluations.[23]

The two technical accounting pronouncements related to interim financial reports are Accounting Principles Board Opinion No. 28 and Financial Accounting Standards Board Statement No. 3. The audit directors may wish to review these pronouncements prior to their meetings with the independent auditors. In particular, they should inquire about the methods of recognizing revenues and expenses and how the annual operating costs are allocated to the interim periods. The major

---

[20] In its 1987 report, the National Commission on Fraudulent Financial Reporting recommended that "the audit committee's oversight responsibilities undertaken on behalf of the board of directors extend to the quarterly reporting process. The audit committee should review the controls that management has established to protect the integrity of the quarterly reporting process. This review should be ongoing" (p. 48). As noted earlier, *Statement on Auditing Standards No. 71* provides the agenda items for the audit committee's review of quarterly reporting. Such a review will help minimize opportunities for managing earnings through improper revenue recognition or deferred expense recognition.

[21] *Statement on Auditing Standards No 71,* par. 20.

[22] Ibid., par. 21.

[23] Ibid., par. 22. More recently, the Blue Ribbon Committee on Improving the Effectiveness of Corporate Audit Committees reaffirmed the National Commission on Fraudulent Financial Reporting position on quarterly reporting (see Chapter 14, Exhibit 14.3).

objective is to identify and comprehend management's methods of reporting interim financial information because the stockholders use the information to predict earnings for the year.

An example of a report on reviewed interim financial information presented in a quarterly report is illustrated in Exhibit 13.5.

Special Reports

According to the Auditing Standards Board, special reports apply to:

- Financial statements that are prepared in conformity with a comprehensive basis of accounting other than generally accepted accounting principles (e.g., cash-basis statements)

- Specified elements, accounts, or items of a financial statement (e.g., working capital position)

- Compliance with aspects of contractual agreements or regulatory requirements related to audited financial statements (e.g., restrictions relative to a bond indenture).

- Financial presentations to comply with contractual agreements or regulatory provisions (e.g., restrictions relative to dividend payments, such as maintaining specified financial ratios)

- Financial information presented in prescribed forms or schedules that require a prescribed form of auditor's report (e.g., filings with a regulatory agency)[24]

Of particular importance to the audit committee are the second and fourth items in the preceding list, because the committee may request the auditors to report on royalties, sales for the purpose of computing a rental fee, employee profit participation, or the adequacy of the provision for taxes. Moreover, the auditors may issue a special report in connection with a proposed acquisition, the claims of creditors, or management's compliance with contractual agreements. While such reports may be appropriate under the preceding circumstances, it is suggested that the committee give consideration to the cost/benefit advantages from such re-

---

[24]*Statement on Auditing Standards, No. 62,* "Special Reports" (New York: American Institute of Certified Public Accountants, 1989), par. 1. With respect to agreed-upon procedures engagements, see *Statement on Auditing Standards, No. 75,* "Engagements to Apply Agreed-Upon Procedures to Specified Elements, Accounts, or Items of a Financial Statement" (New York: American Institute of Certified Public Accountants, 1995). With respect to other agreed-upon procedures engagements, see *Statement on Standards for Attestation Engagements No. 4,* "Agreed-Upon Procedures Engagements" (New York: American Institute of Certified Public Accountants, 1995); also see Thomas A. Ratcliff, "Agreed-Upon Procedures: Applying SAS No. 75 and SSAE No. 4," *CPA Journal* 66, No. 1 (January 1996), pp. 26–22.

Exhibit 13.5 Independent Accountant's Report

Reviewed Interim Financial Information

We have reviewed the accompanying [*describe the statements or information reviewed*] of ABC Company and consolidated subsidiaries as of September 30, 19X1, and for the three-month and nine-month periods then ended. These financial statements (information) are (is) the responsibility of the company's management.

We conducted our review in accordance with standards established by the American Institute of Certified Public Accountants. A review of interim financial information consists principally of applying analytical procedures to financial data and making inquiries of persons responsible for financial and accounting matters. It is substantially less in scope than an audit conducted in accordance with generally accepted auditing standards, the objective of which is the expression of an opinion regarding the financial statements taken as a whole. Accordingly, we do not express such an opinion.

Based on our review, we are not aware of any material modifications that should be made to the accompanying financial statements (information) for them (it) to be in conformity with generally accepted accounting principles.

Source: Statement on Auditing Standards, No. 71, (New York: American Institute of Certified Public Accountants, 1992), par. 28.

ports. As indicated earlier, the committee should give strong consideration to the internal auditing staff regarding its request for special reports.

It is evident that the auditors' professional opinion on the financial statements augments the integrity and objectivity of management's representations in such statements. In addition, the audit committee should be familiar with the auditors' reports because each member has an obligation to provide the impetus to ensure that the proper audit opinion is rendered. Accordingly, the committee should review the audit report during the postaudit review period to determine the audit opinion on the financial statements for the current fiscal period. If an opinion other than an unqualified opinion will be issued, the committee should review and discuss the matters in question with the independent auditors and the senior accounting officers to obtain their concurrence on the auditors' exceptions. Such review meetings may be conducted on a separate or joint basis, depending on the attendant circumstances. The major objective is to identify the particular exceptions and to advise the board of directors in a timely manner of the audit opinion regarding such exceptions so that the board may deal with them.

SOURCES AND SUGGESTED READINGS

American Institute of Certified Public Accountants, *Professional Standards, U.S. Auditing Standards/Attestation Standards,* Vol. 1 (New York: American Institute of Certified Public Accountants, 1998).

Ellingsen, John E., Kurt Pany, and Peg Fagan, "SAS No. 59: How to Evaluate Going Concern." *Journal of Accountancy,* 168, No. 1 (January 1989), pp. 24–31.

National Commission on Fraudulent Financial Reporting, *Report of the National Commission on Fraudulent Financial Reporting* (Washington, D.C.: National Commission on Fraudulent Financial Reporting, 1987).

Robertson, Jack C., "Analysts' Reactions to Auditors' Messages in Qualified Reports." *Accounting Horizons* 2, No. 2 (June 1988), pp. 82–89.

Roussey, Robert S., Ernest L. Ten Eyck, and Mimi Blanco-Best, "Three New SASs: Closing the Communication Gap." *Journal of Accountancy* 166, No. 6, (December 1988), pp. 44–52.

Statement on Auditing Standards, No. 58, "Reports on Audited Financial Statements" (New York: American Institute of Certified Public Accountants, 1988).

Statement on Auditing Standards, No. 59, "The Auditor's Consideration of an Entity's Ability to Continue as a Going Concern" (New York: American Institute of Certified Public Accountants, 1988).

Statement on Auditing Standards, No. 62, "Special Reports" (New York: American Institute of Certified Public Accountants, 1989).

Chapter 14

The Audit Directors' Report and Concluding Observations

The audit committee of the board of directors is elected by the board in order to allow committee members to focus their attention on corporate accountability matters in greater depth than would be practical for the full board. Furthermore, the board of directors sets forth the duties and responsibilities of the audit committee in the committee's charter. It is therefore incumbent upon the committee to report regularly to the board of directors that it is properly performing its responsibilities as set forth in the charter.

The manner in which audit committees report varies from board to board, but, as noted by The Conference Board,[1] substantially all audit committees report to the board at least annually and often more frequently.

The purpose of this chapter is to provide guidance to the chair and members of the audit committee with respect to their reporting responsibilities to the board, whether the reports are submitted orally, following each committee meeting, or in a written format as outlined herein.

This chapter also presents the author's concluding observations and some perspectives on future developments.

PURPOSE OF THE AUDIT DIRECTORS' REPORT

The audit directors' report is the basis for reporting on the board of directors' charge to the committee. It should be addressed to the full board of directors and

---

[1] The Conference Board found that "almost every audit committee in the survey (98 percent, or 664 companies) gives a formal accounting of its activities at least once a year," a finding essentially unchanged from the 1978 survey. However, the frequency of reports to the board has risen, from a median of two for all companies in 1978 to three reports in 1987; just 14 percent report only once a year. See Jeremy Bacon, *The Audit Committee: A Broader Mandate,* Report No. 914 (New York: The Conference Board, 1988), p. 17.

explain their findings and recommendations concerning primarily the overall effectiveness of both the internal and external auditing functions and other areas within their original jurisdiction as defined by the board. In addition, the report should be based on their participation in the audit planning process as well as their monitoring activities, discussed in the preceding chapters. Such a report is critically important to the board for the following reasons:

- It communicates to the board financial, accounting, and auditing matters of particular interest that were noted in the audit directors' reviews and discussions with the internal and external auditing executives and the senior representatives of management, such as the chief financial officer.

- Their report not only contains an independent and objective appraisal of the audit functions but also provides assurance to the board that management is fulfilling its stewardship accountability to its outside constituencies, particularly the stockholders.

- The report reflects the audit directors' responsibility to exercise the legal duty of care in view of the fiduciary principle, discussed in Chapter 4. The reader should reread this chapter prior to the preparation of the report. Also, the reader should refer to Appendix G.

- It calls the board's attention to nonfinancial accounting matters of significance, such as conflicts of interest and other general business practices.

The audit directors are in a unique position within the framework of corporate accountability because they provide a constructive dimension to the board in helping the directors discharge their fiduciary responsibility to the stockholders. Through a review of their functions (discussed in Chapter 1), it is clearly evident that the scope of their position is broad based. Such a position enables the audit directors to obtain a broad perspective of the entity's business operations and its industry. As a result of their knowledge and their exposure to the subjects discussed in this text, they are in a position to recognize the auditing needs of the entity as well as to understand compliance matters with corporate policies. Although they are not directly involved in the day-to-day accounting and auditing management activities, their seasoned business experience permits them to monitor the changes in accounting and auditing standards that affect the financial reporting responsibilities of both the board of directors and the officers of the corporation. Furthermore, because of their independent posture in the corporate framework and their broad overview of the entity, they are not restricted to one particular function in the organization. Equally important, they can anticipate potential financial reporting problems as well as communicate management's course of action regarding the solutions to such problems.

In short, the audit directors have a critical role in developing their report for the board because of their responsibility to formulate recommendations based on their meetings with the auditors and senior financial officers. Such recommendations are a result of their review of the coordinated efforts of the above executives and their discussions with those executives. Consequently, it is incumbent on the audit directors to develop a report that is responsive to the needs and interests of the board of directors.

GUIDELINES FOR PREPARING THE REPORT

General Comments

In view of their oversight, monitoring, and advisory capacity, it is important to recognize that the audit directors' report should convey this position to the other board members. Moreover, the audit directors should communicate their findings and recommendations and avoid any final decisions, since such decisions are not within the province of the committee. Therefore, it is desirable to reexamine the committee's charge from the board and develop the report in response to this charge. This particular charge has been discussed in Chapter 1, and it is suggested that the reader review the committee's functions at this time.

In developing their report, the audit directors should be particularly alert to present or potential financial reporting and compliance problems. Such a charge is a difficult task for a member of the committee. However, subsequent to their orientation program as outlined in Chapter 7 along with their continuous committee meetings, each member's ability to recognize such problems will be enhanced. Obviously, such a skill is not acquired as the result of only a few meetings. Nevertheless, through an understanding of the entity's business and other subjects as discussed in this text, each member can assess his or her own strengths and weaknesses and develop the necessary proficiency. Furthermore, the quality of their report will be contingent on not only each member's perceptiveness and inquisitiveness but also their creativity concerning appropriate recommendations to the board. For example, during the committee's preaudit planning segment of the auditing cycle, discussed in Chapters 6 and 7, the committee should inquire and discuss with auditors and management any particular matters they should be aware of regarding the audit examination. Such inquiries will enable the committee to identify potential areas for possible recommendations to the board. For example, in Chapter 10 it was observed that the audit committee of McKesson Corporation reviews the changes in accounting policy. Thus it can be seen that the committee has a key role in evaluating and understanding the accounting policies of the corporation. Clearly, the audit directors should plan their agenda to allow each member sufficient time to study and review the subjects for the report. In summary, each member should keep the board's expectations in proper perspective during the report development period and realize that fellow board members will be relying on the report regarding the board's overall final decisions.

Sources of Information for the Report

Although the sources of information for the report will vary among different audit committees, the following recapitulation of the common sources discussed in the text is applicable:

1. Independent auditors
   a. Engagement letter
   b. Management letter
   c. Interim financial audit reports
   d. Annual auditors' report in the corporate annual report
   e. Special audit reports, if applicable
2. Corporate management
   a. Lawyer's letter for the outside auditors
   b. Management's letter of representation to the outside auditors
   c. Minutes of meetings of the board and its other standing committees, such as the audit and finance committees[2]
   d. Minutes of the annual stockholders meeting
   e. The annual corporate report and proxy materials
   f. Compliance reports with the regulatory agencies, particularly the SEC and the IRS
   g. Management report in the annual report
   h. Releases to employees and the general report through the public relations office
3. Internal auditors
   Reports on the following:
   a. Compliance audits
   b. Operational audits
   c. Financial audits
   d. Internal control structure

---

[2]Obviously, the minutes of the audit committee's meetings should be documented. Such a record of the committee's proceedings during the year facilitate the preparation of the report. The chairman of the audit committee should be satisfied that the recorded minutes of each committee meeting are sufficient and adequate in terms of the committee's findings, conclusions, and recommendations.

 e. Long-form internal audit report, if available

 f. Special survey reports, such as conflicts of interest and fraud prevention measures

4. Other sources of information

 a. Audit directors' professional development program as discussed in Chapter 7

 b. Interviews with the chief executive officer, chief financial officer, and legal counsel

 c. Bulletins within the organization and outside the organization, such as the newsletters from the professional accounting firms

Report Preparation

The audit directors' report is essentially an informational report that contains their overall assessment of the preceding sources of information along with their separate or joint meetings with the auditors and the representatives of management. Ordinarily, such a report will be prepared by the chair of the committee prior to the issuance of the annual corporate report and subsequent to the committee's postaudit conference. However, it may be desirable to issue an interim committee report with respect to special matters, such as interim financial information, so that such matters are communicated to the board in a timely manner. Thus it is highly probable that the audit committee may issue more than one report during the fiscal period.

During the phases of the auditing cycle, discussed in Chapters 6 and 7, the audit directors will have several review meetings concerning the auditing activities and compliance matters. Such review meetings along with the minutes of those meetings assist the committee in the preparation of the report. Although the content of the report may evolve from the transcripts of their meetings, it is important that the audit directors provide sufficient time to develop their report. Moreover, they should be satisfied not only that the facts are properly documented in the minutes but also that their proposal recommendations are practical and reasonable.

In contrast to the independent auditors' report, discussed in Chapter 13, the audit directors' report is not standardized by a professionally recognized accounting organization, such as the AICPA. Nonetheless, their report should describe the activities of their meetings, which consist primarily of their reviews, discussions, findings, and recommendations. In developing the content of the report, the committee's comments should not contradict the audit report opinion of the external auditors or the conclusions of the director of internal auditing. Therefore, subsequent to the preparation of the first draft of the report, the report content should be checked against the sources of information, primarily the audit reports, to avoid potential misunderstandings among the other board members.

While there are no definitive rules on the subjects, length, and format for the report, the committee should give consideration to the following points[3]:

1. The title of the report should be Audit Directors' Report.
2. The report should be addressed to the board of directors and dated.
3. The charge of the audit committee should be stated in the beginning of the report. Such information should be taken from the corporate bylaws or from a formal resolution passed by the board.
4. The report should contain a statement of the scope of the committee's review. For example, the scope of the report may include the following statement:
   We have made a review of the corporate audit policy statement and related internal and external auditing plans and results for the (period of review) in order to determine whether such functions were being performed in an effective manner. Our review included a discussion of the following: (1) a summary of the entity's financial reporting requirements and the annual report and proxy materials; (2) the system of internal accounting control and the scope of the audit; (3) the coordinated activities between the internal and external auditors regarding the scope of the audit; (4) management's judgment in the selection and application of accounting principles in the preparation of the financial statements; and (5) the entity's compliance with the applicable laws and regulations, particularly the federal securities laws and income tax laws, with the independent auditors and legal counsel.
5. A summary of the committee's review activities and a general discussion of such activities for the current fiscal period. The report should contain a chronological account of the committee's meeting activities. The subjects for the report will consist of the committee's reviews during the phases of the auditing cycle. For example, the committee should describe all significant accounting changes and related accounting policy disclosure matters that were approved during the postaudit review segment of the auditing cycle. For additional guidance on the subjects for the report, the reader should review the check list and other guidelines as discussed in the preceding chapters.
6. A summary of the committee's recommendations regarding such matters as the selection of the public accounting firm and changes in the internal auditing policies. Such recommendations may be incorporated with the preceding step. The reader should review the salient points in Chapter 7 regarding the selection or reappointment of the public accounting firm. Also, the committee will approve certain matters, such as financial statement disclosure matters (e.g., changes in accounting policies) and the audit fees.

---

[3] The author believes it may be desirable to prepare a formal report (as illustrated) in view of not only the potential legal liability of the committee but also the professionalism of the audit directors.

Exhibit 14.1 Illustrative Audit Directors' Report

The Audit Directors' Report

(Date of report)

(To Board of Directors)

(Charge of the audit committee)

(Scope of committee's reviews)

(Summary of the committee's review activities in chronological order)

(Summary of the committee's recommendations)

Respectfully Submitted,

Signed by: _____

(Name of chairman)

(Names of other committee members)

(Attachments, if appropriate)

---

7. The report should be signed by the chair, and names of other committee members should be disclosed in the report.
8. The committee may wish to provide attachments of principals' reports, such as the independent auditors' management letter, management's letter of representation to the auditors, and other special reports based on its discretion.

A suggested format for the report is presented in Exhibit 14.1. Subsequent to their recommendations, the audit directors may wish to use the following paragraph:

> Based upon our reviews, we are confident that management has fulfilled its reporting stewardship accountability in connection with the financial statements, and we are assured that both the internal and external auditors have properly discharged their appropriate auditing responsibilities.

Finally, several publicly held corporations are disclosing a report of the audit committee's activities in their annual reports. Such action exemplifies the committee's role as representatives of the stockholders. An example of the committee's report in the annual report of Ameritech Corporation is shown in Exhibit 14.2.[4]

---

[4]In 1987 the National Commission on Fraudulent Financial Reporting recommended that "the Securities and Exchange Commission require all annual reports to stockholders to include a letter from the chairman of the audit committee describing the committee's responsibilities and activities." For further reference, see the *Report of the National Commission on Fraudulent Financial Reporting* (Washington, D.C.: National Commission on Fraudulent Financial Reporting, 1987). In addition, in 1988 the

Exhibit 14.2   Report of Audit Committee Chairman

The audit committee (the committee) of the Board of Directors is composed of three independent directors who are not officers or employees of the company. The committee, which held three meetings during 1992, oversees the company's financial reporting process on behalf of the Board of Directors.

In fulfilling its responsibility, the committee recommended to the Board of Directors, subject to shareowner ratification, the selection of the company's independent public accountants. The committee discussed with the internal auditors and the independent public accountants the overall scope and specific plans for their respective audits. The committee also discussed the company's consolidated financial statements and the adequacy of the company's system of internal control. The committee met regularly with the company's internal auditors and independent public accountants, without management present, to discuss the results of their audits, their evaluation of the system of internal control, and the overall quality of the company's financial reporting. The meetings also were designed to facilitate any private communications with the committee desired by the internal auditors or the independent public accountants.

Hal C. Kuehl
Chairman, Audit Committee

February 5, 1993

Source: Ameritech Corporation, *1992 Annual Report,* p. 28.

CONCLUDING OBSERVATIONS

Over the past two decades, the audit committee of the board of directors has evolved into a viable mechanism (an independent oversight group) in promoting a high degree of integrity in both the internal and external auditing processes as well as the financial reporting process. While the evolutionary process that created the audit committee was relatively slow, the major impetus toward the

---

MacDonald Commission in Canada supported the recommendation of the National Commission on Fraudulent Financial Reporting: "Indeed, we would go further. We advocate a publicly stated mandate from the board to the audit committee. The committee's annual reporting to the shareholders would then describe specifically what it did to discharge its mandate." See the *Report of the Commission to Study the Public's Expectations of Audits* (Toronto: Canadian Institute of Chartered Accountants, 1988), p. 36. For further reference, see Marilyn R. Kintzel, "The Use of Audit Committee Reports in Financial Reporting," *Internal Auditing* 6, No. 4 (Spring 1991), pp. 16–24; and Frank Urbancic, "The Usefulness of Audit Committee Reports: Assessments and Perceptions," *Journal of Applied Business Research* 7, No. 3 (Summer 1991), pp. 36–41. As noted in Chapter 10, Exhibit 10.1, the Blue Ribbon Committee on Improving the Effectiveness of Corporate Audit Committees recommends that the SEC require all reporting companies to include a letter from the auditee in the company's annual report to shareholders and Form 10-K Annual Report (see Exhibit 14.3 for further details).

mandatory establishment of the committee came from the New York Stock Exchange in June 1978. Their adoption of mandatory audit committees as a listing requirement on the stock exchange has established standards to improve the accountability of corporate boards of directors and managers to their outside constituencies. Since the adoption of the aforementioned listing requirement, the stock exchange(s) of an increasing number of countries with developed or emerging equity markets have adopted audit committees to increase transparency in their stock exchanges, which, in turn, helps facilitate foreign investment. Indeed, it is reasonable to expect that this trend will continue. The managements of stock exchanges have accepted the audit committee as a key mechanism within the corporate framework to help the board of directors not only address the needs of information users who rely on dependable financial reporting but also properly discharge its financial and fiduciary responsibilities to shareholders and other constituencies. Thus to the extent that the audit committee can monitor the internal and external audit processes and understand the perceived financial accounting information needs of the entity's constituencies, it can provide a balance in the corporate financial reporting process.

As Harold M. Williams, former chairman of the SEC, once stated in an address before the Securities Regulation Institute:

> Although the American Institute of Certified Public Accountants recently concluded that it should not compel public companies to establish audit committees as a precondition to obtaining an independent auditor's certification, it reiterated its support for the audit committee concept. In addition, the Foreign Corrupt Practices Act, and the importance which it places on establishing mechanisms to insure that the company has a functioning system of internal accounting controls, has given added impetus to the audit committee movement.
>
> Thus, at this point, the central task is to define the audit committee's responsibilities and enhance the quality of the committee's work.[5]

In light of Chairman William's comments, the first edition of this book was written to respond to the central task of clearly defining the audit committee's responsibilities as well as to enhance the quality of the committee's work. The audit committee is fundamental to the improvement of the board of directors' stewardship accountability to its constituencies.

It is clearly evident from the public and private-sector initiatives in the 1980s and early 1990s that the concept of audit committees has continued as an integral part of corporate governance and accountability. Both sectors have recognized that audit committees have made important contributions in promoting the invest-

---

[5]Harold M. Williams, "Corporate Accountability—One Year Later," Address presented at the Sixth Annual Securities Regulation Institute, San Diego, California, January 18, 1979.

ing public's confidence in the integrity of the auditing processes and the financial reporting process. Equally important, audit committees have become a key element in the entity's system of internal control to help engender a high degree of credibility of financial reporting, which, in turn, helps safeguard the securities market. Their independent oversight responsibility in the internal control environment helps to ensure the independence of both internal and external auditors. As a result, the full board of directors is assured of objective financial reporting by management.

Future Perspectives Revisited

The 14 years since the first edition and 5 years since the second edition of this book were published have been years of dynamic changes in corporate governance, particularly as it has affected audit committees. In the author's view, the future will continue to bring further changes and added duties and responsibilities for members of audit committees.

The intent here is not to comment fully on each of these possible developments but merely to use a "crystal ball," presenting the views of one informed commentator on audit committee activities.

Reporting

- As recommended by the Treadway Report, reports of audit committees will increasingly be included in corporate annual reports.

- Corporate management will be required to include in its annual report a statement about the adequacy of the company's internal control, and the company's external auditors will be required to comment on that statement.

- Future legislation will require the external auditor to report to appropriate authorities, such as the SEC, suspected illegalities discovered by the auditor if the company's management or board of directors (i.e., audit committee) fails to take appropriate action.

- The form and content of financial statements will be revised over time, as suggested by the Public Oversight Board. In addition, disclosures relating to business risks and uncertainties will result in further disclosures in financial reports and in modification to the standard auditor's reports. Both of these factors will have future implications for audit committees.

- The Treadway Report included a recommendation that corporate audit committees have additional responsibilities with respect to an entity's unaudited quarterly earnings report. Although this recommendation has not been adopted by many corporations, it is the author's belief that audit committees' oversight in the future will include quarterly reporting to further ensure the integrity of the interim reporting process.

Other Areas of Future Change

Internal Auditing   As noted in the 1988 Conference Board Research Report ("The Audit Committee: A Broader Mandate"), audit committees are believed to have significantly improved procedures and practices related to the internal auditing function. It is expected that this will continue.

The report of the Treadway Commission recommended that all public companies have an internal audit function. Despite this, many companies, particularly those in the middle and small "cap" range, have not adopted this recommendation for a variety of reasons, including those related to the current economic environment.

It is the author's belief that there will be continued demand to require an internal audit function for all public companies. Furthermore, in those instances in which it may not be economically feasible or practicable to establish a fully staffed internal audit function, this service will be procured from outside firms that specialize in providing such services to the middle and small markets.

Enhanced Audit Committee Liability   The Conference Board Report ("The Audit Committee: A Broader Mandate") indicated that CEOs and CFOs could be deemed to have a special responsibility or knowledge that could increase the possibility of their being sued in a class action. However, most believed that corporate indemnification, D & O insurance, and state statutory protection would be sufficient to offset the additional exposure.

Nevertheless, in view of increasing litigation against members of boards serving on corporate audit committees, it is prudent for audit committee directors to follow the guidance of the Treadway Report and good audit committee practices, as set forth in this book. It is increasingly important from a litigation point of view for an audit committee to do its job well and to document that fact.

Independent Advisors

The Federal Deposit Insurance Corporation Improvement Act of 1991 (FDICIA) sets forth a number of requirements with respect to audit committees, as noted elsewhere in this book. It further requires larger depository financial institutions to provide independent counsel to audit committees. The Treadway Report also recommended that audit committees have the authority to retain expert consultants or advisors to assist them as needed in meeting their duties and responsibilities, or possibly to evaluate the committee's performance.

In view of the ever-expanding duties and responsibilities of audit committees and, perhaps, increased liability in the future, it is not unreasonable to assume that committees will increasingly seek outside independent advisors to assist them in the effective performance of their charter.

During the latter half of the 1990s, several initiatives have occurred in response to the aforementioned observations of one informed commentator on audit committee activities.

- The Private Securities Litigation Reform Act of 1995 requires the external auditors who detect illegal acts to report their findings to the SEC if the client company fails to take appropriate action on such acts that have a material effect on the financial statements.

- SOP 94-6, "Disclosure of Certain Risks and Uncertainties," requires disclosures of certain risks and uncertainties, including nature of operations, use of estimates in financial statements, certain significant estimates, and current vulnerability due to concentration.

- SAS No. 78, "Consideration of Internal Control in a Financial Statement Audit: An Amendment to SAS No. 55," requires that the external auditors gain an understanding of management's risk assessment process. This requirement includes gaining an understanding about how management estimates the significance of those risks and assesses the likelihood of their occurrence. This process may be described as identifying types of potential misstatements and designing controls to prevent or detect those misstatements.

- SIAS No. 18 (Guidelines 220.02), "Use of Outside Service Providers," provides guidance and assistance to companies that have outsourced a portion or all of the internal audit function.

While the dynamic changes in corporate governance and the financial reporting needs of investors continue to impact the role and responsibility of audit committees, to limit the potential litigation risk, the board of directors should consider the overall performance of the committee and reexamine periodically the terms of reference in the committee's charter, as set forth in this book.

Recognizing that audit committees have an independent oversight function and operate on a part-time basis, the board and management should avoid diluting the activities of the committee by inappropriately expanding the scope of its charter. Thus the board should approve any modifications in the terms of reference of the audit committee.

Clearly, the rapidly changing environment in both the corporate and financial communities necessitates the need for a continuing education program for audit committees. Such a program would enable the committee to cope with recent accounting, auditing, and financial reporting developments and thus enable them better to assist their full boards of directors with discharging their fiduciary responsibilities to the shareholders. Professor Jane F. Mutchler has proposed "a more holistic view of auditing." She combines the dictionary definition of auditing and the definition of assurance services from the AICPA Special Committee on Assurance Services (Elliott Committee) as follows:

an independent, methodological examination and review of a situation or condition and a reporting of the results of the examination to improve the quality of information or its context for decision makers.[6]

Given this definition, Professor Mutchler concludes:

If we view auditing in this context, a whole new world beyond financial statement auditing opens up. Now we are talking about systems auditing, operational auditing, ethics auditing, risk auditing, management auditing, business process auditing. This not only provides a vision for new services to be offered but also, and perhaps more important for our organization, provides a whole new vision for curriculum and research issues.[7]

More recently, Arthur Levitt, chairman of the SEC, stated that:

"qualified, committed, independent and toughminded audit committees represent the most reliable guardians of the public interest. Sadly, stories abound of audit committees whose members lack expertise in the basic principles of financial reporting as well as the mandate to ask probing questions."[8]

As a result of SEC Chairman Arthur Levitt's comments and his call for action, the New York Stock Exchange and the National Association of Securities Dealers formed a Blue Ribbon Committee on Improving the Effectiveness of Corporate Audit Committees. See Exhibit 14.3 for a summary of the committee's recommendations. Audit committees and boards of directors may wish to communicate their views on these recommendations to the Securities and Exchange Commission, self-regulatory organizations, and the accounting profession prior to implementation (see Appendix N).

In a study dealing with boards of directors and corporate governance over the next 10 years, Oxford Analytica reported the following with respect to the oversight function:

The key question regarding the oversight function of corporate boards concerns their ability to discipline or even replace management for poor performance before a company is overtaken by a crisis. This is no easy task: challenging the management of a company, even if it is not performing well, requires board members to be well-informed and confident. They are also very likely to need the backing of powerful stakeholders as a counterweight to the power of the CEO.

[6] Jane F. Mutchler, "Report of the Chairperson," Auditing Section/American Accounting Association, *Auditor's Report* 20 (Fall 1996), pp. 1–2.
[7] Ibid., 2.
[8] See Remarks by Chairman Arthur Levitt, Securities and Exchange Commission, *The "Numbers Game,"* NYU Center for Law and Business, New York, September 28, 1998 (http://www.sec.gov/news/speeches/spch220. txt.).

Exhibit 14.3 Summary of Recommendations of the Blue Ribbon Committee on Improving the Effectiveness of Corporate Audit Committees

The first two recommendations are aimed at strengthening the independence of the audit committee:

Recommendation 1

The Committee recommends that both the New York Stock Exchange (NYSE) and the National Association of Securities Dealers (NASD) adopt the following definition of independence for purposes of service on the audit committee for listed companies with a market capitalization above $200 million (or a more appropriate measure for identifying smaller-sized companies as determined jointly by the NYSE and the NASD):

Members of the audit committee shall be considered independent if they have no relationship to the corporation that may interfere with the exercise of their independence from management and the corporation. Examples of such relationships include:

- a director being employed by the corporation or any of its affiliates for the current year or any of the past five years;
- a director accepting any compensation from the corporation or any of its affiliates other than compensation for board service or benefits under a tax-qualified retirement plan;
- a director being a member of the immediate family of an individual who is, or has been in any of the past five years, employed by the corporation or any of its affiliates as an executive officer;
- a director being a partner in, or a controlling shareholder or an executive officer of, any for-profit business organization to which the corporation made, or from which the corporation received, payments that are or have been significant* to the corporation or business organization in any of the past five years;
- a director being employed as an executive of another company where any of the corporation's executives serves on that company's compensation committee.

A director who has one or more of these relationships may be appointed to the audit committee, if the board, under exceptional and limited circumstances, determines that membership on the committee by the individual is required by the best interests of the corporation and its shareholders, and the board discloses, in the next annual proxy statement subsequent to such determination, the nature of the relationship and the reasons for that determination.

Recommendation 2

The Committee recommends that in addition to adopting and complying with the definition of independence set forth above for purposes of service on the audit committee, the NYSE and the NASD require that listed companies with a market capitalization above $200 million (or a more appropriate measure for identifying smaller-sized companies as

---

*The Committee views the term "significant" in the spirit of Section 1.34(a)(4) of the American Law Institute Principles of Corporate Governance and the accompanying commentary to that section.

Exhibit 14.3 (*Continued*)

determined jointly by the NYSE and the NASD) have an audit committee comprised solely of independent directors.

The Committee recommends that the NYSE and the NASD maintain their respective current audit committee independence requirements as well as their respective definitions of independence for listed companies with a market capitalization of $200 million or below (or a more appropriate measure for identifying smaller-sized companies as determined jointly by the NYSE and the NASD).

Our second set of recommendations is aimed at making the audit committee more effective:

Recommendation 3

The Committee recommends that the NYSE and the NASD require listed companies with a market capitalization above $200 million (or a more appropriate measure for identifying smaller-sized companies as determined jointly by the NYSE and the NASD) to have an audit committee comprised of a minimum of three directors, each of whom is financially literate (as described in the section of this report entitled "Financial Literacy") or becomes financially literate within a reasonable period of time after his or her appointment to the audit committee, and further that at least one member of the audit committee have accounting or related financial management expertise.

The Committee recommends that the NYSE and the NASD maintain their respective current audit committee size and membership requirements for companies with a market capitalization of $200 million or below (or a more appropriate measure for identifying smaller-sized companies as determined jointly by the NYSE and the NASD).

Recommendation 4

The Committee recommends that the NYSE and the NASD require the audit committee of each listed company to (i) adopt a formal written charter that is approved by the full board of directors and that specifies the scope of the committee's responsibilities, and how it carries out those responsibilities, including structure, processes, and membership requirements, and (ii) review and reassess the adequacy of the audit committee charter on an annual basis.

Recommendation 5

The Committee recommends that the Securities and Exchange Commission (SEC) promulgate rules that require the audit committee for each reporting company to disclose in the company's proxy statement for its annual meeting of shareholders whether the audit committee has adopted a formal written charter, and, if so, whether the audit committee satisfied its responsibilities during the prior year in compliance with its charter, which charter shall be disclosed at least triennially in the annual report to shareholders or proxy statement and in the next annual report to shareholders or proxy statement after any significant amendment to that charter.

The Committee further recommends that the SEC adopt a "safe harbor" applicable to all disclosure referenced in this Recommendation 5.

(*continues*)

Exhibit 14.3   (*Continued*)

Our final group of recommendations addresses mechanisms for accountability among the audit committee, the outside auditors, and management:

Recommendation 6
The Committee recommends that the listing rules for both the NYSE and the NASD require that the audit committee charter for every listed company specify that the outside auditor is ultimately accountable to the board of directors and the audit committee, as representatives of shareholders, and that these shareholder representatives have the ultimate authority and responsibility to select, evaluate, and, where appropriate, replace the outside auditor (or to nominate the outside auditor to be proposed for shareholder approval in any proxy statement).

Recommendation 7
The Committee recommends that the listing rules for both the NYSE and the NASD require that the audit committee charter for every listed company specify that the audit committee is responsible for ensuring its receipt from the outside auditors of a formal written statement delineating all relationships between the auditor and the company, consistent with Independence Standards Board Standard 1, and that the audit committee is also responsible for actively engaging in a dialogue with the auditor with respect to any disclosed relationships or services that may impact the objectivity and independence of the auditor and for taking, or recommending that the full board take, appropriate action to ensure the independence of the outside auditor.

Recommendation 8
The Committee recommends that Generally Accepted Auditing Standards (GAAS) require that a company's outside auditor discuss with the audit committee the auditor's judgments about the quality, not just the acceptability, of the company's accounting principles as applied in its financial reporting; the discussion should include such issues as the clarity of the company's financial disclosures and degree of aggressiveness or conservatism of the company's accounting principles and underlying estimates and other significant decisions made by management in preparing the financial disclosure and reviewed by the outside auditors. This requirement should be written in a way to encourage open, frank discussion and to avoid boilerplate.

Recommendation 9
The Committee recommends that the SEC require all reporting companies to include a letter from the audit committee in the company's annual report to shareholders and Form 10-K Annual Report disclosing whether or not, with respect to the prior fiscal year: (i) management has reviewed the audited financial statements with the audit committee, including a discussion of the quality of the accounting principles as applied and significant judgments affecting the company's financial statements; (ii) the outside auditors have discussed with the audit committee the outside auditors' judgments of the quality of those principles as applied and judgments referenced in (i) above under the circumstances; (iii) the members of the audit committee have discussed among themselves, without management or the outside auditors present, the information disclosed to the audit committee described in (i) and (ii) above; and (iv) the audit committee, in reliance on the review and discussions conducted with management and the outside auditors pursuant to (i) and (ii)

Exhibit 14.3 (*Continued*)

above, believes that the company's financial statements are fairly presented in conformity with Generally Accepted Accounting Principles (GAAP) in all material respects.

The Committee further recommends that the SEC adopt a "safe harbor" applicable to any disclosure referenced in this Recommendation 9.

Recommendation 10

The Committee recommends that the SEC require that a reporting company's outside auditor conduct a SAS 71 Interim Financial Review prior to the company's filing of its Form 10-Q.

The Committee further recommends that SAS 71 be amended to require that a reporting company's outside auditor discuss with the audit committee, or at least its chairman, and a representative of financial management, in person, or by telephone conference call, the matters described in AU Section 380, Communications With the Audit Committee, prior to the filing of the Form 10-Q (and preferably prior to any public announcement of financial results), including significant adjustments, management judgments and accounting estimates, significant new accounting policies, and disagreements with management.

Source: Blue Ribbon Committee on Improving the Effectiveness of Corporate Audit Committees, *Report and Recommendations of the Blue Ribbon Committee on Improving the Effectiveness of Corporate Audit Committees*, (New York: The Blue Ribbon Committee on Improving the Effectiveness of Corporate Audit Committee, 1999), pp. 10–16.

Oversight is thus likely to be most effective where directors:

Possess and have a reputation for considerable expertise relevant to evaluating the firm's performance; and

Respond to the interests of major shareholders, or are individuals who enjoy the backing of major shareholders.

Certain organizational and structural changes may enhance the ability of the board to keep a watchful eye on management's actions. The rise of the audit committee in US, Canadian, and UK corporations is one of the most important such developments and merits careful examination.[9]

This third edition has examined the chronological events and developments in both the public and private sectors associated with audit committees. Such examination is essential in order to enhance their effectiveness. Finally, given the increasing pervasiveness and the number of audit committees, it is reasonable to expect that they will continue to receive a high level of attention from the investing public.

[9] Oxford Analytica, *Board Directors and Corporate Governance, Trends in the G7 Countries over the Next Ten Years, Executive Report* (Oxford: Oxford Analytica, 1992), p. 7. For an expanded discussion of forward-looking activities of audit committees, see Arthur L. Ruffing, Jr., "The Future Role of the Audit Committee," *Directors & Boards* 18, No. 3 (Spring 1994), pp. 51–54. Also, the reader may wish to review Exhibit B.1 in Appendix B to see the rise of audit committees in certain countries and to see the 1998 speeches on the Internet by Lynn Turner, chief accountant of the SEC, that address the role of audit committees: http://www.sec.gov/news/speeches/spch226.htm.

SOURCES AND SUGGESTED READINGS

Ameritech Corporation, *1992 Annual Report.*

Bacon, Jeremy, *The Audit Committee: A Broader Mandate,* Report No. 914 (New York: The Conference Board, 1988).

Canadian Institute of Chartered Accountants, *Report of the Commission to Study the Public's Expectations of Audits* (Toronto: Canadian Institute of Chartered Accountants, 1988).

Kintzel, Marilyn R., "The Use of Audit Committee Reports in Financial Reporting." *Internal Auditing* 6, No. 4 (Spring 1991), pp. 16–24.

Levitt, Arthur, "The Numbers Game," NYU Center for Law and Business (Washington, D.C.: Securities and Exchange Commission, September 28, 1998).

Blue Ribbon Committee on Improving the Effectiveness of Corporate Audit Committees, *Report and Recommendations of the Blue Ribbon Committee on Improving the Effectiveness of Corporate Audit Committees* (New York: The Blue Ribbon Committee on Improving the Effectiveness of Corporate Audit Committees, 1999).

Mutchler, Jane F., "Report of the Chairperson." *The Auditor's Report* 20 (Fall, 1996), pp. 1–2.

National Commission on Fraudulent Financial Reporting, *Report of the National Commission on Fraudulent Financial Reporting* (Washington, D.C.: National Commission on Fraudulent Financial Reporting, 1987).

Oxford Analytica, *Board Directors and Corporate Governance, Trends in the G7 Countries over the Next Ten Years, Executive Report* (Oxford: Oxford Analytica, 1992).

Ruffing, Arthur L., Jr., "The Future Role of Audit Committee." *Directors & Boards* 18, No. 3 (Spring 1994), pp. 51–54.

Urbancic, Frank, "The Usefulness of Audit Committee Reports: Assessments and Perceptions." *Journal of Applied Business Research* 7, No. 3 (Summer 1991), pp. 36–41.

Williams, Harold M., "Corporate Accountability—One Year Later," January 18, 1979. Address presented at the Sixth Annual Securities Regulation Institute, San Diego, California.

Glossary

Accounting control. Plan of organization and the procedures and records that are concerned with the safeguarding of assets and the reliability of the financial records. See **internal control.**

Accounting policy disclosures. Disclosures that relate to the significant accounting policies with respect to management's selection and application of generally accepted accounting principles in the preparation of the financial statements. The disclosure matters are governed by Accounting Principles Board Opinion No. 22, "Disclosure of Accounting Policies."

Accounting Principles Board (APB). AICPA's accounting rule-making body. It has been succeeded by the Financial Accounting Standards Board, which is separate and distinct from the AICPA.

Administrative control. Plan of organization and the procedures and records that are concerned with the decision processes leading to management's authorization of transactions. See **internal control.**

Adverse opinion. Statement made in the independent auditor's report indicating that the financial statements are not presented fairly in accordance with generally accepted accounting principles. Such a statement is rendered where the auditor's exceptions are so material that the statements as a whole are not fairly presented.

Agreed-on procedures engagement. The CPA firm and the client company agree that certain procedures will be performed with respect to specified elements, accounts, or items of a financial statement, and the report of the engagement is distributed to designated parties.

American Accounting Association. An association of accounting educators although the membership is open to others.

American Institute of Certified Public Accountants (AICPA). The national professional organization of certified public accountants.

Analytical procedures. Procedures consisting of comparative financial information, financial ratios, nonfinancial information, and industry statistics. Independent auditors use these procedures in planning the audit and for the year-end review of the financial statements.

Attest engagement. The independent auditors are engaged by the client to express a conclusion about the reliability of an assertion that is the responsibility of another party (e.g., a report from the independent auditors on management's assertion about the effectiveness of the internal control structure).

Audit Directors' Report. An informational report addressed to the full board of directors regarding their activities during the fiscal accounting period. Such a report also may be disclosed in the annual report on a summary basis.

Audit risk. The risk of independent auditors to modify their audit report with respect to financial statements that are materially misstated. Independent auditors attempt to minimize audit risk by assessing both inherent risk and control risk.

Auditing cycle. The phases of an audit examination, which consist of the initial planning segment, preaudit planning segment, and postaudit review segment.

Auditing Standards Board. The auditing rule-making body of the AICPA.

Auditing Standards of Field Work. Plans for an overall strategy for the expected conduct and scope of the examination for a particular audit engagement.

Certified Fraud Examiner. A person who has completed the necessary requisites of the program administered by the Association of Certified Fraud Examiners.

Certified Internal Auditor Program. A professional development program administered by the Institute of Internal Auditors and designed to prepare individuals for the Certified Internal Auditor (CIA) certificate.

Change in accounting estimate. Refers to a change owing to additional information or more experience on behalf of management whereby management's original estimates are revised to present a fair representation of the financial position and results of operating the business.

Change in accounting principle. A change resulting from the adoption of a generally accepted accounting principle that is different from the one used previously.

Change in reporting entity. A change occurring as a result of restructuring an entity, for example, through a corporate merger.

Compliance audits. Type of audit oriented toward the employees' compliance with management policies. It also refers to the entity's adherence to the rules and regulations of the various government agencies.

Consistency. Concept related to the second generally accepted auditing standard of reporting regarding the consistent application of generally accepted accounting principles to maintain comparability in the current and prior periods' financial statements.

Corporate accountability. Refers to corporate management's reporting responsibility of its stewardship for the economic resources of the enterprise to its outside constituencies.

Corporate auditing independence. Reporting relationship of the internal auditing staff should be structured so that the auditors have an independent posture in the corporate framework. The audit staff should report to an executive whose authority is sufficient to maintain the audit staff's independence. Also, the internal audit executive should have free access to the audit committee.

Corporate auditing philosophy. Refers to the internal auditing staff's approaches to the internal audit function. The current thought concerning such philosophies is espoused by the Institute of Internal Auditors.

Corporate audit plan. Plan that comprises the scope of the overall audit plans, which is an amalgamation of internal and external auditing activities.

Cost Accounting Standards Board. Board established by Congress to develop and maintain cost accounting standards and monitor the cost accounting practices of corporations engaged in government defense contracts.

Disclaimer of opinion. Statement made by independent auditors in their audit report that, as a result of insufficient information, they are unable to form an opinion regarding the financial statements.

Disclosure. An accounting principle stating that management has a reporting responsibility to its constituencies to disclose financial information that is necessary for a proper understanding of the financial statements.

Engagement letter. Document that sets forth the nature and scope of the audit engagement as well as other professional services of the CPA firm.

Errors. Unintentional and acting-in-good-faith misrepresentations of financial statements or disclosures.

Facilitating (grease) payments. Small payments covering ministerial activities, such as for custom documents or minor permits in countries other than the United States.

Fairness. The fourth auditing standard of reporting requires that the independent auditors express their opinion on the fairness of management's representations in the financial statements.

Federal Deposit Insurance Corporation Improvement Act. Legislation enacted December 19, 1991, providing for the establishment of audit committees of insured depository institutions with total assets of $150,000,000 or more.

Financial Accounting Standards Board. The current accounting rule-making body, which succeeded the Accounting Principles Board on July 1, 1973.

Financial audit. An examination of the entity's financial statements in accordance with generally accepted auditing standards. The examination is also made to determine whether the statements are fairly presented in conformity with generally accepted accounting principles. Such an examination may be conducted on an interim or quarterly basis and is known as an interim financial audit for internal managerial purposes.

Financial control system. Refers to the internal accounting controls designed to safeguard the assets and establish sound methods of record keeping in compliance with the Foreign Corrupt Practices Act. See also **accounting control.**

Financial Executive Institute. An association of financial and accounting officers, such as vice presidents of finance, treasurers, and controllers.

Foreign Corrupt Practices Act. Legislation enacted December 19, 1977, providing for the establishment and maintenance of a sound system of internal accounting control and record-keeping requirements. The law states that any direct or indirect payment or offer that is intended to promote business constitutes foreign bribery.

Fraud. In a financial statement audit context, an intentional and acting-in-bad-faith misrepresentation of financial statements or disclosures and misstatements due to misappropriation of assets.

Generally accepted accounting principles. The conventions, rules, and methods of accounting that are widely accepted among accounting practitioners.

Generally accepted auditing standards. A framework for measuring the quality of an auditor's professional performance concerning the audit examination and the audit report.

Governmental Accounting Standards Board. The current accounting rule-making body that issues pronouncements for state and local governmental entities.

Illegal acts. Acts that are a violation of laws and regulations.

Independence Standards Board. A board established to deal with auditor independence questions governed by independence rules with a principles-based system.

Initial Audit Planning Segment. The first phase of the auditing cycle regarding the preliminary audit planning activities.

Institute of Internal Auditors. The international organization of internal auditors.

Internal control. A process, effected by an entity's board of directors, management, and other personnel, designed to provide reasonable assurance regarding the achievement of objectives in the following categories: (1) effectiveness and efficiency of operations; (2) reliability of financial reporting; and (3) compliance with applicable laws and regulations.

International Accounting Standards Committee. A committee that promulgates international accounting standards which provide for uniformity in financial reporting.

International Federation of Accountants. A global organization of national accounting groups in 89 countries. The International Auditing Practices Committee (IAPC) issues international standards on auditing.

Introductory paragraph. First paragraph of the independent auditors' standard audit report. It states that management is responsible for the financial statements and that the auditors' objective is to express an opinion on such statements.

Lawyers' Letter. Legal opinion letter with respect to potential litigation, such as a pending lawsuit. This document is submitted to the independent auditors.

Letter of Management's Representations. A letter originated by the chief executive officer and chief financial officer to the independent accounting firm with respect to the entity's representations concerning the financial position and the results of operations.

Logistical matters. Matters related to the audit reporting and coverage of a multinational corporation on a centralized and decentralized basis regarding the corporate and resident auditors.

Long-form report. The independent auditor's report form used in the examination for the purpose of including details of the items in the financial statements as well as statistical data, explanatory comments, and a description of the scope in greater detail than in the short-form report.

Management assertions. Representations of management contained in the financial statements. See **Letter of Management's Representations.**

Management audit. Audit conducted by independent auditors. The nature of this audit is the same as that of the operational audit, which is conducted by internal auditors. Such an audit is conducted to determine the operating efficiency of the functions or departments within the organization.

Management Letter. Letter containing independent auditors' recommendations as a result of their evaluation of the system of internal accounting control.

Management Report. An acknowledgment by management of its responsibility for the content of the corporate annual report.

Materiality. An accounting principle stating that the financial statements should include only that information which is significant with respect to the entity's financial position and results of operations. This principle is based on the professional judgment of the independent auditors regarding the disclosure of the financial information.

Monitoring function. The responsibility of the audit directors to oversee the corporation's accounting and auditing activities and other matters as defined by the board of directors. Such activities include the system of internal control, the internal audit function, accounting policies, and certain business practices, such as questionable foreign payments.

National Association of Accountants (now Institute of Management Accountants). A professional association of management accountants who are employed in industry, government, and nonprofit organizations.

Operational audit. An audit conducted by the internal audit staff to review and appraise the activities of a certain function within the corporation. The objective is to determine the operational efficiency of the corporate function or department.

Opinion paragraph. The third paragraph of the independent auditors' standard short-form audit report. It contains the auditors' expression of an opinion on the fairness of management's representations in the financial statements in accordance with generally accepted accounting principles.

Peer review. See **quality review standards.**

Planning function. The development of a coordinated plan of administration whereby the audit committee can fulfill its responsibility to oversee and monitor the financial accounting and auditing processes.

Postaudit segment. Refers to the third phase of the auditing cycle whereby the audit committee should review the results of both the internal and external audit activities and recommend the selection or reappointment of the public accounting firm to the board of directors.

Preaudit planning segment. Refers to the second phase of the auditing cycle whereby the audit committee should discuss the internal and external audit plans regarding matters such as audit coverage and assignment of audit personnel.

Private Securities Litigation Reform Act of 1995. Legislation enacted December 22, 1995, providing reforms to curb the number of abusive securities class action suits. The law deals also with such matters as proportionate liability, safe-harbor for forward-looking statements, and loss causation principle.

Public Oversight Board. An independent oversight group of individuals other than public accountants who monitor the AICPA's SEC Practice Section.

Qualified opinion. An opinion used by the independent auditors when there are exceptions regarding management's representations in the financial statements.

Quality control standards. A system of quality control for a CPA firm that consists of policies and procedures to ensure adherence with professional standards.

Quality review standards. Standards for performing and reporting on quality reviews of a CPA firm by another CPA firm.

Related-party transactions. Such transactions occur when one party is able to significantly influence another party that would render a non-arm's-length negotiation (e.g., a director or officers may have a conflict of interest because of loans to the company or from the company that must be disclosed in the financial statements).

Relative risk. Related not only to the financial accounts but also to corporate locations, such as subsidiaries or divisions that are subject to a high exposure of risk based on their susceptibility to irregularities. The elements of materiality and relative risk are correlated closely with respect to the scope of audit planning activities.

Report on internal control. See **management letter** and **attest engagement.**

Reporting function. The responsibility of the audit committee to present a summary of its findings and recommendations to the board of directors based on its review of the audit planning and monitoring activities.

Representation Letters of Compliance. Letters used to obtain acknowledgment from corporate managers regarding their compliance with the entity's policies and practices with respect to corporate conduct and responsibility.

SEC Annual Report 10-K. Report containing additional information beyond the information in the corporate annual report in accordance with the federal securities disclosure laws.

SEC Interim Report 10-Q. Report containing quarterly financial information reported in accordance with the federal securities laws.

SEC Special Report 8-K. Interim report containing information regarding certain special events; must be filed on the occurrence of such events as a change in the independent accounting firm or a change in control of the registrant.

Scope paragraph. Second paragraph of the independent auditors' standard short-form audit report. It sets forth the statements to be examined and the nature of the audit work.

Securities Act of 1933. Legislation that provides financial information regarding the public sale of securities. This act also provides for civil and criminal liability of the directors with respect to fraud in the registration statements.

Securities and Exchange Commission. A regulatory government agency that requires public disclosure of the relevant facts in connection with the issuance of new securities and securities listed on the stock exchange.

Securities Exchange Act of 1934. Legislation that regulates the public sales of securities through the securities exchanges or brokers after the original sale of the securities.

Special Reports. The reports of the independent auditors regarding their review of certain activities as requested by management.

Standard Short-Form Unqualified Report. See **unqualified opinion.**

Unqualified opinion. An audit report used by the independent auditors when they find no exceptions concerning management's representations in the financial statements. Such an opinion is disclosed in the third paragraph of the standard short-form audit report.

U.S. General Accounting Office. A federal agency that issues government auditing standards (the "Yellow Book").

Working capital position. Represents the relationship between the cash and near-cash assets and the short-term liabilities. Such a position is also expressed as the relationship of the current assets to the current liabilities of the entity.

Historical Perspective on Audit Committees

As disclosed in Accounting Series Release No. 19, "In the Matter of McKesson & Robbins, Inc.," in 1940 the SEC recommended that outside members of the board of directors nominate the outside auditors and, in turn, the shareholders elect the public accounting firm. There was doubt as to whether the external auditors were truly independent of management. Of course, the issue relative to this case involved the reporting of consolidated total assets approximating $90 million, which included nonexistent inventories valued at approximately $10 million and overstated accounts receivable by approximately $9 million.[1] Moreover, because of the McKesson & Robbins debacle, the New York Stock Exchange issued a similar recommendation, which stated, "Where practicable, the selection of the auditors by a special committee of the board composed of directors who are not officers of the company appears desirable."[2] Although the term *audit committee* was not mentioned as such, several companies, for example, General Motors, established audit committees as a result of the McKesson & Robbins scandal.[3] This scandal alerted the corporate community and the accounting profession that appointment of an audit committee by the board of directors should be recognized as an important action.

Until 1967 the concept of the audit committee received very little support, and the functions of this committee remained undefined. For example, John L. Carey wrote that a "direct channel of communication between the board and the auditors" is essential in reviewing the financial statements, the "most important representation to the stockholders and the public."[4] In July 1967 the Executive

---

[1] Commerce Clearing House, *Accounting Series Releases* (July 1978), Chicago, Ill.: Commerce Clearing House Exchange Act Release No. 2707, December 5, 1940, par. 3020.
[2] New York Stock Exchange, "Independent Audit and Audit Procedures," *Accountant* 122, No. 4 (April 6, 1940), p. 383.
[3] General Motors, *1979 Proxy Statement*, p. 2.
[4] John L. Carey, "Relations of Auditors with Boards of Directors," *Journal of Accountancy* 95, No. 6 (June 1953), p. 380.

Committee of the American Institute of Certified Public Accountants recommended that publicly held corporations establish audit committees of members outside the board of directors, because "the auditors should communicate with the audit committee whenever any significant question having material bearing on the company's financial statements has not been satisfactorily resolved at the management level."[5]

During the 1970s, the role and responsibilities of audit committees in the United States received a great deal of attention because of the post-Watergate discoveries of corporate slush funds, illegal political contributions, and overseas bribes. Thus the investing public demanded greater corporate accountability to increase the confidence in the quality of financial reporting. In view of the separation of ownership and management, shareholders and other constituencies needed more assurance with respect to both the internal and external auditing processes and the financial reporting process.

In response to these demands, in March 1972 the SEC issued Accounting Series Release No. 123, "Standing Audit Committees Composed of Outside Directors," which stated in part:

> . . . [The SEC] endorses the establishment by all publicly held companies of audit committees composed of outside directors and urges the business and financial communities and all shareholders of such publicly held companies to lend their full and continuing support to the effective implementation of the above cited recommendations in order to assist in affording the greatest possible protection to investors who rely upon such financial statements.[6]

On December 20, 1974, the SEC issued Accounting Series Release No. 165, "Notice of Amendments to Require Increased Disclosure of Relationships Between Registrants and Their Independent Public Accountants," which stated in part:

> Disclosure is required of the existence and composition of the audit committee of the board of directors. The Commission has already expressed its judgment that audit committees made up of outside directors have significant benefits for the company and its shareholders (ASR 123). This disclosure will make stockholders aware of the existence and composition of the committee. If no audit or similar committee exists, the disclosure of that fact is expected to highlight its absence.[7]

---

[5]American Institute of Certified Public Accountants, "Executive Committee Statements on Audit Committees of Boards of Directors." *Journal of Accountancy* 124, No. 1 (July 1967), p. 10.
[6]Commerce Clearing House, *Accounting Series Releases* (July 1978), Exchange Act Release No. 5237, March 23, 1972, par. 3124.
[7]Ibid., Exchange Act Release No. 11147, December 20, 1974, par. 3167.

Essentially, this release not only made the disclosure of an audit committee mandatory but also emphasized the importance of selecting a committee of stature and ability.

While the SEC issued the directive in ASR No. 165, the New York Stock Exchange made the first official mandatory recognition of the need for an audit committee. More specifically, the Exchange issued an audit committee policy statement, which stated in part:

> Each domestic company with common stock listed on the Exchange, as a condition of listing and continued listing of its securities on the Exchange, shall establish no later than June 30, 1978, and maintain thereafter an Audit Committee, composed solely of directors independent of management and free from any relationship that, in the opinion of its Board of Directors, would interfere with the exercise of independent judgment as a committee member. Directors who are affiliates of the company or its subsidiaries would not be qualified for Audit Committee membership.[8]

Such a mandate for an independent oversight group enhances the reliability of the financial reporting system, which is an essential element of an efficient securities market.

With respect to American Stock Exchange companies and over-the-counter companies, the SEC found in a recent survey that 87 percent of AMEX companies and 79 percent of OTC companies have audit committees.[9] It should be noted that the AMEX did not exact the mandatory listing requirement because a significant number of their members voluntarily establish audit committees.[10] Thus the national stock exchanges have accepted the fact that a watchdog committee helps engender the integrity of a public company's financial reporting process and audit processes.

In addition to the aforementioned events, there were a series of court actions with respect to the establishment of audit committees. For example, in the Penn Central Case, the SEC emphasized the "critical importance" of the director's responsibility as well as "greater utilization of public and independent directors."[11] The Commission was pointing toward the need for an advisory committee of outside directors. The audit committee would fulfill this purpose. In the Mattel Case, the SEC sought a consent injunction against the registrant for false financial

---

[8] New York Stock Exchange, *Statement of the New York Stock Exchange on Audit Committee Policy* (January 1977), p. 1.

[9] Securities and Exchange Commission, "Analysis of Results of 1981 Proxy Statement Disclosure Monitoring Program," Title 17 *Code of Federal Regulations,* Sec. 241 (March 1982), p. 7–8.

[10] "The AMEX Board Recommends Audit Committees," *The Wall Street Journal* (December 14, 1979), p. 2, col. 2.

[11] Commerce Clearing House, *Federal Securities Law Reporter,* Chicago (1972–73, 1974–75, 1977–78 Transfer Binder), par. 78931.

reporting. The Commission charged not only that Mattel's financial statements for 1971 were overstated by $14 million in sales but also that the pretax income was overstated by $10.5 million because of inadequate accounting provisions. As a result, a court order was issued requiring Mattel to establish and maintain an audit committee.[12]

Similarly, a U.S. District Court ordered Lum's, Inc. to establish a standing audit committee because the registrant was charged with proxy fraud in connection with future acquisition of businesses.[13] Finally, in the Killearn Properties Case, the court ordered the establishment of an audit committee because the registrant failed to provide a prospectus in accordance with the securities laws. In this particular case the court outlined the specific functions for the committee, which included a review of the independent audit engagement, the internal accounting controls, the internal audit function, the code of conduct, all public releases of financial information, and the activities of the officers and directors.[14] There is little question that the court actions provided a framework for the functions of audit committees. The question of what constitutes proper standards and practices for these committees was emerging through court settlements.

Although the increase in the establishment of audit committees can be traceable to court actions, the SEC and AICPA recommendations, and the NYSE mandate, it is evident that such committees increase the awareness of boards of directors in discharging their stewardship accountability to their constituencies. Felix Pomeranz asserted that "audit committees have become the guardians of corporate morality within the existing organizational framework."[15]

In view of the legal liability of the board of directors and the SEC rule relative to the directors' signature requirement of Form 10-K, it is obvious that the audit committee must be active. For example, Ernst & Whinney (Ernst & Young) found that in a survey of 419 publicly held clients, about one-half of the companies had all directors sign the Form 10-K; 182 of the companies had a majority of directors sign the form.[16] The extent of the committee's activities depends on the complexities of the business and the quality of management. As weaknesses are disclosed, they can be monitored by the audit committee until corrections have been made. Accordingly, the committee can make inquiries of senior management personnel but need not become involved in the day-to-day management. It must be emphasized that the committee has oversight responsibility and serves in an advisory capacity to the board.

[12] Ibid., par. 94807.
[13] Ibid., par. 94504.
[14] Ibid., par. 96256.
[15] Felix Pomeranz, "How the Audit Committee Should Work," *Journal of Accounting, Auditing and Finance* 1, No. 1 (January 1977), p. 46.
[16] Ernst & Whinney, "Survey of Director's Involvement with Financial Information" (February 1982), p. 1.

In response to a rash of well-publicized cases of fraudulent financial reporting, the National Commission on Fraudulent Financial Reporting (Treadway Commission) recommended that the boards of directors of all public companies be required by SEC rule to establish audit committees composed solely of independent directors.[17] In turn, the Auditing Standards Board responded to the Treadway Commission and adopted a Statement on Auditing Standards entitled "Communication with Audit Committees." The major objective of this standard is to ensure communication of the results of the audit to the audit committee.[18] In addition, the National Association of Securities Dealers (NASD), for its National Market System (NMS) companies,[19] and the American Stock Exchange[20] have adopted requirements for the establishment of audit committees as a condition of listing. More recently, the U.S. Congress adopted banking reform legislation (FDIC Improvement Act of 1991) that included provisions mandating the establishment of independent audit committees.

In Canada, several legislative acts have called for the establishment of audit committees. For example, the Ontario Business Corporation Act (1979) mandates that a corporation is legally required to submit its financial statements to its audit committee before such statements are submitted to the board of directors. Nelson Luscombe notes in an interview with Alan J. Dilworth, former chairman of Touche Ross, Canada, that the MacDonald Commission (1988) in Canada is calling for an expanded scope of the audit committee's work.[21] The major objective is to foster a constructive relationship between the audit committee, the internal and external auditors, and management so that all parties fulfill their financial reporting responsibilities.[22]

Moreover, although such committees are not legally required in the United Kingdom, but are required by law in Australia, the boards of directors of certain publicly held corporations in these countries have, voluntarily or involuntarily, formed audit committees to meet the changing regulatory requirements and finan-

---

[17]*Report of the National Commission on Fraudulent Financial Reporting,* (Washington, D.C.: National Commission on Fraudulent Financial Reporting, 1987), p. 40.

[18]*Statement on Auditing Standards, No. 61,* "Communication with Audit Committees" (New York: American Institute of Certified Public Accountants), par. 1.

[19]National Association of Securities Dealers, *NASD Manual* (Chicago, Ill.: Commerce Clearing House, 1987), Part III, section (d) of schedule D of the NASD bylaws.

[20]American Stock Exchange, *American Stock Exchange Guide,* vol. 2 (Chicago, Ill.: Commerce Clearing House, 1993), Sec. 121, "Independent Directors."

[21]Nelson Luscombe, "More Power to Audit Committees," *CA Magazine* 122, No. 5 (May 1989), p. 27.

[22]See the *Report of the Commission to Study the Public's Expectations of Audits* (The Macdonald Commission), published by the Canadian Institute of Chartered Accountants, for further discussion. Also see the *Canadian Securities Administrators Notice on Audit Committees* (1990), which is a general mandate to achieve uniformity of the policies of Canada's provincial securities commissions.

cial reporting needs of shareholders and others.[23] For example, Linda English found that nonexecutive directors of companies in Australia can stand up to forceful CEOs and thereby monitor and discipline management's actions. Such nonexecutive directors need to implement institutional arrangements that will ensure corporate accountability to the stockholders. English concluded that audit committees are the answer for the nonexecutive directors' problem.[24]

Similarly, the Committee on the Financial Aspects of Corporate Governance (Cadbury Committee) in the United Kingdom (1992) has issued a report that includes a *Code of Best Practice*. The Committee recommended that the boards of all listed companies registered in the United Kingdom establish and maintain audit committees. The code stated, in part:

> There should be a minimum of three members. Membership should be confined to the nonexecutive directors of the company and a majority of the nonexecutives serving on the committee should be independent.[25]

As discussed in the Preface, the motivation and rationale for the presence of audit committees in both developed and emerging equity markets has become widespread in the corporate governance arena. Exhibit B.1 summarizes the requirements and/or recommendations for audit committees of publicly held companies by country.[26]

In sum, over the past two decades there has been an evolutionary process in the development of the role and responsibilities of audit committees. Their role has evolved into an independent oversight responsibility for the audit processes and the financial reporting process. Although management is responsible for the integrity of the financial statements, the board of directors has overall responsibility for the financial reporting disclosures because of its fiduciary responsibility to the shareholders. Accordingly, the audit committee is responsible for assuring the full board that management fulfills its responsibilities in the preparation of financial statements. For example, a review of the proxy statement of any U.S. corporation that is subject to the periodic reporting requirements of the Securities Act of 1934 reveals many of the normal functions of audit committees. Such

---

[23] Louis Braiotta, Jr., "An Inquiry into the Operational Effectiveness of Corporate Audit Committees," *Proceedings of the American Accounting Association's Western Regional Meeting* (San Francisco, CA: American Accounting Association, April 28–30, 1983), p. 18.

[24] Linda English, "Non-Executive Directors," *Australian Accountant* (November 1989), p. 41.

[25] The Committee on the Financial Aspects of Corporate Governance, *The Code of Best Practice* (London, England: Gee and Co., 1992), p. 10. As a follow-up to the Cadbury Committee's report, see Christy Chapman, "Cadbury II Begins Work," *Internal Auditor* 53, No. 2 (April 1996), p. 9.

[26] For further discussion, see Louis Braiotta, Jr., "An Exploratory Study of Adopting Requirements for Audit Committees in International Capital Markets," *Advances in International Accounting,* vol. 11 (Stamford, Conn.: JAI Press, 1998), pp. 169–187.

Exhibit B.1 Summary of Requirements and/or Recommendations for Audit Committees of Companies listed on Stock Exchange(s) by Country

Country	Reference
Australia	Working Group on Corporate Practices and Conduct (Borsch Committee), *Corporate Practices and Conduct,* 1990.
Canada	The Bank Act; The Trust and Loan Companies Act, and the Insurance Company Act, 1992, Canadian Business Corporation Act 1975, Commission to Study the Public's Expectations of Audits (MacDonald Commission) 1988, Canadian Securities Administrators Notice on Audit Committees 1990, *Auditing and Related Service Guidelines,* "Commission with Audit Committees," 1991.
France	1995 Vienot Report on Corporate Governance.
Hong Kong	Hong Kong Society of CPAs and The Stock Exchange of Hong Kong, Amendments to Appendix 14 of its Listing Rules, May 1998.
India	Confederation of Indian Industry, Desirable Corporate Governance in India, A Code, Recommendation No. 8, 1997.
Israel	Israeli Companies Ordinance (New Version) 5743-1983, Section 96-15.
Malaysia	Kuala Lumpur Stock Exchange 1995 and Companies Act 1995.
Netherlands	1995 Peters Report on Corporate Governance.
New Zealand	Institute of Directors' *1992 Draft Code of Practice for Boards of Directors.*
Saudi Arabia	Ministry of Commerce (for joint stock companies) regulations 1994.
Singapore	Companies Act of 1989.
South Africa	Johananburg Stock Exchange *Listed Companies Manual,* 1989; King Committee Report on Corporate Governance, Code of Corporate Practices and Conduct, 1994.
Thailand	Stock Exchange of Thailand 1999.
United Kingdom	Recommendations of a Working Party Established by the Institute of Chartered Accountants of Scotland, *Corporate Governance—Directors' Responsibilities for Financial Statements,* 1992; The Committee on the Financial Aspects of Corporate Governance, *The Code of Best Practice* (Cadbury Committee) 1992; *Statement of Auditing Standards 610,* "Reports to Directors of Management," 1995. Committee on Corporate Governance, *The Combined Code: Principles of Good Governance and Code of Best Practice,* 1998.
United States	American Law Institute, *Principles of Corporate Governance: Analysis and Recommendations,* 1994.
	American Stock Exchange Guide, Vol. 2, Sec. 121, 1993.
	FDIC Improvement Act of 1991.

(*continued*)

Exhibit B.1 (*Continued*)

Country	Reference
United States	Connecticut General Statutes, Sec. 33-318 (b) (1) and (b) (2).
	Statement on Auditing Standards No. 61 "Communication with Audit Committees," 1988.
	COCO Report—"Internal Control—Integrated Framework" 1992.
	National Association of Securities Dealers, *NASD Manual,* Part III, Section (d) of Schedule D of the NASD bylaws, 1987.
	New York Stock Exchange Listed Company, 1993.
	Public Oversight Board, *A Special Report by the Public Oversight Board of the SEC Practice Section,* AICPA, 1993.
	Report of the National Commission on Fraudulent Financial Reporting (Treadway Commission) 1987.
	Statement on Internal Auditing Standards No. 7, "Communication with the Board of Directors" 1989.
	U.S. Federal Sentencing Commission, *Federal Sentencing Guidelines for Organizations,* 1991.

functions usually include reviewing the engagement of the external auditors, reviewing the scope of internal and external audit plans, reviewing the internal audit department, and reviewing the adequacy of the corporation's system of internal accounting control.[27] This particular action on the part of the audit committee is important because it enables the committee not only to reinforce the independence of the external auditors from management—and thereby enhance the quality of the company's financial reporting practices—but also to detect key problem areas that may impair the company's integrity and securities in the financial community. Thus the audit committee's review process causes both management and the external auditors to take a more aggressive strategy for corrective action. Clearly, the benefits of such committees outweigh the costs of potential legal liability to the board of directors.[28]

[27]General Motors, *1992 Proxy Statement,* p. 6.

[28]For a more detailed discussion of audit committees in certain countries, see Rocco R. Vanasco, "The Audit Committee: An International Perspective," *Managerial Auditing Journal* 9, No. 8 (1994), pp. 18–42; and *The Audit Committee: An International Perspective* (Altamonte Springs, Fla.: Institute of Internal Auditors, 1994); Price Waterhouse, *Improving Audit Committee Performance: What Works Best* (Altamonte Springs, Fla.: Institute of Internal Auditors, 1993); Linda English, "Making Audit Committees Work," *Australian Accountant* 64, No. 3 (April 1994), pp. 10–18; Brenda Porter and Philip Gendall, "Audit Committees: Panacea for Failure," *Chartered Accountants Journal of New Zealand* 74, No. 5 (June 1995), pp. 28–31; Etienne Barbier, "Audit Committees ala Francaise," *Internal Auditor* 55, No. 3 (June 1998), pp. 77–80; International Task Force on Corporate Governance, *Who Holds the Reins?* (London: International Capital Markets Group, 1995).

Section 182 of the Business Corporations Act—Ontario, Canada

182 (1) The directors of a corporation that is offering its securities to the public shall elect annually from among their number a committee to be known as the audit committee to be composed of not fewer than three directors, of whom a majority shall not be officers or employees of the corporation of an affiliate of the corporation, to hold office until the next annual meeting of the shareholders.

(2) The members of the audit committee shall elect a chairman from among their members.

(3) The corporation shall submit the financial statement to the audit committee for its review and the financial statement shall thereafter be submitted to the board of directors.

(4) The auditor has the right to appear before and be heard at any meeting of the audit committee and shall appear before the audit committee when required to do so by the committee.

(5) Upon the request of the auditor, the chairman of the audit committee shall convene a meeting of the committee to consider any matters the auditor believes should be brought to the attention of the directors of shareholders.

Foreign Corrupt Practices Act Amendments[1]

SEC. 5001. SHORT TITLE.

This part may be cited as the "Foreign Corrupt Practices Act Amendments of 1988."

SEC. 5002. PENALTIES FOR VIOLATIONS OF ACCOUNTING STANDARDS.

Section 13(b) of the Securities Exchange Act of 1934 (15 U.S.C. 78m(b)) is amended by adding at the end thereof the following:

"(4) No criminal liability shall be imposed for failing to comply with the requirements of paragraph (2) of this subsection except as provided in paragraph (5) of this subsection.

"(5) No person shall knowingly circumvent or knowingly fail to implement a system of internal accounting controls or knowingly falsify any book, record, or account described in paragraph (2).

"(6) Where an issuer which has a class of securities registered pursuant to section 12 of this title or an issuer which is required to file reports pursuant to section 15(d) of this title holds 50 per centum or less of the voting power with respect to a domestic or foreign firm, the provisions of paragraph (2) require only that the issuer proceed in good faith to use its influence, to the extent reasonable under the issuer's circumstances, to cause such domestic or foreign firm to devise and

---

[1]The amendments are contained in Title V of Public Law No. 100-418, August 23, 1988. The material contained in this text excludes section 104, which deals with domestic concerns.

maintain a system of internal accounting controls consistent with paragraph (2). Such circumstances include the relative degree of the issuer's ownership of the domestic or foreign firm and the laws and practices governing the business operations of the country in which such firm is located. An issuer which demonstrates good faith efforts to use such influence shall be conclusively presumed to have complied with the requirements of paragraph (2).

"(7) For the purpose of paragraph (2) of this subsection, the terms 'reasonable assurances' and 'reasonable detail' mean such level of detail and degree of assurance as would satisfy prudent officials in the conduct of their own affairs."

SEC. 5003. FOREIGN CORRUPT PRACTICES ACT AMENDMENTS.

(a) PROHIBITED TRADE PRACTICES BY ISSUERS.—Section 30A of the Securities Exchange Act of 1934 (15 U.S.C. 78dd-1) is amended to read as follows:

"PROHIBITED FOREIGN TRADE PRACTICES BY ISSUERS"

"Sec. 30A. (a) PROHIBITION—It shall be unlawful for any issuer which has a class of securities registered pursuant to section 12 of this title or which is required to file reports under section 15(d) of this title, or for any officer, director, employee, or agent of such issuer or any stockholder thereof acting on behalf of such issuer, to make use of the mails or any means or instrumentality of interstate commerce corruptly in furtherance of an offer, payment, promise to pay, or authorization of the payment of any money, or offer, gift, promise to give, or authorization of the giving of anything of value to—

"(1) any foreign official for purposes of—

"(A)(i) influencing any act or decision of such foreign official in his official capacity, or (ii) inducing such foreign official to do or omit to do any act in violation of the lawful duty of such official, or

"(B) inducing such foreign official to use his influence with a foreign government or instrumentality thereof to affect or influence any act or decision of such government or instrumentality,

in order to assist such issuer in obtaining or retaining business for or with, or directing business to, any person;

"(2) any foreign political party or official thereof or any candidate for foreign political office for purposes of—

"(A)(i) influencing any act or decision of such party, official, or candidate in its or his official capacity, or (ii) inducing such party, official, or candidate to do or omit to do an act in violation of the lawful duty of such party, official, or candidate,

"(B) inducing such party, official, or candidate to use its or his influence with a foreign government or instrumentality thereof to affect or influence any act or decision of such government or instrumentality, in order to assist such issuer in obtaining or retaining business for or with, or directing business to, any person; or

"(3) any person, while knowing that all or a portion of such money or thing of value will be offered, given, or promised, directly or indirectly, to any foreign official, to any foreign political party or official thereof, or to any candidate for foreign political office, for purposes of—

"(A)(i) influencing any act of decision of such foreign official, political party, party official, or candidate in his or its official capacity, or (ii) inducing such foreign official, political party, party official, or candidate to do or omit to do any act in violation of the lawful duty of such foreign official, political party, party official, or candidate, or

"(B) inducing such foreign official, political party, party official, or candidate to use his or its influence with a foreign government or instrumentality thereof to affect or influence any act or decision of such government or instrumentality,

in order to assist such issuer in obtaining or retaining business for or with, or directing business to, any person.

"(b) EXCEPTION FOR ROUTINE GOVERNMENTAL ACTION.—Subsection (a) shall not apply to any facilitating or expediting payment to a foreign official, political party, or party official the purpose of which is to expedite or to secure the performance of a routine governmental action by a foreign official, political party, or party official.

"(c) AFFIRMATIVE DEFENSES.—It shall be an affirmative defense to actions under subsection (a) that—

"(1) the payment, gift, offer, or promise of anything of value that was made, was lawful under the written laws and regulations of the foreign official's, political party's, party official's, or candidate's country; or

"(2) the payment, gift, offer, or promise of anything of value that was made, was a reasonable and bona fide expenditure, such as travel and lodging expenses, incurred by or on behalf of a foreign official, party, party official, or candidate and was directly related to—

"(A) the promotion, demonstration, or explanation of products or services; or

"(B) the execution or performance of a contract with a foreign government or agency thereof.

"(d) GUIDELINES BY THE ATTORNEY GENERAL.—Not later than one year after the date of the enactment of the Foreign Corrupt Practices Act Amendments of 1988, the Attorney General, after consultation with the Commission, the Secretary of Commerce, the United States Trade Representative, the Secretary of State, and the Secretary of the Treasury, and after obtaining the views of all interested persons through public notice and comment procedures, shall determine to what extent compliance with this section would be enhanced and the business community would be assisted by further clarification of the preceding provisions of this section and may, based on such determination and to the extent necessary and appropriate, issue—

"(1) guidelines describing specific types of conduct, associated with common types of export sales arrangements and business contracts, which for purposes of the Department of Justice's present enforcement policy, the Attorney General determines would be in conformance with the preceding provisions of this section; and

"(2) general precautionary procedures which issuers may use on a voluntary basis to conform their conduct to the Department of Justice's present enforcement policy regarding the preceding provisions of this section.

The Attorney General shall issue the guidelines and procedures referred to in the preceding sentence in accordance with the provisions of subchapter II of chapter 5 of title 5, United States Code, and those guidelines and procedures shall be subject to the provisions of chapter 7 of that title.

"(e) OPINIONS OF THE ATTORNEY GENERAL.—(1) The Attorney General, after consultation with appropriate departments and agencies of the United States and after obtaining the views of all interested persons through public notice and comment procedures, shall establish a procedure to provide responses to specific inquiries by issuers concerning conformance of their conduct with the Department of Justice's present enforcement policy regarding the preceding provisions of this section. The Attorney General shall, within 30 days after receiving such a request, issue an opinion in response to that request. The opinion shall state whether or not certain specified prospective conduct would, for purposes of the Department of Justice's present enforcement policy, violate the preceding provisions of this section. Additional requests for opinions may be filed with the Attorney General regarding other specified prospective conduct that is beyond the scope of conduct specified in previous requests. In any action brought under the applicable provisions of this section, there shall be a rebuttable presumption that conduct, which is specified in a request by an issuer and for which the Attorney General has issued an opinion that such conduct is in conformity with the Department of Justice's present enforcement policy, is in compliance with the preceding provisions of this section. Such a presumption may be rebutted by a preponderance of the evidence. In considering the presumption for purposes of this paragraph, a court shall weigh all relevant factors, including but not limited to whether the information submitted to the Attorney General was accurate and complete and whether it was within the scope of the conduct specified in any request received by the Attorney General. The Attorney General shall establish the procedure required by this paragraph in accordance with the provisions of subchapter II of chapter 5 of title 5, United States Code, and that procedure shall be subject to the provisions of chapter 7 of that title.

"(2) Any document or other material which is provided to, received by, or prepared in the Department of Justice or any other department or agency of the United States in connection with a request by an issuer under the procedure established under paragraph (1), shall be exempt from disclosure under section 552 of title 5, United States Code, and shall not, except with the consent of the issuer, be made publicly available, regardless of whether the Attorney General responds to such a request or the issuer withdraws such request before receiving a response.

"(3) Any issuer who has made a request to the Attorney General under paragraph (1) may withdraw such request prior to the time the Attorney General issues an opinion in response to such request. Any request so withdrawn shall have no force or effect.

"(4) The Attorney General shall, to the maximum extent practicable, provide timely guidance concerning the Department of Justice's present enforcement policy with respect to the preceding provisions of this section to potential exporters and small businesses that are unable to obtain specialized counsel on issues pertaining to such provisions. Such guidance shall be limited to responses to requests under paragraph (1) concerning conformity of specified prospective conduct with the Department of Justice's present enforcement policy regarding the preceding provisions of this section and general explanations of compliance responsibilities and of potential liabilities under the preceding provisions of this section.

"(f) DEFINITIONS.—For purposes of this section:

"(1) The term 'foreign official' means any officer or employee of a foreign government or any department, agency, or instrumentality thereof, or any person acting in an official capacity for or on behalf of any such government or department, agency, or instrumentality.

"(2)(A) A person's state of mind is 'knowing' with respect to conduct, a circumstance, or a result if—

"(i) such person is aware that such person is engaging in such conduct, that such circumstance exists, or that such result is substantially certain to occur; or

"(ii) such person has a firm belief that such circumstance exists or that such result is substantially certain to occur.

"(B) When knowledge of the existence of a particular circumstance is required for an offense, such knowledge is established if a person is aware of a high probability of the existence of such circumstance, unless the person actually believes that such circumstance does not exist.

"(3)(A) The term 'routine governmental action' means only an action which is ordinarily and commonly performed by a foreign official in—

"(i) obtaining permits, licenses, or other official documents to qualify a person to do business in a foreign country;

"(ii) processing governmental papers, such as visas and work orders;

"(iii) providing police protection, mail pick-up and delivery, or scheduling inspections associated with contract performance or inspections related to transit of goods across country;

"(iv) providing phone service, power and water supply, loading and unloading cargo, or protecting perishable products or commodities from deterioration; or

"(v) actions of a similar nature.

"(B) The term 'routine governmental action' does not include any decision by a foreign official whether, or on what terms, to award new business to or to continue business with a particular party, or any action taken by a foreign official involved in the decisionmaking process to encourage a decision to award new business to or continue business with a particular party."

(b) VIOLATIONS.—Section 32(c) of the Securities Exchange Act of 1934 (15 U.S.C. 78ff) is amended to read as follows:

"(c)(1)(A) Any issuer that violates section 30A(a) shall be fined not more than $2,000,000.

"(B) Any issuer that violates section 30A(a) shall be subject to a civil penalty of not more than $10,000 imposed in an action brought by the Commission.

"(2)(A) Any officer or director of an issuer, or stockholder acting on behalf of such issuer, who willfully violates section 30A(a) shall be fined not more than $100,000, or imprisoned not more than 5 years, or both.

"(B) Any employee or agent of an issuer who is a United States citizen, national, or resident or is otherwise subject to the jurisdiction of the United States (other than an officer, director, or stockholder acting on behalf of such issuer), and who willfully violates section 30A(a), shall be fined not more than $100,000, or imprisoned not more than 5 years, or both.

"(C) Any officer, director, employee, or agent of an issuer, or stockholder acting on behalf of such issuer, who violates section 30A(a) shall be subject to a civil penalty of not more than $10,000 imposed in an action brought by the Commission.

"(3) Whenever a fine is imposed under paragraph (2) upon any officer, director, employee, agent, or stockholder of an issuer, such fine may not be paid, directly or indirectly, by such issuer."

(c) PROHIBITED TRADE PRACTICES BY DOMESTIC CONCERNS.—Section 104 of the Foreign Corrupt Practices Act of 1977 (15 U.S.C. 78dd-2).

Federal Deposit Insurance Corporation Improvement Act[1]

SEC. 112. INDEPENDENT ANNUAL AUDITS OF INSURED DEPOSITORY INSTITUTIONS.

(a) IN GENERAL.—The Federal Deposit Insurance Act (12 U.S.C. 1811 et seq.) is amended by adding at the end the following new section:

"SEC. 36. EARLY IDENTIFICATION OF NEEDED IMPROVEMENTS IN FINANCIAL MANAGEMENT.

"(a) ANNUAL REPORT ON FINANCIAL CONDITION AND MANAGEMENT.—

"(1) REPORT REQUIRED.—Each insured depository institution shall submit an annual report to the Corporation, the appropriate Federal banking agency, and any appropriate State bank supervisor (including any State bank supervisor of a host State).

"(2) CONTENTS OF REPORT.—Any annual report required under paragraph (1) shall contain—

"(A) the information required to be provided by—

"(i) the institution's management under subsection (b); and

"(ii) an independent public accountant under subsections (c) and (d); and

"(B) such other information as the Corporation and the appropriate Federal banking agency may determine to be necessary to assess the financial condition and management of the institution.

---

[1]The act is contained in Title 1 of Public Law No. 102-242 December 19, 1991.

"(3) PUBLIC AVAILABILITY.—Any annual report required under paragraph (1) shall be available for public inspection.

"(b) MANAGEMENT RESPONSIBILITY FOR FINANCIAL STATEMENTS AND INTERNAL CONTROLS.—Each insured depository institution shall prepare—

"(1) annual financial statements in accordance with generally accepted accounting principles and such other disclosure requirements as the Corporation and the appropriate Federal banking agency may prescribe; and

"(2) a report signed by the chief executive officer and the chief accounting or financial officer of the institution which contains—

"(A) a statement of the management's responsibilities for—

"(i) preparing financial statements;

"(ii) establishing and maintaining an adequate internal control structure and procedures for financial reporting; and

"(iii) complying with the laws and regulations relating to safety and soundness which are designated by the Corporation or the appropriate Federal banking agency; and

"(B) an assessment, as of the end of the institution's most recent fiscal year, of—

"(i) the effectiveness of such internal control structure and procedures; and

"(ii) the institution's compliance with the laws and regulations relating to safety and soundness which are designated by the Corporation and the appropriate Federal banking agency.

"(c) INTERNAL CONTROL EVALUATION AND REPORTING REQUIREMENTS FOR INDEPENDENT PUBLIC ACCOUNTANTS.—

"(1) IN GENERAL.—With respect to any internal control report required by subsection (b)(2) of any institution, the institution's independent public account shall attest to, and report separately on, the assertions of the institution's management contained in such report.

"(2) ATTESTATION REQUIREMENTS.—Any attestation pursuant to paragraph (1) shall be made in accordance with generally accepted standards for attestation engagements.

"(d) ANNUAL INDEPENDENT AUDITS OF FINANCIAL STATEMENTS.—

"(1) AUDITS REQUIRED.—The Corporation, in consultation with the appropriate Federal banking agencies, shall prescribe regulations requiring that each insured depository institution shall have an annual independent audit made of the institution's financial statements by an independent public accountant in accordance with generally accepted auditing standards and section 37.

"(2) SCOPE OF AUDIT.—In connection with any audit under this subsection, the independent public accountant shall determine and report whether the financial statements of the institution—

"(A) are presented fairly in accordance with generally accepted accounting principles; and

"(B) comply with such other disclosure requirements as the Corporation and the appropriate Federal banking agency may prescribe.

"(3) REQUIREMENTS FOR INSURED SUBSIDIARIES OF HOLDING COMPANIES.— The requirements for an independent audit under this subsection may be satisfied for insured depository institutions that are subsidiaries of a holding company by an independent audit of the holding company.

"(e) DETECTING AND REPORTING VIOLATIONS OF LAWS AND REGULATIONS.—

"(1) IN GENERAL.—An independent public accountant shall apply procedures agreed upon by the Corporation to objectively determine the extent of the compliance of any insured depository institution or depository institution holding company with laws and regulations designated by the Corporation, in consultation with the appropriate Federal banking agencies.

"(2) ATTESTATION REQUIREMENTS.—Any attestation pursuant to paragraph (1) shall be made in accordance with generally accepted standards for attestation engagements.

"(f) FORM AND CONTENT OF REPORTS AND AUDITING STANDARDS.—

"(1) IN GENERAL.—The scope of each report by an independent public accountant pursuant to this section, and the procedures followed in preparing such report, shall meet or exceed the scope and procedures required by generally accepted auditing standards and other applicable standards recognized by the Corporation.

"(2) CONSULTATION.—The Corporation shall consult with the other appropriate Federal banking agencies in implementing this subsection.

"(g) IMPROVED ACCOUNTABILITY.—

"(1) INDEPENDENT AUDIT COMMITTEE.—

"(A) ESTABLISHMENT.—Each insured depository institution (to which this section applies) shall have an independent audit committee entirely made up of outside directors who are independent of management of the institution, and who satisfy any specific requirements the Corporation may establish.

"(B) DUTIES.—An independent audit committee's duties shall include reviewing with management and the independent public accountant the basis for the reports issued under subsections (b)(2), (c), and (d).

"(C) CRITERIA APPLICABLE TO COMMITTEES OF LARGE INSURED DEPOSITORY INSTITUTIONS.—In the case of each insured depository institution which the Corporation determines to be a large institution, the audit committee required by subparagraph (A) shall—

"(i) include members with banking or related financial management expertise;

"(ii) have access to the committee's own outside counsel; and

"(iii) not include any large customers of the institution.

"(2) REVIEW OF QUARTERLY REPORTS OF LARGE INSURED DEPOSITORY INSTITUTIONS.—

"(A) IN GENERAL.—In the case of any insured depository institution which the Corporation has determined to be a large institution, the Corporation may require the independent public accountant retained by such institution to perform reviews of the institution's quarterly financial reports in accordance with procedures agreed upon by the Corporation.

"(B) REPORT TO AUDIT COMMITTEE.—The independent public accountant referred to in subparagraph (A) shall provide the audit committee of the insured depository institution with reports on the reviews under such subparagraph and the audit committee shall provide such reports to the Corporation, any appropriate Federal banking agency, and any appropriate State bank supervisor.

"(C) LIMITATION ON NOTICE.—Reports provided under subparagraph (B) shall be only for the information and use of the insured depository institution, the Corporation, any appropriate Federal banking agency, and any State bank supervisor that received the report.

"(3) QUALIFICATIONS OF INDEPENDENT PUBLIC ACCOUNTANTS.—

"(A) IN GENERAL.—All audit services required by this section shall be performed only by an independent public accountant who—

"(i) has agreed to provide related working papers, policies, and procedures to the Corporation, an appropriate Federal banking agency, and any State bank supervisor, if requested; and

"(ii) has received a peer review that meets guidelines acceptable to the Corporation.

"(B) REPORTS ON PEER REVIEWS.—Reports on peer reviews shall be filed with the Corporation and made available for public inspection.

"(4) ENFORCEMENT ACTIONS.—

"(A) IN GENERAL.—In addition to any authority contained in section 8, the Corporation or an appropriate Federal banking agency may remove, suspend, or bar an independent public accountant, upon a showing of good cause, from performing audit services required by this section.

"(B) JOINT RULEMAKING.—The appropriate Federal banking agencies shall jointly issue rules of practice to implement this paragraph.

"(5) NOTICE BY ACCOUNTANT OF TERMINATION OF SERVICES.—Any independent public accountant performing an audit under this section who subsequently ceases to be the accountant for the institution shall promptly notify the Corporation pursuant to such rules as the Corporation shall prescribe.

"(h) EXCHANGE OF REPORTS AND INFORMATION.—

"(1) REPORT TO THE INDEPENDENT AUDITOR.—

"(A) IN GENERAL.—Each insured depository institution which has engaged the services of an independent auditor to audit such institution shall transmit to the auditor a copy of the most recent report of condition made by the institution (pursuant to this Act or any other provision of law) and a copy of the most recent report of examination received by the institution.

"(B) ADDITIONAL INFORMATION.—In addition to the copies of the reports required to be provided under subparagraph (A), each insured depository institution shall provide the auditor with—

"(i) a copy of any supervisory memorandum of understanding with such institution and any written agreement between such institution and any appropriate Federal banking agency or any appropriate State bank supervisor which is in effect during the period covered by the audit; and

"(ii) a report of—

"(I) any action initiated or taken by the appropriate Federal banking agency or the Corporation during such period under subsection (a), (b), (c), (e), (g), (i), (s), or (t) of section 8;

"(II) any action taken by any appropriate State bank supervisor under State law which is similar to any action referred to in subclause (I); or

"(III) any assessment of any civil money penalty under any other provision of law with respect to the institution or any institution-affiliated party.

"(2) REPORTS TO BANKING AGENCIES.—

"(A) INDEPENDENT AUDITOR REPORTS.—Each insured depository institution shall provide to the Corporation, any appropriate Federal banking agency, and any appropriate State bank supervisor, a copy of each audit report and any qualification to such report, any management letter, and any other report within 15 days of receipt of any such report, qualification, or letter from the institution's independent auditors.

"(B) NOTICE OF CHANGE OF AUDITOR.—Each insured depository institution shall provide written notification to the Corporation, the appropriate Federal banking agency, and any appropriate State bank supervisor of the resignation or dismissal of the institution's independent auditor or the engagement of a new independent auditor by the institution, including a statement of the reasons for such change within 15 calendar days of the occurrence of the event.

"(i) REQUIREMENTS FOR INSURED SUBSIDIARIES OF HOLDING COMPANIES.—Except with respect to any audit requirements established under or pursuant to subsection (d), the requirements of this section may be satisfied for insured depository institutions that are subsidiaries of a holding company, if—

"(1) services and functions comparable to those required under this section are provided at the holding company level; and

"(2) either—

"(A) the institution has total assets, as of the beginning of such fiscal year, of less than $5,000,000,000; or

"(B) the institution—

"(i) has total assets, as of the beginning of such fiscal year, of more than $5,000,000,000 and less than $9,000,000,000; and

"(ii) has a CAMEL composite rating of 1 or 2 under the Uniform Financial Institutions Rating System (or an equivalent rating by any such agency under a comparable rating system) as of the most recent examination of such institution by the Corporation or the appropriate Federal banking agency.

"(j) EXEMPTION FOR SMALL DEPOSITORY INSTITUTIONS.—This section shall not apply with respect to any fiscal year of any insured depository institution the total assets of which, as of the beginning of such fiscal year, are less than the greater of—

"(1) $150,000,000; or

"(2) such amount (in excess of $150,000,000) as the Corporation may prescribe by regulation."

(b) EFFECTIVE DATE.—The requirements established by the amendment made by subsection (a) shall apply with respect to fiscal years of insured depository institutions which begin after December 31, 1992.

SEC. 121. ACCOUNTING OBJECTIVES, STANDARDS, AND REQUIREMENTS.

(a) IN GENERAL.—The Federal Deposit Insurance Act (12 U.S.C. 1811 et seq.) is amended by inserting after section 36 (as added by section 112 of this title) the following new section:

"SEC. 37. ACCOUNTING OBJECTIVES, STANDARDS, AND REQUIREMENTS.

"(a) In General.—

"(1) Objectives.—Accounting principles applicable to reports or statements required to be filed with Federal banking agencies by insured depository institutions should—

"(A) result in financial statements and reports of condition that accurately reflect the capital of such institutions;

"(B) facilitate effective supervision of the institutions; and

"(C) facilitate prompt corrective action to resolve the institutions at the least cost to the insurance funds.

"(2) Standards.—

"(A) Uniform accounting principles consistent with gaap.—Subject to the requirements of this Act and any other provision of Federal law, the accounting principles applicable to reports or statements required to be filed with Federal banking agencies by all insured depository institutions shall be uniform and consistent with generally accepted accounting principles.

"(B) Stringency.—If the appropriate Federal banking agency or the Corporation determines that the application of any generally accepted accounting principle to any insured depository institution is inconsistent with the objectives described in paragraph (1), the agency or the Corporation may, with respect to reports or statements required to be filed with such agency or Corporation, prescribe an accounting principle which is applicable to such institutions which is no less stringent than generally accepted accounting principles.

"(3) Review and implementation of accounting principles required.—Before the end of the 1-year period beginning on the date of the enactment of the Federal Deposit Insurance Corporation Improvement Act of 1991, each appropriate Federal banking agency shall take the following actions:

"(A) Review of accounting principles.—Review—

"(i) all accounting principles used by depository institutions with respect to reports or statements required to be filed with a Federal banking agency;

"(ii) all requirements established by the agency with respect to such accounting procedures; and

"(iii) the procedures and format for reports to the agency, including reports of condition.

"(B) MODIFICATION OF NONCOMPLYING MEASURES.—Modify or eliminate any accounting principle or reporting requirement of such Federal agency which the agency determines fails to comply with the objectives and standards established under paragraphs (1) and (2).

"(C) INCLUSION OF 'OFF BALANCE SHEET' ITEMS.—Develop and prescribe regulations which require that all assets and liabilities, including contingent assets and liabilities, of insured depository institutions be reported in, or otherwise taken into account in the preparation of any balance sheet, financial statement, report of condition, or other report of such institution, required to be filed with a Federal banking agency.

"(D) MARKET VALUE DISCLOSURE.—Develop jointly with the other appropriate Federal banking agencies a method for insured depository institutions to provide supplemental disclosure of the estimated fair market value of assets and liabilities, to the extent feasible and practicable, in any balance sheet, financial statement, report of condition, or other report of any insured depository institution required to be filed with a Federal banking agency.

"(b) UNIFORM ACCOUNTING OF CAPITAL STANDARDS.—

"(1) IN GENERAL.—Each appropriate Federal banking agency shall maintain uniform accounting standards to be used for determining compliance with statutory or regulatory requirements of depository institutions.

"(2) TRANSITION PROVISION.—Any standards in effect on the date of the enactment of the Federal Deposit Insurance Corporation Improvement Act of 1991 under section 1215 of the Financial Institutions Reform, Recovery, and Enforcement Act of 1989 shall continue in effect after such date of enactment until amended by the appropriate Federal banking agency under paragraph (1).

"(c) REPORTS TO BANKING COMMITTEES.—

"(1) ANNUAL REPORTS REQUIRED.—Each appropriate Federal banking agency shall annually submit a report to the Committee on Banking, Finance and Urban Affairs of the House of Representatives and the Committee on Banking, Housing, and Urban Affairs of the Senate containing a description of any difference between any accounting or capital standard used by such agency and any accounting or capital standard used by any other agency.

"(2) EXPLANATION OF REASONS FOR DISCREPANCY.—Each report submitted under paragraph (1) shall contain an explanation of the reasons for any discrepancy between any accounting or capital standard used by such agency and any accounting or capital standard used by any other agency.

"(3) PUBLICATION.—Each report under this subsection shall be published in the Federal Register."

(b) REPEAL OF PROVISION SUPERSEDED BY SUBSECTION (a) AMENDMENTS.—Section 1215 of the Financial Institutions Reform, Recovery, and Enforcement Act of 1989 (12 U.S. C. 1833d) is hereby repealed.

Excerpt from *The Code of Best Practice*[1]

The Committee's recommendations on audit committees are as follows:

(a) They should be formally constituted as subcommittees of the main board to whom they are answerable and to whom they should report regularly; they should be given written terms of reference which deal adequately with their membership, authority, and duties; and they should normally meet at least twice a year.

(b) There should be a minimum of three members. Membership should be confined to the nonexecutive directors of the company, and a majority of the nonexecutives serving on the committee should be independent of the company, as defined in paragraph 2.2 of the Code.

(c) The external auditor and, where an internal audit function exists, the head of internal audit should normally attend committee meetings, as should the finance director. Other board members should also have the right to attend.

(d) The audit committee should have a discussion with the auditors at least once a year, without executive board members present, to ensure that there are no unresolved issues of concern.

(e) The audit committee should have explicit authority to investigate any matters within its terms of reference, the resources which it needs to do so, and full access to information. The committee should be able to obtain outside professional advice and if necessary to invite outsiders with relevant experience to attend meetings.

(f) Membership of the committee should be disclosed in the annual report, and the chairman of the committee should be available to answer questions about its work at the Annual General Meeting.

[1]The Committee on the Financial Aspects of Corporate Governance (Cadbury Committee), *The Code of Best Practice* (London: Gee and Co., 1992), pp. 10–11.

Exhibit F.1 Excerpt from Part 2 Code of Best Practice[a]

D. ACCOUNTABILITY AND AUDIT

D.1 Financial Reporting

Principle The board should present a balanced and understandable assessment of the company's position and
prospects.

Code Provisions

D.1.1 The directors should explain their responsibility for preparing the
accounts and there should be a statement by the auditors about
their reporting responsibilities.

D.1.2 The board's responsibility to present a balanced and understandable assessment extends to interim and other price-sensitive
public reports and reports to regulators as well as to information
required to be presented by statutory requirements.

D.1.3 The directors should report that the business is a going concern,
with supporting assumptions or qualifications as necessary.

D.2 Internal Control

Principle The board should maintain a sound system of
internal control to safeguard shareholders' investment and
the company's assets.

Code Provisions

D.2.1 The directors should, at least annually, conduct a review of the
effectiveness of the group's system of internal controls and
should report to shareholders that they have done so. The review
should cover all controls, including financial, operational and
compliance controls and risk management.

D.2.2 Companies which do not have an internal audit function should
from time to time review the need for one.

D.3 Audit Committee and Auditors

Principle The board should establish formal and transparent arrangements for considering how they should apply the financial reporting and internal control principles and for maintaining an appropriate relationship with the company's auditors.

Code Provisions

D.3.1 The board should establish an audit committee of at least three directors, all non-executive, with written terms of reference which deal clearly with its authority and duties. The members of the committee, a majority of whom should be independent non-executive directors, should be named in the report and accounts.

D.3.2 The duties of the audit committee should include keeping under review the scope and results of the audit and its cost effectiveness and the independence and objectivity of the auditors. Where the auditors also supply a substantial volume of non-audit services to the company, the committee should keep the nature and extent of such services under review, seeking to balance the maintenance of objectivity and value for money.

[a]Committee on Corporate Governance *The Combined Code: Principles of Good Governance and Code of Best Practice* (London: Gee and Co., 1998), pp. 11–12.

Model Business Corporation Act— Chapter 8: Directors and Officers[1]

Subchapter A.
BOARD OF DIRECTORS

§8.01. REQUIREMENT FOR AND DUTIES OF BOARD OF DIRECTORS

(a)   Except as provided in section 7.32, each corporation must have a board of directors.

(b)   All corporate powers shall be exercised by or under the authority of, and the business and affairs of the corporation managed under the direction of, its board of directors, subject to any limitation set forth in the articles of incorporation or in an agreement authorized under section 7.32.

§8.02. QUALIFICATIONS OF DIRECTORS

The articles of incorporation or bylaws may prescribe qualifications for directors. A director need not be a resident of this state or a shareholder of the corporation unless the articles of incorporation or bylaws so prescribe.

---

[1]Adopted by the Committee on Corporate Laws of the Section of Business Law with the support of the American Bar Foundation (Chicago, Ill.: American Bar Association, 1994). The material contained in this text excludes the official comments and statutory cross-references revised through 1998 as well as Subchapter D, Officers, Subchapter E, Indemnification, and Subchapter F, Directors' Conflicting Interest Transactions.

§8.03. NUMBER AND ELECTION OF DIRECTORS

(a)   A board of directors must consist of one or more individuals, with the number specified in or fixed in accordance with the articles of incorporation or bylaws.

(b)   If a board of directors has power to fix or change the number of directors, the board may increase or decrease by 30 percent or less the number of directors last approved by the shareholders, but only the shareholders may increase or decrease by more than 30 percent the number of directors last approved by the shareholders.

(c)   The articles of incorporation or bylaws may establish a variable range for the size of the board of directors by fixing a minimum and maximum number of directors. If a variable range is established, the number of directors may be fixed or changed from time to time, within the minimum and maximum, by the shareholders or the board of directors. After shares are issued, only the shareholders may change the range for the size of the board or change from a fixed to a variable-range size board or vice versa.

(d)   Directors are elected at the first annual shareholders' meeting and at each annual meeting thereafter unless their terms are staggered under section 8.06.

§8.04. ELECTION OF DIRECTORS BY CERTAIN CLASSES OF SHAREHOLDERS

If the articles of incorporation authorize dividing the shares into classes, the articles may also authorize the election of all or a specified number of directors by the holders of one or more authorized classes of shares. A class (or classes) of shares entitled to elect one or more directors is a separate voting group for purposes of the election of directors.

§8.05. TERMS OF DIRECTORS GENERALLY

(a)   The terms of the initial directors of a corporation expire at the first shareholders' meeting at which directors are elected.

(b)   The terms of all other directors expire at the next annual shareholders' meeting following their election unless their terms are staggered under section 8.06.

(c)   A decrease in the number of directors does not shorten an incumbent director's term.

(d) The term of a director elected to fill a vacancy expires at the next share-holders' meeting at which directors are elected.

(e) Despite the expiration of a director's term, he continues to serve until his successor is elected and qualified or until there is a decrease in the number of directors.

§8.06. STAGGERED TERMS FOR DIRECTORS

If there are nine or more directors, the articles of incorporation may provide for staggering their terms by dividing the total number of directors into two or three groups, with each group containing one-half or one-third of the total, as near as may be. In that event, the terms of directors in the first group expire at the first annual shareholders' meeting after their election, the terms of the second group expire at the second annual shareholders' meeting after their election, and the terms of the third group, if any, expire at the third annual shareholders' meeting after their election. At each annual shareholders' meeting held thereafter, directors shall be chosen for a term of two years or three years, as the case may be, to succeed those whose terms expire.

§8.07. RESIGNATION OF DIRECTORS

(a) A director may resign at any time by delivering written notice to the board of directors, its chairman, or to the corporation.

(b) A resignation is effective when the notice is delivered unless the notice specifies a later effective date.

§8.08. REMOVAL OF DIRECTORS BY SHAREHOLDERS

(a) The shareholders may remove one or more directors with or without cause unless the articles of incorporation provide that directors may be removed only for cause.

(b) If a director is elected by a voting group of shareholders, only the share-holders of that voting group may participate in the vote to remove him.

(c) If cumulative voting is authorized, a director may not be removed if the number of votes sufficient to elect him under cumulative voting is voted against his removal. If cumulative voting is not authorized, a director may be removed only if the number of votes cast to remove him exceeds the number of votes cast not to remove him.

(d)   A director may be removed by the shareholders only at a meeting called for the purpose of removing him and the meeting notice must state that the purpose, or one of the purposes, of the meeting is removal of the director.

§8.09.   REMOVAL OF DIRECTORS BY JUDICIAL PROCEEDING

(a)   The [name or describe] court of the county where a corporation's principal office (or, if none in this state, its registered office) is located may remove a director of the corporation from office in a proceeding commenced either by the corporation or by its shareholders holding at least 10 percent of the outstanding shares of any class if the court finds that (1) the director engaged in fraudulent or dishonest conduct, or gross abuse of authority or discretion, with respect to the corporation and (2) removal is in the best interest of the corporation.

(b)   The court that removes a director may bar the director from reelection for a period prescribed by the court.

(c)   If shareholders commence a proceeding under subsection (a), they shall make the corporation a party defendant.

§8.10.   VACANCY ON BOARD

(a)   Unless the articles of incorporation provide otherwise, if a vacancy occurs on a board of directors, including a vacancy resulting from an increase in the number of directors:

(1)   the shareholders may fill the vacancy;

(2)   the board of directors may fill the vacancy; or

(3)   if the directors remaining in office constitute fewer than a quorum of the board, they may fill the vacancy by the affirmative vote of a majority of all the directors remaining in office.

(b)   If the vacant office was held by a director elected by a voting group of shareholders, only the holders of shares of that voting group are entitled to vote to fill the vacancy if it is filled by the shareholders.

(c)   A vacancy that will occur at a specific later date (by reason of a resignation effective at a later date under section 8.07(b) or otherwise) may be filled before the vacancy occurs but the new director may not take office until the vacancy occurs.

§8.11.   COMPENSATION OF DIRECTORS

Unless the articles of incorporation or bylaws provide otherwise, the board of directors may fix the compensation of directors.

Subchapter B.
MEETINGS AND ACTION OF THE BOARD

§8.20.   MEETINGS

(a)   The board of directors may hold regular or special meetings in or out of this state.

(b)   Unless the articles of incorporation or bylaws provide otherwise, the board of directors may permit any or all directors to participate in a regular or special meeting by, or conduct the meeting through the use of, any means of communication by which all directors participating may simultaneously hear each other during the meeting. A director participating in a meeting by this means is deemed to be present in person at the meeting.

§8.21.   ACTION WITHOUT MEETING

(a)   Unless the articles of incorporation or bylaws provide otherwise, action required or permitted by this Act to be taken at a board of directors' meeting may be taken without a meeting if the action is taken by all members of the board. The action must be evidenced by one or more written consents describing the action taken, signed by each director, and included in the minutes or filed with the corporate records reflecting the action taken.

(b)   Action taken under this section is effective when the last director signs the consent, unless the consent specifies a different effective date.

(c)   A consent signed under this section has the effect of a meeting vote and may be described as such in any document.

§8.22.   NOTICE OF MEETING

(a)   Unless the articles of incorporation or bylaws provide otherwise, regular meetings of the board of directors may be held without notice of the date, time, place, or purpose of the meeting.

(b)   Unless the articles of incorporation or bylaws provide for a longer or shorter period, special meetings of the board of directors must be preceded by at least two days' notice of the date, time, and place of the meeting. The notice need not describe the purpose of the special meeting unless required by the articles of incorporation or bylaws.

§8.23. WAIVER OF NOTICE

(a)   A director may waive any notice required by this Act, the articles of incorporation, or bylaws before or after the date and time stated in the notice. Except as provided by subsection (b), the waiver must be in writing, signed by the director entitled to the notice, and filed with the minutes or corporate records.

(b)   A director's attendance at or participation in a meeting waives any required notice to him of the meeting unless the director at the beginning of the meeting (or promptly upon his arrival) objects to holding the meeting or transacting business at the meeting and does not thereafter vote for or assent to action taken at the meeting.

§8.24. QUORUM AND VOTING

(a)   Unless the articles of incorporation or bylaws require a greater number or unless otherwise specifically provided in this Act, a quorum of a board of directors consists of:

   (1)   a majority of the fixed number of directors if the corporation has a fixed board size; or

   (2)   a majority of the number of directors prescribed, or if no number is prescribed the number in office immediately before the meeting begins, if the corporation has a variable-range size board.

(b)   The articles of incorporation or bylaws may authorize a quorum of a board of directors to consist of no fewer than one-third of the fixed or prescribed number of directors determined under subsection (a).

(c)   If a quorum is present when a vote is taken, the affirmative vote of a majority of directors present is the act of the board of directors unless the articles of incorporation or bylaws require the vote of a greater number of directors.

(d)   A director who is present at a meeting of the board of directors or a committee of the board of directors when corporate action is taken is deemed to have assented to the action taken unless: (1) he objects at the beginning of the meeting (or promptly upon his arrival) to holding it or transacting business at the meeting; (2) his dissent or abstention from the action taken is entered in the minutes of the meeting; or (3) he delivers written notice of his dissent or abstention to the presiding officer of the meeting before its adjournment or to the corporation immediately after adjournment of the meeting. The right of dissent or abstention is not available to a director who votes in favor of the action taken.

§8.25. COMMITTEES

(a) Unless the articles of incorporation or bylaws provide otherwise, a board of directors may create one or more committees and appoint members of the board of directors to serve on them. Each committee must have two or more members, who serve at the pleasure of the board of directors.

(b) The creation of a committee and appointment of members to it must be approved by the greater of (1) a majority of all the directors in office when the action is taken or (2) the number of directors required by the articles of incorporation or bylaws to take action under section 8.24.

(c) Sections 8.20 through 8.24, which govern meetings, action without meetings, notice and waiver of notice, and quorum and voting requirements of the board of directors, apply to committees and their members as well.

(d) To the extent specified by the board of directors or in the articles of incorporation or bylaws, each committee may exercise the authority of the board of directors under section 8.01.

(e) A committee may not, however:

(1) authorize distributions;

(2) approve or propose to shareholders action that this Act requires be approved by shareholders;

(3) fill vacancies on the board of directors or on any of its committees;

(4) amend articles of incorporation pursuant to section 10.02;

(5) adopt, amend, or repeal bylaws;

(6) approve a plan of merger not requiring shareholder approval;

(7) authorize or approve reacquisition of shares, except according to a formula or method prescribed by the board of directors; or

(8) authorize or approve the issuance or sale or contract for sale of shares, or determine the designation and relative rights, preferences, and limitations of a class or series of shares, except that the board of directors may authorize a committee (or a senior executive officer of the corpo-

ration) to do so within limits specifically prescribed by the board of directors.

(f)   The creation of, delegation of authority to, or action by a committee does not alone constitute compliance by a director with the standards of conduct described in section 8.30.

Subchapter C.
STANDARDS OF CONDUCT

§8.30.   GENERAL STANDARDS FOR DIRECTORS

(a)   A director shall discharge his duties as a director, including his duties as a member of a committee:

　　(1) in good faith;

　　(2) with the care an ordinarily prudent person in a like position would exercise under similar circumstances; and

　　(3) in a manner he reasonably believes to be in the best interests of the corporation.

(b)   In discharging his duties a director is entitled to rely on information, opinions, reports, or statements, including financial statements and other financial data, if prepared or presented by:

　　(1) one or more officers or employees of the corporation whom the director reasonably believes to be reliable and competent in the matters presented;

　　(2) legal counsel, public accountants, or other persons as to matters the director reasonably believes are within the person's professional or expert competence; or

　　(3) a committee of the board of directors of which he is not a member if the director reasonably believes the committee merits confidence.

(c)   A director is not acting in good faith if he has knowledge concerning the matter in question that makes reliance otherwise permitted by subsection (b) unwarranted.

(d)   A director is not liable for any action taken as a director, or any failure to take any action, if he performed the duties of his office in compliance with this section.

§8.31. [RESERVED]

The text of §8.31 of the 1984 Model Act is printed and discussed in the Annotation to §8.60.

§8.32. [RESERVED]

§8.33. LIABILITY FOR UNLAWFUL DISTRIBUTIONS

(a) A director who votes for or assents to a distribution made in violation of section 6.40 or the articles of incorporation is personally liable to the corporation for the amount of the distribution that exceeds what could have been distributed without violating section 6.40 or the articles of incorporation if it is established that he did not perform his duties in compliance with section 8.30. In any proceeding commenced under this section, a director has all of the defenses ordinarily available to a director.

(b) A director held liable under subsection (a) for an unlawful distribution is entitled to contribution:

    (1) from every other director who could be held liable under subsection (a) for the unlawful distribution; and

    (2) from each shareholder for the amount the shareholder accepted knowing the distribution was made in violation of section 6.40 or the articles of incorporation.

(c) A proceeding under this section is barred unless it is commenced within two years after the date on which the effect of the distribution was measured under section 6.40(e) or (g).

Committee of Sponsoring Organizations of the Treadway Commission, *Internal Control-Integrated Framework—Volume I, Executive Summary*[1]

EXECUTIVE SUMMARY

Senior executives have long sought ways to better control the enterprises they run. Internal controls are put in place to keep the company on course toward profitability goals and achievement of its mission, and to minimize surprises along the way. They enable management to deal with rapidly changing economic and competitive environments, shifting customer demands and priorities, and restructuring for future growth. Internal controls promote efficiency, reduce risk of asset loss, and help ensure the reliability of financial statements and compliance with laws and regulations.

Because internal control serves many important purposes, there are increasing calls for better internal control systems and report cards on them. Internal control is looked upon more and more as a solution to a variety of potential problems.

---

[1]Reprinted with permission from *Internal Control-Integrated Framework*, Copyright © 1992 by the Committee of Sponsoring Organizations of the Treadway Commission. It should be noted that the three additional volumes may be obtained from the American Institute of Certified Public Accountants. See Appendix N.

What Internal Control Is

Internal control means different things to different people. This causes confusion among businesspeople, legislators, regulators and others. Resulting miscommunication and different expectations cause problems within an enterprise. Problems are compounded when the term, if not clearly defined, is written into law, regulation or rule.

This report deals with the needs and expectations of management and others. It defines and describes internal control to:

- Establish a common definition serving the needs of different parties
- Provide a standard against which business and other entities—large or small, in the public or private sector, for profit or not—can assess their control systems and determine how to improve them

Internal control is broadly defined as a process, effected by an entity's board of directors, management and other personnel, designed to provide reasonable assurance regarding the achievement of objectives in the following categories:

- Effectiveness and efficiency of operations
- Reliability of financial reporting
- Compliance with applicable laws and regulations

The first category addresses an entity's basic business objectives, including performance and profitability goals and safeguarding of resources. The second relates to the preparation of reliable published financial statements, including interim and condensed financial statements and selected financial data derived from such statements, such as earnings releases, reported publicly. The third deals with complying with those laws and regulations to which the entity is subject. These distinct but overlapping categories address different needs and allow a directed focus to meet the separate needs.

Internal control systems operate at different levels of effectiveness. Internal control can be judged effective in each of the three categories, respectively, if the board of directors and management have reasonable assurance that:

- They understand the extent to which the entity's operations objectives are being achieved.
- Published financial statements are being prepared reliably.
- Applicable laws and regulations are being complied with.

While internal control is a process, its effectiveness is a state or condition of the process at one or more points in time.

Internal control consists of five interrelated components. These are derived from the way management runs a business, and are integrated with the management process. Although the components apply to all entities, small and midsize companies may implement them differently than large ones. Its controls may be less formal and less structured, yet a small company can still have effective internal control. The components are:

- *Control Environment*—The control environment sets the tone of an organization, influencing the control consciousness of its people. It is the foundation for all other components of internal control, providing discipline and structure. Control environment factors include the integrity, ethical values and competence of the entity's people; management's philosophy and operating style; the way management assigns authority and responsibility, and organizes and develops its people; and the attention and direction provided by the board of directors.

- *Risk Assessment*—Every entity faces a variety of risks from external and internal sources that must be assessed. A precondition to risk assessment is establishment of objectives, linked at different levels and internally consistent. Risk assessment is the identification and analysis of relevant risks to achievement of the objectives, forming a basis for determining how the risks should be managed. Because economic, industry, regulatory and operating conditions will continue to change, mechanisms are needed to identify and deal with the special risks associated with change.

- *Control Activities*—Control activities are the policies and procedures that help ensure management directives are carried out. They help ensure that necessary actions are taken to address risks to achievement of the entity's objectives. Control activities occur throughout the organization, at all levels and in all functions. They include a range of activities as diverse as approvals, authorizations, verifications, reconciliations, reviews of operating performance, security of assets and segregation of duties.

- *Information and Communication*—Pertinent information must be identified, captured and communicated in a form and timeframe that enables people to carry out their responsibilities. Information systems produce reports, containing operational, financial and compliance-related information, that make it possible to run and control the business. They deal not only with internally generated data, but also information about external events, activities and conditions necessary to informed business decision-making and external reporting. Effective communication also must occur in a broader sense, flowing down, across and up to the organization. All personnel must receive a clear message from top management that control responsibilities must be taken seriously. They must understand their own role in the internal control system, as well as how individual activities relate to the work of others. They must have a means of communicating significant information upstream. There also needs to be effective communication with external parties, such as customers, suppliers, regulators and shareholders.

- *Monitoring*—Internal control systems need to be monitored—a process that assesses the quality of the system's performance over time. This is accomplished through ongoing monitoring activities, separate evaluations or a combination of the two. Ongoing monitoring occurs in the course of operations. It includes regular management and supervisory activities, and other actions personnel take in performing their duties. The scope and frequency of separate evaluations will depend primarily on an assessment of risks and the effectiveness of ongoing monitoring procedures. Internal control deficiencies should be reported upstream, with serious matters reported to top management and the board.

There is synergy and linkage among these components, forming an integrated system that reacts dynamically to changing conditions. The internal control system is intertwined with the entity's operating activities and exists for fundamental business reasons. Internal control is most effective when controls are built into the entity's infrastructure and are a part of the essence of the enterprise. "Built in" controls support quality and empowerment initiatives, avoid unnecessary costs and enable quick response to changing conditions.

There is a direct relationship between the three categories of objectives, which are what an entity strives to achieve, and components, which represent what is needed to achieve the objectives. All components are relevant to each objectives category. When looking at any one category—the effectiveness and efficiency of operations, for instance—all five components must be present and functioning effectively to conclude that internal control over operations is effective.

The internal control definition—with its underlying fundamental concepts of a process, effected by people, providing reasonable assurance—together with the categorization of objectives and the components and criteria for effectiveness, and the associated discussions, constitute this internal control framework.

What Internal Control Can Do

Internal control can help an entity achieve its performance and profitability targets, and prevent loss of resources. It can help ensure reliable financial reporting. And it can help ensure that the enterprise complies with laws and regulations, avoiding damage to its reputation and other consequences. In sum, it can help an entity get to where it wants to go, and avoid pitfalls and surprises along the way.

What Internal Control Cannot Do

Unfortunately, some people have greater, and unrealistic, expectations. They look for absolutes, believing that:

- Internal control can ensure an entity's success—that is, it will ensure achievement of basic business objectives or will, at the least, ensure survival.

  Even effective internal control can only *help* an entity achieve these objectives. It can provide management information about the entity's progress, or lack of it, toward their achievement. But internal control cannot change an inherently poor manager into a good one. And, shifts in government policy or programs, competitors' actions or economic conditions can be beyond management's control. Internal control cannot ensure success, or even survival.

- Internal control can ensure the reliability of financial reporting and compliance with laws and regulations.

  This belief is also unwarranted. An internal control system, no matter how well conceived and operated, can provide only reasonable—not absolute—assurance to management and the board regarding achievement of an entity's objectives. The likelihood of achievement is affected by limitations inherent in all internal control systems. These include the realities that judgments in decision making can be faulty, and that breakdowns can occur because of simple error or mistake. Additionally, controls can be circumvented by the collusion of two or more people, and management has the ability to override the system. Another limiting factor is that the design of an internal control system must reflect the fact that there are resource constraints, and the benefits of controls must be considered relative to their costs.

Thus, while internal control can help an entity achieve its objectives, it is not a panacea.

Roles and Responsibilities

Everyone in an organization has responsibility for internal control.

- *Management*—The chief executive officer is ultimately responsible and should assume "ownership" of the system. More than any other individual, the chief executive sets the "tone at the top" that affects integrity and ethics and other factors of a positive control environment. In a large company, the chief executive fulfills this duty by providing leadership and direction to senior managers and reviewing the way they're controlling the business. Senior managers, in turn, assign responsibility for establishment of more specific internal control policies and procedures to personnel responsible for the unit's functions. In a smaller entity, the influence of the chief executive, often an owner-manager, is usually more direct. In any event, in a cascading responsibility, a manager is effectively a chief executive of his or her sphere of responsibility. Of particular significance are financial officers and their staffs, whose control activities cut across, as well as up and down, the operating and other units of an enterprise.

- *Board of Directors*—Management is accountable to the board of directors, which provides governance, guidance and oversight. Effective board members are objective, capable and inquisitive. They also have a knowledge of the entity's activities and environment, and commit the time necessary to fulfill their board responsibilities. Management may be in a position to override controls and ignore or stifle communications from subordinates, enabling a dishonest management which intentionally misrepresents results to cover its tracks. A strong, active board, particularly when coupled with effective upward communications channels and capable financial, legal and internal audit functions, is often best able to identify and correct such a problem.

- *Internal Auditors*—Internal auditors play an important role in evaluating the effectiveness of control systems, and contribute to ongoing effectiveness. Because of organizational position and authority in an entity, an internal audit function often plays a significant monitoring role.

- *Other Personnel*—Internal control is, to some degree, the responsibility of everyone in an organization and therefore should be an explicit or implicit part of everyone's job description. Virtually all employees produce information used in the internal control system or take other actions needed to effect control. Also, all personnel should be responsible for communicating upward problems in operations, noncompliance with the code of conduct, or other policy violations or illegal actions.

A number of external parties often contribute to achievement of an entity's objectives. External auditors, bringing an independent and objective view, contribute directly through the financial statement audit and indirectly by providing information useful to management and the board in carrying out their responsibilities. Others providing information to the entity useful in effecting internal control are legislators and regulators, customers and others transacting business with the enterprise, financial analysts, bond raters and the news media. External parties, however, are not responsible for, nor are they a part of, the entity's internal control system.

Organization of this Report

This report is in four volumes. The first is this *Executive Summary,* a high-level overview of the internal control framework directed to the chief executive and other senior executives, board members, legislators and regulators.

The second volume, the *Framework,* defines internal control, describes its components and provides criteria against which managements, boards or others can assess their control systems. The *Executive Summary* is included.

The third volume, *Reporting to External Parties,* is a supplemental document providing guidance to those entities that report publicly on internal control over preparation of their published financial statements, or are contemplating doing so.

The fourth volume, *Evaluation Tools,* provides materials that may be useful in conducting an evaluation of an internal control system.

What to Do

Actions that might be taken as a result of this report depend on the position and role of the parties involved:

- *Senior Management*—Most senior executives who contributed to this study believe they are basically "in control" of their organizations. Many said, however, that there are areas of their company—a division, a department or a control component that cuts across activities—where controls are in early stages of development or otherwise need to be strengthened. They do not like surprises. This study suggests that the chief executive initiate a self-assessment of the control system. Using this framework, a CEO, together with key operating and financial executives, can focus attention where needed. Under one approach, the chief executive could proceed by bringing together business unit heads and key functional staff to discuss an initial assessment of control. Directives would be provided for those individuals to discuss this report's concepts with their lead personnel, provide oversight of the initial assessment process in their areas of responsibility and report back findings. Another approach might involve an initial review of corporate and business unit policies and internal audit programs. Whatever its form, an initial self-assessment should determine whether there is a need for, and how to proceed with, a broader, more in-depth evaluation. It should also ensure that ongoing monitoring processes are in place. Time spent in evaluating internal control represents an investment, but one with a high return.
- *Board Members*—Members of the board of directors should discuss with senior management the state of the entity's internal control system and provide oversight as needed. They should seek input from the internal and external auditors.
- *Other Personnel*—Managers and other personnel should consider how their control responsibilities are being conducted in light of this framework, and discuss with more senior personnel ideas for strengthening control. Internal auditors should consider the breadth of their focus on the internal control

system, and may wish to compare their evaluation materials to the evaluation tools.

- *Legislators and Regulators*—Government officials who write or enforce laws recognize that there can be misconceptions and different expectations about virtually any issue. Expectations for internal control vary widely in two respects. First, they differ regarding what control systems can accomplish. As noted, some observers believe internal control systems will, or should, prevent economic loss, or at least prevent companies from going out of business. Second, even when there is agreement about what internal control systems can and can't do, and about the validity of the "reasonable assurance" concept, there can be disparate views of what that concept means and how it will be applied. Corporate executives have expressed concern regarding how regulators might construe public reports asserting "reasonable assurance" in hindsight after an alleged control failure has occurred. Before legislation or regulation dealing with management reporting on internal control is acted upon, there should be agreement on a common internal control framework, including limitations of internal control. This framework should be helpful in reaching such agreement.

- *Professional Organizations*—Rule-making and other professional organizations providing guidance on financial management, auditing and related topics should consider their standards and guidance in light of this framework. To the extent diversity in concept and terminology is eliminated, all parties will benefit.

- *Educators*—This framework should be the subject of academic research and analysis, to see where future enhancements can be made. With the presumption that this report becomes accepted as a common ground for understanding, its concepts and terms should find their way into university curricula.

We believe this report offers a number of benefits. With this foundation for mutual understanding, all parties will be able to speak a common language and communicate more effectively. Business executives will be positioned to assess control systems against a standard, and strengthen the systems and move their enterprises toward established goals. Future research can be leveraged off an established base. Legislators and regulators will be able to gain an increased understanding of internal control, its benefits and limitations. With all parties utilizing a common internal control framework, these benefits will be realized.

Example of a Code of Business Conduct— Some Broad Guidelines[1]

A LETTER FROM THE CHAIRMAN

Dear Colleague:

Despite the fact that our industry, our business and our jobs are changing rapidly, the Business Conduct Guidelines have changed little—until now.

What follows is a major revision of this document. It recognizes some of the things many of you have been seeing: the fierce competition and the importance of using all of the advantages IBM has because of its size and scale, to name a few. At the same time, we all continue to be responsible and accountable for exercising good judgment and for acting ethically.

Ethical behavior is important in its own right. However, it is also good for our business because it fosters one of our greatest assets—customer loyalty. So take the time to read these guidelines and continue to live, with pride, by the code of ethical conduct that has served us so well.

Louis V. Gerstner, Jr.
Chairman & Chief Executive Officer

May 1995

---

[1]International Business Machines, *Business Conduct Guidelines* (New York: International Business Machines, 1995). The material contained in this text excludes pp. 10–23.

INTRODUCTION

In IBM, the Chief Executive Officer and senior executives are responsible for setting standards of business ethics and overseeing compliance with these standards. It is the individual responsibility of each IBM employee to comply with these standards.

As IBM employees, we frequently encounter a variety of ethical and legal questions. We should decide these questions in ways which are consistent with IBM's basic values and principles. IBM expects all employees to obey the law and to act ethically. IBM's Business Conduct Guidelines provide general guidance for resolving a variety of legal and ethical questions for employees of IBM and its subsidiaries. Employees who work in marketing and specialized areas such as government procurement and regulatory matters (e.g., environmental, export, tax and customs) must also comply with additional functional guidelines.

Our industry continues to undergo significant changes. As a whole, these changes make the ways in which we do business more complex. Because of the continuing need to reassess and clarify our practices, the contents of these Guidelines will be kept online and updated as required.

Each section of these Guidelines covers an area in which we have responsibilities to IBM as employees:

- Personal conduct and protection of IBM's assets
- Obligations in conducting IBM's business with other people and organizations
- Conflicts of interest and other considerations affecting IBM that may arise on our own time

Because rapid changes in our industry constantly present new ethical and legal issues, no set of guidelines should be considered the absolute last word under all circumstances. If you have any questions about interpreting or applying these Guidelines—or about guidelines and procedures published by IBM or its operating units, subsidiaries or specific functions—it is your responsibility to consult your manager or IBM counsel. A violation of any IBM guidelines can result in disciplinary action, including dismissal.

YOU AND YOUR JOB IN IBM

Communications Channels

If you know of an unlawful or unethical situation, you should immediately tell IBM whatever you know or have heard about it; you can do so in one of several ways. Contacting your manager is the best place to start, but you can also contact IBM counsel, use the "Speak Up" program or "Open Door" to higher management. IBM will promptly review your report of unlawful or unethical conduct, and IBM will not tolerate threats or acts of retaliation against you for making that report.

Personal Conduct

IBM's reputation for integrity and business ethics should never be taken for granted. To maintain that reputation, you must follow all of IBM's business conduct guidelines and exercise good judgment in your decisions and actions. It's no exaggeration to say that IBM's integrity and reputation are in your hands.

If IBM management finds that your conduct on or off the job adversely affects your performance, that of other employees, or IBM's legitimate business interests, you will be subject to disciplinary measures, including dismissal.

Work Environment

IBM strives to maintain a healthy, safe and productive work environment which is free from discrimination or harassment based on race, color, religion, sex, sexual orientation, age, national origin, disability, veteran status, membership or an application for membership in a uniformed service, such as the military or a public health service, or other factors that are unrelated to IBM's legitimate business interests. IBM will not tolerate sexual advances, actions, comments or any other conduct in the workplace that creates, in the judgment of IBM management, an intimidating or otherwise offensive environment. Similarly, the use of racial or religious slurs—or any other remarks, jokes or conduct that, in the judgment of IBM management, encourages or permits an offensive work environment—will not be tolerated.

If you believe that you are subject to such conduct, you should let IBM know through any of IBM's communication channels. Your complaint of such conduct will be reviewed promptly. Employees who are found to have engaged in harassment or discrimination, or to have misused their positions of authority in this regard, will be subject to disciplinary measures, including dismissal.

Other conduct that is prohibited because of its adverse impact on the work environment includes: (1) threats; (2) violent behavior; (3) the possession of weapons of any type; (4) the use of recording devices for other than management approved purposes; and (5) the use, distribution, sale or possession of illegal drugs or any other controlled substance, except for approved medical purposes. In addition, employees should not be on IBM premises or in the IBM work environment if they are under the influence of or affected by illegal drugs, controlled substances used for non-medical purposes or alcoholic beverages. Consumption of alcoholic beverages on IBM premises is only permitted, with prior management approval, for company-sponsored events.

Employee Privacy

IBM and IBM authorized companies and individuals collect and maintain personal information which relates to your employment, including medical and benefit information. Access to such information is restricted to people with a need to know. Personal information is normally released to outside parties only with employee approval, except that IBM and authorized companies and individuals may also release personal information to verify employment, to satisfy the legitimate requirements of a company or other entity which is considering acquiring some of IBM's business operations, or for appropriate investigatory, business or legal reasons. Employees who have access to personal information must ensure that the information is not disclosed in violation of IBM's policies or practices.

Personal items, messages or information that you consider private should not be placed or kept anywhere in the IBM workplace, such as in telephone systems, office systems, desks, credenzas, lockers, or offices. IBM management has the right to access those areas and any other IBM furnished facilities. Additionally, in order to protect its employees and assets, IBM may ask to search an employee's personal property, including briefcases and bags, located on or being removed from IBM locations; the employee is expected to cooperate with such a request. Employees, however, should not access another employee's work space, including electronic files, without prior approval from management.

Protecting IBM's Assets

IBM has a large variety of assets. Many are of great value to IBM's competitiveness and success as a business. They include our physical assets and our extremely valuable proprietary information, such as IBM's intellectual property and IBM confidential information.

Protecting all of these assets is critical. Their loss, theft or misuse jeopardizes the future of IBM.

You are personally responsible for protecting IBM property entrusted to you and for helping to protect the company's assets in general. To do this, you should be aware of and understand IBM's security procedures. You should be alert to any situations or incidents that could lead to the loss, misuse or theft of company property. You should report all such situations to the security department or your manager as soon as they come to your attention.

What types of assets should you be concerned about protecting? And what are your responsibilities in this regard?

Physical Assets   IBM's physical assets, such as equipment, systems, facilities, corporate charge cards and supplies, must be used only for conducting IBM's business or for purposes authorized by management.

Internal IBM Information Systems   The increasing reliance placed on internal information and communications facilities in carrying out IBM business makes it absolutely essential to ensure their integrity. Like other IBM assets, these facilities and the information they make available through a wide variety of databases should be used only for conducting IBM business or for purposes authorized by management. Their unauthorized use, whether or not for personal gain, is a misappropriation of IBM assets. It is your responsibility to make sure that each use you make of any IBM system is authorized and proper.

Proprietary Information   IBM proprietary information is any information that is owned by IBM. Much, but not all, IBM proprietary information is confidential. It may also be subject to copyright, patent or other intellectual property or legal rights. Proprietary information includes such things as: IBM's technical or scientific information relating to current and future products, services or research; business or marketing plans or projections; earnings and other financial data; personnel information including executive and organizational changes; and software.

IBM's proprietary information is the result of the ideas and hard work of many of your fellow employees and of substantial investments by IBM in planning, research and development. This information, particularly IBM confidential information, gives IBM a competitive advantage in the marketplace, and IBM would be damaged if its competitors discovered it.

The value of IBM's proprietary information is well known not only to IBM's competitors, but also to others in the industry, such as security analysts, members of the press, and consultants. IBM would be harmed by unauthorized disclosures of its proprietary information to, or the unauthorized use of that information by, any of those people. For example, unauthorized disclosure of an unannounced IBM product can hurt IBM by giving competitors more time to match our product. Another example is unauthorized disclosure of an unannounced executive or organizational change which can adversely affect employee morale and can interfere with IBM's plans.

As an IBM employee, you will have access to information that IBM considers proprietary. Given the widespread interest in IBM and the increasingly competitive nature of the industry, you will probably come into contact with someone who is interested in acquiring IBM proprietary information. It is critical that you do not disclose or distribute that information except as authorized by IBM and that you follow all IBM safeguards for protecting that information.

Inadvertent Disclosure   You should be careful to avoid the inadvertent disclosure of proprietary information.

To avoid inadvertent disclosure, never discuss with any unauthorized person proprietary information that IBM considers confidential or which IBM has not made public. Furthermore, you should not discuss such information even with authorized IBM employees if you are in the presence of others who are not authorized—for example, at a trade show reception or in a public area, such as an airplane, or when using a cellular or wireless telephone or an electronic bulletin board or database. You should also not discuss such information with family members or with friends, who might innocently or unintentionally pass the information on to someone else.

Finally, keep in mind that a harmful disclosure may start with the smallest leak of bits of information. Fragments of information you disclose may be pieced together with fragments from other sources to form a fairly complete picture.

Direct Requests for Information and Contacts with the Press, Analysts, and Others IBM's business activities are monitored closely by reporters, consultants and securities analysts. You should not initiate contact with these individuals or groups or respond to their inquiries without authorization as follows:

- Reporters—IBM Communications
- Consultants—IBM Consultant Relations
- Securities Analysts—IBM Investor Relations

Similarly, if you receive a request for information on IBM's business from an attorney, investigator or law enforcement official, you should refer the request to an IBM attorney. If you do not know what functional area a questioner should be referred to, ask your manager.

Using Proprietary Information Besides your obligation to protect IBM proprietary information from unauthorized disclosure or distribution, you are also required as an employee to use such information only in connection with IBM's business. This obligation applies whether or not you developed the information yourself, and it applies by law in virtually all countries where IBM does business.

IBM Intellectual Property Rights When you joined IBM, you were required to sign an agreement under which you, as an employee of IBM, assumed specific obligations relating to intellectual property as well as the treatment of confidential information. Among other things in the agreement, you assign to IBM all of your right, title, and interest in intellectual property you develop when you are employed in certain capacities, such as a managerial, technical, product planning, programming, scientific or other professional capacity. The intellectual property you assign includes such things as ideas, inventions, computer programs and documents which relate to IBM's actual or anticipated business, research or development or that are suggested by, or result from, work or tasks you perform for, or on behalf of, IBM. Subject to the laws of each country, this obligation applies no matter where or when—at work or after hours—such intellectual property is created. That intellectual property must be reported to IBM, and the property must be protected like any other proprietary information of the company. However, if you believe that your idea, invention or computer program neither falls within the area of IBM's actual or anticipated business interests, nor resulted from, nor was suggested by, any of your work assignments in IBM, you should discuss it with your local intellectual property law department. Throughout your IBM employment, you should seek advice and direction from your local intellectual property law department before you file for a patent. You should provide that department with copies of any patent you have applied for or obtained.

Leaving IBM If you leave the company for any reason, including retirement, you must return all IBM property, including documents and media which contain IBM proprietary information, and you may not disclose or use IBM proprietary information, including IBM confidential information. Also, IBM's ownership of intellectual property that you created while you were an IBM employee continues after you leave the company.

Legal Remedies Regrettably, there have been significant cases in which IBM's physical or intellectual property assets have been wrongfully taken or misused. In some of these instances, IBM has not limited its response to disciplinary action against offending employees, but has taken legal action as well. Also, a number of individuals, including former IBM employees, have been prosecuted for their actions by government authorities and convicted of crimes for their part in stealing IBM assets.

IBM will continue to take every step necessary, including legal measures, to protect its assets.

Recording and Reporting Information

You should record and report all information accurately and honestly.

Every employee records information of some kind and submits it to the company. For example: an engineer fills out a product test report; a marketing representative reports orders; an accountant records revenues and costs; a scientist prepares a research report; and, a customer engineer completes a service call report. Each employee must accurately and honestly fill in reports.

One very important report that many employees use is the expense account. Employees are entitled to reimbursement for reasonable expenses—but only if those expenses were actually incurred. To submit an expense account for meals not eaten, miles not driven, airline tickets not used or for any other expense not incurred is dishonest reporting and is prohibited.

Dishonest reporting within IBM, for example to IBM management or IBM auditors, or to organizations and people outside the company, is strictly prohibited. This includes not only reporting information inaccurately, but also organizing it in a way that is intended to mislead or misinform those who receive it. Employees must ensure that they do not make false or misleading statements in external financial reports, environmental monitoring reports and other documents submitted to or maintained for government agencies, or status reports on contracts, particularly in situations where IBM is selling goods or providing services to a government customer. Dishonest reporting can lead to civil or even criminal liability for you or IBM.

American Institute of Certified Public Accountants, Code of Professional Conduct[1] as Amended October 28, 1997

COMPOSITION, APPLICABILITY, AND COMPLIANCE

The Code of Professional Conduct of the American Institute of Certified Public Accountants consists of two sections—(1) the Principles and (2) the Rules. The Principles provide the framework for the Rules, which govern the performance of professional services by members. The Council of the American Institute of Certified Public Accountants is authorized to designate bodies to promulgate technical standards under the Rules, and the bylaws require adherence to those Rules and standards.

The Code of Professional Conduct was adopted by the membership to provide guidance and rules to all members—those in public practice, in industry, in government, and in education—in the performance of their professional responsibilities.

---

[1]Copyright © 1997 by the American Institute of Certified Public Accountants and reprinted with permission. It should be noted that the Institute has issued interpretations under the rules of conduct, and the reader may wish to consult such interpretations. See AICPA, *Professional Standards,* Vol. 2, (New York: American Institute of Certified Public Accountants, 1998).

Compliance with the Code of Professional Conduct, as with all standards in an open society, depends primarily on members' understanding and voluntary actions, secondarily on reinforcement by peers and public opinion, and ultimately on disciplinary proceedings, when necessary, against members who fail to comply with the Rules.

OTHER GUIDANCE

The Principles and Rules as set forth herein are further amplified by interpretations and rulings contained in *AICPA Professional Standards* (volume 2).

Interpretations of Rules of Conduct consist of interpretations which have been adopted, after exposure to state societies, state boards, practice units and other interested parties, by the professional ethics division's executive committee to provide guidelines as to the scope and application of the Rules but are not intended to limit such scope or application. A member who departs from such guidelines shall have the burden of justifying such departure in any disciplinary hearing.

Ethics Rulings consist of formal rulings made by the professional ethics division's executive committee after exposure to state societies, state boards, practice units and other interested parties. These rulings summarize the application of Rules of Conduct and interpretations to a particular set of factual circumstances. Members who depart from such rulings in similar circumstances will be requested to justify such departures.

Publication of an interpretation or ethics ruling in the *Journal of Accountancy* constitutes notice to members. Hence, the effective date of the pronouncement is the last day of the month in which the pronouncement is published in the *Journal of Accountancy*. The professional ethics division will take into consideration the time that would have been reasonable for the member to comply with the pronouncement.

A member should also consult, if applicable, the ethical standards of his state CPA society, state board of accountancy, the Securities and Exchange Commission, and any other governmental agency which may regulate his client's business or use his report to evaluate the client's compliance with applicable laws and related regulations.

SECTION I—PRINCIPLES

Preamble

Membership in the American Institute of Certified Public Accountants is voluntary. By accepting membership, a certified public accountant assumes an obligation of self-discipline above and beyond the requirements of laws and regulations.

These Principles of the Code of Professional Conduct of the American Institute of Certified Public Accountants express the profession's recognition of its responsibilities to the public, to clients, and to colleagues. They guide members in the performance of their professional responsibilities and express the basic tenets of ethical and professional conduct. The Principles call for an unswerving commitment to honorable behavior, even at the sacrifice of personal advantage.

Article I

Responsibilities

In carrying out their responsibilities as professionals, members should exercise sensitive professional and moral judgments in all their activities.

As professionals, certified public accountants perform an essential role in society. Consistent with that role, members of the American Institute of Certified Public Accountants have responsibilities to all those who use their professional services. Members also have a continuing responsibility to cooperate with each other to improve the art of accounting, maintain the public's confidence, and carry out the profession's special responsibilities for self-governance. The collective efforts of all members are required to maintain and enhance the traditions of the profession.

Article II

The Public Interest

Members should accept the obligation to act in a way that will serve the public interest, honor the public trust, and demonstrate commitment to professionalism.
A distinguishing mark of a profession is acceptance of its responsibility to the public. The accounting profession's public consists of clients, credit grantors, governments, employers, investors, the business and financial community, and others who rely on the objectivity and integrity of certified public accountants to maintain the orderly functioning of commerce. This reliance imposes a public interest responsibility on certified public accountants. The public interest is defined as the collective well-being of the community of people and institutions the profession serves.

In discharging their professional responsibilities, members may encounter conflicting pressures from among each of those groups. In resolving those conflicts, members should act with integrity, guided by the precept that when members fulfill their responsibility to the public, clients' and employers' interests are best served.

Those who rely on certified public accountants expect them to discharge their responsibilities with integrity, objectivity, due professional care, and a genuine interest in serving the public. They are expected to provide quality services, enter into fee arrangements, and offer a range of services—all in a manner that demonstrates a level of professionalism consistent with these Principles of the Code of Professional Conduct.

All who accept membership in the American Institute of Certified Public Accountants commit themselves to honor the public trust. In return for the faith that the public reposes in them, members should seek continually to demonstrate their dedication to professional excellence.

Article III

Integrity

To maintain and broaden public confidence, members should perform all professional responsibilities with the highest sense of integrity.

Integrity is an element of character fundamental to professional recognition. It is the quality from which the public trust derives and the benchmark against which a member must ultimately test all decisions.

Integrity requires a member to be, among other things, honest and candid within the constraints of client confidentiality. Service and the public trust should not be subordinated to personal gain and advantage. Integrity can accommodate the inadvertent error and the honest difference of opinion; it cannot accommodate deceit or subordination of principle.

Integrity is measured in terms of what is right and just. In the absence of specific rules, standards, or guidance, or in the face of conflicting opinions, a member should test decisions and deeds by asking: "Am I doing what a person of integrity would do? Have I retained my integrity?" Integrity requires a member to observe both the form and the spirit of technical and ethical standards; circumvention of those standards constitutes subordination of judgment.

Integrity also requires a member to observe the principles of objectivity and independence and of due care.

Article IV

Objectivity and Independence

A member should maintain objectivity and be free of conflicts of interest in discharging professional responsibilities. A member in public practice should be in-

dependent in fact and appearance when providing auditing and other attestation services.

Objectivity is a state of mind, a quality that lends value to a member's services. It is a distinguishing feature of the profession. The principle of objectivity imposes the obligation to be impartial, intellectually honest, and free of conflicts of interest. Independence precludes relationships that may appear to impair a member's objectivity in rendering attestation services.

Members often serve multiple interests in many different capacities and must demonstrate their objectivity in varying circumstances. Members in public practice render attest, tax, and management advisory services. Other members prepare financial statements in the employment of others, perform internal auditing services, and serve in financial and management capacities in industry, education, and government. They also educate and train those who aspire to admission into the profession. Regardless of service or capacity, members should protect the integrity of their work, maintain objectivity, and avoid any subordination of their judgment.

For a member in public practice, the maintenance of objectivity and independence requires a continuing assessment of client relationships and public responsibility. Such a member who provides auditing and other attestation services should be independent in fact and appearance. In providing all other services, a member should maintain objectivity and avoid conflicts of interest.

Although members not in public practice cannot maintain the appearance of independence, they nevertheless have the responsibility to maintain objectivity in rendering professional services. Members employed by others to prepare financial statements or to perform auditing, tax, or consulting services are charged with the same responsibility for objectivity as members in public practice and must be scrupulous in their application of generally accepted accounting principles and candid in all their dealings with members in public practice.

Article V

Due Care

A member should observe the profession's technical and ethical standards, strive continually to improve competence and the quality of services, and discharge professional responsibility to the best of the member's ability.

The quest for excellence is the essence of due care. Due care requires a member to discharge professional responsibilities with competence and diligence. It imposes the obligation to perform professional services to the best of a member's ability with concern for the best interest of those for whom the services are performed and consistent with the profession's responsibility to the public.

Competence is derived from a synthesis of education and experience. It begins with a mastery of the common body of knowledge required for designation as a certified public accountant. The maintenance of competence requires a commitment to learning and professional improvement that must continue throughout a member's professional life. It is a member's individual responsibility. In all engagements and in all responsibilities, each member should undertake to achieve a level of competence that will assure that the quality of the member's services meets the high level of professionalism required by these Principles.

Competence represents the attainment and maintenance of a level of understanding and knowledge that enables a member to render services with facility and acumen. It also establishes the limitations of a member's capabilities by dictating that consultation or referral may be required when a professional engagement exceeds the personal competence of a member of a member's firm. Each member is responsible for assessing his or her own competence—of evaluating whether education, experience, and judgment are adequate for the responsibility to be assumed.

Members should be diligent in discharging responsibilities to clients, employers, and the public. Diligence imposes the responsibility to render services promptly and carefully, to be thorough, and to observe applicable technical and ethical standards.

Due care requires a member to plan and supervise adequately any professional activity for which he or she is responsible.

Article VI

Scope and Nature of Services

A member in public practice should observe the Principles of the Code of Professional Conduct in determining the scope and nature of services to be provided.

The public interest aspect of certified public accountants' services requires that such services be consistent with acceptable professional behavior for certified public accountants. Integrity requires that service and the public trust not be subordinated to personal gain and advantage. Objectivity and independence require that members be free from conflicts of interest in discharging professional responsibilities. Due care requires that services be provided with competence and diligence.

Each of these Principles should be considered by members in determining whether or not to provide specific services in individual circumstances. In some instances, they may represent an overall constraint on the nonaudit services that might be offered to a specific client. No hard-and-fast rules can be developed to help members reach these judgments, but they must be satisfied that they are meeting the spirit of the Principles in this regard.

In order to accomplish this, members should

- Practice in firms that have in place internal quality-control procedures to ensure that services are competently delivered and adequately supervised.

- Determine, in their individual judgments, whether the scope and nature of other services provided to an audit client would create a conflict of interest in the performance of the audit function for that client.

- Assess, in their individual judgments, whether an activity is consistent with their role as professionals (for example, Is such activity a reasonable extension or variation of existing services offered by the member or others in the profession?).

SECTION II—RULES

Applicability

The bylaws of the American Institute of Certified Public Accountants require that members adhere to the Rules of the Code of Professional Conduct. Members must be prepared to justify departures from these Rules.

INTERPRETATION OF APPLICABILITY SECTION

[The professional ethics executive committee has issued the following interpretation of the applicability section of the Code, effective November 30, 1989.]

For purposes of the applicability section of the Code, a "member" is a member or international associate of the American Institute of CPAs.

1. The Rules of Conduct that follow apply to all professional services performed except (a) where the wording of the rule indicates otherwise and (b) that a member who is practicing outside the United States will not be subject to discipline for departing from any of the rules stated herein as long as the member's conduct is in accord with the rules of the organized accounting profession in the country in which he or she is practicing. However, where a member's name is associated with financial statements under circumstances that would entitle the reader to assume that U.S. practices were followed, the member must comply with the requirements of rules 202 and 203.

2. A member may be held responsible for compliance with the rules by all persons associated with him or her in the practice of public accounting who are either under the member's supervision or are the member's partners or shareholders in the practice.

3. A member shall not permit others to carry out on his or her behalf, either with or without compensation, acts which, if carried out by the member, would place the member in violation of the rules.

Definitions*

Client.   A client is any person or entity, other than the member's employer, that engages a member or a member's firm to perform professional services or a person or entity with respect to which professional services are performed. The term "employer" for these purposes does not include those entities engaged in the practice of public accounting.

Council.   The Council of the American Institute of Certified Public Accountants.

Enterprise.   For purposes of the Code, the term "enterprise" is synonymous with the term "client."

Financial statements.   A presentation of financial data, including accompanying notes, if any, intended to communicate an entity's economic resources and/or obligations at a point in time or the changes therein for a period of time, in accordance with generally accepted accounting principles or a comprehensive basis of accounting other than generally accepted accounting principles.

Incidental financial data to support recommendations to a client or in documents for which the reporting is governed by Statements on Standards for Attestation Engagements and tax returns and supporting schedules do not, for this purpose, constitute financial statements. The statement, affidavit, or signature of preparers required on tax returns neither constitutes an opinion on financial statements nor requires a disclaimer of such opinion.

Firm.   A form of organization permitted by state law or regulation whose characteristics conform to resolutions of Council that is engaged in the practice of public accounting, including the individual owners thereof.

Holding out.   In general, any action initiated by a member that informs others of his or her status as a CPA or AICPA-accredited specialist constitutes holding

---

*Pursuant to its authority under the bylaws (section 3.6.2.2) to interpret the Code of Professional Conduct, the professional ethics executive committee has issued these definitions of terms appearing in the Code effective November 30, 1989 (revised April 1992 and May 1996).

out as a CPA. This would include, for example, any oral or written representation to another regarding CPA status, use of the CPA designation on business cards or letterhead, the display of a certificate evidencing a member's CPA designation, or listing as a CPA in local telephone directories.

Institute. The American Institute of Certified Public Accountants.

Interpretations of Rules of Conduct. Pronouncements issued by the division of professional ethics to provide guidelines concerning the scope and application of the Rules of Conduct.

Member. A member, associate member, or international associate of the American Institute of Certified Public Accountants.

Practice of public accounting. The practice of public accounting consists of the performance for a client, by a member or a member's firm, while holding out as CPA(s), of the professional services of accounting, tax, personal financial planning, litigation support services, and those professional services for which standards are promulgated by bodies designated by Council, such as Statements of Financial Accounting Standards, Statements on Auditing Standards, Statements on Standards for Accounting and Review Services, Statement on Standards for Consulting Services, Statements of Governmental Accounting Standards, Statements on Standards for Attestation Engagements, and Statement on Standards for Accountants' Services on Prospective Financial Information.

However, a member or a member's firm, while holding out as CPA(s), is not considered to be in the practice of public accounting if the member or the member's firm does not perform, for any client, any of the professional services described in the preceding paragraph.

Professional services. Professional services include all services performed by a member while holding out as a CPA.

Rules

Rule 101 Independence

A member in public practice shall be independent in the performance of professional services as required by standards promulgated by bodies designated by Council.

Rule 102 Integrity and Objectivity

In the performance of any professional service, a member shall maintain objectivity and integrity, shall be free of conflicts of interest, and shall not knowingly misrepresent facts or subordinate his or her judgment to others.

Rule 201   General Standards

A member shall comply with the following standards and with any interpretations thereof by bodies designated by Council.

A. *Professional Competence.*   Undertake only those professional services that the member of the member's firm can reasonably expect to be completed with professional competence.
B. *Due Professional Care.*   Exercise due professional care in the performance of professional services.
C. *Planning and Supervision.*   Adequately plan and supervise the performance of professional services.
D. *Sufficient Relevant Data.*   Obtain sufficient relevant data to afford a reasonable basis for conclusions or recommendations in relation to any professional services performed.
      (See implementing resolutions, pages 15–17.)

Rule 202   Compliance With Standards

A member who performs auditing, review, compilation, management consulting, tax, or other professional services shall comply with standards promulgated by bodies designated by Council.
      (See implementing resolutions, pages 15–17.)

Rule 203   Accounting Principles

A member shall not (1) express an opinion or state affirmatively that the financial statements or other financial data of any entity are presented in conformity with generally accepted accounting principles or (2) state that he or she is not aware of any material modifications that should be made to such statements or data in order for them to be in conformity with generally accepted accounting principles, if such statements or data contain any departure from an accounting principle promulgated by bodies designated by Council to establish such principles that has a material effect on the statements or data taken as a whole. If, however, the statements or data contain such a departure and the member can demonstrate that due to unusual circumstances the financial statements or data would otherwise have been misleading, the member can comply with the rule by describing the departure, its approximate effects, if practicable, and the reasons why compliance with the principle would result in a misleading statement.

Rule 301   Confidential Client Information

A member in public practice shall not disclose any confidential client information without the specific consent of the client.

This rule shall not be construed (1) to relieve a member of his or her professional obligations under rules 202 and 203, (2) to affect in any way the member's obligation to comply with a validly issued and enforceable subpoena or summons, or to prohibit a member's compliance with applicable laws and government regulations, (3) to prohibit review of a member's professional practice under AICPA or state CPA society or Board of Accountancy authorization, or (4) to preclude a member from initiating a complaint with, or responding to any inquiry made by, the professional ethics division or trial board of the Institute or a duly constituted investigative or disciplinary body of a state CPA society of Board of Accountancy.

Members of any of the bodies identified in (4) above and members involved with professional practice reviews identified in (3) above shall not use to their own advantage or disclose any member's confidential client information that comes to their attention in carrying out those activities. This prohibition shall not restrict members' exchange of information in connection with the investigative or disciplinary proceedings described in (4) above or the professional practice reviews described in (3) above.

Rule 302 Contingent Fees

A member in public practice shall not

(1) Perform for a contingent fee any professional services for, or receive such a fee from, a client for whom the member or the member's firm performs

    (a) an audit or review of a financial statement; or

    (b) a compilation of a financial statement when the member expects, or reasonably might expect, that a third party will use the financial statement and the member's compilation report does not disclose a lack of independence; or

    (c) an examination of prospective financial information;

    or

(2) Prepare an original or amended tax return or claim for a tax refund for a contingent fee for any client.

The prohibition in (1) above applies during the period in which the member or the member's firm is engaged to perform any of the services listed above and the period covered by any historical financial statements involved in any such listed services.

Except as stated in the next sentence, a contingent fee is a fee established for the performance of any service pursuant to an arrangement in which no fee will be charged unless a specified finding or result is attained, or in which the amount of the fee is otherwise dependent upon the finding or result of such service. Solely for purposes of this rule, fees are not regarded as being contingent if fixed by courts or other public authorities, or, in tax matters, if determined based on the results of judicial proceedings or the findings of governmental agencies.

A member's fees may vary depending, for example, on the complexity of services rendered.

Rule 401   [*There are currently no rules in the 400 series.*]

Rule 501   Acts Discreditable

A member shall not commit an act discreditable to the profession.

Rule 502   Advertising and Other Forms of Solicitation

A member in public practice shall not seek to obtain clients by advertising or other forms of solicitation in a manner that is false, misleading, or deceptive. Solicitation by the use of coercion, over-reaching, or harassing conduct is prohibited.

Rule 503   Commissions and Referral Fees

A. *Prohibited Commissions*

A member in public practice shall not for a commission recommend or refer to a client any product or service, or for a commission recommend or refer any product or service to be supplied by a client, or receive a commission, when the member or the member's firm also performs for that client

(a) an audit or review of a financial statement; or

(b) a compilation of a financial statement when the member expects, or reasonably might expect, that a third party will use the financial statement and the member's compilation report does not disclose a lack of independence; or

(c) an examination of prospective financial information.

This prohibition applies during the period in which the member is engaged to perform any of the services listed above and the period covered by any historical financial statements involved in such listed services.

B. *Disclosure of Permitted Commissions*

A member in public practice who is not prohibited by this rule from performing services for or receiving a commission and who is paid or expects to be paid a commission shall disclose that fact to any person or entity to whom the member recommends or refers a product or service to which the commission relates.

C. *Referral Fees*

Any member who accepts a referral fee for recommending or referring any service of a CPA to any person or entity or who pays a referral fee to obtain a client shall disclose such acceptance or payment to the client.

Rule 504 [*There is currently no rule 504.*]

Rule 505 Form of Organization and Name

A member may practice public accounting only in a form of organization permitted by state law or regulation whose characteristics conform to resolutions of Council.

A member shall not practice public accounting under a firm name that is misleading. Names of one or more past owners may be included in the firm name of a successor organization.

A firm may not designate itself as "Members of the American Institute of Certified Public Accountants" unless all of its owners are members of the Institute.

COUNCIL RESOLUTIONS TO IMPLEMENT CODE OF PROFESSIONAL CONDUCT

Under Rules 201, 202, and 203   Designating Bodies to Promulgate Technical Standards

Financial Accounting Standards Board

WHEREAS: In 1959 the Council designated the Accounting Principles Board to establish accounting principles, and

WHEREAS: The Council is advised that the Financial Accounting Standards Board (FASB) has become operational, it is

RESOLVED: That as of the date hereof the FASB, in respect of statements of financial accounting standards finally adopted by such board in accordance with its rules of procedure and the bylaws of the Financial Accounting Foundation, be, and hereby is, designated by this Council as the body to establish accounting principles pursuant to rule 203 and standards on disclosure of financial information for such entities outside financial statements in published financial reports containing financial statements under rule 202 of the Rules of the Code of Professional Conduct of the American Institute of Certified Public Accountants provided, however, any accounting research bulletins, or opinions of the accounting principles board issued or approved for exposure by the accounting principles board prior to April 1, 1973, and finally adopted by such board on or before June 30, 1973, shall constitute statements of accounting principles promulgated by a body designated by Council as contemplated in rule 203 of the Rules of the Code of Professional Conduct unless and until such time as they are expressly superseded by action of the FASB.

Governmental Accounting Standards Board

WHEREAS: The Governmental Accounting Standards Board (GASB) has been established by the board of trustees of the Financial Accounting Foundation

(FAF) to issue standards of financial accounting and reporting with respect to activities and transactions of state and local governmental entities, and

WHEREAS: The American Institute of Certified Public Accountants is a signatory to the agreement creating the GASB as an arm of the FAF and has supported the GASB professionally and financially, it is

RESOLVED: That as of the date hereof, the GASB, with respect to statements of governmental accounting standards adopted and issued in July 1984 and subsequently in accordance with its rules of procedure and the bylaws of the FAF, be, and hereby is, designated by the Council of the American Institute of Certified Public Accountants as the body to establish financial accounting principles for state and local governmental entities pursuant to rule 203, and standards on disclosure of financial information for such entities outside financial statements in published financial reports containing financial statements under rule 202.

AICPA COMMITTEES AND BOARDS

WHEREAS: The membership of the Institute has adopted rules 201 and 202 of the Rules of the Code of Professional Conduct, which authorizes the Council to designate bodies to promulgate technical standards with which members must comply, and therefore it is

Accounting and Review Services Committee

RESOLVED: That the AICPA accounting and review services committee is hereby designated to promulgate standards under rules 201 and 202 with respect to unaudited financial statements or other unaudited financial information of an entity that is not required to file financial statements with a regulatory agency in connection with the sale or trading of its securities in a public market.

Auditing Standards Board

RESOLVED: That the AICPA auditing standards board is hereby designated as the body authorized under rules 201 and 202 to promulgate auditing and attest standards and procedures.

RESOLVED: That the auditing standards board shall establish under statements on auditing standards the responsibilities of members with respect to standards for disclosure of financial information outside financial statements in published reports containing financial statements.

Management Consulting Services Executive Committee

RESOLVED: That the AICPA management consulting services executive committee is hereby designated to promulgate standards under rules 201 and 202 with respect to the offering of management consulting services, provided, however, that such standards do not deal with the broad question of what, if any, services should be proscribed.

AND FURTHER RESOLVED: That any Institute committee or board now or in the future authorized by the Council to issue enforceable standards under rules 201 and 202 must observe an exposure process seeking comment from other affected committees and boards, as well as the general membership.

Attestation Standards

RESOLVED: That the AICPA accounting and review services committee, auditing standards board, and management consulting services executive committee are hereby designated as bodies authorized under rules 201 and 202 to promulgate attestation standards in their respective areas of responsibility.

Under Rule 505   Form of Organization and Name

RESOLVED: That with respect to a firm or organization which performs (1) any audit or other engagement performed in accordance with the Statements on Auditing Standards, (2) any review of a financial statement or compilation of a financial statement performed in accordance with the Statements on Standards for Accounting and Review Services, or (3) any examination of prospective financial information performed in accordance with the Statements on Standards for Attestation Engagements, or which holds itself out as a firm of certified public accountants or uses the term "certified public accountant(s)" or the designation "CPA" in connection with its name, the characteristics of such a firm or organization under rule 505 are as set forth below. The characteristics of all other firms or organizations are deemed to be whatever is legally permissible under applicable law or regulation.

1. A majority of the ownership of the firm in terms of financial interests and voting rights must belong to CPAs. The non-CPA owner would have to be actively engaged as a firm member in providing services to the firm's clients as his or her principal occupation. Ownership by investors or commercial enterprises not actively engaged as firm members in providing services to the firm's clients as their principal occupation is against the public interest and continues to be prohibited.

2. There must be a CPA who has ultimate responsibility for all the services provided by the firm and by each business unit performing financial statement attest and compilation services and other engagements governed by Statements on Auditing Standards or Statements on Standards for Accounting and Review Services.

3. Non-CPA owners could not assume ultimate responsibility for any financial statement attest or compilation engagement.

4. Non-CPAs becoming owners after adoption of Council's resolution would have to possess a baccalaureate degree and, beginning in the year 2010, have obtained 150 semester hours of education at an accredited college or university.

5. Non-CPA owners would be permitted to use the title "principal," "owner," "officer," "member" or "shareholder," or any other title permitted by state law, but not hold themselves out to be CPAs.

6. Non-CPA owners would have to abide by the AICPA Code of Professional Conduct. AICPA members may be held responsible under the Code for acts of co-owners.

7. Non-CPA owners would have to complete the same work-related CPE requirements as set forth under AICPA bylaw section 2.3 for AICPA members.

8. Owners shall at all times own their equity in their own right and shall be the beneficial owners of the equity capital ascribed to them. Provision would have to be made for the ownership to be transferred to the firm or to other qualified owners if the non-CPA ceases to be actively engaged in the firm.

9. Non-CPA owners would not be eligible for membership in the AICPA.

The Institute of Internal Auditors, Inc., Summary of General and Specific Standards for the Professional Practice of Internal Auditing[1] and Code of Ethics[2]

100 **INDEPENDENCE**—INTERNAL AUDITORS SHOULD BE INDE-PENDENT OF THE ACTIVITIES THEY AUDIT.

    110 **Organizational Status**—The organizational status of the internal auditing department should be sufficient to permit the accomplishment of its audit responsibilities.

    120 **Objectivity**—Internal auditors should be objective in performing audits.

200 **PROFESSIONAL PROFICIENCY**—INTERNAL AUDITS SHOULD BE PERFORMED WITH PROFICIENCY AND DUE PROFESSIONAL CARE.

The Internal Auditing Department

    210 **Staffing**—The internal auditing department should provide assurance that the technical proficiency and educational background of internal auditors are appropriate for the audit to be performed.

[1]Copyright 1998 by the Institute of Internal Auditors, Inc. and reprinted with permission.
[2]Copyright 1998 by the Institute of Internal Auditors, Inc. and reprinted with permission.

220 **Knowledge, Skills, and Disciplines**—The internal auditing department should possess or should obtain the knowledge, skills, and disciplines needed to carry out its audit responsibilities.

230 **Supervision**—The internal auditing department should provide assurance that internal audits are properly supervised.

The Internal Auditor

240 **Compliance with Standards of Conduct**—Internal auditors should comply with professional standards of conduct.

250 **Knowledge, Skills, and Disciplines**—Internal auditors should possess the knowledge, skills, and disciplines essential to the performance of internal audits.

260 **Human Relations and Communications**—Internal auditors should be skilled in dealing with people and in communicating effectively.

270 **Continuing Education**—Internal auditors should maintain their technical competence through continuing education.

280 **Due Professional Care**—Internal auditors should exercise due professional care in performing internal audits.

300 **SCOPE OF WORK**—THE SCOPE OF INTERNAL AUDITING SHOULD ENCOMPASS THE EXAMINATION AND EVALUATION OF THE ADEQUACY AND EFFECTIVENESS OF THE ORGANIZATION'S SYSTEM OF INTERNAL CONTROL AND THE QUALITY OF PERFORMANCE IN CARRYING OUT ASSIGNED RESPONSIBILITIES.

310 **Reliability and Integrity of Information**—Internal auditors should review the reliability and integrity of financial and operating information and the means used to identify, measure, classify, and report such information.

320 **Compliance with Policies, Plans, Procedures, Laws, and Regulations**—
Internal auditors should review the systems established to ensure compliance with those policies, plans, procedures, laws, and regulations which could have a significant impact on operations and reports and should determine whether the organization is in compliance.

330 **Safeguarding of Assets**—Internal auditors should review the means of safeguarding assets and, as appropriate, verify the existence of such assets.

340 **Economical and Efficient Use of Resources**—Internal auditors should appraise the economy and efficiency with which resources are employed.

350   **Accomplishment of Established Objectives and Goals for Operations or Programs**—Internal auditors should review operations or programs to ascertain whether results are consistent with established objectives and goals and whether the operations or programs are being carried out as planned.

400 **PERFORMANCE OF AUDIT WORK**—AUDIT WORK SHOULD INCLUDE PLANNING THE AUDIT, EXAMINING AND EVALUATING INFORMATION, COMMUNICATING RESULTS, AND FOLLOWING UP.

410   **Planning the Audit**—Internal auditors should plan each audit.

420   **Examining and Evaluating Information**—Internal auditors should collect, analyze, interpret, and document information to support audit results.

430   **Communicating Results**—Internal auditors should report the results of their audit work.

440   **Following Up**—Internal auditors should follow up to ascertain that appropriate action is taken on reported audit findings.

500 **MANAGEMENT OF THE INTERNAL AUDITING DEPARTMENT**—THE DIRECTOR OF INTERNAL AUDITING SHOULD PROPERLY MANAGE THE INTERNAL AUDITING DEPARTMENT.

510   **Purpose, Authority, and Responsibility**—The director of internal auditing should have a statement of purpose, authority, and responsibility for the internal auditing department.

520   **Planning**—The director of internal auditing should establish plans to carry out the responsibilities of the internal auditing department.

530   **Policies and Procedures**—The director of internal auditing should provide written policies and procedures to guide the audit staff.

540   **Personnel Management and Development**—The director of internal auditing should establish a program for selecting and developing the human resources of the internal auditing department.

550   **External Auditors**—The director of internal auditing should coordinate internal and external audit efforts.

560   **Quality Assurance**—The director of internal auditing should establish and maintain a quality assurance program to evaluate the operations of the internal auditing department.

The Institute of Internal Auditors
CODE OF ETHICS

PURPOSE: A distinguishing mark of a profession is acceptance by its members of responsibility to the interests of those it serves. Members of The Institute of Internal Auditors (Members) and Certified Internal Auditors (CIAs) must maintain high standards of conduct in order to effectively discharge this responsibility. The Institute of Internal Auditors (Institute) adopts this *Code of Ethics* for Members and CIAs.

APPLICABILITY: This *Code of Ethics* is applicable to all Members and CIAs. Membership in The Institute and acceptance of the "Certified Internal Auditor" designation are voluntary actions. By acceptance, Members and CIAs assume an obligation of self-discipline above and beyond the requirements of laws and regulations.

The standards of conduct set forth in this *Code of Ethics* provide basic principles in the practice of internal auditing. Members and CIAs should realize that their individual judgment is required in the application of these principles.

CIAs shall use the "Certified Internal Auditor" designation with discretion and in a dignified manner, fully aware of what the designation denotes. The designation shall also be used in a manner consistent with all statutory requirements.

Members who are judged by the Board of Directors of The Institute to be in violation of the standards of conduct of the *Code of Ethics* shall be subject to forfeiture of their membership in The Institute. CIAs who are similarly judged also shall be subject to forfeiture of the "Certified Internal Auditor" designation.

STANDARDS OF CONDUCT

    I.   Members and CIAs exercise honesty, objectivity, and diligence in the performance of their duties and responsibilities.

   II.   Members and CIAs shall exhibit loyalty in all matters pertaining to the affairs of their organization or to whomever they may be rendering a service. However, Members and CIAs shall not knowingly be a party to any illegal or improper activity.

  III.   Members and CIAs shall not knowingly engage in acts or activities which are discreditable to the profession of internal auditing or to their organization.

  IV.   Members and CIAs shall refrain from entering into any activity which may be in conflict with the interest of their organization or which would prejudice their ability to carry out objectively their duties and responsibilities.

    V.   Members and CIAs shall not accept anything of value from an employee, client, customer, supplier, or business associate of their organization which would impair or be presumed to impair their professional judgment.

  VI.   Members and CIAs shall undertake only those services which they can reasonably expect to complete with professional competence.

 VII.   Members and CIAs shall adopt suitable means to comply with the *Standards for the Professional Practice of Internal Auditing*.

VIII. Members and CIAs shall be prudent in the use of information acquired in the course of their duties. They shall not use confidential information for any personal gain nor in any manner which would be contrary to law or detrimental to the welfare of their organization.

IX. Members and CIAs, when reporting on the results of their work, shall reveal all material facts known to them which, if not revealed, could either distort reports of operations under review or conceal unlawful practices.

X. Members and CIAs shall continually strive for improvement in their proficiency, and in the effectiveness and quality of their service.

XI. Members and CIAs, in the practice of their profession, shall be ever mindful of their obligation to maintain the high standards of competence, morality, and dignity promulgated by The Institute. Members shall abide by the *Bylaws* and uphold the objectives of The Institute.

Association of Certified Fraud Examiners, Professional Standards and Practices for Certified Fraud Examiners[1] and Code of Ethics[2]

I. GENERAL STANDARDS

A. Independence and Objectivity

CFEs are responsible for maintaining independence in attitude and experience, approaching and conducting fraud examinations in an objective and unbiased manner, and assuring that examining organizations they direct are free from impairments to independence.

B. Qualifications

CFEs must possess the skills, knowledge, abilities, and experience needed to perform examinations proficiently and effectively. CFEs responsible for directing fraud examinations must assure they are performed by personnel who collectively possess the skills and knowledge necessary to complete examinations in accordance with these Standards. CFEs must maintain their qualifications by fulfilling continuing education requirements and adhering to the Code of Ethics of the Association of Certified Fraud Examiners.

[1]Copyright 1991 by the Association of Certified Fraud Examiners and reprinted with permission.
[2]Copyright 1988 by the Association of Certified Fraud Examiners and reprinted with permission.

C. Fraud Examinations

CFEs must conduct fraud examinations using due professional care, with adequate planning and supervision to provide assurance that objectives are achieved within the framework of these Standards. Evidence is to be obtained in an efficient, thorough, and legal manner; and reports of the results of fraud examinations must be accurate, objective and thorough.

D. Confidentiality

CFEs are responsible for assuring that they and examining organizations they direct exercise due care to prevent improper disclosure of confidential or privileged information.

II. SPECIFIC STANDARDS

A. Independence and Objectivity

1. **Attitude and Appearance**
   Independence of attitude requires impartiality and fairness in conducting examinations and in reaching resulting conclusions and judgments. CFEs must also be sensitive to the appearance of independence so that conclusions and judgments will be accepted as impartial by knowledgeable third parties. CFEs who become aware of a situation or relationship that could be perceived to impair independence, whether or not actual impairment exists, should inform management immediately and take steps to eliminate the perceived impairment, including withdrawing from the examination if necessary.
2. **Objectivity**
   To assure objectivity in performing examinations, CFEs must maintain an independent mental attitude, reach judgments on examination matters without undue influence from others and avoid being placed in positions where they would be unable to work in an objective professional manner.
3. **Organizational Relationship**
   The CFEs reporting relationship should be such that the attitude and appearance of independence and objectivity are not jeopardized. Organizational independence is achieved when the CFE's function has a mandate to conduct independent examinations throughout the organization, or by a reporting relationship high enough in the organization to assure independence of action.

B. Qualifications

1. Skills, Knowledge, Abilities and Experience

CFEs cannot be expected to have an expert level of skill and knowledge for every circumstance that might be encountered in a fraud examination. Nevertheless, CFEs must have sufficient skill and knowledge to recognize when additional training or expert guidance is required. It is the responsibility of a CFE to assure that necessary skills, knowledge, ability and experience are acquired or available before going forward with a fraud examination.

CFEs must be skilled in obtaining information from records, documents and people; in analyzing and evaluating information and drawing sound conclusions; in communicating the results of fraud examinations, both orally and in writing; and in serving as an expert witness when appropriate.

CFEs must be knowledgeable in investigative techniques, applicable laws and rules of evidence, fraud auditing, criminology and ethics.

2. Continuing Education

CFEs are required to fulfill continuing education requirements established by the Association of Certified Fraud Examiners. Additionally, CFEs are responsible for securing other education necessary for specific fraud examinations and related fields in which they are individually involved.

3. Code of Ethics

CFEs are to adhere to the code of Professional Ethics of the Association of Certified Fraud Examiners.

C. Fraud Examinations

1. Due Professional Care

Due professional care is defined as exercising the care and skill expected of a prudent professional in similar circumstances. CFEs are responsible for assuring that there is sufficient predication for beginning a fraud examination; that said examinations are conducted with diligence and thoroughness; that all applicable laws and regulations are observed; that appropriate methods and techniques are used; and that said examinations are conducted in accordance with these Standards.

2. Planning and Supervision

CFEs must plan and supervise fraud examinations in a manner to assure that objectives are achieved within the framework of these Standards.

3. Evidence

CFEs must collect evidence, whether exculpatory or incriminating, that supports fraud examination results and will be admissible in subsequent proceedings, by obtaining and documenting evidence in a manner to ensure that all necessary evidence is obtained, and the chain of custody is preserved.

4. Reporting

CFE reports of the results of fraud examinations, whether written or verbal, must address all relevant aspects of the examination, and be accurate, objective and understandable.

In rendering reports to management, clients or others, CFEs shall not express judgments on the guilt or innocence of any person or party, regardless of the CFE's opinion of the preponderance of evidence. CFEs must exercise due professional care when expressing other opinions related to an examination, such as the likelihood that a fraud has or has not occurred, and whether or not internal controls are adequate.

D. Confidentiality

CFEs, during fraud examinations, are often privy to highly sensitive and confidential information about organizations and individuals. CFEs must exercise due care so as not to purposefully or inadvertently disclose such information except as necessary to conduct the examination or as required by law.

Richard F. Brodfuehrer, CFE, CIA
Chairman, Professional Standards and Practices Committee, CIA

Code of Ethics

   I. A CFE shall, at all times, demonstrate a commitment to professionalism and diligence in the performance of his or her duties.

  II. A CFE shall not engage in any illegal or unethical conduct, or any activity which would constitute a conflict of interest.

 III. A CFE shall, at all times, exhibit the highest level of integrity in the performance of all professional assignments, and will accept only assignments for which there is reasonable expectation that the assignment will be completed with professional competence.

 IV. A CFE will comply with lawful orders of the courts, and will testify to matters truthfully and without bias or prejudice.

  V. A CFE, in conducting examinations, will obtain evidence or other documentation to establish a reasonable basis for any opinion rendered. No opinion shall be expressed regarding the guilt or innocence of any person or party.

 VI. A CFE shall not reveal any confidential information obtained during a professional engagement without proper authorization.

VII. A CFE shall reveal all material matters discovered during the course of an examination, which, if omitted, could cause a distortion of the facts.

VIII. A CFE shall continually strive to increase the competence and effectiveness of professional services performed under his or her direction.

Accounting, Auditing, and Attestation Standards Topical Index of References to Accounting Principles Board (APB), Financial Accounting Standards Board (FASB), Statement on Auditing Standards (SAS), Statement on Standards for Attestation Engagements (SSAE), and Accounting Standards Executive Committee (AcSEC) Pronouncements as of December 31, 1998

Accounting/Auditing Topic	APB Reference Number	FASB Standard Reference Number	FASB Interpretation Reference Number	SAS Reference Number	SSAE Reference Number
Accounting changes	20*	32,* 56, 73, 83	1, 20	58	
Accounting estimate	20*			57	
Accounting policies	22				
Accounts receivable and payable—interest on transfers	21	77	2	67	
Accounts receivable confirmation				67	
Adequacy of disclosurer in financial statements				32	
Agreed-upon procedures				75	4
Analytical review procedures				56	
Attestation standards					1*
Audited financial statements—other information				8	
Audit planning and supervision				22	
Audit risk and materiality				47	
Audit sampling				39	
Audits of governmental entities				74	
Auditors' reports				26, 29, 35, 42, 50, 51, 58* 62, 69, 79, 87	
Business combinations	16*	10, 38, 79	4, 9*		
Business segment report		14,* 18, 21, 24, 30, 131		21	

Accounting/Auditing Topic	APB Reference Number	FASB Standard Reference Number	FASB Interpretation Reference Number	SAS Reference Number	SSAE Reference Number
Capitalization of interest cost		34,* 42, 58, 62	33		
Cash flows		95,* 102, 104			
Certain marketable securities		12,* 115	10,* 11, 12, 13, 16		
Client representations				85	
Communication between predecessor and successor auditors				84	
Communication with audit committees				61	
Compensated absences		43			
Compliance auditing/attestation				68	3
Comprehensive income		130			
Computer software		86			
Concepts of financial reporting		Concept Statements Nos. 1–6			
Consideration of omitted procedures				46	
Contingencies and commitments		5,* 11	14, 34	12	
Contribution received/made		116			
Convertible debt	14	84			
Deferred compensation plans	25		38		
Depreciation	1	93,* 99			
Development stage enterprise		7	5, 7		
Disclosure of information about					

			FASB		FASB
capital structure		129			
Disclosure of long-term obligation	47				
Discontinued operations	30*				
Early extinguishment of debt	26*	4, 64, 76, 84			
Earnings per share	15*	21, 55, 85, 128	31	31,* 80	
Evidential matter	30				
Extraordinary items				37	
Filing under Federal Securities Statutes					1*
Financial forecasts and projections			39		
Financial instruments		105,* 107,* 119,* 126, 133			
Financial reporting and changing prices		39,* 40, 41, 33,* 46, 54, 82, 89, 70 117			
Financial statements-not-for-profit					
Foreign currency exchange		8, 20, 52	15, 17, 37		
Franchise fee revenue		45			
Fraud				82	
Future contracts		80			
Illegal client acts				54	
Income taxes	11,* 23,* 24	9, 31, 37, 109	18, 22, 29	12	
Inquiry of a client's lawyer				12	
Intangible assets	17*	44, 72, 121		71	
Interim financial information	28	3		65	
Internal audit effects on the audit				48	
Internal control—EDP				55,* 60	
Internal control—communication of weakness					2,* 6

Accounting/Auditing Topic	APB Reference Number	Standard Reference Number	Interpretation Reference Number	SAS Reference Number	SSAE Reference Number
Investments in common stock	18*	94	35	81	
Investments in securities		115, 124			
Investment tax credit	2,* 4	13,* 17,* 22, 23, 26,* 27, 28, 29, 98	25, 32 19, 21, 23, 24, 26, 27		
Leases					
Letters for underwriters				72, 79, 86	
Loan impairment		114, 118			
Management discussion and analysis				87	8
Mortgage-backed securities		134			
Nonmonetary transactions	29		30		
Obligations callable by the creditor	78				
Pension plans	8*	35,* 36, 75, 87, 88, 110, 132	3		
Postretirement benefits other than pension		81, 106, 112			
Preacquisition contingencies of purchased enterprises					
Prior period adjustments		38			
Processing of transactions by service organizations		16			
Product financing arrangements		49		70	
Quality control for CPA firms				25	
Question about an entity's continued existence				59	
Refinancing of expected short-term obligations		6			
Related-party transactions		57		45	
Reporting on pro forma financial information					1

*Partially or fully amended.

AICPA ACCOUNTING STANDARDS EXECUTIVE COMMITTEE (AcSEC), STATEMENTS OF POSITION (SOP)

SOP 94-1, Inquiries of State Insurance Regulators

SOP 94-2, The Application of the Requirements of Accounting Research Bulletins, Opinions of the Accounting Principles Board, and Statements and Interpretations of the Financial Accounting Standards Board to Not-for-Profit Organizations

SOP 94-3, Reporting of Related Entities for Not-for-Profit Organizations

SOP 94-4, Reporting of Investment Contracts Held by Health and Welfare Benefit Plans and Defined-Contribution Pension Plans

SOP 94-5, Disclosures of Certain Matters in the Financial Statements of Insurance Enterprises

SOP 94-6, Disclosure of Certain Significant Risks and Uncertainties

SOP 95-1, Accounting for Certain Insurance Activities of Mutual Life Insurance Enterprises

SOP 95-2, Financial Reporting by Nonpublic Investment Partnerships

SOP 95-3, Accounting for Certain Distribution Costs of Investment Companies

SOP 95-4, Letters for State Insurance Regulators to Comply With the NAIC Model Audit Rule

SOP 95-5, Auditors' Reporting on Statutory Financial Statements of Insurance Companies

SOP 96-1, Environmental Remediation Liabilities

SOP 97-1, Accounting by Participating Mortgage Loan Borrowers

SOP 97-2, Software Revenue Recognition—supersedes SOP 91-1

SOP 97-3, Accounting by Insurance and Other Enterprises for Insurance-Related Assessments

SOP 98-1, Accounting for the Costs of Computer Software Developed or Planned for Internal Use

SOP 98-2, Accounting for Costs of Activities of Not-For-Profit Organizations and State and Local Governmental Entities That Include Fund-Raising

SOP 98-3, Audits of States, Local Governments, and Not-For-Profit Organizations Receiving Federal Awards—supersedes SOP 92-9, Audits of Not-For-Profit Organizations Receiving Federal Awards.

SOP 98-4, Deferral of the Effective Date of a Provision of SOP 97-2, Software Revenue Recognition

SOP 98-5, Reporting on the Costs of Start-up Activities

SOP 98-9, Modification of SOP 97-2

Professional Accounting Associations, Business Organizations, Boards, Commissions, and Directors Publications

The American Assembly
Columbia University
475 Riverside Drive
New York, NY 10115-0456
(212) 870-3500
www.columbia.edu/cu/amassembly/

American Bar Association
750 N. Lake Shore Drive
Chicago, IL 60611
1-800-285-2221
www.abanet.org

American Accounting Association
5717 Bessie Drive
Sarasota, FL 34233
(813) 921-7747
www.AAA.edu.org

American Institute of Certified Public
  Accountants
1211 Avenue of the Americas
New York, NY 10036-8775
(212) 596-6200 or 1-888-777-7077
www.aicpa.org

American Law Institute
4025 Chestnut Street
Philadelphia, PA 19104
1-800-253-6397
www.ali-aba.org

American Society of Bank Directors
P.O. Box 2739
Alexandria, VA 22301
(703) 683-3030

American Society of Corporate
  Secretaries, Inc.
521 Fifth Avenue
New York, NY 10175
(212) 681-2000
www.ascs.org

Association for Investment
  Management and Research
5 Boar's Head Lane
P.O. Box 3668
Charlottesville, VA 22903
(804) 977-6600
www.aimr.org

Association of Certified Fraud
   Examiners
The Gregor Building
716 West Avenue
Austin, TX 78701
(512) 478-9070
1-800-245-3321
www.cfenet.com

Association of Government
   Accountants
2200 Mount Vernon Avenue
Alexandria, VA 22301
(703) 684-6931
www.rutgers.edu/accounting/raw/aga/
   home.htm

Australian Institute of Company
   Director
Company Director House
3rd Floor
71 York Street
Sydney, NSW, Australia
(02) 299-8788

Blue Ribbon Commission on Audit
   Committees
The Center for Board Leadership
1215 17th Street, NW
Suite 402
Washington, D.C. 20036
(202) 467-8076

Blue Ribbon Committee on Improving
   the Effectiveness of Corporate
   Audit Committees

The Business Roundtable
1615 L Street N.W.
Washington, D.C. 20036
(202) 872-1260
www.brtable.org

The Canadian Institute of Chartered
   Accountants
277 Wellington Street West
Toronto, Canada M5V 3H2
(416) 977-3222
www.cica.ca

Committee of Sponsoring
   Organizations of the Treadway
   Commission (COSO)
American Institute of Certified Public
   Accountants
1211 Avenue of the Americas
6th Floor
New York, NY 10036-8775
(212) 575-6656
www.aicpa.org

The Conference Board
845 Third Avenue
New York, NY 10022
(212) 759-0900
www.conference-board.org

The Corporate Board
4440 Hagadorn Road
Okemos, MI 48864
(517) 336-1700
www.corporateboard.com/

Directorship
Directors Publications, Inc.
8 Sound Shore Drive
Greenwich, CT 06830
(203) 861-7000
www.directorship.com

Financial Accounting Standards Board
401 Merritt 7
P.O. Box 5116
Norwalk, CT 06856
(203) 847-0700
www.fasb.org

Financial Executives Institute
10 Madison Avenue, P.O. Box 1938
Morristown, NJ 07960
1-800-336-0773
www.fei.org

Government Accounting Standards
  Board
401 Merritt 7
P.O. Box 5116
Norwalk, CT 06856
(203) 847-0700
www.fasb.org

Heidrick and Struggles
245 Park Avenue
New York, NY 10167
(212) 867-9876
www.H-S.com

Independence Standards Board
6th Floor
1211 Avenue of the Americas
New York, NY 10036
(212) 596-6200
www.cpaindependence.org

The Institute of Internal Auditors, Inc.
249 Maitland Avenue
Altamonte Springs, FL 32701
(407) 830-7600
www.theiia.org

International Accounting Standards
  Committee (IASC)
167 Fleet Street
London EC4A 2ES
England
(44) 713530565
www.iasc.org.uk

International Auditing Practices
  Committee (IAPC)

114 West 47th Street
Suite 2410
New York, NY 10022
(212) 302-5952
www.ifac.org

International Federation of
  Accountants (IFAC)
114 West 47th Street
Suite 2410
New York, NY 10036
(212) 286-9344
www.ifac.org

International Forum for Corporate
  Directors
4130 La Jolla Village Drive
Suite 107-152
La Jolla, CA 92037
(619) 597-4718
www.ifcd.org/

International Organization of
  Securities Commissions (IOSCO)
800 Square Victoria
17th Floor
Montreal, Quebec H4Z 1G3
Canada
(514) 875-8278
www.iosco.org/

Institute for Research on Boards of
  Directors, Inc.
1654 Starling Drive
Sarasota, FL 34231
(813) 923-2988

Institute of Corporate Directors
55 St. Clair Avenue West
Suite 255
Toronto, Ontario M4V 2Y7
(416) 944-8282

Institute of Management Accountants
10 Paragon Drive
Montvale, NJ 07645
1-800-638-4427
www.imanet.org

Investor Responsibility Research
  Center
Suite 600
1755 Massachusetts Avenue N.W.
Washington, D.C. 20036
(202) 833-0700
www.irrc.org

Korn/Ferry International
237 Park Avenue
New York, NY 10017
(212) 687-1834
www.futurestep.com

MLR Holdings, Inc.
Directors & Boards
229 South 18th Street
Philadelphia, PA 19103
(215) 567-3200

National Association of Corporate
  Directors
1701 L Street N.W.
Suite 560
Washington, D.C. 20036
(202) 775-0509
www.nacd.org

National Association of Securities
  Dealers, Inc.
1735 K Street, NW
Washington, D.C. 20006
(202) 728-8000
www.nasd.com

National Investor Relations Institute
2000 L Street N.W.
Suite 701
Washington, D.C. 20036
(202) 861-0630
www.niri.org

New York State Society of Certified
  Public Accountants
530 Fifth Avenue
New York, NY 10036-5101
1-800-633-6320
www.luca.com

New York Stock Exchange, Inc.
Eleven Wall Street
New York, NY 10005
(212) 656-2017
www.nyse.com

Organization for Economic
  Co-operation and Development
2 Rue André-Pascal
75775 Paris, Cedex 16
France
www.oecd.org

Oxford Analytica, Ltd.
52 New Inn Hall Street
Oxford OX1 2QB, England
(44) 865-244442

Paula Lowitt, Esq.
Weil, Gotshal, & Manger, LLP
767 Fifth Avenue
New York, NY 10153
(212) 310-8000
www.weil.com

Pro NED
Devonshire House
Mayfair Place, Picadilly
GB-London W1X 5FH
Great Britain
44 (171) 493-4567

Public Oversight Board
One Station Place
Stamford, CT 06902
(201) 353-5300

Russell Reynolds Associates
200 Park Avenue
New York, NY 10166
(212) 351-2000
www.russreyn.com

U.S. General Accounting Office
Washington, D.C. 20548
(202) 275-6241
www.gao.gov/

U.S. Securities and Exchange
    Commission
450 Fifth Street N.W.
Washington, D.C. 20549
(202) 942-2770
www.sec.gov/

Women Directors of the Top
    Corporate 1000
National Women's Economic Alliance
    Foundation
808 17th Street, N.W.
Suite 600
Washington, D.C. 20006
(202) 393-5257

Index